AUSTRALIAN DREAMING

40,000 Years of Aboriginal History

AUSTRALIAN DREAMING

40,000 Years of Aboriginal History

compiled and edited by
JENNIFER ISAACS

LANSDOWNE PRESS
Sydney • Auckland • London • New York

Above: 'My own people, the Riratjingu, are descended from the great Djankawu who came in his canoe with his two sisters, following the morning star which guided them to the shores of Yelangbara on the eastern coast of Arnhem Land. My painting is the design of Yelangbara, our Ancestral homelands.' Wandjuk Marika. *photo R. Morrison*

Endpapers: Detail from a bark painting by Banapana Maymuru from Yirrkala, Northern Territory. *photo P. Tweedie*

Half Title Page: Aboriginal oral tradition tells of their continued existence on this continent for over 40,000 years. *photo R. Edwards*

Title Page: In the desert, knowledge of the location of freshwater springs is vital. Children are taught of them in many legends. *photo R. Edwards*

WELDON-HARDIE
GROUP OF COMPANIES

Published by Lansdowne Press, Sydney
176 South Creek Road, Dee Why West
Australia 2099
First published 1980
Reprinted 1984
Reprinted 1986
© Copyright (this anthology) Jennifer Isaacs
and Aboriginal Arts Board 1980
Typeset in Australia by S.A. Typecentre Pty.
Limited, Adelaide
Printed in Hong Kong by Toppan Printing
Company

National Library of Australia
Cataloguing-in-Publication Data

Isaacs, Jennifer

  Australian dreaming.

  Index.
  Bibliography.
  ISBN 0 7018 1330X

  1. Australia — History. 2. Aborigines,
    Australian — Legends.
  I. Title.

994

Designed by Robin James
Edited by Sue Wagner

Foreword

In the world today men discuss whether our ancestors came to Australia by land across a land bridge that has now gone, or by boat, across the sea from Asia. Scientists who study faces say we look like some of the southern Indian people and like some of the hill people of the Celebes. Well let them continue to try to find the answer.

The truth, of course, is that my own people, the Riratjingu, are descended from the great Djankawu who came from the island of Baralku far across the sea. Our spirits return to Baralku when we die. Djankawu came in his canoe with his two sisters, following the morning star which guided them to the shores of Yelangbara on the eastern coast of Arnhem Land. They walked far across the country following the rain clouds. When they wanted water they plunged their digging stick into the ground and fresh water flowed. From them we learnt the names of all the creatures on the land and they taught us all our Law.

That is just a little bit of the truth. Aboriginal people in other parts of Australia have different origins and will tell you their own stories of how the mountains came to be, and the rivers, and how the tribes grew and followed the way of life of their Spirit Ancestors.

The huge Wandjina, makers of thunder, rain and lightning, soared over the sea to Western Australia. Their faces stare at us from the cave walls of the Kimberley Ranges and the spears that fought their giant battles are still in the sands on the coast north of Derby. The giant Rainbow Serpent emerged from beneath the earth and as she moved, winding from side to side, she forced her way through the soil and rocks, making the great rivers flow in her path, and carving through mountains she made the gorges of northern Australia. From the Rainbow Serpent sprang many tribes, and tales about her are told all over Arnhem Land — over to Western Australia, in central Australia and even to New South Wales. Our paintings on rocks illustrate this true story about one of our Ancestors.

In Victoria Bunjil the eagle hawk made the mountains and rivers; it was he that created the men and the animals. He taught all men how to behave on this earth and when he had finished his work he became a star in the sky. The women down there were created by Balayung the bat, the brother of Bunjil.

Our legends tell us how the country was formed. Totyerquil, the great Ancestor of the Wotjobaluk tribe, pursued the cod fish and as the cod weaved from side to side fleeing from his adversary he formed the bends and banks of the Murray River.

Our people of the desert in the centre of the continent speak of the Creation period, the Tjukirita time when the land was a flat disc, a vast featureless plain which stretched to the horizon without rivers or hills. But as the ages passed many different giant mythical beings emerged from beneath this crust and wandered about. They had the form of animals, insects, and other creatures, snake, kangaroo, euro, owl, honey ants and termites, yet lived and behaved as men do today. When this time was passed these creatures left their life essence behind them and at various places where they camped or where an event took place a rock, waterhole, tree, cave or boulder now marks the site, and these natural features are full of this essence, this Kuranita. Our people must preserve these areas for ceremonies or the animals, plants and people cannot survive.

In Queensland Giroo Gurrll, part man and part eel, rose out of the water near Hinchinbrook Island and named the animals, birds and all the places there, while the great Ancestor Chivaree the Seagull paddled his canoe from the Torres Islands down the western coast of Cape York to Sandy Beach where his canoe turned into stone.

Some of the legends of our tribes, especially those of the southern and south-eastern areas, are now recalled only through the work and in the words of the Europeans who wrote them down long ago before the people disappeared.

But in the areas where my people are still leading their traditional life our legends are strong and our history can be told today, just as my father taught me and his father and grandfather the same before that. We want to tell you our story, not the inner secrets of our deepest beliefs — these we keep sacred for our generations to come so that our culture can remain whole — but the story as we tell it to our young people before they become initiated into the sacred Law.

The scientists can give you a small story of our origins possibly 40,000 years ago, but we can tell you many more. The stories in this book told by Aboriginal people each add a little bit to the history of this continent Australia, and tell of how we have come to live here since before time could be counted, since the Dreaming.

WANDJUK MARIKA, O.B.E.

The great snake continued its journeys and came to rest in a
cave at Gibb River, Western Australia. *photo I. Crawford*

*The Aboriginal people's own story of the continent of Australia,
the origin of the landscape, the people, and their way of life.*

This book is produced with the assistance of the Aboriginal Arts Board of
the Australia Council as part of its continuing program to present
Aboriginal culture through the Aboriginal people themselves.

The use of the printed word as a means of communication is relatively
new to the Aboriginal people, whose own culture and history is proudly
retained as an oral tradition. The literature program of the Aboriginal
Arts Board is bridging that gap and endeavouring to present Aboriginal
history and culture direct from the people themselves.

Contents

Introduction

Aboriginal history is Australian history. The history of mankind on the Australian continent did not commence when Captain Cook first landed on the eastern coast but 40,000 years before that when the ancient predecessors of the Aboriginal people began their sea voyages south. This history is not lost: it has been retained in the memories of successive generations of Aboriginal people and passed on through the rich oral tradition of song-poetry and legend. The early history of the Australian Aboriginal people, of their origins and way of life, their laws, social organization and customs can be found in legends and song-cycles. Aboriginal oral literature can provide us with accounts of the geological changes that have occurred over the ages since the first discovery of the continent, accounts of dramatic landscape changes and the activities of great Spirit Beings.

Many collections of Aboriginal legends have been published in the past. This book is different. It presents the Aboriginal people's own account of their history and gives their explanation for the formation of the landscape, their own origins and the origin of their way of life. Selections have been made from translations of traditional mythology and song-poetry, combined with contemporary Aboriginal stories and commentaries. Individual styles of prose obviously vary, and these have been retained.

Each Aboriginal group in Australia has its own version of the great stories. Some legends overlap different tribal areas, some stories are known by many groups, while others are the province of a few people only. Traditional Aboriginal life was quickly disrupted in the southern areas of the continent after European settlement. I have therefore relied heavily on stories and myths from the people of these areas which were recorded earlier this century. Some of the researchers have recorded the names of tribes and individual storytellers, others have not; wherever possible the Aboriginal origins of the story have been indicated. Elsewhere in Australia also, the work of anthropologists throughout this century has provided us with a large repository of translated legends and songs which give the Aboriginal people's own story of their country and people. I am deeply indebted to the original research of those whose works have been selected for inclusion in this collection, particularly to Professor R. M. Berndt. I have indicated sources for all stories in the footnotes.

In a growing number of Aboriginal communities the people themselves are setting up their own literature centres where they are tape-recording, transcribing and translating their stories. These centres have ensured the emergence of a written Aboriginal literature. Many stories contributed from these sources appear in this publication, largely from Milingimbi in the Northern Territory and Mowanjum in Western Australia.

In traditional Aboriginal communities the rituals remain strong and beliefs in the origin of man and the landscape are unaltered. Here the deeper truths are the province of the older men, and will only be passed on to others as they fulfil their ceremonial obligations. The wishes of the Aboriginal people in regard to sacred stories have been strictly adhered to and only the public versions have been included in this collection. Also, in deference to the wishes of the Aboriginal people, the names of the deceased have been deleted so that their spirits may rest in peace.

In telling the story of 40,000 years of Australian history I have chosen stories from a cross-section of communities and areas which illustrate the variation in beliefs of the different Aboriginal groups. In editing the material, rather than develop each theme by using extracts from Aboriginal stories which specifically relate only to the subject matter under consideration, I have purposely included the entire story, with all its other implications for life and behaviour. In this manner I hope that the unique Aboriginal way of story-telling has been preserved, and the Aboriginal presence retained. Legends may touch on many aspects of life and human behaviour and many included here obviously relate to several chapters simultaneously. The Zebra Finch Journeys, for example, tell of the great journeys of the Zebra Finch men, but incidentally relate the bringing of fire to women for the first time. This is the essence of Aboriginal teaching, to recount the lessons of life in story form, as allegories or cautionary tales.

In initiating this publication, the Aboriginal Arts Board, which is comprised of Aboriginal people from all over Australia, felt the need to explain the history of the Australian continent as seen by the Aboriginal people. It is impossible, the Aboriginal people believe, to successfully present their case for occupancy/ownership of their own land if their basic beliefs about the formation of the land and its laws are not understood by white Australians and accepted as part of every Australian's history of their own continent.

JENNIFER ISAACS

CHAPTER ONE

The Reality of Myth

THE EARLIEST MEMORIES

Aboriginal oral traditions which describe the origin of Australia from ancient times are frequently dramatic, involving great beings and amazing events, however they do contain the essence of the truth. The legends when distilled create a story of the origins of man in Australia and of the Australian landscape as it is today of which much can be substantiated by scientific investigation. The ancient racial memory of a people whose traditions and culture remained largely unaltered for thousands of years can recount great geological changes — the rising of the seas, the change from lush vegetation to desert, and the eruption of volcanoes as well as the very first arrival of man on this continent.

THE ARRIVAL OF THE FIRST AUSTRALIANS

Aboriginal people have lived on the Australian continent for an extraordinary length of time. About 40,000 years ago before even North and South America were inhabited, the first small groups of people began arriving in Australia. At this time, in the Pleistocene era, Australia had a very different climate and geography. The second last Ice Age was drawing to a close and there were enormous amounts of ice in the North and South Poles of the world. The ocean was as much as 120 to 180 metres (400 to 600 feet) lower than its present levels, the coastline of Australia extended far into what is now ocean, and New Guinea and Tasmania were part of one great land mass. To the north, Java, Sumatra and Borneo were all part of the Asian land mass. Under these circumstances it was quite possible for people to migrate to Australia from South-East Asia by island-hopping, never having to lose sight of land in their short canoe trips from one island to another between the land masses and it is therefore likely that the first people stepped ashore on the southern land mass somewhere on the west coast of the bridge joining Australia to New Guinea, long ago submerged.

Why the first people came, and who they were, is lost in aeons of time. Stone tools found in Australia at various sites dated to the Pleistocene era, suggest however that Aboriginals may be connected to island South-East Asian peoples. Theories put forward as to why they came suggest that over-population, famine, war, and accident caused people to gradually push south to unknown lands. Small groups may have continued to arrive on the shores of Australia until about 10,000 B.P. (before the present) when the last Ice Age ended and the melting ice caused sea levels to gradually rise to those we know today. Australia and its original inhabitants were from that time on effectively isolated from the rest of mankind.

Aboriginal people have important stories of their own to tell about this early time, as memories of the ancient period when men first came to Australia persist in myths and stories. Many accounts relate the original journeys to Australia of men and animals, such as the following myth of the Thurrawal people of coastal New South Wales.

The Coming of the First Australians to the Coast of New South Wales:
the Arrival of the Thurrawal Tribe

Long ago in the distant past all the animals that are now in Australia lived in another land far beyond the sea; they were at that time in human form. One day they met together and decided to set out in a canoe in order to find better hunting grounds over the sea. The whale, who was much larger than any of the rest, had a bark canoe

Opposite: About 40,000 years ago the first small groups of people began arriving in Australia. It is likely that they stepped ashore somewhere on the west coast of the bridge joining Australia to New Guinea, long ago submerged. *photo H. Herbert*

11

of great dimensions but would not lend it to any of the others. As the small canoes of the other animals were unfit for use far from the land, they kept watch daily in the hope that the whale might leave his boat, so that they could get it, and start away on their journey. The whale however always watched it closely and never let his guard down.

The starfish, a close friend of the whale, formed a plan with the other people to take the attention of the whale away from his canoe, and so give them a chance to steal it. One day, the starfish said to the whale: 'You have a great many lice in your head; let me catch them and kill them for you.' The whale, who had been much pestered with the parasites, readily agreed to his friend's kind offer, and, tying up his canoe alongside a rock, they sat down. The starfish immediately gave the signal to some of the others, who assembled on the beach in readiness to sneak quietly into the canoe as soon as the whale was distracted.

The starfish rested the head of the whale in his lap and began to remove the lice from his head. The whale was lulled into passivity and did not notice the others quickly get into his canoe and push off shore. Now and then he would ask, 'Is my canoe all right?' The starfish in reply tapped a piece of loose bark near his leg and said, 'Yes, this is it which I am tapping with my hand,' and vigorously scratched near the whale's ears so he could not hear the splashing of oars. This continued until the canoe was nearly out of sight, when suddenly the whale became agitated and jumped up. Seeing the canoe disappearing in the distance, he was furious at the betrayal of the starfish and beat him unmercifully. Jumping into the water, the whale then swam away after his canoe, and the starfish, mutilated and tattered, rolled off the rock on which they had been sitting, into the water, and lay on the sand at the bottom. It was this terrible attack of the whale which gave the starfish his present ragged appearance and his habit of keeping on the sea floor.

The whale pursued the canoe in a fury and spurted water into the air through the wound in the head he had received during his fight with the starfish, a practice which he has retained ever since. Although the whale swam strongly, the forearms of the koala pulled the oars with great strength for many days and nights until they

The whale, exhausted after his long swim, turned back along the coast. He still cruises there today with his descendants, spouting water furiously through the hole in his head. *photo R. Morrison*

finally sighted land and beached the canoe safely. The native companion bird, however, could not stay still and stamping his feet up and down made two deep holes in the canoe. As it was no longer of use, he pushed it a little way out to sea where it settled and became the small island known as Gan-man-gang near the entrance to the ocean of Lake Illawarra.

The whale, exhausted after his long swim, turned back along the coast. He still cruises there today with his descendants, spouting water furiously through the hole in his head.

Thurrawal tribe[1]

Another myth was told by Alexander Vesper of the Gullibul tribe in New South Wales, also telling of men coming to Australia from across the sea, this time in a sailing ship.

The Three Brothers

This story has been handed down by the Aboriginal people through their generations. This story cannot be altered.

I am sixty-seven years of age. I heard this story from my grandfather who was a full-blood of the Ngarartbul tribe near Murwillumbah. On my grandmother's side the tribe was Gullibul, from Casino and Woodenbong. I heard this story also from many old Aboriginals who came from other tribes.

The first finding of this unknown land, Australia, was made by three brothers who came from the central part of the world. The names of these three brothers were Mamoon, Yar Birrain and Birrung. They were compelled to explore for land on the southerly part of the world because they were forced out of the centre of the world by revolutions and warfare of those nations of the central part.

They came in a sailing ship. As they made direct for the south, coming across different islands and seeing the people in these islands, they kept in the sea all the time until they came to Australia, to the eastern part of this continent.

Their first coming into the land was at Yamba Head on the Clarence River. They anchored just on the mouth of the Clarence. This was the first landing of men in this empty continent. They camped, taking out of their empty ship all their camping belongings, such as a steel axe and many other things of the civilized race in the central part of the world.

After they had rested from the voyage, through the night a storm started to rise from the west. The force of wind broke the anchor and deprived them of the ship, which was driven out to sea and never seen again.

These three brothers had each a family of his own and they had their mother. Their three wives were with them. When they knew that the ship was gone, they reasoned among themselves and said, 'The only possible chance is to make a canoe and return from here from island to island.' So they went up the Clarence River and they came across a blackbutt tree. They stripped the bark off it, made a big fire, a long fire, and heated the bark until it was flexible, until you could bend it about as you pleased. Out of this long sheet of bark, they made a canoe. Three of these canoes were made.

They went back to their families and told them to get everything packed up as they were about to leave. Their families said, 'Yes, we'll pack up, but mother has gone out for some yams. She was looking for something to eat.' So they sang out. They searched along the beach, among the honeysuckle and the tea-tree along the coast, trying to find the old woman. But she had wandered too far out of the reach of their search. She thought within herself that her sons would not be able to make the canoes so quickly.

The three brothers said, 'Well, she might have died. We'll have to go back into the sea.' So they packed up and took to the ocean in the three canoes with the intention of returning to where they came from.

After they got a distance out from Yamba Head, the old woman arrived back at the camp they had left. She went up to the top of the hill and started singing out for them. And then she saw them far out on the ocean. She was trying to wave them back, but it seemed to be impossible for her to draw their attention. So she was angry with them. She cursed the families and said to the ocean to be rough. As she cursed

13

them and spoke to the ocean to be rough, the ocean started to get fierce. They attempted to continue on against the tempest, but they were driven back to the northern shore beyond Yamba. They were compelled to come in to land at the place which is now known as Evans Head.

They made the first settling place in Australia at Evans Head. One of the sons returned to Yamba when the ocean was calm and found the mother still alive. She had lived on yams. That is how Yamba got its name. Well, that word 'yam', it comes from a civilized word. It means 'sweet spud'. So that word alone will give you a clue as to where those first people came from.

So one brother went back to Yamba and brought the mother to Evans Head. When they settled there, in the course of time, they increased their families. One family race generated northwards on the Australian coast, one to the west and one to the south. As they were generating, they were keeping on extending, and they kept in touch with each other all the time.

They went on in that manner and eventually they became tribal races, and the first language of their origin we call Jabilum, that means, 'The Originals'. Tabulam is the word the white man made out of this word. The first language of these Jabilum was the Birrein tongue. And the second was Gumbangirr, of the Grafton tribe. Weervul is the Ballina lot. And Gullibul, that is between the two. Gullibul sprang out of the centre from Tweed Heads. The race of the Aboriginals as it was continually generated had often a knowledge of the other races across the sea in the other islands. We call these islands Ngareenbil, that is, other countries that are not contactable to Australia. The coastal Aboriginal often took a canoe to these islands and was married there.

During the period of the increase of the Aboriginals, they started to make a tribal law which is notable through the other races in the world. And by these laws which they made they were able to check up on different things. They were compelled to use the stone tomahawk. They had to climb trees after possums and hunt for food such as kangaroos, wallabies and many other things, such as fishes.

As far as making weapons, they made shields, they made boomerangs, discovering and imitating swifts and swallows. They saw it was possible to make a boomerang take to the air and come back. And they made boomerangs for fighting, especially the straight boomerang which will cut through the air. Their shields, buggarr, came from the central part of the world. Also their spears. They never used the woomera, the spear-thrower. The spear they threw with their hand, holding the spear in the middle. In warfare they used mainly the shield and the boomerang.

Well, that's how the Aboriginals came to be in Australia.

Gullibul tribe[2]

Important Creation stories which are remembered clearly in northern Australia and which form the basis of elaborate rituals and ceremonies tell of the arrival of the great Spirit Ancestors in canoes. Djankawu* the great Ancestor of the Riratjingu came by canoe to the coast of north-east Arnhem Land, and Chivaree the seagull man, the Ancestor of the Mapoon people, travelled down the west coast of Cape York from the Torres Islands and then up again in his canoe.

The gradual movement of the original Australians over this vast continent must have taken generations, as people spread out and adjusted to different climates and conditions within the continent. By 30,000 B.P., however, there is ample evidence that men were well established throughout the whole of Australia.

THE GIANTS

In Pleistocene times huge animals inhabited Australia; the great rhinoceros-like Diprotodon, the giant kangaroo standing 3 metres (10 feet) high, the giant marsupial wombat, as well as the flightless birds, Genyornis (giant emu) and Dromornis which matched the great Moa in size. These animals mysteriously disappeared in Australia about 15,000 years ago; however, Aboriginal stories which have been recorded throughout Australia indicate clearly that the animals were a part of the environment of early man on this continent, remembered with both fear and awe for generations.

*See Chapter 2, The Creation Era

The giant Diprotodon once lived on the Australian continent and was part of the environment of early man. Legends recall these giant animals with fear and awe. Courtesy South Australian Museum.

Archaeological evidence suggesting the coexistence of Aboriginal people with the extinct animals and giant marsupials is found in a number of places. One of the most important sites containing the fossil bones of twelve extinct giant marsupials is at Lake Menindee on the Darling River in western New South Wales where extinct animals were found along with stone flake tools of man.

At Keilor near Melbourne a group of animals were found including the bones of a Diprotodon, seemingly corresponding in time to the remains of an Aboriginal camp site dated about 31,000 B.P. Similarly at the Balladonia homestead in the Great Australian Bight, bones of the Tasmanian devil; marsupial lion, large wombat, and Diprotodon were discovered in the same layer of conglomerate rock as the stone implements of Aboriginals.

At another site in western New South Wales the remains of a giant kangaroo were found in an Aboriginal camp oven dated to about 26,000 B.P., which seemed definite evidence that they lived at the same time until it was pointed out that the remains could have been a large example of a still-living species of kangaroo. Aboriginals are content to leave the arguments to the scientists. Their own oral traditions give them the answers.

In the 1890s the explorer and geologist J. W. Gregory heard an account of a myth of the Dieri tribe in central Australia which told of giant bones revealed in the desert. At Lake Callabonna, where he investigated this legend, he found the bones of extinct giant animals, and among them a Diprotodon, a wombat-like creature as large as a rhinoceros, whose skeleton is now assembled in the Adelaide museum. This story also tells of a time when the climate of the desert was different. The vegetation was lush and green, as could have been the case before the end of the last Ice Age. The legends of the northern Aranda also describe the country of the MacDonnell Ranges and the plains north of Alice Springs as once well watered. In earliest times the plain was green with herbs and grasses, the mountains decked brightly with a multi-coloured covering of wild flowers.[3]

Once the deserts of central Australia were fertile plains. Giant trees grew there. In this sky-land lived the monsters called the Kadimakara. *photo R. Edwards*

The fresh smell of green plants on earth often rose to this sky-land, tempting the Kadimakara to climb down the gum trees to the earth below. *photo D. Roff*

The Giant Kadimakara

Once the deserts of central Australia were fertile plains. Forests of giant trees grew there. Rivers, lakes and lagoons were thickly fringed with waving reeds. The sky was covered by clouds so dense that it appeared solid. The air, that is now filled with blinding, salt-laden dust, was washed by soft, cooling rains.

The deep, rich loam of this land supported luxurious vegetation which spread, from lake shores and river banks, far out across the plains. The trunks of lofty gum trees held up the distant sky with their inter-lacing branches and foliage. In this sky-land lived the monsters called the Kadimakara. The fresh smell of green plants on earth often rose to this sky-land, tempting the Kadimakara to climb down the gum trees to the earth below.

Once, when the monsters had climbed down the gum trees and were quietly feeding on the earth, three gum trees which were the pillars of the sky fell down. The Kadimakara were cut off from their sky-land. They were forced to roam on the earth and to wallow in the marshes of Lake Eyre until they died. To this day, their bones lie where they died. After the three gum trees had fallen down, all the sky became one continuous hole, called 'Pura wilpanina', which means, 'great hole'.

At times, when the country is parched during prolonged drought, the Dieri Aboriginals make journeys to the bones of the Kadimakara and hold ceremonies to appease the spirits of the dead Kadimakara and to persuade them to intercede with those who still dwell in the sky and control the clouds and rain.

Aranda, central Australia[4]

Another story from the Dieri tribe describes giant frogs, which were common in Australia in the Pleistocene era.

16

The Giant Frogs

In the Dreamtime two giant frogs, who were then men, went on a long walkabout. Leaving their country, Malooka, which is where Mataranka is, they travelled north until they came to the Katherine River where they met two other frog-men from a different country, also on a walkabout. These four frog-men camped together. Then the elder of the two Malooka frogs, whose name was Koit-nong-mee, asked the other two frogs to go and get them some water.

'We are old-men frogs,' said Koit-nong-mee, 'and you two are young-men. You should therefore carry water for us.'

But the other two frogs refused to carry water for Koit-nong-mee and his companion, and soon the four frogs were fighting. Koit-nong-mee and his companion killed the two younger frogs and then started the journey back to their own country. After this some frog-men of the same tribe as the two who had been killed came to this place. When they found their two tribesmen lying dead, they picked them up and carried them back to their country. Then these frog-men began to gather an army together to go and make war with Koit-nong-mee and his tribe.

However Koit-nong-mee heard about the army that was being formed, and he too began to call and gather all his fellows into an army. Koit-nong-mee and his army of frogs travelled and met the opposing army on the plains called Jartee-kundar-wenai, which is near the Katherine River. As the two great frog-armies formed up into long lines across the plain to begin the battle, far out on the plain alone, sat an old woman, watching.

The frog-armies fought with stone-headed spears and with shields, with clubs and stone axes. And as the battle went on they fought in scattered groups, killing each other and falling backwards in heaps. They fought until all had been killed and were lying in lines and heaps across the plain.

The lines and heaps of these huge frogs who had slain each other were turned into stone and they remain on the plain of Jartee-kundar-wenai to this day. And, far out on the plain sits the old woman who watched the battle and who also was turned into stone long ago.

Dieri, central Australia[5]

References to giant animals who lived in the Dreamtime are found abundantly in myths from many tribes. The giant emu (Genyornis) appears in several stories.

The Giant Emu

Ngindyal or Tchingal was a giant of the Dreamtime, a sorceress, who killed many people and ate them. She was bird-like with the shape and feathers of an enormous emu. She made her huge nest at Wambagruk, and there laid one huge egg, on which she sat. Her peace was disrupted one day by a prying crow and leaping up onto her giant legs she strode across the land, chasing him as fast as she could. The crow slipped into a crack in the side of a mountain, but the Ngindyal with one hard kick split it in two, forming what is now known as Rose's Gap. The Ngindyal split mountain after mountain as she pursued the crow until the crow was safe at its spirit waters where the Ngindyal could not intrude. So she returned to her nest.

Some time later the crow met the Bram-bam-bult brothers near Jeparit and told them how he had outrun the Ngindyal. The brothers were keen to avenge the deaths of many of their people who had been caught and eaten by the Ngindyal, and they asked the crow to show them where to find her. The three then travelled over the land in search of the legendary giant until in the distance they saw a bright shining star. The crow said, 'That is her eye; she is there sitting on her nest.'

The three circled her; the younger brother stood in front of her and as she leapt up to attack him the older brother hurled his spear into her breast. The younger one then had his chance to attack, and finally the spears had caused such loss of blood she weakly ran off towards what is now called Horsham Plain. When Wity-gurk, the lark, saw the Ngindyal coming, pursued by the Bram-bam-bults, he came out carrying a bough to camouflage himself. When he was within range, he threw a spear with all his force which struck the Ngindyal in the chest and killed her.

The Bram-bam-bults then split each feather of the Ngindyal down the middle, putting one half of the feathers on the right-hand side and the other half on the left, making two heaps. One of these heaps of feathers was converted into a cock and the other heap into a hen of the present race of emus, which are much much smaller than the Ngindyal. It was also arranged by the sorcery of the Bram-bam-bults that all future emus should lay a number of eggs, instead of only one. The splitting of the feathers is still easily observable in the double feathers of all emus, which consist of two independent shafts.

All the people then journeyed away to Wambagruk to get the egg on which the Ngindyal had been sitting. Although they tried their best, none of them could lift the egg, till Babim'bal the wattle-bird came. He picked it up and, putting it into his bag, carried it to Horsham Plain, where it was cooked and a great feast was held. The nest in which the large egg lay is said to be still visible at Wambagruk. The Ngindyal now occupies the black patch in the constellation of the Southern Cross, and the crow was changed to Argus, at some distance from his ancient pursuer.

Wotjobaluk tribe[6]

Skeletons of this ancient giant emu have been found in the Western District of Victoria which corroborate the great legends.

Many of the great Spirit Beings of the Dreaming, both animal and human, were envisaged as giants and evidence of their epic feats is pointed out today. Huge bones found in many places in Aboriginal Australia are traced to the great Spirits.

The greatest of local landmarks at Brewarrina in New South Wales are the stone fisheries made in the bed of the Barwon. This is the work of the Great Spirit Baiame and his giant sons. At Boogira on the Narran Lake is an imprint in stone of Baiame's hand and foot, while at Cuddie, a spring in the Brewarrina district, every now and then huge bones of animals now extinct emerge from the banks. Legends say that these bones are the remains of the victims of Mullyan the eagle hawk, whose camp was in a tree by the spring.

At Cuddie, the only permanent water between Brewarrina and Walgett, New South Wales, bones of enormous fossilized animals were found which included the Diprotodon, Phascolonus, Genyornis, Megalania, Procoptidon and large crocodiles. The legend of Mullyan's Tree, a gum over 27 metres (90 feet) tall, observed by Sturt as he crossed this area, explains these bones.

Legend of Mullyan and the Big Dry

A legend of this Big Dry tells of the people camped on one of the remaining waterholes, named Geerah, half-way between Brewarrina and Walgett. Lining this waterhole were giant gums and in the tallest was the nest of Mullyan the eagle. When the young eagles hatched, Mullyan couldn't fill their empty bellies, although he hunted skilfully and long over the desolate land. It was then that the giant eagles swooped down on the camps in the shade of their tree, tearing babies from screaming mothers, clutching them in cruel claws and lifting them to their nest high above. Great was the distress and anger in the camps whenever the shadow of Mullyan passed over until, in desperation, the men gathered in a tight body, protected under their raised spears, like Piggi-billa the echidna, and attacked the base of the enormous tree with their stone axes. As the tree crashed heavily to the ground, killing the eagles, its hollow trunk slid into the waterhole, allowing the water to flow along its massive length to the nest, sinking it and the bones of animals eaten by Mullyan into the parched earth. Since that time the Aboriginals have called the spot Cuddie, which means 'natural water'.[7]

Among the tribes of the Murray River area a legend is told of a fiercesome creature, the Whowie, who devoured many people and was the most feared animal in existence.[8] His length was somewhere about 6 metres (20 feet). He looked like a goanna, except that he had six legs instead of four and an enormous head like a frog. He was very slow in his movements and lived in a cave on the banks of the Murray River. He attacked and ate any living thing, eating people in great numbers. The Whowie legend is most probably a recollection of giant crocodiles which

The crow slipped into a crack in the side of a mountain, but Ngindyal, the giant emu, with one hard kick split it in two. *photo B. Thompson*

Images of emus from Creation times are carved on rock surfaces in many parts of the continent. This engraving is from Dampier, Western Australia. *photo R. Morrison*

in previous climates were known to have lived in many parts of Australia. The myth tells how the clever water rat organized the other tribes, and when they were sure the Whowie was deep in his cave, they carried wood into the entrance of it. When a great pile had accumulated the fire was lit, and at last the Whowie was forced out, blinded and dazed by the smoke and flames, so that he was able to be killed by spears, stone axes and nulla-nullas.

The fossilized bones of giant animals that were often visible in the ground were seen as physical evidence in support of myths. The following myth tells of a giant serpent but could equally well relate to large crocodiles, known to have existed in these areas.

The Kurrea and the Warrior

On the main road from Kunopia to Goondiwindi, on the New South Wales side of the Barwon River, is a large sheet of water several miles long, known as Boobera Lagoon. Some parts of this lagoon are very deep, and according to the legends at one particular place it is bottomless. In the depths dwells the Kurrea, a huge snake-like monster. He belongs to the Kupathin group, and his wife is the daughter of the bumble tree, of the Dilbi group. The Kurrea burrows as he moves across the land, and as he moves the waters flow behind in the troughs he creates, allowing him to remain beneath the water as he travels. Many hollow channels around Boobera which are now dry except in time of floods were formed long, long ago by the Kurrea.

19

If any man ever went to that part of Boobera Lagoon to swim, or sat on the bank fishing, or paddled out in his canoe in pursuit of waterfowl, the Kurrea was sure to seize and devour him. Not being able to hunt here was a serious loss to the people as fish, mussels, ducks, swans and other animals abounded in the lagoon.

Long ago a headman named Toolalla, of Noona on the Barwon, who was a great warrior, decided to kill the Kurrea and rid his people of their enemy. He stood on the southern bank of the lagoon armed with the best of his weapons and watched for the Kurrea. When the giant snake saw him, he immediately swam towards him. Although Toolalla threw several spears and clubs with all his force, they had no effect and he had soon used all his weapons. He was forced to turn and flee across the plain. The Kurrea gave chase, forming a channel in his usual manner, winding about like a huge snake and travelling at a great pace. He was gaining rapidly on Toolalla, who was running for his life, but just as he was tiring he saw a bumble tree growing on the edge of the plain. He made a final effort to reach it, because it was the mother-in-law of the Kurrea, and he knew he would not dare approach it. When the Kurrea saw that Toolalla had reached the bumble tree, he stopped suddenly, and digging a small waterhole in which he could turn his body round, he returned to the lagoon along the channel he had made.

When the lake or rivers dried up in this area the Kurreas perished and many people have found the huge bones in the banks of deep, dry watercourses. The children of the Kurreas appear in many forms, one of which is the Gowarkee, which resembles a giant emu with black feathers and red legs.[9]

The giant marsupial kangaroo is well documented geologically, and appears vividly in a story of the people of the Lachlan River, collected in the 1920s. This myth may reflect something of how the giant animals became extinct, which is still a subject of controversy. Changing climate may not have been completely responsible, and it may be that the Aboriginals themselves were instrumental in their gradual extinction, partly through their weapons and hunting techniques, but also through their sometimes catastrophic use of fire.

The Clash between Man and the Giant Kangaroo of the Dreamtime

The tribes of the Lachlan River area have a story which tells of a time in the ancient past when bands of marauding giant Kangaroos preyed on weak and defenceless men. It tells of the way in which a clever young man sought the aid of the Great Spirit and with the discovery of fire and weapons, subdued these monsters so that men could live peacefully from that time on.

Long ago, many people were camped at the confluence of the Lachlan and Murrumbidgee Rivers. The day was very hot and a haze rose from the windless plain so that the horizon danced, and mirages distorted the landscape. Everyone lay motionless, resting in the heat. Suddenly, a tribe of giant Kangaroos were seen away in the distance and the headman leapt to his feet with a galvanizing cry. The camp became a scene of wild excitement and fear. Children were quickly seized and everyone dispersed into the bush. In those times, however, the men had no weapons and were defenceless against the enemy. The Kangaroos relentlessly advanced on them through the bush and without mercy crushed their victims with their powerful arms. When the animals were finished, few of the tribe remained. The headman, however, lived, and in desperation he called the remaining band together to discuss methods of defence. At that meeting the men devised the weapons of spears, shields, clubs and boomerangs, some of which are still used today in many parts of Australia. Many young women had lost their children as they fled, and needing a device in which to carry their babies they made the ingenious bark cradle.

But Wirroowaa, the cleverest of the men, thought of enlisting the help of the Great Spirit. To do this, however, he needed to paint his chest with sacred designs in white clay which had to be collected from the banks of the river bed where the giant Kangaroos were camped.

Opposite: In the ancient past, bands of marauding giant Kangaroos preyed on weak and defenceless men. *photo D. Roff*

A fire was made which quickly spread across the grassy plain. The people rushed to the treeless area and the Kangaroos were driven back. *photo B. Thompson*

A fire still burnt in the base of a gum tree. The hole it had made, the old man said, could shelter a man. This was to be done to the old large trees throughout the land. *photo B. Thompson*

Fearlessly he set out across the plain for the river bed. He turned over a hollow log with his foot and found a big, brown-banded goanna, his beady eyes blinking and his wide yellow jaws apart. Quickly killing the goanna, Wirroowaa slit the belly open with a stone tool and extracted the body fat. This he smeared all over his skin until it glistened in the hot sun; then he rolled in the dust until he was as brown as the earth, and then picked up a branch of leaves to hold before him. This was the first time a man had used the technique of camouflage. Completely disguised, he quietly crept on towards the Kangaroo camp and without being observed stole the sacred clay.

Behind him a small breeze had come up, and the nearer he got to the river bed the stronger the breeze became. Two sticks which first were gently rubbing together soon became warm, then red hot, and suddenly a spark flew from the smoking twigs into a patch of dry grass. A fire was made. Wirroowaa quickly smeared his body with the clay, making sacred designs which would bring the presence of the Great Spirit to him.

The wind gradually grew in volume and spread over the grassy plain. The little breeze became a gale. The Great Spirit came and told Wirroowaa to keep to the dry patches of ground. Some of the people had already been caught in the fire, but others, picking up their babies in the bark cradles, rushed to the treeless area. The giant Kangaroos appeared on the horizon but were driven back immediately by the fire. The danger from them was over for a while.

But the leader, the headman, was dying and Wirroowaa painted him with the sacred clay so that the power of the Great Spirit would be with him. Then the old man spoke. He said that one day the giant Kangaroos would be overcome. Each man must carry spears and clubs, and bark must be stripped from trees to make shelters for each family, so that the sun would not weaken the people as it had in the past. Shields were also to be used in defence.

Opposite: Ancient stone tools for cutting, scraping and hacking have been found at all the earliest archaeological sites. The culture of these first Australians was to remain for thousands of years. *photo R. Edwards*

With a weak arm he pointed to a fire that still burnt in the base of a gum tree. The hole it had made, he said, could shelter a man. This was to be done to the old large trees throughout the land. The old man then died and was buried where he lay. A bark shield was made and put in the grave with him. Spears and nullas and his yam stick were laid beside him, and he was placed in a sitting position. His skin cloak was kept and the clever Wirroowaa, who succeeded him, wore it from that time on.[10]

THE WAY OF LIFE OF THE FIRST PEOPLE

Archaeological evidence at Lake Mungo in western New South Wales gives a vivid picture of the life of the first Aboriginal people. At that time the climate in this area was colder, and the ice that covered the Great Dividing Range provided plentiful water for Lake Mungo. Whether the rainfall was actually heavier than today has not been established, but the abundant fresh water in the lake gave rise to a prolific population of animals, birds and fish that have long since vanished.

Small groups of people camped by the shores of the lake, probably staying for several months in a good season and then moving on to hunt and gather in another area when food became depleted or they wanted a change of diet. Freshwater shellfish were collected, and these shells have survived until today in piles called 'middens'. They hunted the bettong, a small hopping animal the size of a hare, as well as kangaroos, brown hare wallabies, western native cats, hairy-nosed wombats, and they may possibly have collected the eggs of the giant emu. All this can be deduced from bone and shell remains excavated at the lake. The fossil relics of their meals also show that they caught golden perch weighing more than 14 kilograms (30 pounds). The Tasmanian tiger was also living on the shores of the lake at that time. This animal became extinct on the Australian mainland some 10,000 years ago, surviving only in Tasmania. Examples of the Tasmanian tiger occur in both

Early Aboriginal rock engravings of bird tracks reproduce the imprint of birds' feet in the wet sand. *photos P. Tweedie, R. Edwards*

In prehistoric times giant animals wandered the continent of Australia. The footprint of one of these creatures is embedded in rock beneath the tide near Broome in Western Australia. This cast taken from the original has been set on rocks nearby. *photo R. Morrison*

Sharpening grooves made by the stone tools of ancient Australians in a rock shelter in western Arnhem Land. *photo P. Tweedie*

Aboriginal rock paintings and rock engravings in northern Australia. Plentiful stone tools for cutting, scraping and hacking were found around their ancient hearths by the lake and evidence of one of the world's oldest cremations was discovered here, that of a young woman who had been cremated and then buried near the lake. It should be remembered that at this time Australia and South-East Asia were connected by a land bridge. It was therefore possible for ideas and inventions to slowly percolate from northern Australia to the south and back again. Apart from hunting skills, the first people in Australia must obviously have possessed simple boats and known how to make fire.

The earliest camp site so far discovered in northern Australia is at Oenpelli, at Malangangerr Nawamoyn, with stone tools dating back to 20,000 B.P. Among these were edge-ground axes, possibly the earliest recorded evidence in the world for a relatively 'advanced' stone tool. (Elsewhere in Australia these edge-ground axes do not appear until about 5000 B.P.) The nearest comparison to those ground axes, in near-Pleistocene contexts, is found in New Guinea, suggesting that the early colonists of Australia brought their techniques with them from the north.

The food-debris in the Oenpelli camp sites shows that the diet of these people included tortoises, bandicoots, possums, fish, shellfish, nuts, and the root of the lotus-lily, foods still abundant in the area, and used by Aboriginal people leading a traditional life style today. The sophisticated axes with their well shaped and sharpened cutting edges would have been used to chop wood and shape wooden tools, while the stone flakes, also abundant at the site, would have been used to cut vegetables, food and meat, and to scrape skins.

Another very early southern site is at Keilor, near Melbourne, where stone flake tools have been dated to earlier than 17,000 B.P. A human skull possibly 15,000 years old has been recovered from this area.

Tasmania was not cut off from the mainland until the end of the last Ice Age, about 11,000 years ago, and there the earliest archaeological evidence of Aboriginal inhabitation is at Rocky Cape dating back to 8000 B.P. Before that time, the extremely cold climate would have made all but the northern part very inhospitable to man.

THE RISING OF THE SEAS: AUSTRALIA AND ITS PEOPLE ARE ISOLATED

Towards the end of the last Ice Age the environment of the Aboriginals slowly but perceptibly changed as the ice melted and the seas rose. It has been calculated that on the gentle slopes of plains the sea could cover 5 kilometres (3 miles) in one year. Every tribe living on what was the coastal land in the last Ice Age must have gradually lost its entire territory, causing great disruption to every aspect of life.

Along the southern shores from Gippsland to the Nullarbor Plain legends relate events of the distant past when the sea level was lower and the coast extended further south.

The Kurnai of Victoria believed that long ago there was land south of Gippsland which the sea has now covered.[11] At that time some children were playing and inadvertently found a sacred object and showed it to the women. Immediately as vengeance the earth crumbled away and it was all water and many people were drowned.

Georgiana McCrae records a similar story about the Port Phillip Bay area from the Mornington Peninsula Aboriginals.[12] This was previously a flat and fertile hunting area but a violent storm blew up, with thunder and lightning, and the sea flooded the area.

Perhaps the many myths about disastrous floods in the Dreamtime relate to an ancient memory of climatic changes. The following legend tells one such story of a great flood in the ancient Dreaming era.

The Flood and the Bird Men

In the time long ago called Kardoorair when all the animals were men, a big rain began to fall. It fell for many days and nights until finally it covered all the country of the Murinbata people called Darimun. Soon it swelled the creek and covered all the land. There was only water.

All the people who were then at Port Keats were worried. Karan the curlew, Pulloo-pulloo the eagle, Kar Kork the frogmouth bird, Tarduk the friar bird and Weirk the white cockatoo talked incessantly amongst themselves about the flood, wondering what to do. Karan the curlew, the wise father of all the bird-men, knew more than the others. Suddenly he changed his form and became a bird, he flapped his wings and flew into the sky, calling the strange cry of the curlew. The water rose higher; seizing the firestick the curlew called to the other men to follow him. The bird-men followed; they had no other solution. The small group moved from one resting point to another but each time the waters came up and put out their fire. They rested at Doothawa, or Table Hill, and met there Yalngook, the King quail man who was also escaping the flood.

Yalngook tried to send the other bird-men away but Karan's power equalled that of the great Kunmanngur, the Rainbow Serpent, and they stayed. Karan cut the top joint off one of the young bird-men's fingers and let the blood run into the flood waters. They slowly subsided and finally all the bird-men changed into the bird forms they have today and flew back to their own tribal countries. Karan flew away high into the sky and sat down alongside Meerk the moon.

Kianoo Tjeemairee, Murinbata tribe[13]

Legends tell of a time long ago when it rained day and night; the seas rose and water covered all the land. *photo D. Roff*

Another fascinating myth from the north coast of New South Wales tells of the arrival of the first people who, using the rainbow as a bridge, travelled from a land across the sea. In this myth the first people arrive on the continent after the rising of the seas, after the 'great flood', and therefore it could relate to later migrations of Aboriginal people who still retained their links in memory to the peoples of the north.

A Flood Separated the Countries of the World

One time all the land in the world was joined up in one big country. Then a big flood came and the world was covered.

As the water began to go down, the streams and currents of water divided the land up into islands. There were some people left on one of these islands. It might have been that country called Africa. These people were cut off, living on that island. They were great throwers of the boomerang. They could split a tree with the boomerang. They could throw their boomerangs into the sky until they went out of sight. They were hard throwers in those times.

One man was throwing his boomerang in that country. He threw it hard and far. It travelled into the sky, away out of sight. The boomerang flew and hit a tree in the country of Australia. That tree was near the beach at Middle Head, down from Macksville.

'Oh,' those people on the island cried. 'There's land over there.' But they didn't know how to get back to this country.

Then a little boy started to cry. He was crying and crying and crying. All his people tried to give him witchetty grub, honey, paddy-melon, carpet-snake, wallaby. All kinds of tucker they brought to him. But the little boy would take that tucker and throw it away and go on crying and crying.

The little boy's brother-in-law, Ngudgeegullum, came along. He brought with him a dungirr, a koala. He said to the little boy, 'Do you want this?' 'Ngee!' said the little boy. The brother-in-law took the bear and killed it. He opened it up and took out the guts. Then he took the intestines and threw them at the boy and hit him in the stomach with them.

'Yarree, jagurr, yarngoo yarri,' said the boy. 'I'm going down to the beach now.' He took the koala's intestines down to the beach and started to blow them up with his mouth.

'Yes, that's right,' said his brother-in-law. The little boy started to laugh then.

Those intestines started to go right up into the sky. The little boy blew into them, boombi, we call them. They began to curve over the sky and make a bridge.

All those people, those tribes on the island, started to walk across on that bridge. Ngudgeegullum, the brother-in-law, went first and the little boy followed him. As they walked across the bridge, Ngudgeegullum kept saying, 'I'll cut it off now! I'll cut it off!' He wanted to cut the bridge with his stone axe.

But the little boy said, 'Don't do that! Wait until we are all over there.'

When all the people landed on the beach at Middle Head — that's where the bridge ended when it went across the sky — Ngudgeegullum cut it off with his stone tomahawk. 'Now,' he said, 'you can float away. I don't want to see you any more. Now you can turn into a rainbow.' So the bridge turned into a rainbow and floated away.

There was no sea at that time. It was all calm water. 'Now,' said Ngudgeegullum to the water, 'you've got to chase me now.' The water started to roll. It started to roll in to the beach in big waves. Ngudgeegullum ran up and down the beach crying out, 'Come on! Chase me!' The water, it rolled and it rolled, trying to chase Ngudgeegullum. That's how the sea started. That's how it is today.

'Now,' said Ngudgeegullum to the little boy, 'you must turn into the koala and I must turn into the native cat. Our names are Dungirr and Barnjull.' So these two turned into the koala and the native cat.

Then all those people who landed at that place split up into different tribes. They went to different rivers. That's why the tribes talk different languages all over Australia.[14]

VOLCANOES

From the Pleistocene era to as late as 5000 B.P. the awe-inspiring sight of erupting volcanoes was witnessed by Aboriginal people in the southern part of the continent. A myth collected many years ago may well describe the eruption of Mount Wilson in the Blue Mountains near Sydney.

The Story of the Eruption of the Earth and the Waratah

This legend tells of the time when the earth blew up, great flames filled the sky and rocks and debris flowed over the land. Disaster and destruction of the whole of the tribes was averted only by the magic of the waratah. The area this took place is now called Mount Wilson, in New South Wales, and the beautiful waratah grows there still shining red amongst the green of the surrounding eucalypts.

Long ago in the Dreamtime, from the valleys of the Hawkesbury River and from the Hartley district, many tribes had pushed south and established a big camp on the heights (now Kurrajong Heights) together with the Mount Wilson people. There was plenty of game here — red rock wallabies everywhere. Their skins were striped and beautiful — rugs and cloaks were stitched from them to keep the men warm in the coolness of the winter. These were trimmed with the red crests of the gang-gangs (cockatoos) and made fine clothes.

They were on the watch for the Hunter Valley tribes, however, who were drawing closer, and one young man from the camp crept out in darkness one night, wrapped in a wombat skin, to spy on the enemy. He brought news back of their strength and the Mount Wilson mob then decided to drive them away.

Down in the gully a clearing was made and stones were placed in position for a great corroboree. The day was very hot; a dark mist gathered and the mountains seemed expectant. As darkness fell, all the adult men and some of the women went down to the ceremonial ground. The uninitiated young men, children and younger women stayed behind at the camp. The sound of chanting filled the night and the nullah-nullahs rhythmically beat the ground.

Then the whole world shook. The sky lit up and the hillside seemed to split open as flames leapt to the sky, and a great roar was heard. The hillside was tumbling down. There was nowhere to run. All eyes turned with fear and anguish to the camp site where the young people were. They would all die unless the fire could be stopped. Even now, cries of anguish and pain could be heard.

Then a young man named Camoola leapt up and called to his friend who had cleverly acted as scout and hidden in a wombat skin. He must know how to put the fire out! Seizing a clump of waratah stems and leaves this young 'wombat-skin' ran off into the night, followed closely by Camoola who brought as many waratahs as he could carry. Camoola pursued Wombat-skin until they came to a cave. Just then the sky became light and the stars shone clearly — they could see the injured, sick and maimed in their camp; but could not reach them.

The waratahs had long been used by the people for wrapping the hand to hold hot things as they repel heat and fire. Holding the waratahs before them, they entered the cave in the ground, and winding through cavernous passages they came suddenly upon the fire. It seemed to be coming from the underground, up a tunnel and along the new crack in the mountain. Camoola and Wombat-skin knew they had to stop up that hole if their people were to be saved.

They needed more waratah leaves desperately and headed back to the cave-hole entrance to collect them. There they found they could not get out. There were no footholes and although they jumped repeatedly they could not make it. There was an evil spirit near, preventing them. Wombat-skin was more highly trained in Tribal Law than the young Camoola and hastily snatching some pipeclay from the side of the hole he made sacred designs on his body. Then he uttered a yell. It was the yell to send the evil away by reaching the Great Spirit Ancestor. Camoola heard the call, and, although he was uninitiated, he understood its meaning. It was to be his death.

A third time Wombat-skin yelled, and then the strange thing happened. Wombat-skin could jump no higher, but the leaves of the waratah grew out. The petiole — the stalk that joined them to the stem — grew longer. Both men saw that,

The awe-inspiring sight of erupting volcanoes was witnessed by Aboriginal people in the southern part of the continent. *photo D. Roff*

and both men leapt again. They grasped the leaf and drew the stalks closer until they could hold them, and a quick, sharp tug broke them from the great thick root. Soon they had gathered enough.

But Camoola grew strangely weak. His arms and legs burned and withered. Wombat-skin, however, had enough waratahs and, completely covering himself with them, he returned to the seat of the flame. He lay across the hole. The flames were stopped, and the power of the waratah stems acted. He was not burned.

The tribe shrieked with delight when they saw that the flames had ceased. All they had to do was to twine some pliable waratah stems about their feet and they could step on the hot stones and cross the fissure. This they did, and wearily tramped up the hill to the blackened camp. They reached their people to find that all were burned and some were dead.

Wombat-skin, when he knew the fire had ceased, arose and went back to Camoola who lay still in death. He had clutched a waratah too tightly after it had been touched by the Great Spirit and before the Spirit had left it. The petioles were still growing. His uninitiated hand stopped the growth, and that is why most of the leaves of waratahs are imperfect. They twist and curl and do not fully grow. Wombat-skin left him there, and many ages afterwards they say his bones were found by a white man.

The Mount Wilson district shows signs of a volcanic eruption. The trespassing blacks saw the fire and felt the quake, and they made all haste back to the Hunter Valley. The tribes that had amalgamated separated again, and each bore their dead back to their own territory. All but Camoola. No one dared touch him. The clearing that was made for the corroboree is still at the foot of Mount Wilson. The great volcanic crack may be seen today, and all agree that ages ago volcanic disturbance did take place about this great mountain. It and Mount Hay and Mount Tomah are to be seen plainly from the outskirts of Sydney, and some say that the petioles of the State emblem flower are longer there than anywhere else.[15]

It is possible that such references distantly reflect the great climatic and geological changes that have occurred in Australia since man first arrived. Over the millennia Aboriginal people, who by this time were living in widely dispersed groups throughout Australia, had observed the gradual but great climatic changes that occurred. They had witnessed the drying up of the huge interior lakes which previously teemed with life, and watched the progressive spreading aridity of the interior of the continent. They had watched as the sea waters encroached on their coastal lands, changing the shape of their tribal country and forcing them to retreat to the lands of their neighbours further inland where conflict and death were the inevitable results. To the south-east, along the ranges of New South Wales, western Victoria and South Australia, terrifying happenings had taken place. Mountains burst into flame and hurled rocks in every direction. Only after the burning lava had cooled and the bush vegetation taken over, could the tribespeople and the animals, their quarry, wander here once again.

Aboriginal history is an oral tradition; long-remembered stories are told around campfires and enacted in dance. The history of the people emerges as a living thread spun from the mouths of storytellers and ritual song-men throughout the continent as they tell of the dawn of time, the creation of life, their great Spirit Ancestors and the way in which this country was formed. The scientists follow behind, piecing together the evidence. The Aboriginals ask us to open our ears to their own stories, to hear the history of this land Australia from those who were here at the beginning.

The Mount Wilson district shows signs of ancient volcanic eruption and the fertile volcanic soils have now given rise to rainforest vegetation. *photo G. & J. Eadie*

CHAPTER TWO

The Creation Era

According to Aboriginal belief, all life as it is known today, human, animal, bird and fish, is part of one unchanging interconnected system, one vast network of relationships which can be traced to the great Spirit Ancestors of the Dreamtime, Alcheringa or Tjukurpa.

Aeons ago, when the earth was barely formed, these great Spirits, in both human and animal form, made their dramatic entrances onto the barren featureless landscape. Some, like the giant Serpents, came from beneath the ground, and as they pushed upward created huge ridges, mountains and gorges. Others came from the sky, or from distant islands across the sea. After their arrival on this continent, an era then followed when the spirits made their epic journeys across the land, creating rivers, trees and rocks, and naming plants and animals as sacred species for their descendants. At times, they clashed with others, both animal and human, and metamorphosis from human to animal form was a common feat.

The Ancestors are responsible for the whole pattern of life as Aboriginal people know it today. They govern the seasons and therefore the growth of natural vegetation, the natural reproduction of animal species and the cycle of life from birth to death.

The Dreamtime is not only an ancient era of Creation, but continues as the 'Dreaming' in the spiritual lives of Aboriginal people today. The journeys and events of the Dreamtime are enacted in ceremonies, danced in mime form by living embodiments of Dreamtime creatures — human goannas, serpents or giant figures — each painted and elaborately decorated with traditional symbolic designs. Song-poetry, chanted incessantly to the accompaniment of didjeridu or clapsticks, relates the story of the events of those early times and brings the power of the Dreaming to bear on life today.

THE DESERT ANCESTORS

Amongst the desert nomads the very existence of the people is traced to Creation times or in Pitjantjatjara language Tjukurpa times — the era when the great totemic heroes performed many mighty deeds. The beings of the Tjukurpa not only formed the geography of the desert lands and the creatures which were thereafter hunted for food, but they also fashioned the first weapons and utensils for the people. They gave the Law the people still follow today and the stories and legends of these times are accepted as the absolute truth by Aboriginal people, providing an answer to the universal questions and problems of man throughout the ages: the origins of the universe, the spirit world, the laws of nature, relations between the sexes, family life, death and life after death.

Before the Tjukurpa, the earth was a flat desolate and parched plain; there were no hills, no desert trees or grasses, no beautiful waterholes and no animals, birds, insects or living creatures. Life did not exist above the surface. But in the depths of the earth great beings dwelt, and emerged one by one, pushing the earth up as they came. These were the great Spirit Ancestors and gradually, as the ages passed, they began their journeys across the land. Although legends give them the appearance of creatures and plants, they behaved in the same manner as human beings: they made camps, made fire and cooked food, dug for water, performed ceremonies, made love and gave birth to children. They differ in that wherever they stopped, wherever any event took place in their lives, they left behind them features of the landscape which remain today.

Opposite: Wherever the great Creation Ancestors stopped, they left behind them features of the landscape which remain today. *photo R. Edwards*

In a deep rock hole on the summit of Ayers Rock dwells the serpent Wanambi. When offended, he raises himself into the sky and takes the form of a rainbow. *photo D. Roff*

In the arid centre of Australia there is no one great Spirit Ancestor responsible for life as it is known today, but numerous totemic beings who existed contemporaneously with each other in the distant Dreaming and from whom each man and his family still claim descent. The path of each man's Ancestor as he wandered the land forms his own 'Dreaming' path and at various times of the year particular rocks, waterholes, trees or caves which mark the route are visited for the performance of ceremonies.

During these rituals, a miraculous transformation takes place. Over successive days and nights of song-poetry chanted into the dawn, the dancers methodically stamp and move in rhythmic imitation of the events which befell the Ancestor at this site. Their bodies are decorated totally with feathers, ochre and grass seeds, stuck to their bodies with dried sacred blood let from their veins. Dancers at different Dreamings become Nintaka the perentie, Windaru the bandicoot, Kalaia the emu, Kanga the crow, Malu the kangaroo or Mala the hare-wallaby.

THE ORIGIN OF THE DESERT TORS

AYERS ROCK

Ayers Rock, that great monolith south-east of Alice Springs, rises more than a thousand feet above the flat surrounding plain and is 9 kilometres (5½ miles) in perimeter. The sheer immensity of this great rock in the middle of an extensive level plain, and its extraordinary colouring which changes from orange to purple at sunrise and sunset, makes it one of the great geographical wonders of the world. Its rugged surface contains many waterholes, some of which are permanent, and numerous caves. The run-off of rain from the rock has created a narrow fertile area at its base where many plants grow and animals frequently visit to drink and to feed. The rock therefore assumes great significance to a desert nomadic people,

At the end of the Creation era the camp of the Mala men became etched into the rock. *photo D. Roff*

perpetually seeking food and water. The great rock has for the Pitjantjatjara and Yangkuntjatjara always been the same from the Creation period, when it changed miraculously from a low sandhill to its present form. they believe the many topographical features of the rock were created by several different totemic beings.

The Kuniya and Liru

Long ago in the Tjukurpa, the Kuniya or non-venomous carpet snakes journeyed from Paku-Paku, a waterhole near Mount Conner west of Ayers Rock, until they came to a large flat sandhill in the centre of which was a waterhole. They made their camp there and for a time life was very good. Each day the Kuniya women were able to find plenty of food which they carried home to the camp in their curved wooden carrying dishes. They prepared their bread from seeds gathered from grasses on the plain and cooked it in the ashes of their fires. The Kuniya men, after hunting kangaroos, emus and wallabies, liked to lie resting at the edge of the sandhill as the sun set. This sandhill at the close of the Creation era turned to rock. The Kuniya people themselves were changed into various features of what is now called Ayers Rock. The women seated in their camp became large boulders in Tjukiki Gorge while their 'piti', wooden carrying dish, became a tall slab of rock at the head of the gorge. A rockhole represents their campfire and small grasses and bushes which grow in tufts in the gorge are their hairs. The sleeping Kuniya men turned into boulders which now lie motionless in the sun on the plain beneath.

While the Kuniya people were staying at Ayers Rock, however, life did not remain peaceful. A party of venomous snake men, the Liru, were travelling around in the Pitjantjatjara country causing a lot of trouble. The Liru camped at Katatjuta (Mount Olga) and then decided to approach Ayers Rock to attack the Kuniya. They were led by the great warrior Kulikudgeri, and travelling in a large

When Kurpannga the dingo attacked, the Mala fled to safety. The marks of their retreat route form furrows on the surface of the rock. *photo R. Beeche*

group they crossed the sandhills and arrived at the camp of a powerful Kuniya woman named Pulari. Pulari had separated herself from the rest of her people as she had just given birth to a child. Enraged and desperate to protect her child, she sprang at the Liru with her child in her arms, spitting out the essence of disease and death, or arukwita. Many of the Liru were killed, but they continued to attack. A young Kuniya warrior challenged Kulikudgeri to a fight to the death and the Liru man, after an arduous battle, fatally wounded the Kuniya man who crawled away over the sandhill.

Kuniya Inkridi, the mother of the slain youth, then rose in a fury and struck Kulikudgeri a great blow on the nose with her digging stick. He died in agony, his blood streaming over the surface of the land, leaving stains on the rock that remain today. Kuniya Inkridi mourned for her lost son. She covered her body in red ochre and sang and wailed into the night. She spat out arukwita, the essence of death and disease, and any man approaching that site today will be stricken.

Meanwhile a huge battle took place between the Liru and the Kuniya at the waterhole on the top of the sandhill. The Liru speared a great many Kuniya and, victorious, left the area and went back to Katatjuta. Kuniya Inkridi the great mother carpet snake despaired; hearing of the death of her people, she sang the arukwita song to kill herself and the remaining Kuniya.

At the close of the Tjukurpa period, when the giant sandhill turned to stone, these epic events were enshrined in stone also. The route of the Liru men from Katatjuta to Ayers Rock is marked by rows of desert oaks, the metamorphosed bodies of the invaders, while the tracks of the Liru men were turned into deep fissures on the south-western face of the Rock. The spears the Liru men threw made indentations in the sand which are now potholes on the vertical cliff face. A large split boulder was once the body of the Kuniya woman Pulari who gave birth

Cave of the Mala women. Each geographical feature of Ayers Rock marks the activities of the totemic Ancestors. *photo R. Beeche*

at this place; within the boulder is a small cave in which her child was born. Near the Pulari stone is a shallow cave with stones in front, which were once Pulari and her child. Until recently, pregnant women tried to give birth in this cave, believing that Pulari would help them have an easier delivery.

When the young wounded Kuniya warrior crawled away, the track he left became a watercourse. He died at a place where today there are three waterholes, each of which contains the blood of the dying man transformed into water. His victor, the leader of the Liru, Kulikudgeri, became the large square boulder, while his nose which was cut off by Kuniya Inkridi stands out as a huge slab that has split off the main rock.

The bodies of Kuniya Inkridi and her husband remain today as large and small boulders and rocks, the fig trees that tenaciously grip the smooth rock surface and send roots burrowing into the crevices are believed to be their hair. These boulders remain very important sites for the descendants of the Kuniya, as increase or fertility centres for carpet snakes.

Pitjantjatjara–Yangkuntjatjara, central Australia[1]

The Hare-Wallabies, Mala, and the Spirit Dingo, Kurpannga

While the carpet snake people were camped at the waterhole on the south-eastern part of Ayers Rock, a party of hare-wallabies, the Mala, left their camp in the country north-west of Mount Liebig and travelled to Ayers Rock in order to put their young boys through ceremonies which would make them men. The route the Mala took is now a line of bare rock on the north-western corner.

The Mala women and children set up their own camp; each day while the ceremonies were going on they went out to search for edible seeds, berries and small game. They gathered plenty of fruit and cooked it for the evening meal. One old Mala man did not take part in the ritual. He was sent to watch the women, to

Camp site of Linga, the lizard man. *photo D. Roff*

The totemic place of the lizard, Kandju. The holes Kandju dug while searching for his boomerang are now potholes and vertical chasms. *photo D. Roff*

The Mulga-seed men created a giant dingo called Kurpannga and sent him to Ayers Rock to punish the Mala wallabies. *photo D. Roff*

make sure no one came near the secret ceremonies. These matters were the sacred business of the men and women were compelled to keep away or the power of the Ancestral Spirits would be broken.

The young boys were guarded by the old men, and the actual rituals were performed on a hard patch of ground, which was transformed into the back wall of a long cylindrical cave on the side of the Rock. This cave is absolutely forbidden to women, who were not even allowed to look in that direction when passing. While the Mala ceremony was proceeding, the Wintalyka or Mulga-seed men of Kikingkura in the Petermann Ranges, sent their messenger, the bellbird Panpanpanala, to Ayers Rock to invite the Mala people to a ceremony and ask them to bring material for decorations with them so that they could use some for body designs. The Mala people were angry at this request and sent back some white ash and a discourteous reply.

The Mulga-seed men were furious and urged their sorcerers, their knowledgeable medicine men who knew the greatest secrets and had the power to communicate with the Spirits, to devise a revenge. The medicine men created a malevolent giant Spirit dingo called Kurpannga, and sent him to Ayers Rock. Kurpannga had the appearance of a dingo with very little hair. His teeth were savagely sharp and the songs of the medicine men filled him with the urge to fight and kill strangers.

When Kurpannga reached the Mala camp it was the hot midday; all the Mala people were asleep, except the old kingfisher woman, Lunba, who kept watch. She saw the movement of Kurpannga and gave the alarm. Kurpannga, however, crept up to the camp and with his ferocious teeth he killed two men. The rest of the Mala escaped. The Mala men managed to save their sacred emblems and then the Mala fled eastward with the young men and with the kingfisher woman.

As with the story of the Kuniya and Liru, the camps of the mythical people, their battles and their deeds were transformed into boulders, clefts and natural features of Ayers Rock at the close of the Tjukurpa. The main camp of the Mala women and children is now a large cave in the north-western corner of the Rock. The erosion patterns of the cliff face represent the transformed features of the women. The men carried out sacred ceremonies on the northern and north-western sides of the Rock. A long curving line of caves in a large eroded area were once the young men lying on the ground, being decorated by the old Mala men. A dark water stain on the rock face was the bark brush used to paint ceremonial designs.

Pitjantjatjara–Yangkuntjatjara, central Australia[1]

The importance of Ayers Rock in the ceremonial and ritual life of the desert people has never waned, and now that the area has become a major tourist attraction, there is constant anxiety and distress amongst the old men whose origins are there and who regard it as sacred to themselves and their descendants. The story of the dingo and his revenge on the Mala is told by Tony Tjamiwa, a Pitjantjatjara man. When the Mala left Ayers Rock they scattered to his country, where he now guards the sacred emblems of the Mala rituals.

'The Mala rejected that man from Wintalyka (Docker River). He tried to call them for a ceremony, and because of this they created an evil Mamu spirit there, Kurpannga, a dog, and they created it there because they were unable to call the Mala for a ceremony. Having come from Wintalyka the Spirit dog arrived there and having found it, bit a young eagle. Kurpannga bit the young eagle at Ayers Rock and all the Mala scattered and some of them came round this way to Ulkiya.

'You white fellows do not know about Ulkiya. You have not seen it. There are other things on the other side which have not been seen. That is my camp. Listen! My father told me a little about this and I am looking after it properly and I have always been looking after it, not just now. I have been continually looking after it. And having heard of Ayers Rock, having heard of tourists at the sacred cave, I have been thinking to make this known. Having received this from my father, I have been looking after this. But he is finished. I am speaking plainly and telling you men and you white people that this is holy. And we rise for one ceremony, the ceremony of the Mala (plains wallaby), this is our ceremony.'

Tony Tjamiwa, Pitjantjatjara[2]

Even more desperate in his appeal for white people not to desecrate his sacred area is old Paddy, the traditional owner of the area, in particular the Mala wallaby sites. His Pitjantjatjara name is the same as that of the rock, signifying his descent from and unity with it. An emotional meeting was held at Ernabella in 1971 with Paddy and some of the other Pitjantjatjara men who were linked to Ayers Rock where a sacred cave had recently been entered by a white woman. The old men tried to explain the reasons for their anguish in an attempt to prevent the march of tourism to the area. Their words are those of desperation: if Ayers Rock is desecrated there is no future; their Dreaming of the Mala, the plains wallaby, is destroyed. They, the Mala, are no more.

'Ayers Rock is my camp. This is mine, this holy cave. Yes, this is a holy cave. I alone truly know about this place. I was put into this place. Yes, my fathers and grandfathers entrusted me with this cave. This holy cave. And girls have broken this thing of mine. And I have become very sad. This is my great ceremony, my holy ceremony, my great camp with its holy tree and Mutitjulu on this side is holy. Ayers Rock is holy. I am Ayers Rock and these things are mine. And now white people have broken that which is ours, our Law, ours, our great ceremony, the ceremony of the Mala wallaby from which we are taught. And I am speaking truly to you. Mutitjulu is the main place at Ayers Rock and white people have gone through it. A white fellow, having frightened me, chased me away. Having gone from that place I wandered around, having left my things there I moved around. That was my camp, my home, mine, and I was going around from there. Finished! My fathers are finished. They are finished.

'Having become one in that place I left it. This having happened I let everything go and later a white girl went through there. I do not know where she came from, from a long way away, but she went through this holy place. She broke this holy place. It is broken completely. They get rich from seeing this flash place. We do not know about it but the white fellows get rich. They come from a long way away, from the west, and they get rich from Ayers Rock. I don't know. They are a

In the Tjukurpa or Creation times Kandju the blue-tongued
lizard created many features of Ayers Rock. *photo D. Roff*

long way away. Yes, but from my camp they become rich. Yes, and now I am
obtaining a motor car and I am coming to that place. I am going to live there at
Ayers Rock. Yes, here I am coming to you. Yes.'*[3]

The Lizard Man, Kandju or Linga

While the snakes and wallaby were camped at Ayers Rock, a little lizard man lived
alone, somewhere to the west. One day, while he was trying out a boomerang, the
weapon spun away and buried itself in the soft sand of the mound which later
turned to rock. Kandju, upset over his loss, dug everywhere in the sand until he
found it. Many of the spectacular features in the Kandju Gorge are the result of his
desperate search — the holes and gutters he dug in the sand are now the deep
potholes and vertical chasms of the gorge.

The lizard stayed in this area for a while, and then moved to another side of
Ayers Rock, near Taputji, the camp of the Mala women, and here the
Yangkuntjatjara call him Linga. Linga lived mainly on honey ants, but the worker
ants chased and bit him every time he stole the honey. As he was unable to find any
other food, he became very hungry, and almost starved to death. One day he saw a
young carpet snake girl asleep in front of her wet-weather shelter and killed her to
eat. The body of the Kuniya girl changed into a boulder, the wound in her neck
into a rock fissure. Having eaten the girl, Linga left the area and travelled away
into the distance towards the Musgrave Ranges.

Pitjantjatjara–Yangkuntjatjara, central Australia[4]

* Paddy Uluru did return to Ayers Rock. He stayed there until he died, and he was buried there. His five sons survive him
and these men together with several Yangkuntjatjara men are now the traditional owners of the area. Paddy Uluru died at
Ayers Rock while this book was in preparation and in deference to the wishes of the Pitjantjatjara people his name and the
Aboriginal name of Ayers Rock have been deleted.

41

The Sleepy Lizard Man, Lunkana

During Creation times, an unmarried sleepy lizard man called Lunkana lived by himself at Ayers Rock. Despite Aboriginal law about sharing food, he was so mean that he kept all the meat he caught for himself. When he caught emus, he would bring them secretly back to his camp and eat after dark. His cooking place became a small rockhole. After a while the carpet snake people became angry at such meanness and decided to kill Lunkana. While he was asleep in his wet-weather shelter of boughs, the Kuniya men set fire to it and the lizard died in agony. The windbreak where he slept was turned into a cave, the smoke is now a large area of lichen and the dead body of Lunkana is a low boulder at the base of the Rock.

This low rock is the increase centre for sleepy lizards and is full of Kurunba or the life essence of the lizards.

Pitjantjatjara–Yangkuntjatjara, central Australia[4]

Willy Wagtail Woman

Tjinderi-Tjinderiba was a willy wagtail woman who set up camp with her children at the northern end of Ayers Rock — now transformed into a rockhole. Not far away is a long cylindrical boulder which is the body of the wagtail woman, who was speared by a Liru man. Her numerous children are now large and small boulders. In a nearby shallow cave are four small rocks, once four infants. This cave is believed to contain an inexhaustible supply of spirit children who will become human babies if they find the right mother. The Pitjantjatjara have a deep fear of the willy wagtail and believe it will do great harm if hurt in any way.

Pitjantjatjara–Yangkuntjatjara, central Australia[4]

Below: Lunkana the sleepy lizard who was very greedy once lived at Ayers Rock. He was killed by the Kuniya carpet snakes as punishment for not sharing his food. *photo D. Roff*

Opposite: The Wanambi are giant serpents with flowing manes, beards and sharp teeth who live in deep waterholes. It is forbidden to light fire in a Wanambi's area or drink at his waterhole or, rising into the air in the form of a rainbow, he will kill the intruder by taking his spirit. *photo R. Edwards*

The Mythical Snake, Wanambi

On the summit of Ayers Rock is a steep-sided rockhole in which a mythical snake, Wanambi, lives. This snake, which is very dangerous and unfriendly, lives in huge caverns beneath the water. It is hundreds of yards long and can assume the form of a rainbow when offended. The Wanambi will take the water from all the springs and rockholes in the area as another means of hurting his enemies. This Wanambi is not in the same category as the totemic beings of Creation times, as he has not created any of the topography of the rock, and remains the same today as he always was.

Pitjantjatjara-Yangkuntjatjara, central Australia[4]

KATATJUTA — THE OLGAS

Katatjuta, literally 'the place of many heads', is a spectacular group of enormous rock domes that rise precipitously from the level sandy desert. Apart from the group of domes to the south where the poisonous Liru snakes camped before setting out for Ayers Rock some distance away, the Olgas do not link to the Rock, but were created by many different mythical beings.

Wanambi, the Mythical Snake

The largest monolith in the Olgas is the permanent home of an immense, highly-coloured Wanambi similar to the one that lives at Ayers Rock, with a flowing beard, a mane and long teeth. During the Wet Season the Wanambi lives in one of the waterholes on the top of the mountain, but during the Dry Season he makes his

Katatjuta, the 'place of many heads'. *photo D. Roff*

home in a waterhole in one of the gorges. If these dry up, he retreats inside the rock itself. A wind blows constantly in the gorge, sometimes gently, sometimes like a hurricane. This is the breath of Wanambi when angered. It is forbidden to light fire in this area or to drink at his waterhole or, rising into the air in the form of a rainbow, he will kill the intruder by taking his spirit from him.

Most major boulders, domes of rock and caves that occur throughout the Olgas are associated with Totemic Ancestors. The caves in the southern side of Walpa Gorge, probably more than 490 metres (1500 feet) high, were once piles of corkwood tree blossoms collected by the corkwood tree sisters in Tjukurpa times. From these they obtained a sweet drink by soaking them in their wooden dishes. The stories of the mice women and the curlew man are lost in time as their descendants have long gone; their camps, however, remain as the series of large monoliths on the eastern side of Katatjuta.

Katatjuta is still guarded by the traditional owners, however, who can relate stories of their creation and the Totemic Beings associated with them. One highly spectacular pillar of rock on the eastern side, with the smaller one leaning against its side, is the transformed body of Malu the kangaroo man who is arrested in stone as he dies in the arms of his sister Mulumura, a lizard woman. He was killed at this place by a pack of dingoes after his long travels from the west. His wound is an erosion in the rock and his intestines which spilled out appear as a rock mound at the base. One of the most interesting stories which tell the history of Katatjuta is that of the Pungalunga men, giant cannibals who lived in distant times and preyed on man and who appear as domes on the western side.[5]

The Pungalunga Men of Katatjuta

The Pungalunga were huge men who lived entirely on the flesh of Aboriginal men, women and children. Each day they killed people, tucked them into the hair-string belts around their waists and carried them home to be cooked and eaten. Their jaws and teeth were extremely powerful and they ate the whole body, crushing the bones completely. They broke the backs of their victims into sections and swallowed these whole. They were particular about the way they cooked their victims. After the removal of the intestines, the body was buried in an earth trench and the fire lit above it, similar to the method of cooking kangaroos today. The body was dismembered after cooking; it was first broken in half at the base of the spine and then the chest and ribs were severed from the spinal column using a sharp-edged stone. The heads, unless the Pungalunga were extremely hungry, were generally kept in the fork of a tree to be eaten the next day.

The Pungalunga men were a terrifying sight as they strode across the countryside in search of victims, but gradually the Aboriginal people began to grow in numbers as the Pungalunga disappeared one by one. Finally only one Pungalunga remained.

One day, two men went out hunting Malu kangaroos and did not reach camp until it was getting dark. Their wives went to the waterhole to collect water and as the day left and night came the men became worried for their safety. They climbed a hill and seeing a huge campfire burning in the distance, they knew the Pungalunga man had caught their wives and was eating them. That night the men decided to end the terror of the Pungalunga for ever. They straightened their spears over the fire and made sure their spear-throwers were strong. The next morning both men walked towards the waterhole. The Pungalunga watched from behind some trees. One man acted as a decoy and kept going to the waterhole while the other crept around behind the monster and speared him in the back. Screaming with pain, the Pungalunga ran into the scrub to escape, but he was finally speared to death, and died in the Kuniula Cave, near Mulara Spring. The two hunters then lit a huge fire at the mouth of the cave and destroyed all traces of the last of these cannibals.[6]

Overleaf: The gorges, waterholes, caves and boulders of central Australia were formed by the totemic Ancestors in the Creation era. *photo R. Edwards*

45

THE ORIGIN OF LAKE EYRE

Lake Eyre is a huge arid lake bed swelling with water only in times of flood. It lies in a vast region of shifting sandhills, claypans and impermanent rivers between the Birdsville Track and the Central Australian Railway. The wildlife includes myriads of waterbirds, packs of dingoes and unusually resilient fauna and flora.

The formation of Lake Eyre is linked to the great travels of the Tjukurpa kangaroo, which form an extremely important Dreaming path across the desert areas. Most of the songs which relate to this story and the features of the country associated with it are still considered sacred by the desert people, the exclusive knowledge of fully initiated men, and must never be heard by women. These stories are therefore closed to us. However, the following legend of the Arabana tribe recounts how Lake Eyre, that vast inland lake, was formed in Tjukurpa times.

An old woman was out hunting when she saw a huge kangaroo in the distance. From her belly a young boy, Wilkuda, jumped out and chased the kangaroo west, hoping to spear it. He chased it until his spear finally reached its mark and, thinking it was dead, he threw it over his fire to cook and went to sleep. When he awoke the kangaroo had jumped off and escaped him. Wilkuda followed that kangaroo from sunrise to sunset for many days, until finally he grew weary. An old man with a dog came across their path, and with the aid of his dog, killed the kangaroo. Wilkuda said the old man could have the meat from his kangaroo, but he needed the skin.

Then Wilkuda travelled back east and threw the skin down east of Anna Creek, where it changed into a huge lake, Lake Eyre. Wilkuda is today seen as a boulder by the shores of the lake.

Arabana tribe[7]

The Nullarbor Plain hides beneath its desolate surface an extensive cave system which has provided scientists with evidence of some of the earliest art of mankind, as well as skeletons of extinct Australian animals. *photo R. Edwards*

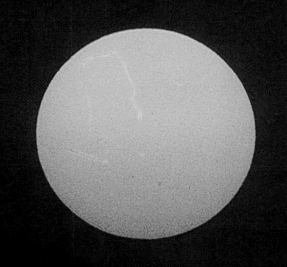

Once the earth was completely dark and silent. Inside a cave
slept a beautiful woman, the Sun. *photo R. Morrison*

THE NULLARBOR PLAIN

The Nullarbor Plain, that vast limestone plateau which appears so barren and inhospitable, hides beneath its desolate surface an extensive cave system with cathedral chambers and mirror-surfaced lakes. The depths of the Koonalda Cave have provided scientists with evidence of some of the earliest art of mankind, as well as skeletons of extinct Australian animals. They also give rise to this legend about the creation of mankind which was recorded from an old woman, Kardin-Nilla of the Karraru tribe of the west coast of South Australia.

Once the earth was completely dark and silent; nothing moved on the barren surface. Inside a deep cave below the Nullarbor Plain slept a beautiful woman, the Sun. The Great Father Spirit gently woke her and told her to emerge from her cave and stir the universe into life. The Sun Mother opened her eyes and darkness disappeared as her rays spread over the land; she took a breath and the atmosphere changed, the air gently vibrated as a small breeze blew.

The Sun Mother then went on a long journey, from east to west and from north to south she crossed the barren land and wherever her gentle rays touched the earth, grasses, shrubs and trees grew until the land was covered in vegetation. In each of the deep caverns in the earth, the Sun found living creatures which like herself had been slumbering for untold ages. She stirred the insects into life in all their forms and told them to spread through the grasses and trees, then she woke the snakes, lizards and many other reptiles and they slithered out of their deep hole. Behind the snakes mighty rivers flowed, teeming with all kinds of fish and water life. Then she called for the animals, the marsupials and many other creatures to

49

awake and make their homes on the earth. The Sun Mother then told all the creatures that the days would from time to time change from wet to dry and from cold to hot, and so she made the seasons. One day while all the animals, insects and other creatures were watching, the Sun travelled far in the sky to the west and as the sky shone red, she sank from view and darkness spread across the land once more. The creatures were alarmed and huddled together in fear. Some time later, the sky began to glow on the horizon to the east and the Sun rose smiling into the sky again. The Sun Mother thus provided a period of rest for all her creatures by making this journey each day.

Karraru tribe[8]

The Morning Star is the son of the Sun Woman and the Moon is his wife. The children of the Morning Star and the Moon were the Ancestors of the Aboriginals today.

THE SKY HEROES OF SOUTH-EASTERN AUSTRALIA

The great All-Father was known by many different tribes in Victoria and New South Wales and had different names according to the different language groups. In Victoria he was predominantly known as Bunjil and in New South Wales as Baiame and Dhurramulan. The All-Father, or the Great Spirit Father, is given much of the credit for shaping the world of south-eastern Australia, for creating the natural features of the land, and for instituting important aspects of the culture of the Aboriginal people. Accounts vary, but in many he is said to have dwelt on earth formerly, but then ascended to the sky where he watches the events of mankind today. He returned to earth for the great initiation ceremonies or Bora of the south-eastern people where his terrifying voice was heard in the whirr of the bullroarer warning the women and children to stay away. Baiame is married, with two wives and several sons. Although he has many human attributes, he remains a supernatural transcendental Being who can do anything and sees all that goes on. The great Boras are no longer held and the voice of Baiame is still, yet the people of New South Wales and Victoria will tell you his presence is always felt. He watches over his people even today.

Baiame and the Origin of the Narran Lake

Old Baiame was out searching for the nest of a native honey bee. He stuck a white feather on the back of one small bee and began to follow it to its tree. While he was hunting he sent his two wives, Birrahgnooloo and Cunnunbeillee, to search for yams and frogs and to make camp by the Coorigel Spring. The two women gathered plenty of yams which they dug up with their digging sticks and together with the frogs they had caught, they put these in their goolays, the string bags which they carried on their backs. Although they were tired when they arrived at the spring, they made a shelter to camp in for the night and gathered some firewood. The clear waters of the spring looked too enticing, however, and the women laid down their goolays and their digging sticks and, taking off their young girls' wallaby string skirts, they jumped into the water and splashed happily.

In these waters lived the giant Kurreahs, crocodile-like beings which preyed on man, and the young wives of Baiame had only begun to swim when they were seized and swallowed whole by the two Kurreahs. As the giant monsters swam away the water of the spring rushed behind them through an underground channel which led into the Narran River. As they swam down the river its course as well became dry behind them.

Baiame came to his camp that evening to find his wives missing. He saw they had made camp and gathered plenty of tucker but when he saw their string girdles lying by the water he knew the Kurreahs had them. In a fury, armed with spears and woggarahs (wooden battle-axes), he pursued them from one dried-up waterhole to another along the length of the Narran River, cutting across its meanders so that he was soon ahead of the Kurreahs. As Baiame speared the giant crocodiles, they writhed in pain and lashed around in the mud with their great tails so that a great hollow was formed. When he was close he killed them with his woggarah.

Opposite: The edge of the vast limestone plateau of the Nullarbor Plain falls precipitously to the sea. The Karraru people were descended from the Sun woman who rose from beneath the Nullarbor Plain and aroused all the plants and animals to life. *photo R. Morrison*

Baiame then cut open the Kurreahs and placed his two wives on red ant beds. The young women were covered with slime from the giants' intestines and seemed dead, yet when the ants had cleaned them and bitten them many times, they revived and came to life again.

Baiame told his young wives never to swim in the deep holes of the Narran River again or the Kurreahs may swallow them. The place where the giants lashed with their tails filled with water to become a beautiful lake where black swans, pelicans, ducks and wildfowl made their home.[9]

An interesting aspect of the legend of the Narran Lake is that crocodiles, although not now found south of the tropics, would most certainly have lived in the Narran Lake area at the close of the last Ice Age.

The Stone Fish Trap of Baiame

During Creation times a great drought came to the country in western New South Wales. The once plentiful waters of the Ngemba, Ualarai, Kamilaroi and Weilwan tribes, who lived on the fertile country above Brewarrina, began to disapppear. Fish drained away to the west; the country slowly browned, as the fierce drought shrunk the waters further, leaving strings of fading green waterholes. The rich grasses yellowed, the trees withered, the usually abundant animal life was reduced. The survivors crowded to the drying lakes and waterholes where they were trapped by the clinging mud or became easy prey for the hungry hunters.

As the drought continued, the Ngemba of Brewarrina faced a famine as the depleted waters of Gurrungga were swallowed by the Sun. Their suffering became known to Baiame who returned to Brewarrina with his sons, Booma-ooma-nowi and Ghinda-inda-mui. Using the scattered stones and boulders dug up by Baiame they set them out in the pattern of a great fish net. First the boulders, then higher to a man's thigh with smaller stones, until the stone mesh stretched down the slope of the wall of Gurrungga and across the dry watercourse. Baiame showed how to open the stone traps at either end and to set the stones securely so that they would always be kept in good repair.

That evening, the people gathered on the bare banks and held a corroboree for Baiame, who took a coolamon and showed some of the old men how to call the rain. For hours the hard ground rumbled under the stamping feet, while the fine dust rose up through the clapping boomerangs, clouding the camps, before the dancers flung themselves down to sleep around the dimming campfires. Slowly the dust clouds drifted higher and higher into the night sky where they ringed Bahloo the moon, who filled them with rain. The exhausted dancers were awakened by big heavy drops of rain which thudded onto their stiff dusty bodies and thumped into the soft powdered earth. For several days the rain poured down, clouding the green water of Gurrungga which rose slowly before the excited people. Suddenly they were startled by a growing roar as a foaming wall of brown water rushed into Gurrungga, over the rock wall, covering Baiame's stone net or Ngunnhu, and on down the dry Callewatta.

Gradually the flood fell, exposing the sharp black pattern of Baiame's net, to show the fins and mouths of thousands of fish breaking the surface of the water. The watchers, overjoyed at the return of the fish, rushed into the river and herded the teeming fish through the stone meshes, killing them with their sticks and short spears or just grabbing them in their hands. One grunted like a wounded animal when caught; this was one of Baiame's black fish, the black bream or grunter, which all grunt as the great fish Baiame first speared. The older and wiser men followed behind the excited hunters and blocked the entry to the stone traps, preventing the escape of any fish back down the river to warn others of the trap.

Long thin black lines scribbled themselves across the blue sky as the waterfowl answered their ancient call, and everyone was grateful to Baiame. This is how the Rock Fisheries came to Brewarrina.[10]

Opposite: The clear waters of the spring looked enticing, so the women laid down their goolays and digging sticks and jumped into the water. *photo H. Herbert*

Baiame's Camp

Near the town of Byrock in the west of New South Wales there is a large outcrop of
granite where Baiame is said to have had his home. He dug a waterhole at one edge
of the rock with his stone axe and as it became blunt, he whetted it on the rock
surface near him. The reddish-brown stains on the rock, caused by oxides, are
believed to be the result of Baiame laying down his magical weapons on the
surface.[11]

The Bora of Baiame

As the season was good it was decided to have a great gathering of the tribes at
Googooreewon. Old Baiame said he would take his sons, Ghinda-inda-mui and
Booma-ooma-nowi, as it was time they should be made young men so that they
could marry, eat emu flesh and learn to fight. However, although the men knew
there was to be a Bora, a ceremony for the initiation of the young men, the women
were on no account to find out.

Each tribe arrived at Googoorewon and camped at various points on the ridges
surrounding the open space where the ceremonies were to be held. The Wahn
(crows) were at one point, the Dummerh (pigeons) at another, and round about
were the Dog tribe, the Black Swans, the Blue-tongued Lizard tribe, and many
others. Hundreds and hundreds of people performed in the mighty corroborees,
each tribe trying to excel in dancing and singing. By day there was much hunting
and feasting, pledges of friendship exchanged, young daughters given to old
warriors, old women given to young men, babies promised to grown men, with the
Wireenun or doctors of the tribe being consulted at every stage.

After some days the Wireenun told the men they were going to hold a Bora, but
as the women must not know, they must all go out each day as if to hunt and then
prepare the Bora ground in secret. Out went the men each day. They cleared a very
large circle, then they built an earth dam around this circle and cleared a pathway
leading into the thick bush, with a bank on either side of the pathway.

When the Bora ground was finished, the tribes as usual held a corroboree at
night. Two Wireenuns pretended to have a fight to distract the people's attention.
Suddenly there came a strange whizzing whirring noise from the scrub around.
The women and children shrank together, for the sudden uncanny noise
frightened them. They knew it was made by Spirits who were coming to assist at the
initiation of boys.

The next day all the people moved camp to the big ring that the men had made.
The Mahthi, or dog tribe, however, had so angered Baiame by their incessant
chattering and laughter when he was trying to speak that he took away their power
of human speech. When the dogs realized that they could only bark and howl, a
look of yearning and entreaty came into their eyes, which is still seen in the eyes of
their descendants. The other tribes were awed by the power of Baiame.

Baiame came back to his camp and asked the women why they were sitting so
idly and not grinding grass seeds on their grinding stones or dayoorl. The women
said, 'Our dayoorls have gone, and we don't know where they are.'

'You're lying,' said Baiame, 'you lent them to the Pigeon tribe.' 'No,' they said 'we
didn't,' but because they were frightened of Baiame they went and asked at each
camp for their dayoorls and at each camp the answer was the same: the dayoorls
had all vanished. As the women went on they heard a strange noise like the cry of
spirits, a sound like a smothered 'oom, oom, oom' coming from high in the air and
then low in the trees, until it seemed as if spirits were everywhere. Baiame flashed a
fire stick at the sound and saw two dayoorls speeding over the ground by their own
momentum.

Next morning the camp of the Dummerh or pigeons was empty. As they saw the
dayoorls gliding through their camp they knew they had to follow them or they
would anger the spirits. They followed the dayoorls to a mountain called Diran-
gibirrah where the dayoorls piled themselves up. For the future the people had to
go to this mountain to get good dayoorls, and the Dummerh were changed to
pigeons with a cry like the spirits' 'oom, oom, oom.' That night when the Bora

Above: Cave shelter at Milbrodale, New South Wales. *photo National Parks and Wildlife Service*

Below: Detail of painting inside cave shelter at Milbrodale of a giant Ancestor Being, possibly Baiame. The arms of the figure are extended the width of the cave in either direction. *photo National Parks and Wildlife Service*

corroboree began, all the women relations of the boys to be initiated danced all night. At the end of the night all the young women were ordered into bough humpies, while the old women stayed on. Meanwhile each man seized one of the initiates and carried him off down the track to the scrub. The old women said goodbye to the boys and then went into the humpies with the young women, so they could see nothing further. The women knew that questions about what happened to the boys would get no answer. In a few months time they would see their boys return minus a front tooth and with some extra scars, and apart from these few facts, they knew nothing.

The next day the tribes made ready to go to another little Bora ring about twelve miles away. However, just as they were about to leave, the widow Millindooloonubbah staggered into the camp crying, 'You all left me to travel alone with my large family of children. How could the little feet of my children keep up with you? Have I more than two arms and one back? How could I come swiftly with so many children? Yet none of you stayed to help me. And as you went from each waterhole you drank all the water. When, tired and thirsty, I reached a waterhole and my children cried for a drink, what did I find to give them? Mud, only mud! As we reached hole after hole and found only mud, one by one my children lay down and died, died for want of a drink which their mother could not give them.'

As she spoke a woman went to her with water. 'Too late, too late!' she said. 'Why should a mother live when her children are dead?' But as she felt the water cool her parched mouth and swollen tongue, she made a final effort and, standing up, waved her hands at the tribes, crying aloud, 'You were in such haste to get here. You shall stay. Turn into trees.' And she died. As she fell back all the tribes standing round were changed into trees. The tribes in the background were changed each according to the name they were known by, into bird or animal.

There at the place of the big Bora you can see the trees standing tall and gaunt, sad-looking in their sombre colours, waving their branches with a sad wailing towards the lake which covers the place where the Bora was held. This place, now called Googoorewon, is known as a great meeting place for birds that are called by the names of the old tribes — the black swans, the pelicans and the ducks. Blue-tongued lizards glide through the grass, and pigeons call 'oom, oom, oom.'

The men and boys with Baiame who were at the place of the little Bora escaped being changed into trees, birds and animals. At last they realized the rest of the tribes would never arrive, and fearing that some fierce enemy might be close by, they went quickly to Noondoo.

And today, in the thick scrub on one of the Noondoo ridges, lives the old man Baiame, the Great Spirit, who lives forever, the strongest of the Wireenun.[12]

Dhurramulan

Dhurramulan was considered by some New South Wales tribes to be the All-Father himself, and by others to be a half-brother or near relative of Baiame. He was said to have only one leg. He lived in trees and had a voice like the rumbling of distant thunder. He separated the youths from their mothers and taught them the ceremonies of the tribe. The boys were brought to a place in the bush with rugs over their heads so that they did not know where they were going, or what was going on. Dhurramulan would hit a boy on the back of his head, which caused one of his front incisors to fall out. He would then throw the youth in the fire and scorch all his hair off. Sometimes he would even burn a boy to ashes, and by the power of his sorcery would bring him to life again. He fed the boys on a species of small wood lizard which thay ate raw.

Eventually the spirit of Dhurramulan entered different trees, in which he still lives except when initiation ceremonies are going on. A piece of wood cut from a tree will make a bull-roarer, which is also called Dhurramulan as the humming sound represents his voice. He likes to live on the large irregular protuberances characteristic of many eucalypt trees, and old men say they have found the upper side of these protuberances worn smooth by the occupation of Dhurramulan. Like many other mythical heroes he has the power of changing his shape from the size of a little bird to that of a giant.[13]

56

Bunjil the eagle hawk made the mountains and rivers, the animals and insects, and laid down the Laws for man. *photo D. Roff*

Bunjil, the Great Eagle Hawk

Amongst the Kulin Aboriginals of Victoria, the Great Ancestor Spirit is known as Bunjil. It was he who made the mountains and rivers, the animals and insects, who created man and who taught him how to behave on earth and how to make the necessary weapons for his survival.

Stories tell how Bunjil had two wives and a son named Binbeal, the rainbow, whose wife was the second bow, sometimes seen showing fainter than the first. When Bunjil had finished creating the landscape and animals, and instructing men, he became tired of staying upon the earth. So he gathered his family about him and told Bellin-bellin the musk crow, who looked after the winds: 'Open your bags and let out some wind.' So Bellin-bellin opened one of the bags in which he kept the whirlwinds and let out a blast that blew great trees into the air, roots and all. Bunjil said, 'That is not enough, let out more wind.' Bellin-bellin opened all his bags at once, and a huge wind came out and blew Bunjil and all his people to the sky, where they now live looking down on the world as stars.[14]

The Bram-bam-bult Brothers

These two brothers also belong to the myths of the Wotjobaluk people of Victoria; they moved about the country in the Dreaming era creating various features of the landscape and making sure that justice was done. They pursued Wembelin the triantelope, who had savagely killed and eaten their nephew, Doan the flying squirrel, and killed him and his wives. They also killed the Great White Owl at Lake Coorong, when they found him eating his relatives. The mopoke, who hoarded water in a tree until all the country was parched with drought, was also punished by the Bram-bam-bult brothers by being enclosed in a tree himself. And the epic hunt

57

for Ngindyal the giant emu has already been told in Chapter 1. The Bram-bam-bult brothers are therefore Creation Ancestors of the south-eastern area who are remembered largely for their role as guardians of Tribal Law and punishers of wrongdoing.

THE EARTH MOTHER

One of the major themes in Aboriginal beliefs about the supernatural pantheon of Ancestor Beings of northern Australia concerns the Great Earth Mother, the symbol of fertility and creator of life. Sacred ceremonies associated with the mother ensure the reproduction of all the species, her power animates and increases both human and animal life, it is responsible for the fluctuation of the seasons from plenty to scarcity and from wet to dry, and the continuation of the well-being of the world of the Aboriginal people.

Amongst the Kakadu, the now vanished people of the Alligator Rivers region after whom the beautiful Kakadu National Park in that area is named, the Great Earth Mother was called Imberombera. She was the original great ancestress from whom all things emanated.

Imberombera came from across the sea and arrived at Malay Bay on the coast of Arnhem Land. Her stomach was filled with children and from her head were suspended woven dilly bags in which she carried yams, bulbs and tubers. She held a digging stick in her hand. She travelled far and wide over Western Arnhem Land and everywhere she went she planted yams, bamboo, cyprus palms and waterlilies. She formed the hills, creeks, animals and plants and left behind her many spirit children, giving each group a different language.[15]

Another great fertility mother, Ungulla, made her journeys after Imberomba and as she crossed the country she met the children of Imberomba. She carried some of her children on her shoulders, others on her hips and some of them walked. Ungulla herself wore sheets of paperbark and showed the Kakadu women how to make bark aprons. Finally, having borne many children, she tore out her vagina and uterus and threw them to the women saying, 'From now on this will be yours. You can have the children from now on.' And then she took her breasts and fighting stick and gave these to the women also. To the men she gave a flat spear-thrower and a reed spear.

Amongst the Gunwinggu people a similar story is told of the origins of mankind. Their story is of Waramurungundji, who also travelled across the sea from north-west Indonesia to land on the northern coast, at the beginning of the Creation times.

Waramurungundji

Waramurungundji — the 'mother' — came from over the sea from the north-west, in the direction of Indonesia, at the beginning of the world. When she landed on the Australian coast she made children, telling them where they were to live and what language they were to speak. She also created much of the countryside and left various creatures and natural features, bees and wild honey in one place and a banyan tree in another. She tried to circumcise the children she had made but at first she was unsuccessful and the children died. In those areas people do not practise circumcision today. But at last she succeeded and in those places, therefore, people continue to circumcise today. Waramurungundji's husband was called Wuragag, and he too came with her. After some adventures together he left her, and took a second wife named Goringal. Waramurungundji continued her journeys alone. Wuragag had many adventures, and many wives. Finally, at the end of his particular travels, he turned into a high rocky hill, a landmark which dominates the plains north of Oenpelli. This bears his name, Wuragag, because his spirit remains there; in English it is called Tor Rock. Beside this rock stands a smaller one facing east alongside of him and that is his young wife Goringal.[16]

To the south-east of Arnhem Land, along the Roper River, the fertility mother is known as Jingana or Eingana. Here the fertility rites express two main concepts, the fertility mother and the Rainbow Serpent, and both of these are inextricably connected.

58

Eingana – The Mother

That first time, Creation time, we call Biengana. The first Being we call Eingana. We call Eingana our mother. Eingana made everything. Eingana had everything inside herself that first time.

Eingana is snake. She swallowed all the blackfellows. She took them, inside herself, down under the water. Eingana came out. She was big with everything inside her. She came out of the big waterhole near Bamboo Creek. Eingana was rolling about, every way, on the ground. She was groaning and calling out. She was making a big noise with all the blackfellows, everything, inside her belly.

Eingana could not give birth until a man came and speared her.

No one can see Eingana. In the raintime, when the flood water comes, Eingana stands up out of the middle of the flood water. She looks out at the country. She lets go all the birds, snakes, animals, children belonging to us.

Goodoonoo, Djauan tribe, Roper River[17]

Kunapipi

The ceremonies of Kunapipi are extremely widespread across northern Australia, crossing tribal boundaries and encompassing groups who speak different languages but who know the main words and songs of the ritual. It is thought to have spread north-west from the Roper River where the great Kunapipi mother rose from the sea at the mouth of the river and commenced her travels across the land. The sacred Kunapipi ceremonies are for the initiated men only and the secrets of the great Kunapipi Ancestress remain in the keeping of the elder custodians of the ceremony. Throughout northern Australia just before the Wet Season commences, when the air is heavy and humidity reaches its highest, the whisper spreads through the camps — 'Kunapipi'.

The women remain behind, but for days, sometimes up to two weeks, the secret singing and ceremonial dances are enacted in seclusion in the bush, thus perpetuating the ageless link with the source of life and all creation, the great Kunapipi.

In the Wet Season torrential rains swell the rivers of Arnhem Land; swamps cover the grassy plains and animal and bird life increases. *photo R. Edwards*

Opposite: Rock painting of Ngalyod the Rainbow Serpent in a shelter on the Cadell River. Painted by Mandarg about 1965. *photo P. Tweedie*

Above: In Arnhem Land the sinuous bends of the rivers, as they carve through valleys, gorges and open plains, remind us that this is the home of the great serpents, in particular the powerful Rainbow Serpent. *photo R. Morrison*

Below: Ancient red ochre rock painting of a Rainbow Serpent that has swallowed a bandicoot. *photo R. Edwards*

THE GREAT SERPENTS

Travelling across the northern coast of Arnhem Land in a small plane, the ground below becomes a maze of winding rivers with their tributaries and water channels forming vein-like patterns across the coastal saltpans. The sinuous bends of the Alligator and Liverpool Rivers as they carve through valleys, gorges, and open plains, remind us that this is the home of the great serpents, in particular the powerful Rainbow Serpent.

The Rainbow Serpent, known as Ngalyod by the Gunwinggu and Borlung by the Miali, is a serpent of immense proportions which inhabits deep permanent waterholes. One Aboriginal group will say the Rainbow Serpent is female, another will maintain it is male, yet another will tell you it is a male serpent with the breasts of a woman. Lengthy stories of the great deeds of Ngalyod are rare. Still greatly revered and feared, she is spoken of in lowered voices, stories principally relating her physical attributes or methods of vengeance should an unwary person anger her or cross her in any way.

The serpent symbolizes the storms of the wet season when torrential rains swell the rivers, streams and creeks as they make their way to the sea. The Rainbow Serpent is closely associated with the great Ubar ceremonies of western Arnhem Land during which a cylindrical wooden gong is rhythmically beaten and becomes the voice of the 'mother', Waramurungundji, who gave birth to the Rainbow Serpent. One story related to the Ubar ceremony which features the Great Serpent and depicts him as male, is the story of Yirawadbad, sometimes spoken of as the husband of Warramurungundji.[18]

NGALYOD

Ngalyod, the Creator Spirit, is sometimes male and sometimes female, but for the Gunwinggu she is the great fertility mother who gave birth to the first people. Even today, she brings forth the Wet Season after the long Dry, with its teeming waters and abundance of wildlife, and she is therefore the great Creator still, causing plants and animals to multiply and all forms of life to increase. She is the Spirit of the Rainbow, standing on her tail and reaching high into the sky after rain for all the people to see.

In contrast to her role of Creator and protector of life, the Rainbow Serpent is also feared as she will seriously punish the people if any of the taboos and rituals associated with her Dreaming sites or ceremonies are not observed. As the first Creator she taught the people the Laws and ceremonies and failure to abide by these Laws will arouse her fury and desire for vengeance. Many stories tell of her swallowing people who have not observed the taboos, or of her causing natural disasters, such as flash floods, torrential rain, or drought. The Rainbow Serpent is therefore greatly feared by the Gunwinggu and the rituals associated with her are carefully observed by all.

The following Gunwinggu story tells of a young boy whose crying woke the Rainbow Serpent.

An Orphan Who Used to Cry

Long ago the old people used to tell the story of a boy who was always crying, and was eaten by the Rainbow Serpent. They had refused to give him lily roots — he had already tasted that food and found it very tasty. That was why he had to cry — he was always crying. Once when he was walking around an old lady asked him, 'Why are you crying?' Then the orphan said, 'They refuse to give me any manburrangkali lily roots.' 'Is that so?' replied the old lady.

Then that old lady went and got a different kind of lily root for him. She got lots of them for him. But the orphan was still lying down crying, while she was bringing him back a bag full of yaldanj lily roots.

Opposite: Bark painting of Ngalyod the Rainbow Serpent by Njiminjuma from Maningrida. *photo J. Steele*

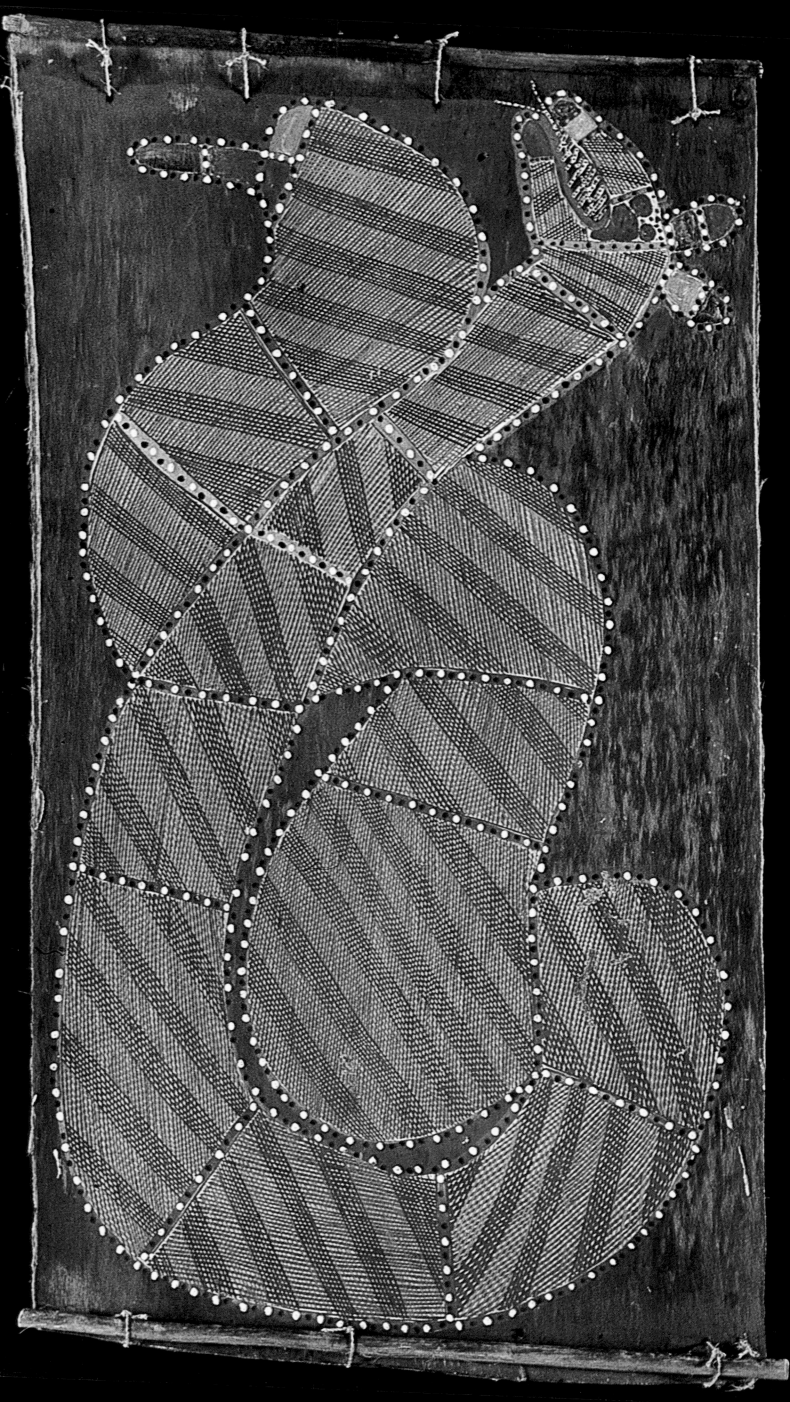

She placed the lily roots on the ground while she went and got some firewood. She returned and lit the fire and cooked them all. The old woman said, 'Come and eat these yaldanj lily roots.' The orphan stood there and said, 'I don't want those lily roots, I don't like them.'

So he kept on crying — he was walking around crying, so another man got up and went to get some bush honey. When he returned he showed the boy and said, 'Come and eat some honey.' The orphan stood there and said, 'I don't want any honey, I don't like it.' 'Is that so?' said the man. 'Okay, you just cry, and leave my honey alone.'

So he just kept crying. Another lady then got up and said, 'Let me go and get some long yams for him, otherwise he will always be crying.' Then she went and got some long yams for him, filled her dilly bag, returned, put them on the ground, went for firewood, lit the fire, and roasted the yams. When they were cooked she said, 'Come and eat some long yams.' The orphan said, 'I don't want those long yams.' 'Is that so?' said the old woman.

The people said to him, 'Okay, you just cry, because you didn't want the long yams, the honey, the yaldanj lily roots, because you are always thinking of the taste of those sweet manburrangkali lily roots.'

Now there were lots of old people sitting there and they said to him, 'Why can't you stop crying? Will you always be crying then? Soon the Rainbow Serpent will eat us.' They told him this, but he did not stop crying — he was always crying. He cried and cried.

Now there was a Rainbow Serpent at Miya, to the north. The Rainbow Serpent lifted up her head, looked around, listened very carefully, and heard him crying at Mayawunj in the south. That rainbow serpent said, 'I will go south to that place and eat them.'

Then the Rainbow Serpent started, she went underground and kept going, she was getting closer to them. When she came near to them, she came out of the ground, lifted her head and saw them. She said, 'Ah, this is the place where that orphan is crying — this is where they are camping.'

Then she appeared near them. The people had been looking to the north and had seen something like a fire or a light shining on them and they cried out in fear.

Then they told the men, 'Quick, spear it! Do you want it to eat us?' They kept trying to spear it, but were always missing it, so they said, 'That's it, bad luck. It's no good, the Rainbow Serpent will just have to eat us.'

In fear they tried to run away. The Rainbow Serpent was watching them and hooked her tail around them all, the orphan with them. That Rainbow Serpent ate the orphan first, biting his head and swallowing it. Then she ate the others. This made the Rainbow Serpent from Miya full up.

That is what happened at Mayawunj in the south — she went under the ground with them and is lying there with them at Mayawunj.

Gunwinggu, Oenpelli[19]

BORLUNG

Borlung is sometimes spoken of as the son of Ngalyod, but invariably he is a male serpent. Like Ngalyod he can be seen high in the sky in the form of a rainbow, sometimes over water or in the spray of a waterfall. Amongst the Dalabon there is belief in many Borlung and a strong link between Borlung and fertility. If a woman is to conceive she must be entered by one of the many Borlung snakes that abound in waterholes. After death, the person's spirit will revert to a Borlung, dwell in water and appear in rainbow form from time to time.

Borlung is the name most frequently given to the Rainbow Serpent in the outstations west of Maningrida in central Arnhem Land. Spider Mururulmi explains the relationship of Borlung to the Creator Mother as follows.

Jingana is the Mother who existed in the Goregun, the beginning of time. She is always painted wearing a head ornament of white cockatoo feathers; she has a beard, and a prominent bulge on her chest like a 'brisket bone'. Her serrated back is like a crocodile and she is both male and female at the same time.

Jingana grew two large eggs in her belly, one became Borlung the male serpent, the other a female Ngalkunburriyaymi who looked more like a fish.[20]

When angered the Rainbow Serpent travels underground, carving deep tunnels through rocks as she goes. *photo B. Thompson*

While Jingana is generally represented as a composite figure in paintings, Ngalyod and Borlung are generally depicted in snake form.

The caves and rockfaces of the escarpment area of Arnhem Land along the Alligator, Liverpool and Cadell Rivers provide us with a magnificent visual historical record of the presence of the Rainbow Serpent for centuries. Paintings of the great serpents range from ancient red ochre Mimi drawings possibly 20,000 years old and still today identified by local people as Ngalyod, to new paintings of her by custodians of the Laws of the Rainbow Serpent.

THE KIMBERLEY SNAKES

The giant snake myths extend right across from Arnhem Land to Western Australia where in the Kimberley region rock paintings of snakes are frequently found in cave shelters. The snakes here have a similar mythological base; they are always associated with water and thunderstorms and also with child spirits and fertility. The name of the snake or python varies: it can be Ungud, Lu, Lumeri or Lumuru, and may appear as the rainbow in the sky signifying the end of the rain, a whirlpool in the sea or as in the following explanation by Albert Barunga, a hollow log floating on the water's surface.

When they see the hollow log on the tide, then they used to say: 'Ah! That's the Lu! That's the snake! We can't cross over — it is dangerous. We have seen Lumeri floating by. She's in the whirlpool — we might drown.'

Lumuru . . . well, it's like a magic stick: it has got power in it, a snake they used to say. It has only turned itself into a log, but inside it is a snake. It will swallow people.

Those people who tried to cross the Prince Regent, those that sank, well, Lumuru swallowed them — that is what the old people believe. Another lot were lost up at Parry Harbour — they tried to cross the water in a canoe, and they drowned. Lumuru got them! When they see the big log floating in the river which they want to cross, they won't dare go into the water.[21]

In the myths of the Kimberley area great pythons travelled from the east around the landscape forming rivers from east to west. They reached the north-west corner of Kimberley and turned south along the coast until they reached the Worora country. The rock python came from the east and headed towards the sea. The snake was travelling with babies and because she was very tired and her babies crying, she came to live at the cave on Gibb River Station called Mandangari ('the gum of the Kurrajong'). She painted herself there and then after resting, travelled on to Manning Creek where she stayed on the cave wall. This story tells of those events.

A mob of snakes, when the snakes were like human beings, were following the rivers. From the Hunter River they came down and they were trying to follow the Prince Regent River. One leader climbed one of the hills to look at the face of the country. 'Oh! That's how the country looks,' she said.

She followed the river up to Mount Waterloo and Mount Trafalgar. Then she went on to Perulba. She was lying across the rocks, and the bowerbirds were running all around as she lay there. Now you see her as a lot of rocks, but she is still there now, lying in the shape of the snake. Another snake was pounding yams, another was burnt by the bushfire, and another two went right up the Glenelg River where they remained in the water.

In the Kimberley area great pythons travelled from the east, forming rivers until they reached the Worora country. The rock python was tired and her babies were crying so she stopped at a cave on Gibb River Station and painted herself there. *photo I. Crawford*

This first snake was killing all the flying foxes and when she was very full, she looked around: 'Where am I going to lie down and be comfortable?' she said.

So she climbed up the foot of the hill, and lay there. She was so full that she was farting and she said: 'Oh! I must lie down in this place to make camp.' So she lay down, and the place is called Djilgu, the farting place.[22]

GIANT SERPENTS OF EASTERN AUSTRALIA

Stories about giant serpents who inhabit rivers and waterholes are found throughout the whole Australian continent. They have many different temperaments. Some are so belligerent that the waterholes where they live can never be approached, whereas others are more tolerant. Fire, the antithesis of water, is often used to ward off the serpents or protect a family camped in the vicinity of a water source where a serpent is known to dwell. Their creative power on the landscape and their association with fertility and child spirits varies also in different areas of Australia.

In eastern Australia, beliefs in the serpent have been reported in many areas ranging from the tip of Cape York to Victoria. A myth from the Wiradjuri tribe in New South Wales describes how the serpent is responsible for the creation of ceremonies and the inspiration of artists.

The Wawi and Song-makers

The Wawi is a serpent-like creature which lives in deep waterholes on the Darling River and burrows into the bank. He has a wife and children who camp close to him, but in a different place. A 'doctor' or clever man can go and see the Wawi, but must not go near his family. When a man is going on a visit to this monster he must paint his body all over with red ochre. He then follows after the rainbow some day when there is a thunder-shower; and the end of the rainbow which rests over the waterhole is where the Wawi lives. The man then dives under the water, where he finds the Wawi who takes him into his hole and sings him a new song for the corroboree. The man repeats the song after the Wawi until he has learnt it sufficiently, and then starts back to his own people. When they see him returning, painted red and singing, they know he has been with the Wawi. This man then takes a few of the other clever men with him into the bush where they strip pieces of bark off trees, and paint different patterns on them with earth ochres. The bark paintings are taken to the corroboree ground, and all the men dance and sing the new song. This is how new songs and dances are made. The Wawi has the magic power of varying his size from a few inches up to enormous proportions. The black streak in the Milky Way, towards the Southern Cross, is one of the Ancestors of the Wawi.

Wiradjuri tribe[23]

The Barwon River in northern New South Wales and the Narran River are the sites of stories about the giant Kurrea, often described as crocodiles but also as serpents. This confusion in interpretation of the form of these giants was reflected also in the description given by Spider Murululmi in Arnhem Land. He stated that the serpent had a serrated back like a crocodile and was both male and female at the same time. One story tells of the hunter Toolalla of the Barwon River who long ago decided to destroy the powerful snake and rid the people of their enemy.

Toolalla and the Kurrea

In the deeper parts of the Boobera Lagoon in the Barwon River is the home of the giant Kurrea, a snake of enormous proportions. He cannot travel on dry land so when he wishes to leave the lagoon he forms a channel by tearing up the ground on its banks, thereby allowing the water to flow and bear him along. There are many shallow channels around Boobera Lagoon which were made by the giant serpent.

Fear of the serpent prevented the men from paddling their canoes far in search of waterfowl or fish and the people grew very hungry. So Toolalla decided to kill the serpent, and one day made a valiant attempt to spear the monster, but he only managed to enrage him. Toolalla fled across the countryside and took refuge in a very tall tree. The snake returned to his waters and remains there now when the waters of the Boobera Lagoon swell with floods.[24]

In Queensland, a number of myths indicate the presence of giant serpents. On the Bloomfield River, for example, the Yero inhabits long deep pools that connect the waterholes and rapids of the Roaring Meg, a stream that rises from a rugged mountain and flows into the river. If a man enters one of these waterholes he will be pulled about by the Yero, who is described as being striped and like a giant eel or serpent with a large head and red hair.[25] In south-eastern Queensland the medicine men acquire their power through a huge supernatural water snake with a manelike head of hair. He is also closely associated with quartz crystals, which occur on the earth where the rainbow ends. These crystals have magical properties used by the medicine men and are believed to have come from the Giant Serpent himself.

In South Australia and Victoria, the legendary Bunyip has many qualities like the Rainbow Serpent. He lives in waterholes and was much feared by the early European settlers who heard first-hand accounts of his powers from Aboriginal people. Arkaroo were serpent-like ancestors of the people of the Flinders Ranges.

The Serpents of Wilpena Pound

Long ago in Creation times the very first circumcision ceremony was performed at Wilpena Pound in the Flinders Ranges. Two Arkaroo heard it was about to take place and travelled to that place planning to destroy all the people. When they reached there they hid, waiting until the ceremony was over. Then they surrounded the group and by creating powerful whirlwinds swept them into their mouths. The only people who escaped were Wala the wild turkey, Yulu the kingfisher and the young man just initiated. These fled in different directions. At the close of the Creation era, the bodies of the two Arkaroo were changed into the steep walls that now surround Wilpena Pound. Their spirits made a home in a waterhole at the entrance to the pound, where they became huge creatures of many colours with manes and beards.

Adnyamatana tribe, Flinders Ranges[26]

In Victoria the Law keeper was Myndie the giant snake, appointed by the Great Creator Bunjil to punish the people who disobeyed the rules of life he had laid down. When Bunjil commanded him, the Myndie would destroy anyone who broke the Laws of the tribe. The Myndie could extend or contract his size. He could climb a tree and, holding onto the branch like a ring-tailed possum, stretch his body across a great forest. He lived in a waterhole near Bukara-bunnal (Puckapunyal).

In the extreme north-west of the continent the power of the Rainbow Serpent is replaced by that of the Wandjina, the great Beings whose staring images are painted on cave walls and rock shelters in the Kimberleys.

THE WANDJINA

The giant staring Wandjina of the north-west have excited the imagination of Europeans since the expedition of George Grey in 1837 reported the findings of painted heads on rockfaces.
'. . . they appeared to stand out from the rock; and I was certainly rather surprised at the moment that I first saw this gigantic head and upper part of a body bending over and staring down at me.' Looking at a group of Wandjina figures Grey commented, 'I imagine them to represent females . . . each had a very remarkable headdress, coloured with a deep bright blue, and one had a necklace on . . . Each of the four faces was marked by a totally distinct expression of countenance, and although none of them had mouths, two, I thought, were otherwise rather good looking.'[27]

Opposite: 'This is Wandjina. He made Earth and Sea and everything. He gave Man to live in this Earth, for this World, this Tribal Country.' *photo I. Crawford*

Wandjina paintings, King Edward River, Western Australia. *photo I. Crawford*

Attributed to a variety of artists in the intervening years and given different interpretations by successive writers, little was known about the great Wandjina for a century or more. The truth is of course that the Wandjina are extremely important Creation Ancestors of the Kimberley Aboriginal people and these images on rock are representations of them in places where they changed their physical form and became Spirits. They left themselves on rock.

The poetic words of one of the finest Aboriginal leaders from the Kimberleys best explains this relationship.

This is Wandjina. There was a time when this Earth — he made Earth and Sea and everything. This is Wandjina — he made people. Wandjina is Wandjina. He gave Man to live in this Earth, for this World, this Tribal Country. He put the Wandjina in the cave for him to remember this Wandjina, to follow his Laws, to go about the right ways.

Wandjina, he said. You must believe Wandjina. If you won't believe Wandjina, you won't live. This is because Wandjina gave us that Law to follow. And then he says, I give you this Land, and you must keep your Tribal Land. You can't touch somebody's land because it is your body, and your body is right here, and the Aborigines believe his body is his own Tribal Land.

Aborigines believe that the Wandjina give rain. Then it says that the Earth is hot and that it breathes; the Earth it breathes — it is like live Earth. When it breathes, it's a steam blow up, and it gives cloud to give rain. Rain gives fruit, and everything grows, and the trees and the grass to feed other things, kangaroos and birds and everything.

Albert Barunga, Mowanjum, north-west Australia[28]

Wandjina paintings, Black Fellow Creek, Western Australia. *photo I. Crawford*

The paintings were made by the Wandjina but Aboriginal people occasionally retouch them today. The wrath of the Wandjina spirits however can cause torrential storms and floods, and the painters must be circumspect and address the spirits in the right way. The following monologue of the Aboriginal artist Charlie Numbulmoore as he addresses the Wandjina is from a record of the Aboriginal people's own accounts of the meaning of the paintings.

'I don't know what happened to you, but all your spirit has gone out of you. No men or women watch over you, for the people who belong to this place — my aunties sisters, fathers and grannies — they are all dead now. Only, I, that belong to another place, came to visit you, but you were lonely for all those people who died and your spirit has gone away now.

'Because you are looking all dull — you're not looking bright — I'll try and draw you. I'll try and put new paint on you people . . . Don't get wild, don't send rain! . . . You must be very glad that I'm going to make you new — don't try and get wild and don't send the rain to me . . . I made you very good now — I don't know how I did it.

'Very good! . . . You must be very glad, because I made your eyes like new. That eye, you know, like this my eye . . . I made them new for you people. My eye has life, and your eye has life too, because I made it new . . .

'Don't try to bring rain, my wife might drown with rain. The rain might drown her.'[29]

The legends surrounding the Wandjina vary from area to area in the Kimberleys but the following story of the great Wandjina is known by all.

The Legend of Wodjin

Two children were playing with the bird Tumbi — they thought it was a honey-sucker but it really was the owl. They did not see the difference in the eyes and they thought the bird was not important.

The children maimed the bird, pulling all the feathers from his tail and head, pushing grass through his nose and blinding him. Then they mocked the bird, throwing him into the air, telling him to fly — but he could not and fell back to earth. Then he did fly and disappeared: the boys did not know where he had gone and they did not worry about it.

Now Tumbi was not just an ordinary bird — he was the owl, the son of a Wandjina, and when he disappeared he went up to Inanunga the Wandjina in the sky and to him he complained.

The news flew to the Wandjinas who determined to punish the people. Wodjin called all the Wandjinas throughout the country together, and the bird incited them to revenge. The Wandjinas assembled their followers — from Munja and from the Calder they came, camping from time to time, fixing their spears for the fight. However, they did not know where to find the people, and the lizards and animals which they sent to scout around for them refused to tell where the people were. The animals were sorry for the people, and tried to hide them, knowing that the Wandjinas would kill them. But Wodjin produced the bicycle lizard from his penis, and the lizard saw the people and beckoned the Wandjinas on.

The Wandjinas saw the people on a wide flat near the spring at Tunbai. The Wandjinas were on the top of one of the hills which surround this flat.

They then held an initiation ceremony, Wodjin saying: 'I want to be light so that I can catch up with those people if they run away.' Wodjin, however, became ill from this cutting ceremony, swelling up so that he was unable to take further part in the fight. However, he was able to bring heavy rain by stroking his beard, so that the flat was flooded.

The Wandjinas divided into two parties and attacked in a pincer movement from the top of the hill and surrounded the people. Meanwhile the Brolgas had been dancing on the wet ground and had turned it into a bog and the Wandjinas drove the people into the boggy ground where they drowned. The people tried to fight back, but they were unable to harm Wandjinas and so they were killed.

The two boys who had harmed the bird escaped from the massacre by running away, but when the Wandjinas realized that they were gone, they set off after them. The boys were very frightened by the fight, the rain and lightning, and when they saw a large boab tree with a split in it, they decided to hide inside. But the tree was really a Wandjina and no sooner were the boys inside than it closed on them and crushed them.

The Wandjinas had achieved their aim and revenged the injuries done to the owl. Now they met to decide their future movements. Wodjin moved to a cave, but in the process, he slipped and injured his foot. So he named the cave Wanalirri and decided that he would stay there. The others decided to go to different places, and so the Wandjinas dispersed.[30]

Namaaraalee

The coastal people of the north-west talk of the great Wandjina Namaaraalee and the epic battle which took place on the beach at Langgi, a small bay on the western coast. Here many Wandjinas perished and numerous giant erect rocks which protrude from the sands are the metamorphosed bodies of those killed in battle.

Namaaraalee was chasing the rock cod, but he could not catch her for she kept slipping through his hands. From this corner, all around he was chasing her at the place called Langgi. He chased her into the eastern corner when his group met another group of Wandjinas. His people told him: 'They are fighting — they've taken your wife!'

Then he went to the fight and with all the strength he had, he belted the whole lot with his club. He knocked the lot down, but they put a spear into his side then.

The mob looked at him saying: 'Hello — he got speared! He's speared in a fatal place — he will die.' Everybody cried for him then.

His group carried him away, made the tree platform where his grave is and painted him on the rocks. The people must use the burial platform because the Wandjina used it: that fellow made the Law for the dead bodies.

Sam Woolgoodja[31]

The cave at Langgi where Namaaraalee was buried contains a large slab supported by pillars of rock and the burial ritual of placing the body on tree platforms is still practised today in order to follow the precedent of the Ancestral Wandjina.

Namaaraalee is remembered however in the beautiful words of Sam Woolgoodja in his poem, *Lalai Dreamtime.*

> *The first one, Namaaraalee, came from the Awararii tribe.*
> *He had been in many fights*
> *before he came to this land.*
> *Here he saw the woman he wanted to keep,*
> *But the Wandjinas all looked, then each one tugged at her.*
> *Backward, forward – hotter and hotter –*
> *At last they flung spears that fell like rain –*
> *and Namaaraalee felt one drop down his side.*
> *Then they had killed him.*
>
> *These rocks are Wandjinas*
> *marking the fight*
> *When they saw he was dead*
> *they carried him over the creek.*
> *"Djirr" – for the first one*
> *They made that dry sound on their tongues.*
> *Then he was laid on a forked stick cradle*
> *High off the ground.*
> *Now, Namaaraalee lies*
> *in his cave on top of the rocks.*
>
> *They speared him in this water,*
> *this water is Namaaraalee.*
> *They carried him along here,*
> *they laid him up there.*
> *We belong to this place,*
> *Strangers must stay away.*

Sam Woolgoodja[32]

If the Wandjinas are angered they will call up the lightning to strike the offender dead, or the rain to flood the land and drown the people, or the cyclone to devastate the country. These are the weapons which the Wandjinas used then they killed the people at Tunbai, and their power to use them remains unabated. The monsoonal rains which fall in Kimberley between late December and March are believed to be the work of the Wandjinas, and the Aborigines sing songs to placate the Spirits at these times; in some areas it has been common practice to put water on faded paintings in order to make them appear brighter (this practice, however, causes a rapid deterioration in the paintings). The Wandjina figures in the paintings appear to be revitalized in the damp conditions.

The Wandjinas are also involved in keeping the repositories of the spirits of children. Aboriginals tell us that these little spirits live in water, particularly in the freshwater pools, and that they belong to the Wandjinas. When a man eats fish, turtles or crocodiles taken from the pool, he may consume a child spirit, or it may simply follow him home from the pool.

Our fathers found us in the form of fish or turtles, but Wandjina is our real father. He put us in the water from the sky. We now call our name from our earthly father, but we came from heaven through the water by dreams . . .

Sam Woolgoodja[33]

Opposite: Detail of painted wooden sculpture of Ancestor figure, north-eastern Arnhem Land. Artist: Mambarrara. *photo P. Tweedie*

Above: At Bilirri the Djankawu saw the sun rise over the hill, spreading its rays across the sky. The clans descended from Djankawu commemorate the great feats of the Creation era in song and ritual. *photo P. Tweedie*

The Wandjinas control the baby spirits not only of human beings but also of animals. The Wandjinas and the Giant Snakes are the sources of fertility in the land and the Aboriginals believe that if their paintings fall into disrepair, or are defiled, the Spirits will leave and the natural species will cease to reproduce.

CREATION ANCESTORS OF NORTH-EASTERN ARNHEM LAND

The people of north-eastern Arnhem Land are broadly divided into two sections or halves called moieties, the Dhuwa and the Yirritja, and each clan falls into one of these two categories. The moieties each have different Ancestor figures from whom all the Laws and rules governing life as we know it today are derived. For the Dhuwa, the great Ancestors are the Djankawu and the Wawilak Sisters, for the Yirritja they are Barama and Laindjung.

The Wawilak Sisters

In the Creation era before man had appeared, the land was very different. The Wawilak Sisters had travelled from Trial Bay in the south-east across to the Arafura Sea. The younger sister was pregnant and the older sister carried her baby under her arm in a paperbark cradle. They both carried stone spears and killed goannas, possums and bandicoots for food, as well as gathering plant foods, which they put in their dilly bags. As they walked along, they gave names to all the animals and plants they saw.

The younger sister suddenly felt the first pains of childbirth and said to her sister they had better make a camp for her baby would soon be born. They were

75

then at the edge of the great Mirarrmina waterhole, and they sat down here. They did not know, however, that in the deep subterranean waters beneath the upper waters of the well dwelt the giant Rainbow Snake. The older sister made a fire and started cooking the bush food they had gathered and the animals they had killed. But as soon as they had thrown the food on the fire, each animal and plant sprang up, jumped out of the fire, ran to the waterhole and jumped into it — first the crab, then yams, goannas, frill-necked lizards, rock pythons, seagulls, sea eagles, brolgas and crocodiles. Each ran and dived into the well and disappeared from sight. They feared the Serpent.

It was then time to build a bark shelter for the night and so the older sister began to collect paperbark. As she walked through the waters of the Mirarrmina well to get paperbark on the other side, her menstrual blood fell into the water and was carried down deep below the floor of the well where the Python lived. He raised his head and sniffed. 'Where does this blood come from?' he said. He opened the bottom of the well by throwing the stone which covers its base out of the well onto the land by the two women's camp where the young sister had now had her child. He crawled out slowly like a snake does from the well, sucking some well water into his mouth. He spat into the sky and a small cloud formed in the centre of the sky. The great snake watched the women and babies and hissed, calling for rain. Still the sisters were unaware of his presence.

Night fell, and a huge dark cloud gathered overhead. The sisters thought it was just lightning from the sky, but it was lightning from that billabong which flashed and lit up the sky. The Serpent was furious at the pollution of his pool. He rose onto his tail and was so huge he reached from the earth to the sky. A great storm blew up and the women and the children huddled frightened in their shelter. Then they saw the Snake. The elder sister stood up and danced frantically, calling out 'Gawarr, Gawarr, Gawarr,' (stop, stop!) and circling around and around but the Snake came straight on and swallowed the younger sister and her baby. The older sister escaped by leaping over the coils of the snake as he was swallowing her sister. She eventually died at another place where she was bitten to death by leeches.

The other snakes came along and asked the Snake what he had eaten and he felt ashamed.

'Come on and tell me, my big brother,' said the Wessel Island snake. After a long time the Snake said, 'I ate the sister and her baby.' When he said this the south-east monsoon started to blow and he roared and fell to the ground. When he fell he split the ground open and made a river. Then he regurgitated the sister and her baby and dropped them into an ant's nest, and then crawled slowly back to his waterhole. Some ants came out then and bit the sister and her baby and they came to life again.

Wandjuk Marika, Yirrkala[34]

Djankawu and His Sisters

On the island of Baralku, far out to sea south-east of Yelangbara, lived the Djankawu. There were three of them, Djankawu himself, his elder sister Bildiwuwiju, who had borne many children, and his younger sister Muralaidj, who was just past puberty and whose breasts were strong and firm. They lived on Baralku for a while, putting people on the island, performing sacred ceremonies and leaving Dreamings, but eventually they were ready to leave and make their journey across the sea. At dusk, they loaded their bark canoe with Dreamings, sacred drawings and emblems which they kept in a woven conical mat, and paddled out to sea. As they dipped into the waters, the morning star shone overhead and they sang.

At last, at sunrise, they came to the coast of Arnhem Land and at Ulpinbuy, they saw two rainbow parakeets perched on a rockhole drying their brilliant red breast feathers in the first rays of the sun. They paddled into the wide beach of Yelangbara, singing with joy, and allowed the surf to carry their canoe into the shallow water. Where they landed on Yelangbara beach is now a sacred place.

They beached their canoe there and it became a rock. Djankawu plunged his mawalan, his walking stick, into the sand and water appeared and a well was formed. His stick is now a she-oak tree. They heard the cry of the black cockatoo and then glancing at the sandhills, they saw the tracks of an animal. It was a goanna. Djankawu named it djunda.

As soon as they had thrown the food on the fire, each animal and plant sprang up, jumped out of the fire, ran to the waterhole and jumped into it. Bark painting by Malangi from Ramangining (detail). *photo P. Tweedie*

The great snake coiled around the Wawilak sisters and swallowed the younger one and her newborn baby. Bark painting by Dhatangu from Ramangining (detail). *photo P. Tweedie*

They left many children in the caves and then travelled on to Bilirri, Borkinya and Ganungyala. At Bilirri the Djankawu saw the sun rise over the hill, spreading the rays across the sky. Bilirri means the spreading rays of the sun. Djankawu sat down there and put many sacred objects or djuta into the ground. From them grew all sorts of yams and special foods and today rocks which mark that place are sacred. Djankawu named the places he saw and all the animals that they came across. At Borkinya, he named the wild turkey, and at Ganungyala the Djankawu stayed until dawn and saw the Morning Star. All these places are Riratjingu people's country. Ours is the first place Djankawu came to and we have the Djankawu ceremonies.

Leaving Riratjingu country, then the Djankawu paddled down to Kambuka at Caledon Bay and made a sacred place with their special emblems. Trees sprang up as the sacred poles were pushed into the ground. While they were here they looked up and saw a big cloud or Wulma coming from Blue Mud Bay, so they went there, leaving many dreamings and making 'shades' to camp under which are now special trees called Gullu. All through the coastal country they left sacred djuta emblems and baskets and they sang as they went.

They followed the rain cloud to Gorminungbuy and here they made camp. There was a beautiful billabong here, and many whistling ducks were living there. Waterlilies covered the surface of the water and Djankawu named them as totems. It was in this billabong that Mundukul the snake dwelt, and although the Djankawu saw him he did not bother them.

Continuing on they reached Nganmarrwi where they made a large shade. While they were here, many people were born from the elder sister. The Djankawu brother said to his sisters: 'We will put the boys in the grass, so that later when they grow up they will have whiskers. These little girls we put under the mat, hiding them there so they will be smooth, soft and hairless, and because girls are really sacred. They must be kept in the mat, just as the sacred emblems are kept.' The children grew up and married and were the progenitors of the present Aboriginals of those parts. After this, the two sisters were always pregnant.

At Woiwiwi they left more children and many Dreamings so that when the children grew up they and their descendants could look after them. They continued to Ngarrwiwi, where they saw wild duck tracks, wild peanuts and frightened some goannas. They made camp here and more children were born from the sisters. After staying a while, they journeyed on to Grogula where they saw the yellow snake. They passed the snake and reached Burirri where they also passed the Thunder Man and at last came to Damiyagaiyu, named after the black cockatoo. The elder sister said to her brother, 'Perhaps we will live at this place, the black cockatoo's cry makes us all happy. It reminds us of the just place, Yelangbara.' They made two shades there, and created many trees and wells.

Travelling on, they passed through many places, singing about the animals and birds they met and making children. They walked along to Duniwi, singing about manal (mangrove shells) and gurumudgi (geese).

On Elcho Island, they left many Dreamings, the red ochre Dreaming being the most important. The Djankawu brother also initiated circumcision ceremonies in this region, making circumcision a new Law. Going on, they came to Wessel Island, then to Galguwiri, making wells and creating people; finally arriving near Milingimbi at Maluwa. They made a big shade and the sisters collected lily roots in the billabong and bore many children.

One day the brother tripped over a creeper and accidentally pushed his pole into the mud and a big sea came up and flooded the country. This formed the sea between Elcho Island (Yawurr Yawurr) and the mainland, leaving them on the mainland.

The Djankawu went on, seeing many kinds of fish and crabs and finally came to Marabay where they put sacred dilly bags and made shades to camp under. A great number of children were born here. While they were living at Marabay the elder sister said to the younger sister, 'We had better put our dilly bags in this shade and leave them for a while, while we look for mangrove shells.' While they were gone foraging, the Djankawu brother and his companions, men who were sons of the sisters, hid in the big shade. The sisters collected many shells and then heard the cry of the mangrove bird Djunmal warning them that something was wrong. They ran back to the shade and found that the sacred dilly bags full of emblems were gone, and on the ground were the tracks of men. They hurried on towards the men, and as they came running the brother began singing with his singing stick Bilma, which caused the sisters to fall to the ground, frightened of the power of the sacred songs. The men had taken from them not only the songs and the sacred emblems but also the power to perform rituals.

The younger sister said, 'What are we going to do? All our dilly bags are gone, all the emblems, all our power for sacred ritual.' The older one replied, 'I think we can leave that. Men can do it now, they can look after it. We can spend our time collecting bush foods for them for it is not right that they should get that food as they have been doing. We know everything. We have really lost nothing, for we remember it all and we can let them have that small part. For aren't we still sacred even if we have lost the bags? Haven't we still our uteri?' So the sisters left all their Dreamings in this place and put a lot of people there too and made a very sacred well, while the Djankawu brother and his companions sang songs and performed the rituals.

Wandjuk Marika, Yirrkala[35]

Barama and Laindjung

Barama emerged from a waterhole in Guludji near the Koolatong River with tresses of freshwater weeds clinging to his arms and carrying special tree rangga. However, these weeds were not really weeds, they were mädayin armbands with long feather pendants attached to them. His whole body was covered with watermarks forming all the patterns and designs which he allocated eventually to the various Yirritja moiety linguistic groups and clans.

Opposite: Bark painting by Wandjuk Marika and his father Mawalan depicting the great Creation story of Djankawu. Collection Art Gallery of New South Wales

The women of Arnhem Land hang their woven dilly bags up today as did the Djankawu sisters in Creation times. Their sacred emblems were stolen by the men. *photo P. Tweedie*

In Creation times the Djankawu sisters dug for roots and tubers; their example is followed today as women dig with digging sticks or machete. *photo P. Tweedie*

Barama saw a tree log in the water and, mounting it, floated down the river. Near Gangan, Galbarrimun, a head man of the Dalwongu mala, saw him coming. Barama said to him, 'Do not be afraid of me, I am Barama, come along and meet me. I have brought you rangga and sacred paintings.' When Barama abandoned the log it embedded itself in the river and bacame a rangga emblem. Barama then washed himself in the river but the sacred pattern on his body did not come off.

Laindjung emerged at Dhalungu at about the same time as Barama. His body was covered with watermarks but he had no rangga emblems. He walked to Gangan and there he met Barama. They talked together and discussed all the paintings and rangga emblems. They called the mythical headmen of all the Yirritja mala together and told them to prepare a sacred dancing ground so that they could perform a mala ritual. Barama was the 'boss' who gave all the instructions in sacred matters, Laindjung and Galbarrimun assisted him. When the Ngara ceremony was over Barama made Galbarrimun guardian of all the mädayin business for the Dalwongu mala. Then he sent him and Laindjung to distribute all the paintings and rangga emblems to the Yirritja people. Laindjung set out in the direction of Milingimbi, and Galbarrimun towards the Rose and Roper Rivers. Thus the majority of the Yirritja linguistic groups and clans of eastern Arnhem Land obtained their ritual knowledge and sacred paraphernalia from Laindjung, but Barama was the 'real big boss'. He belongs to the Dalwongu mala and his 'official' place is Gangan, the mala ground in Gululdji.

Before Barama sent out his emissaries he gave strict instructions to them to stay away from main camps and to keep the sacred objects hidden out of the sight of women and children. Galbarrimun obeyed these commands. However, Laindjung, on his way back from Milingimbi, openly displayed sacred objects and sang sacred songs for everyone to hear. This was very wrong so the old men decided to kill him.

Near Trial Bay when they heard him approach they climbed into trees, and when he passed by they speared him. Laindjung kept on singing as he sank into the swamp until he disappeared. However, he was not dead and, re-emerging from the swamp, walked away towards Blue Mud Bay and changed himself into a paperbark tree, called dhulwu.

Gawerin, Yirrkala[36]

CREATION HEROES OF NORTH-EASTERN AUSTRALIA

Two myths, one from south-eastern Queensland, and one from the north-west coast of Cape York, show how the great Creation heroes, part animal, part man, named the animals and birds and formed the landscape, as well as inventing the principal ceremonies of the tribe.

Girroo Gurrll

Girroo Gurrll rose up out of the ocean, near Hinchinbrook Island (Injun-borr-rorr), part man, mostly eel, and gazed around the newly made countryside. He delighted in every new tree and hill and stream. The animals and birds he saw surprised him by their very shapes and sizes and colours. The rugged landscape of Hinchinbrook impressed him and he arose from the water and pronounced its name loudly. The sea teemed with barramundi in those early days and he said from that time they would be known as Ginbulla. Girroo Gurrll then plunged into the sea and came out on top of the mountains at the back of Cardwell. He saw a freshwater lake surrounded by mangroves and he called it Girringun Lake.

Another journey underground brought him out at the Murray Falls. 'I name you Gweeyouroaree Falls,' he called, and rested awhile to watch the water churning and foaming among the rocks. Coming out of the ground once more he arrived at the rapids in a tributary of the Murray. 'I am now at the Gayeejull Rapids,' he called. On and on he went, naming the birds and the animals, the rocks and streams and mountains. He surprised a flock of parrots feeding on the ground and when they fled up a tree at his approach he told them they would never come down from the tree again and must always feed in the branches. He named them Billngoor. He looked up in the trees and named Boongaree (the tree-climbing kangaroo) and Midinn (the possum). When the dingo (Orlmaburry) scuttled away he was startled and called out in fear, but he did not forget to name the dog as it ran. He named the Goondoyee (cassowary) as it pushed its way through the thick lawyer vines on the bank of the Tully River, and lingered at the water's edge to watch for the fishes. He saw Boogul the black bream, Koolkaa the catfish, and Eeragun the eel. A sudden storm deluged and he was frightened by the lightning. 'Oor-boy shall be your name, O Thunderstorm,' he cried through chattering teeth.

On the way to the cave on Echo Creek he found a parcel of Bungee Gnawr (zamia palm nuts) tied up in leaves and soaking in the water. They were left there by the little crayfish who used them for food. With his long sword he cut the parcel in two, leaving one half for the crayfish and eating the other half himself. At the same time his sword cut a large rock into two pieces and it may still be seen there.

Girroo Gurrll finally came to rest on Mount Mackay (Coot-aa-mee) and there built himself a little humpy. Sometimes he came down from the mountain to swim at Silky Oak Creek, until one day he saw something which frightened him very much. He went back to his hut at the mountain top and died. His hut slowly turned to stone. In his lifetime Girroo Gurrll named every sandbank and lagoon from the sea to the hills, every stream, prominence and valley.[37]

I'wai the crocodile was the principal Ancestor figure among the tribes of the west coast of Cape York. He began the initiation rites and other ceremonies, and many parts of the landscape are indelibly associated with him.

The Story of I'wai

In the beginning when our Ancestors lived, animals were men. At this time, I'wai lived alone on the Upper Pascoe River. One day he was playing with blady grass, and he made four houses, one for play, one for the small boys and initiates, one for the women and his own living house. Then he tried to find the best material to make the long initiation dress and headdress and found hibiscus bark best, which is still used today. Then he held a big meeting. 'Let us all have a good play!' The red kangaroo, the emu, wallaby, cuscus, white cockatoo, scrub turkey and the cassowary were all very glad. 'All right, let us all play!'

I'wai made a mask of hibiscus bark with eyes of nautilus shell. He played by himself for a couple of days and put all the girl and boy initiates in a sacred place. I'wai made the Ompoibo (a masked human figure completely covered in a long black dress of hibiscus bark) to frighten the women and children. He then left the initiates inside one of the houses and went hunting near Werrkimutta.

I'wai had no wife. At Yankingon he found Yanki the python woman who was Ka'oma the echidna's favourite wife. He stayed for a while 'quietening' Yanki and then they ran away together to a mountain on the Upper Pascoe River. I'wai ran away with this woman and when they camped he said, 'You look for my lice, and I'll look for yours.'

Yanki had no female organs when I'wai found her, so he cut a vagina in her, and copulated. A tree called kaiyidji with red sap like blood, grew where this happened.

I'wai wanted to sing to the initiates. He tried sticks to beat time but they were no good, so he tried a hollow tree. When he struck the tree it boomed. He cut it with his stone axe and stretched skin over one end, and put a figure of I'wai on the outside of the drum.

But the boom of the drum attracted the attention of the people of Yankingon and they set out to kill him because he had stolen Yanki. They made spears from a grass tree, but Ka'oma the echidna man did not throw his spears and so he carries them still. I'wai ran away from the spears, dropping his long initiation garment and the drum and leaving behind the house he had made from blady grass. They were all turned to stone and can still be seen at this story place. I'wai ran to Mankal, at the mouth of the Pascoe River.

At low water I'wai walked about and found a sawfish dead on the beach. I'wai found the saw of the sawfish and took it to his camp. He said, 'We'll make a ceremony and dance.' He tried it out. He put on plenty of paint and made the headdress. He tried it over and over again until he made the sawfish dance and headdress as we have it now.

I'wai took some vegetable food, and went to Mankal at the mouth of the Pascoe River, looking for a camp. He thought, 'I have plenty of children, plenty of girls, all sisters. I'll leave the food here for them.' He threw the food down at Mankal and it turned to stone, becoming the totemic centre for this vegetable.

I'wai went on until he reached salt water. He still had the girl and boy initiates with him. The weather was very bad, with heavy rain and a big sea and darkness. He came to the mouth of the Pascoe with all the initiates on his back, and fell into the sea. The strong waves pulled him down with his heavy load. He tried to sing for fine weather, and the sea became quiet, allowing him to carry the girls and boys to Mitirinji (Quoin Island, north-east from the mouth of the Pascoe). Here I'wai dried himself and slept after being so long in the sea. Two of his girls went to the other side of the island where they found a bullroarer. They made a noise with the bullroarer and I'wai woke up. He said, 'What are you making? Let go!' He was ashamed and angry. He took the bullroarer away from the girls, and raped them. Then he left them on the island, took the rest of the initiates on his back, and went away. The girls cried, and made a leaf house, but they were turned to stone and their house became a cave. No woman may see the bullroarer today, or use it, even though it was found by women.

I'wai swam away from the island. In the sea he met the kingfish which he named, and which is now a forbidden food for initiates. He gave names to all the fish. He went up and down the coast, camping at different places At a small island he and his initiates pulled their canoe up on the beach to eat turtle eggs, and while they were asleep the canoe drifted out to sea. I'wai tried to reach it but the tide took it away and the initiates called him back. So I'wai called out to Tappilla the ray and Tiyari the big

Aboriginal shell middens. Heaps of empty shells left
over from shellfish meals line Australia's coasts,
marking the ancient camping sites of Aboriginal
people through the centuries. *photo R. Edwards*

rock cod, and Tappilla the ray heard him and came ashore. I'wai said, 'Can you take
me to the Mainland?'

The ray said, 'I will try, but hold me tight.' I'wai left all the initiates on the island,
even though they were so thirsty their mouths seemed full of maggots. But I'wai was
too heavy, and Tappilla had to take him ashore again.

Then Tiyari the rock cod came ashore, but he couldn't carry I'wai either. Then
Alkon the diamond stingray came, when I'wai sang to him, and he was so big that
the tide came up with him. (Alkon makes the tides.) So I'wai and all the initiates
went to the mainland with Alkon, and then I'wai left Alkon and went to look for
water. [38]

The culture of the people of the Cape York Peninsula differs markedly from that of
the rest of Australia. Here the frequent contacts with the Torres Islands to the
north have influenced the history and culture of the Aboriginal people and ceremonies re-enact travels and deeds of great human heroes as well as animal Ancestors. Dances performed today incorporate drums and masks, both features of the
culture of the northern islands. The story of Chivaree the seagull man which
follows tells of the canoe journey in Creation times of the great seagull man who
came from the islands.

Chivaree the Seagull Man

Chivaree the seagull man paddled his canoe from the Torres Islands down the coast
of western Cape York and then back up the coast to near Mapoon. He was camped
with his brother Ee-all and they were making dances, beating drums made from
hollow logs. Ee-all made a headdress of cockatoo feathers and danced the cockatoo
dance.

Dancers from Cape York mime the ancient dances performed by Chivaree the seagull man and Ee-all his brother who made a headdress of cockatoo feathers and danced the cockatoo dance. *photo P. Tweedie*

After some time Chivaree left his brother and went to Mapoon where he made a big camp at Janie Creek. He made a paddle there for his canoe out of a big mangrove tree. Then he looked at the daughters of Nyungoo the pigeon and wanted them as his wives. Despite Nyungoo, who was against the marriage, Chivaree stole the two women and pushed off in his canoe. As he pushed his paddle in the mud it stuck there and now it marks a freshwater well at Janie Creek.

The canoe however moved by itself and travelled north to the island of Badu. On the way, one of the pigeon women complained of a sore breast and Chivaree put her ashore. She remains abandoned there today as a rock near Verillion Point, and as the tide washes over her she cries salt tears.

In the Torres Islands Chivaree continued his travels, creating waterholes and having many adventures. The story of Chivaree forms a link between the Torres Straits and mainland Australia and elements of the myth are known to people from the islands right down the west coast of Cape York.

Gloria Fletcher and Ernest Hall, Weipa

Opposite: A dancer from Aurukun re-creates the great deeds of the Ancestral heroes in his dance. *photo S. Doring*

CHAPTER THREE

The Great Journeys

The great Spirit Ancestors of Aboriginal tribes throughout Australia undertook many amazing journeys which criss-cross this vast country in a maze of tracks. They performed feats along the way which moulded and formed the Australian landscape as it is known today.

In Australia's arid centre the great Totemic Ancestors of the many tribal groups are remembered in ceremonies which last days, even weeks. Lengthy cycles of songs are performed at particular stopping points where the Ancestor rested, where he may have created a natural boulder, lake or waterhole or where his Spirit remained in a cave. Or the sites chosen may be those where the Ancestors from the Tjurkurpa left the essence of fertility, the kuranita of particular plants or animals, and here ceremonies are held which are designed to release this life-giving power, so that the natural regeneration and procreation of the species of animal or plant will be ensured.

The great Dreaming tracks, as these paths are known, mark the land boundaries of the central tribes in a way which no arbitrary State boundaries can surpass. Today, man-made roads have cut the Dreaming pathways, and fences designed to delineate huge cattle properties have inadvertently severed the path of Malu, the great kangaroo. But the Dreaming paths remain. They are real and very well known by all tribal people of the Centre. When moving over vast distances, navigation is accomplished not by watching the stars, but by noting the well-known Dreaming sites along the way. The traveller may not have passed that way before, but he has a mind's-eye map of the countryside drawn from legend, myth and ceremonial song-cycles describing and laying down the paths of his Dreaming Ancestors and the places and features they created on their travels.

The great Ancestral routes of the Centre extend for hundreds of miles in all directions. The native cat Ancestors, for example, travelled through the lands of many different groups, the Aranda, Unmatjera, Kaititja, Ilpara, Ngalia, and Kukatja. However, each tribe retains only that part of the myth which concerns the native cat in their own territory. The native cats started their journeys at the great Salt Sea, probably Spencer Gulf, and moved in a northerly direction, to the Simpson Desert.

THE ZEBRA FINCH JOURNEYS

The Zebra Finch Ancestors, small birds with red beaks, set out on a long journey in Creation times which commenced in the far north-west corner of South Australia and moved in a wide circle passing through Ceduna and returning to their place of origin, Kultuwa. The detailed song poetry associated with these great journeys remains the sacred core of ceremonial life of the Pitjantjatjara people and little is revealed to outsiders.

Some of the senior men from Indulkana in north-west South Australia have, however, shown a deep concern for teaching traditional songs to their own children and also for teaching non-Aboriginal people the same stories through the songs. They have chosen the following children's ceremony, a section of the Inma Nyi:Nyi (Zebra Finch Ceremony), to tell the story of the travels of the bird Ancestors.

An old Zebra Finch man had many sons. He camped with them and their wives and children at Kultuwa, a special area in the north-west marked by large boulders

Opposite: Painting from Papunya, central Australia. These paintings give a detailed plan of the great journeys of the desert Ancestors through symbols, lines and dots. Reproduced by courtesy of Aboriginal Arts and Crafts Pty Ltd. *photo J. Steele*

The great Spirit Ancestors of Aboriginal tribes throughout Australia undertook many journeys which criss-cross this vast country in a maze of tracks. *photo R. Edwards*

and a fig tree. The sons decided to go out hunting and to find a large group of Zebra Finches at their next camping place. When they had left, the father and the daughters-in-law also set off on their travels. The father sang to the women as they set off:

You, my daughters-in-law, rise!   *Through the coloured flowers*
Go away with me in the early morning   *The pretty colours of the countryside.*

Travelling over the sandhills, they came to a claypan and here they paused to drink and refresh themselves on their journey. As they washed their wooden carrying dishes by scooping up the water and swirling it around, they saw the tracks of the snake.

Scoop the water to clean the carrying dishes, throw it away;
Scoop the water to clean the carrying dishes, throw it away.
See the snake's tracks

Lift the water to clean the carrying dishes, throw it away;
Lift the water to clean the carrying dishes, throw it away;
See the snake's tracks.

As the Nyi:Nyi continued their travels they sang about the other birds they came across, and the events that occurred at each place. They saw dogs following a woman with large breasts and they saw the honey-eater people frighten a scrub wallaby carrying a baby in its pouch.

The honey-eater people are hand-in-hand;
The woman with large breasts
Calls 'Tjau Tjau' to her dogs;
A scrub wallaby with a baby
Takes fright.

88

After travelling all day and singing about many adventures of the honey-eaters and other bird Ancestors, the Zebra Finch women called softly to their children to rest; the children however kept up their little songs about the mallee fowl.

My little children with red ochred noses
My little children with red ochred noses
Come and sleep.

The children sang softly until they fell asleep.

Mallee fowl　　　　　　　　　*Heaping up the sand.*
Heaping up the sand.　　　　*Only one*
Mallee fowl　　　　　　　　　*Only one egg.*

The women travelled on, their sleeping children cradled in their arms, dancing the women's step (nyanpinyi), jumping with feet together, leaving tracks in the sand. They commenced the return journey to Kultuwa.

Hugging the children
Their heads in our arms
We dance along
Nyanpinyi-nyanpinyi.

In the meantime the Zebra Finch men also decided to return to Kultuwa and at an important rock hole, Wantuwantu, they lit a fire which leapt from bush to bush. This gave the signal to the people remaining at Kultuwa that they were returning. The emu wren brothers were also returning to Kultuwa and they lit their signal fire at the same time. When the people at Kultuwa saw the smoke they prepared food for the returning travellers.

We brothers from Wantuwantu
We all make fire
And throw the flames into the trees.

They, the brothers from Wala, are throwing fire
They, the brothers with rounded buttocks, are throwing fire.

Grind the seeds on a flat stone
The flour from the dish tastes good.

Watch as you pound
and winnow the Watalka seed.

The first traveller to return was the old grandmother who had been away a very long time. All the bird children at Kultuwa rushed to meet her, to inspect her closely.

See the red inside Grandmother's ear!　　*See the red inside Grandmother's ear!*
She is home after a long time away.　　　*She is home after a long time away.*

Finally the line of travellers could be seen in the distance and the excited song of Witululun, the full breasted lark, could be heard.

Witululun runs to tell everyone.　　　*Father came back*
He runs quickly to tell them.　　　　*To the high rock on top of another rock,*
His chest is fat　　　　　　　　　　*To Kultuwa.*
His chest is fat.

　　　　　　　　　　　　　　　　　They all came back to Kultuwa
　　　　　　　　　　　　　　　　　And put down their spears.
In the distance　　　　　　　　　　*The wild fig tree is good shelter*
Putiritirilu is carrying the men's fire.　*And makes a windbreak.*

The song cycle concludes as the weary travellers return bringing the fire to the women, who are very pleased and excited to have fire to cook the food.

　　　The Zebra Finches finally rested at Kultuwa, the sacred site where a wild fig tree sheltered them. The boulder at Kultuwa today marks the site where this took place in the Creation times.

Iwantja community, Indulkana[1]

Overleaf: When moving over vast distances, navigation is accomplished by noting the well-known Dreaming sites along the way. *photo R. Edwards*

THE TRAVELS OF THE KANGAROO AND EURO

The route of the travels of the mythical creatures, Kangaroo and Euro, covers approximately 220 kilometres (140 miles) of Central Australian desert, passing through the hunting territory of many Aboriginal groups, each of which knew sections of the myth. Along their journeys, numerous natural features mark their adventures.

The story concerns the revenge of the Kangaroo and Euro on the Ninjuri lizard-men who had killed Nintaka the blue-tongue lizard. The willy wagtail woman, a relative of Nintaka, grieving over his death, cut off her hair and gave it to Kangaroo and Euro to make hair-belts for themselves. The acceptance of the gift of her hair placed Kangaroo and Euro in her debt and they therefore pledged to revenge the death of Nintaka.

The myth tells of the pursuit of the Ninjuri lizard-men by Kangaroo and Euro, and their gradual destruction. Stopping at many places over the long route, the Kangaroo and Euro enticed the lizard-men into caves and then jumped on the cave roofs — causing them to collapse on those inside. Small springs, rocks, trees and caves mark the long journey. The body of Euro is seen in the watermarks on a cave wall, a rock crevice was created by the force of a spear, and a tree is the metamorphosed body of the Ancestor.[2]

Amongst the Pintubi and Anmatjera to the north of Central Australia, Ancestral Dreaming routes are remembered by the men as they carry out commemorative ceremonies at stopping points along the journeys.

The ground is smoothed at the site of the ritual and elaborate patterns of lines and circles are constructed from bird down, clay and ochre which reproduce in symbolic form the paths and journeys of the Ancestors. The story of the blue-tongue lizard man is one of numerous Dreaming routes which is remembered in songs and paintings by the Pintubi–Anmatjera people today.

The Blue-Tongue Lizard Man and the Fire

In the Dreamtime, Lungkata (Jangala) the blue-tongue lizard man travelled through the country, carrying a fire stick. His two sons followed behind, and although they had enjoyed a meal of kangaroo the previous day, they were now hungry again.

Because the sons had not looked after Lungkata's appetite, Lungkata decided to light a fire. He touched his fire stick to a bush — and it exploded into flames! The flames licked out — flicking as the tongue of the blue-tongue, and soon clumps of grass and bushes were ablaze in every direction. The two sons broke branches from trees and beat at the flames. When the fire appeared to be extinguished, the two sons lay down to rest, only to wake and find that it had rekindled. This same thing happened many times, and the fire still continued to lick through the grass, exploding from bush to bush and driving them further and further south. Eventually, the exhausted sons were pushed some 150 kilometres (90 miles) to the south and perished in the desert at the site called Jambijimba-jarra, where the fire burnt itself out.

Dinny Nolan Jambijimba, Anmatjera tribe[3]

The journeys of the Ancestors of the far north and north-west were not as numerous but they did cover vast distances as did those of the centre. Djankawu and his sisters, for example, travelled from Yelangbara to Milingimbi, and the Kunapipi Mother moved from Roper River into the far west of Arnhem Land, while the Wandjina moved around the north-west Kimberley region. The Rainbow Serpent stories are however the most widely dispersed, having travelled from the north into the centre and to the west following the journeys of the great snakes of the Dreaming. Although there is no one great myth which tells of the travels of this important Creation Ancestor, each group retains the segments of the stories which relate to the origins of features such as the rivers or hollow logs according to the

At various places where the Creation Ancestors rested on their journeys they created remarkable natural features of the landscape. *photo R. Edwards*

activities of the great snakes in their own tribal area. In the north-west, legends tell of river-forming snakes which 'came from the north', as do the myths of the tribes north of Alice Springs. Fearsome serpents which live in waterholes or lagoons are known throughout the continent, indicating that the travels of this great Ancestral hero were enormously wide.

The journeys of Great Ancestors are not simply travel tales. These stories are the foundation of the daily lives and thoughts of the Aboriginal people, as well as their own oral history. Often the travels of Ancestors reflect early migration patterns of Aboriginal groups.

The Eagle and Crow stories are almost as widely distributed as those of the Rainbow Serpent. In the southern version the crow is clever and mischievous, while the eagle is a good man, but in the north these roles are reversed. The following story recounts the myth of the Eagle and Crow in South Australia.

Waku and Kanau, Crow and Eagle

Waku the crow and Kanau the eagle lived in the Manara Range in western New South Wales. The homes of the two men stood up like hills, one at each end of the range, and between their camps was the camp of two sisters. These sisters, both of whom were unmarried, stood in a special relationship to Kanau. He called them 'Mother' and it was his duty to protect them within the tribe. Waku called them 'Mother-in-law' and therefore he was not supposed to look in their direction or have anything to do with them.

The wife of Kanau was a sister of Waku and these men called each other 'Brother-in-law'. Under Tribal Law, it was the responsibility of Kanau to provide Waku with a wife, but as he had no sisters, Waku remained unmarried.

One day Waku came to Kanau and said, 'Brother-in-law, you have a wife and I have not received one in return. Give me one, for it will be pleasant to have a woman. If you won't let me have a wife, I will point a bone at you. I will take the two sisters for whom you are caring.' Kanau attempted to placate his brother-in-law and told him to come back some time later, when he might find him a wife. Waku repeatedly visited Kanau, pleading with him to find him a wife, but to no avail. Finally he said: 'I will return to my camp now, brother-in-law. But one day I will return and hold you to your word.'

Waku then returned to his own camp and sat down. However, because he was a very cunning man 'much more clever than the Makwora men (the sorcerers)' he sought ways to overcome the resistance of his mothers-in-law, the two sisters. From his camp in the Manara Range, he watched the sisters squatting down beside a claypan gathering food. His penis became erect and he sang a song of great magic. It then became extremely long like a serpent and, entering the ground, came up first under one of the women, then the other. The younger woman said: 'Older sister, I have a strange feeling something is happening.' The other replied: 'We had better escape. Old man Waku is trying to trick us.' Then both women ran away from that place.

Soon after, both women showed signs of being pregnant and in time the younger sister gave birth to a boy and laid him in a bed of soft grass with a bark covering. The older sister gave birth to a girl and made a similar soft bed for her baby. They hid the children in the bush, fearing the reaction of the tribe if they knew what had happened. But their frequent trips into the bush to feed the babies were soon observed and the sisters were tormented and ridiculed by their own people as a result. When the tribe attacked them saying 'They have broken the rules, they must be punished,' they ran away, travelling all day until they came to the Darling River.

At the Darling River they met an old man called Tulu, or kingfisher. Tulu was an excellent fisherman, very skilled at catching Murray cod. While everyone else ate their food raw, Tulu had fire and was able to cook all he ate. Tulu watched the two fine strange women as they came towards him. 'What is your group?' And they replied 'Makwora.' 'You are the right skin for me, for I am Kilpara.' So the old man took them as his wives, fed them well and for a while they were very happy living by the Darling River.

Waku, however, continued to pursue the sisters and found them in their camp by the river. By cunning and trickery he killed the husband of the two women and attempted again to take them as his wives, but the sisters escaped the old Waku and travelled far away down until they came to the Murray River at Wentworth. They followed the river downstream to Lake Victoria, keeping on the northern bank until they came to Morgan, where the river turned south.

Waku, on discovering the women's escape, attempted to follow them. He was not able to catch them, however, for they had had a long start and, attempting to take a short cut at Loxton, he made a cave into which he crept and tunnelled underground until he reached Swan Reach, where his exit is now a deep cave.

In other versions of stories about the sisters along the Murray River, they became the wives of the Ancestral Hero Ngurunderi, who travelled along the Murray River chasing the legendary Murray cod. Finally the women were turned to stone by Ngurunderi and are now two small islands (the Pages) off the coast of Encounter Bay.

Waku returned to his own country on the Darling River and revisited his brother-in-law. He then took revenge for his ordeal on Kanau, his brother-in-law, by killing his sister's son. After the death of the child, Waku and Kanau were transformed into their bird forms, and became the crow and the eagle.

Maraure tribe[4]

This story therefore traces Ancestral journeys from the Manara Range in New South Wales to the Darling River, south to the Murray River, thence to Lake Victoria. In Victoria the Eagle and Crow myth links to the story of Ngurunderi and carries the journey through into South Australia.

Another story from the far south which recounts the journeys of the mythical Ancestors tells of the giant Lo-An, a Kulin Tribal Ancestor who finally stopped at Wilson's Promontory, the southernmost point of Australia. The myth was also known by the enemies of the Kulin, the Kurnai.

Lo-An of the Kulin

A Kulin named Lo-An lived with his wife Lo-An Tuka on the Yarra Flats. He was of giant stature, very powerfully built, and a great hunter. They lived mainly on eels, which Lo-An Tuka cooked in the marin-a-thung, or 'splendid oven', which was the name for the earth oven used by most tribes.

One day Lo-An speared a fine eel, nice and fat, just as he liked them. Lo-An Tuka proceeded to cook it in the oven, and while Lo-An was waiting he lay down in the shade of a lightwood tree, with his face to the sky. As he lay there a swan's feather, carried by the light southerly breeze, landed on his chest.

Lo-An sat up and examined it carefully. 'There must be some fine swans where that came from,' he said, 'much better than eel.' So when they finished eating the eel he took his spears and they walked towards the breeze to see where the feather had come from.

They walked on until they stood on the shores of Western Port at Yallok, and there Lo-An saw hundreds of beautiful black swans. The swans were startled at his approach and rose into the air with a noise like thunder. Lo-An and his wife camped there for a long time feeding on swans, and then continued their travels in an easterly direction by following the coastline, staying at one inlet after another, and each day enjoying a meal of swan. At last they came to Corner Inlet, and seeing the mountains on Wilson's Promontory before him, Lo-An thought he would make his home there. So they crossed over, and finding a cave in the mountains opposite Rabbit Island, they made their home in it.

The Kulin claimed that Lo-An became the star Sirius, and that his wife Lo-An Tuka became the star Canopus. The Kurnai said that they sometimes saw him upon his mountain gazing towards the sea, and that Lo-An 'watched over' the people living there.

Kulin tribe, Victoria[5]

Although tales such as that of Lo-An are not great Creation stories, they are interesting in the manner in which they explain motives for travel and movement of tribes in the past, and in the case of the Kulin version, the explanations they provide for the formation of certain stars.

Overleaf: Lo-An and his wife journeyed to the shores of Western Port where they saw hundreds of beautiful black swans. *photo H. Herbert*

CHAPTER FOUR

Earth, Fire & Water

THE EARTH

We belong to the ground
It is our power and we must stay
Close to it or maybe
We will get lost.

Narritjin Maymuru, Yirrkala

In recent years the religious relationship of Aboriginal people to their lands has been discussed often. It has been compared with that of other indigenous cultures, analysed and defined, in an attempt to give Australian administrators a clear formula, a set of owners, maps and boundaries that would facilitate negotiations between Aboriginal people and those who wish to utilize the resources of their lands. Reserves have been created, leases given, titles given, all in the legal terms of white men. The essential and timeless nature of the relationship of a man to his Dreaming and of the ownership and power that the land exerts over him has never been fully understood. The Law which existed throughout the land binding the Mala men to their sacred Dreaming route of the mala wallaby, that bound the Riratjingu to the sacred areas where the Djankawu sisters gave birth and that prevented women from venturing close to any sacred Dreaming site on pain of death has never been recognized.

When Ayers Rock rises from the flat plain at dawn, immense, glowing orange against the grey sky and black earth, as if miraculously lit by thousands of spotlights, its supernatural aura can be universally felt. 'Ayers Rock is holy . . . my great ceremony, my holy tree are holy.' These words from the anguished old owner can be fully appreciated.

An enormous number of sacred sites, rocks and natural features which are held in the same regard and are of vital importance to the Dreaming paths of totemic Ancestors and the Laws of Aboriginal communities may not be as visually spectacular as Ayers Rock, but to their owners they remain the essence of life and the reason for their continued existence.

The Aboriginal people who lived throughout Australia for centuries never owned land in the European sense: it owned them. The clans and groups held in sacred trust the chains of Dreaming sites which their Ancestors had visited in the past. Periodically, here, the initiated men re-enact in chant, mime, and dance, the actions of these Ancestors. Without these ceremonies the annual cycle of life could not be ensured and if the sites were destroyed or defiled, the whole functioning of the cosmos would be endangered.

A man deprived of his homeland, and therefore his Dreaming sites, became nothing, a non-person without vitality or hope for the future. Aboriginals accept and revere their land as it is. Their claim is not to an area on behalf of an individual but to the spiritual content of a whole territory on behalf of the clan, so that the special places made sacred in the Dreaming can be carefully safeguarded and tended.

The Creation era extended for a long time. The great hills and mountains of Australia were formed and as we have seen the Dreaming Ancestors lived on the land in much the same way as Aboriginal people.

Opposite: Arnhem Land escarpment area, Northern Territory. To their owners, the sacred sites remain the essence of life and the reason for their own continued existence. *photo R. Morrison*

Cliffs at Point Gantheaume, Western Australia. *photo R. Morrison*

In many areas however, the Dreaming Ancestors, both animal and human, fought over the two most important elements, the necessities of life — water and fire, and accounts of formation of rivers, waterholes and lakes have been universally retained in Aboriginal oral literature. Fire, also, was immeasurably important and every tribe has its own story of the value of fire.

Many elements of the earth have been important to Aboriginal people for centuries. They were not unaware of the different properties of various deposits on the earth's surface but frequently ascribed these to the actions of their great Ancestors. Quartz, coal, copper and gold; the myths teach us how these were deposited in the Dreaming era. Crystal and quartz had sparkling qualities identified with fire, and were associated with sorcery; women frequently being forbidden to see or touch the quartz knives or crystal flakes that were supposed to make murderous cuts in the sorcerer's victims. In north Queensland on the Proserpine River, people believed rain could be made from a quartz crystal found where the arc of the rainbow touched the earth.

A story by Walter Coulthard of the Flinders Ranges also accounts for the formation of copper deposits by the activities of a witchdoctor.

Yudnamutana Story

Two yuras (men) went hunting for wallaby meat and as they were carrying the wallaby back to camp, they looked behind and saw another man with 'yudnumutana' which means big around the belly button. They realized he was a witchdoc-

Circular Aboriginal stone arrangement, central Australia. *photo R. Edwards*

tor, because he was hunting carpet snakes instead of wallabies. The two yuras with wallabies sat down and watched him. They saw the doctor man sit down on the rocks and then they saw coloured lights where he was sitting. They got frightened and went back to camp to tell the other people, who also got frightened so that they all stayed up the whole night.

Near dawn, they went to see where the witchdoctor was sitting, and noticed the rocks were a green colour, which is the trace of copper. Then they saw where the doctor man dragged the carpet snake along towards the Daly River — that is why there is copper all the way from Yudnamutana mine to Daly. The white man calls it Yudnamutana, us yuras call it Yudnu-mutana.[1]

In western New South Wales at the great copper mines of Cobar, there was once a cave in the rock which was one of the camping places of Baiame in Creation times. This hole sloped inwards and there was red ochre on its sides. 'Kubbur' is the Aboriginal word for red ochre and has been corrupted to Cobar by white people. The old Aboriginals of the area used to say that very early this century before the copper mines were worked, there were footmarks, boomerangs, bullroarers and other designs on the rocks. The ore of copper visible on the surface was believed to be Baiame's excretions, deposited there during the time he lived in the cave.[2]

Another Flinders Ranges legend relates how coal was formed by the fires of the Dreaming Ancestors. One of the most beautiful parts of the Flinders Ranges is Wilpena Pound and the most valuable, the Leigh Creek Coalfield.

Long ago there was a big corroboree and initiation ceremony at Wilpena Pound. There was an old Kingfisher man called Yulu Yulura who lived in the west, near Kaurna territory. He entered the Flinders from the north at Mount Termination. At Leigh Creek he lit a large signal fire to let the people know of his coming. The

101

Above: Saltpan, central Australia.
photo R. Edwards

Opposite: Bushfire, Arnhem Land.
photo P. Tweedie

charcoal remains of this fire has formed the coal deposits at Leigh Creek and several small deposits in other places on the way down. The Aborigines called it Yulu's coal long before white man ever came into the country.

When Yulu was passing through Brachina Gorge on his way to the ceremony he saw two huge snakes travelling in the same direction. These snakes, which are Arkaroos, scared Yulu so he crept behind some low hills so that he could not be seen.

Yulu reached the ceremony and in the meantime the two Arkaroos had caught up with him at the Pound. They surrounded the people and between them they swallowed the lot except for Yulu and the Wild Turkey man who went off earlier towards the south and one newly initiated Wilyaru man and a Vadnappa, who fled towards the east.[3]

FIRE

The most common fire theme which pervades Aboriginal legends is that fire was discovered by a bird or other animal who hid it secretly until other creatures forcibly stole it away in order to share the most precious commodity among everyone. In many myths the original owner lit a fire which spread uncontrollably, causing a huge bushfire and from that time on knowledge of fire became universal.

Fire is central to Aboriginal life; wherever a family camps there is fire for warmth, for cooking food, for protection from spirits and as a focal point to gather round. The antithesis of fire is darkness, where Spirits live. Few Aboriginals will walk alone in the dark bush without at least a fire stick. Fires are lit at night both to keep the Spirits of the dead away from the camps of the living, and to propitiate them. The dead have no fire, so the possession of this vital element is the possession of life. Fire was made by drilling or sawing one piece of wood against another; it was

102

commonly carried from one place to another as lighted fire sticks. Fire was most probably invented and discovered in different ways by various tribes, and the myths emphasize how miserable life was before its discovery. On a cold night fire was the only source of warmth, as, except in the south where possum-skin rugs were made, people generally went naked. Especially along coastal areas fire was also used to send messages, by placing bark sheets at intervals over a smoking fire.

When hunting, Aboriginals frequently used fire to drive out animals from long grass, yet once they were caught the fire was left burning. Fires were also lit to encourage the growth of new green shoots to feed kangaroos and other herbivorous animals. In dry seasons enormous grassfires often spread through the land. Calculated use of fire over so many millennia must therefore gradually have altered the whole ecology of Australia. Fire-resistant plants became dominant. The eucalypt which regenerates so quickly and plants like hakeas and banksias which rely on fire to germinate their seed spread. Through continual burning, low forests became grasslands and the number of herbivorous animals able to be supported on the land enormously increased.

A typical fire myth from the Murray River in Victoria shows that the Aboriginals were themselves aware of the changing of the landscape by fire.

The Eagle Steals the Fire

In early times people had no fire, because it was kept by two friends, Koorambin the water rat and Pandawinda the cod fish in their underwater home amongst the river reeds. All efforts by the people to obtain a spark of fire failed.

One day the two friends cooked a large heap of freshwater mussels on the river bank. The fishing eagle noticed the smoke from the fire and, soaring high in the sky, he magically caused a strong wind to blow the fire amongst the dry reeds. The two friends desperately tried to put out the fire, but the eagle caused a whirlwind to blow the fire in all directions, so that it reached as far as the forests which grew

Over the centuries since its discovery, Aboriginals have developed exceptional skill with fire for cooking, light and warmth. *photo R. Edwards*

thickly at that time on the plains bordering the river. The forests were burnt out, and that is the reason for the immense bare plains; but the people were able to get as much fire as they wanted and have kept it ever since.[4]

In this story and in nearly all the stories about the origin of fire, the element of water is associated with the creatures who try to keep, hide, or destroy fire — such as fish, crocodiles or snakes — and the element of air which is akin to fire is the habitat of birds who in many cases save fire from destruction and give it to men. This is very obvious in myths from the northern half of Australia.

In the Arnhem Land area, each tribe has a fragmentary myth about fire; these, when they are all put together, give a general history explaining the origin of fire and the adventures of those who try to steal or hide it, and its eventual repossession by men. The invention of fire through fire sticks is described in the following myth, the first fragment of this history.

Kakan, an old hawk, discovered how to make fire by twirling one stick upon another. In a dispute with a white hawk the country was set on fire. A pine tree, by which every day a number of men, women and children used to climb into the sky and come down again, was burnt, so that the people stayed in the sky. Starlight comes from the crystals implanted in their heads, elbows, knees and other joints.[5]

Once the people had discovered fire, they tried always to keep it alight. A myth from Oenpelli tells how women at first kept fire secret from the men; but eventually the crocodile men learnt how to use the fire sticks.

The Shared Secret

Two men went hunting with their mothers. While the men caught ducks and plovers on the plain, the women collected lily roots and seeds from water pools. The women possessed fire, but sought to keep it secret from the men who were ignorant of firemaking. The women cooked their food while the men were away, and on seeing them returning, hid the live ashes in their vulvas. The men asked where the fire was. The women denied that there was fire and a row broke out, but the women gave the men cooked lily cake, and after they had eaten cake and meat, they all slept. Then the men went hunting and the women cooked.

The weather was very hot. The uneaten remains of the birds went bad. The men brought a fresh supply and again saw the fire burning in the distance. A spur-winged plover flew to warn the women, who hid the fire as before. The men arrived, they argued, the women denied the fire. The men said, 'We saw a big fire; if you have no fire, which way do you cook your food? Has the sun cooked it? If the sun cooks your lilies, why does it not cook our ducks and stop them from going bad?' There was no reply to this. So they slept.

In the morning the men left the women and went away by themselves. After a great deal of effort they discovered that they could make fire by rubbing sticks together. They then decided to turn themselves into crocodiles and so they fashioned crocodile heads, pierced their lungs so that they could breathe under-water, practised swimming, and then hid the heads and returned to camp. Again they saw fire in the distance and again the plover gave warning. The women wanted to know what the men had been doing, but the men said nothing at all. Late in the afternoon the women set their nets for fish. In the morning they went to draw in the nets, but the men had arrived first and turned themselves into crocodiles in the water. They hung onto the nets so that the women could not pull them in. When the women felt under the water to see what made the nets heavy, the crocodiles dragged them under and drowned them.

The men threw away their sticks and spears and everything that they had and changed themselves completely into crocodiles. They then dived into the water where they have lived ever since.[6]

Although the crocodiles knew about the fire sticks, they were very clumsy at actually lighting a fire, as another myth from north-eastern Arnhem Land shows.

The crocodile took a fire stick with which to make a fire, for there was then none in the world. But every time he tried he broke the drill stick. Soon his hands were cut and bleeding and broken fire sticks lay about. Then the frilled lizard arrived. He sat down and continued work on a basket that he had started. The crocodile asked him to try making fire. The frilled lizard, who had fire sticks of his own in the basket, told the crocodile that he had been gripping the drill incorrectly, and then made fire. 'Waku (sister's son) of mine,' said the crocodile, 'it is a good thing you are my relative and it is a good thing that you made fire for us, for all people.' The crocodile took grass, lit it, and built a huge fire.[7]

Finally, a myth from the Dalabon in Beswick Reserve shows how the crocodile selfishly guarded fire for himself only, until he was tricked by the rainbow bird who gave the fire to men.

The crocodile possessed fire sticks. The rainbow bird would ask for fire, but was knocked back every time. The rainbow bird was without fire. He had no light. He slept without a camp fire and ate his food of fish, goanna, lizards and mussels raw. The rainbow bird could not get fire because the crocodile was 'boss' for fire and would knock him back, saying, 'You can't take fire!'

'What am I to do for men? Are they to eat raw food?'

'They can eat it raw. I won't give you fire sticks!'

The crocodile had fire. No man made it. The crocodile had had fire from a long time ago. Then the rainbow bird put fire everywhere. Every tree has fire inside now. It was the rainbow bird who put the fire inside.

The rainbow bird spoke. 'Wirid, wirid, wirid!' He climbed into a tree, a dry place, a dry tree. Down he came, like a jet plane, to snatch the fire sticks, but the crocodile had them clutched to his breast. Again and again the rainbow bird tried.

'You eat raw food,' the crocodile told him. 'I'm not giving you fire.'

'I want fire. You are too mean. If I had had fire I would have given it to you. Wirid, wirid, wirid, wirid, wirid!' Down he came. He missed. He flew up. 'Wirid, wirid, wirid!' They argued again.

'I'm not giving you fire. You are only a little man. Me, I'm a big man. You eat raw food!'

The rainbow bird was angry. 'Why do you knock me back all the time?'

The crocodile turned around for a moment. Snatch! The rainbow bird had the fire stick! 'Wirid, wirid, wirid!' Away he flew.

The crocodile could do nothing. He has no wings. The rainbow bird was above. 'You can go down into the water,' he called. 'I'm going to give fire to men!' The rainbow bird put fire everywhere, in every kind of tree except the pandanus. He made light, he burned, he cooked fish, crocodile, tortoise.

The crocodile had gone down into the water. The two had separated.

'I'll be a bird. I'll go into dry places,' the rainbow bird called out. 'You can go into the water. If you go to dry places you might die. I'll stay on top.'

The rainbow bird put the fire sticks in his behind. They stick out from there now. That was a long time ago.[8]

The theme of the water creature hoarding fire until it is snatched away by a bird is repeated in a story about the great water-dwelling serpent Kunmanggur, from the Murinbata tribe in the Port Keats area.

Kunmanggur took all the fire and entered the water, meaning to take the fire for ever. The fire was on his head. When only his fiery headdress could still be seen, the butcher bird snatched the fire. Then the kestrel made fire with fire sticks, the first time they had been used, and set alight the grass on all sides, giving the country its characteristic fire-scorched appearance.[9]

In the centre of Australia in the desert country of the Pitjantjatjara Kipara the wild turkey stole a burning log, which burned without being consumed, and travelled

Fire remains a source of life and great comfort to Aboriginal tribes throughout the desert regions, where camp is never made without a small fire. *photo R. Edwards*

towards the sea to extinguish the flame in the water. Just as he reached the sea, the two hawk men, Muttja-didju, swooped down unexpectedly and took the fire stick, returning it to men.[10]

Further south, in the area of the Nullarbor Plain, Daisy Bates recorded another version of the fire myth. In this case Kweenda the bandicoot selfishly refused to give fire to men. Kwidderuk the sparrow hawk and his cousin Wata the pigeon pursued him for possession of the fire, which the bandicoot kept under his tail. At last they reached the sea, and the bandicoot cried out to his uncle the sea to take the fire. But a little spark flew out and smouldered in Wata the pigeon's beard and thus the sparrow hawk and pigeon brought fire to men, putting fire into every tree as they passed, to make it burn well.[11]

In the far southern areas of Australia the sky is always an important feature in myth, being the home of the Sky-Father, Bunjil or Baiame. Two fire myths from the far south of the continent relate how the original possessors of fire lost it to men, and went up into the sky as stars.

The Kanatgurk and the Crow

Five women called the Kanatgurk were once the possessors of fire, but would not share it. One day Waang the crow tasted a cooked yam from their fire and liked it so much he resolved to steal the fire. By a trick he put snakes in some anthills as the women were passing to frighten the women, as they carried their fire sticks along. Some coals fell from the sticks to the ground; and pouncing on one Waang carried it to the top of a tree.

Bunjil then gathered all his people around the tree and they shouted to Waang for fire. Waang became scared and flung fire down to them. Bunjil's young men were angry and threw fire back up at him and since then all crows have been black. They also set fire to Waang's country and the conflagration was so great that Bunjil had difficulty in putting it out. He placed some large rocks at the head of the Yarra to stop the fire spreading there; two of his young men were burnt and are now two rocks at the foot of the Dandenong Ranges.

The Kanatgurk were swept up into the sky, where they are now the Pleiades; still glowing at night as they carry fire at the end of their digging sticks.

Kulin tribe, Victoria[12]

A fragmentary myth from Tasmania, where so little evidence of myth has survived, relates how two men were seen by the Aboriginals on top of a hill. They threw down fire to the people, and as it fell amongst them they ran away frightened. Later the people returned to make a fire with wood, and the two men became the stars Castor and Pollux.[13]

Fire remains a source of life and great comfort to Aboriginal tribes throughout the desert regions where camp is never made without a small fire. The enormous importance of fire in the adaptation of man over the millennia has meant that Aboriginal people have grown to be its master and have developed exceptional skills in controlling fire for warmth and light. A small fire is always kept burning in the camp of each family group — often it will stay miraculously alight with only a few sticks from dusk to dawn, keeping all who sleep there warm. In the ritual life of night fire assumes a great dramatic role and as if by magic a small glow will suddenly roar into an explosion of fire and light, or a single lit fire stick will in an instant ignite the fire sticks of possibly twenty dancers as they re-create the great fire started by Lungkata the blue-tongue lizard man, which exploded from bush to bush, driving his sons on their southern journey.[14]

WATER

As the tribes moved and dispersed across the vast continent, water became essential for survival in areas where vegetation was exceedingly sparse and dry. It is not surprising that legends telling of the creation of waterholes, soaks and rivers receive a great deal of attention and are well remembered amongst succeeding generations. On Australia's small offshore islands, varying explanations are given for the separation from the mainland. The Djankawu brother when on Elcho Island tripped and accidentally pushed his stick into the sand, causing the sea to rush in; and on Mornington Island, in the Gulf of Carpentaria, legends tell of the seagull woman, Garnguur, who formed the channels separating the islands from the mainland by dragging her raft backwards and forwards across what was then a peninsula. The people of central Arnhem Land believe the narrow seas between Milingimbi in the Crocodile Islands and the mainland were formed by the Creation Shark, who went on to form the land at the place now known as Nangalala.

The legend of the Shark follows as told by Mayngurrawuy of Milingimbi.

Burrulupurrulu Speared a Shark

One day, Burrulupurrulu and his wives were sitting at that place called Djawal. Well, Burrulupurrulu said to his wives, 'Off you go, you women of mine. I'm going to stay here. I am going to make a barbed spear for myself. I will be sitting over there at Gulkula.'

'Okay, old man, you can wait over there for us. You can make your spear for yourself over there, and we'll meet you when we come back.' Off they went, walking down to the sea. Off they went across the saltpans together, until they reached a place called Gukuk. One of the young wives looked towards the beach and said, 'Well, it's low tide, sister.'

And the sister replied, 'That's right, sister. We might as well get some oysters.' So they went down and started to collect oysters. Suddenly the little sister turned

Opposite: Aboriginal accounts of the formation of rivers, waterholes and lakes have been universally retained in oral literature. *photo P. Tweedie*

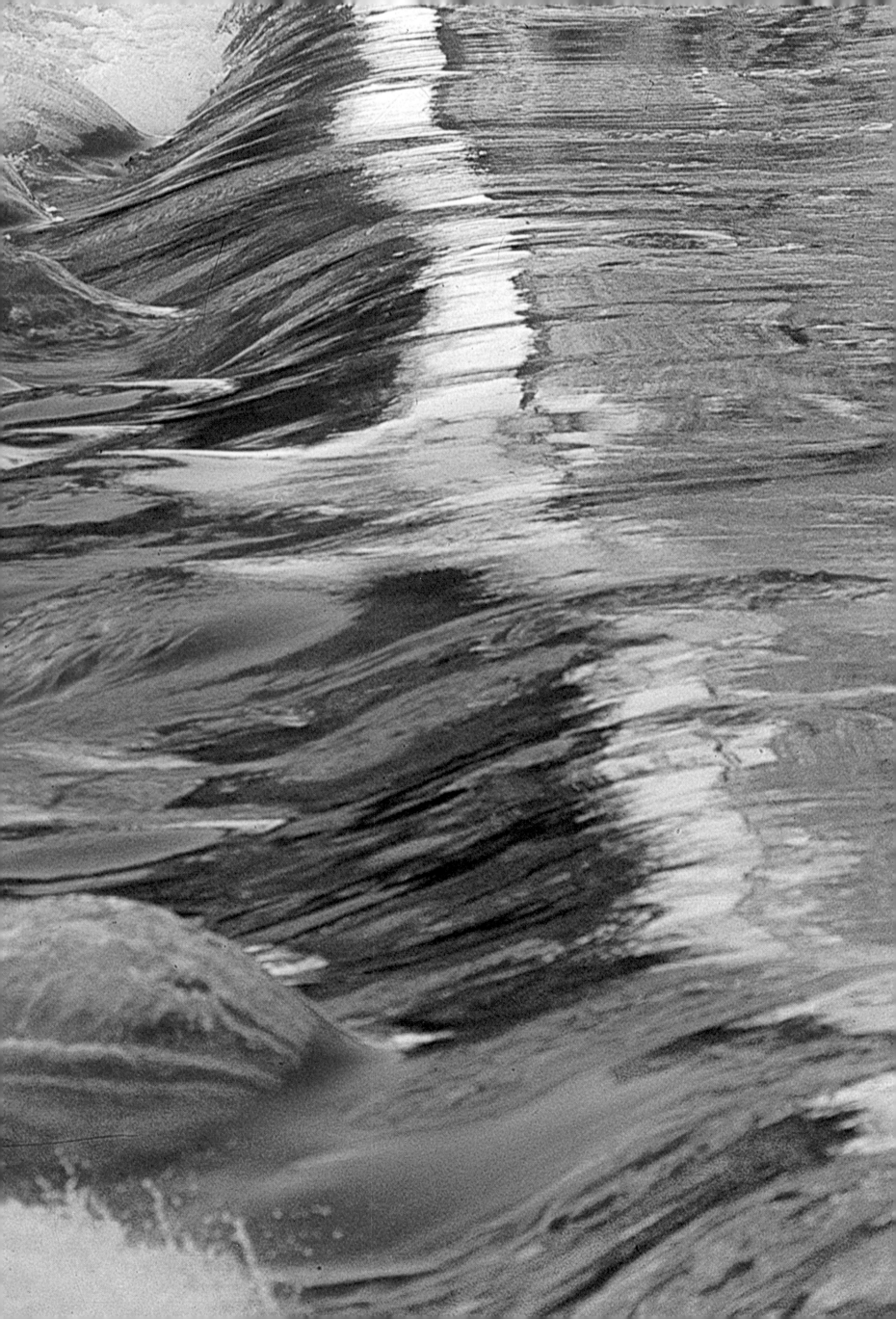

Burrulupurrulu looked down his spear, straightening it, then danced a bungul, a ceremony. *photo S. Doring*

The shark speared by Burrulupurrulu created the land of Nangalala and gave the places names as he went. Detail of bark painting of Shark Dreaming by Mamulunawuy of Milingimbi, Northern Territory. *photo P. Tweedie*

around; she had heard a shark, he was creating land around them. And she said, 'Hey! What is this, sister? There's a big shark, he has been caught in a shallow area when the tide went out.'

The big sister said, 'Come on, let's run to our husband and tell him, because he's making a big barbed spear. But first we'll have a good look and make sure.' They had a closer look and then they said to each other, 'What are we going to do?' The big sister said, 'Off you go and tell him, and I will stay here and keep my eye on the shark.' The little sister agreed.

So the little sister ran and took the news to their husband. She ran and ran and ran. Her husband turned around and saw her running and he said, 'Tell me, what news is in your mind? What have you found for us?'

She replied, 'Come, my husband, wonderful strong arms, it's stuck in the shallow water! It was creating the lands. My sister is keeping her eye on it!'

Burrulupurrulu said, 'Hey! Just wait a minute! Don't force me into anything! Hold on, I'll have to have a look for myself.'

The woman replied, 'Wonderful husband, this is a great Spirit, a land Creator. He came out of the deep water, and he is still there.'

Burrulupurrulu said, 'Yes. Don't you say anything to anyone.' He looked down his spear, straightening it, then he danced and said, 'Wait! What say I run to that hill called Gulkula Rranyirranyi?' And he climbed up the hill Gulkula. He ran up, stayed there a moment, then returned, dancing. He was dancing a bungul, a ceremony. Dancing, closer, closer, closer, and the wives called out to him, 'My husband, dance well!'

So he danced there and back three times, and then he said, 'Right, now show me where he is.' And he broke off the end of his spear shaft to finish it.

Then off they all went together, and when they arrived, Burrulupurrulu said, 'Where is it?'

110

'Here! Here it is, husband with fine arms. Here it is,' said his wives. He climbed up a sandhill and he saw the shark; it was lying with its back sticking up.

'What is this, the poor thing that you have found for us here? Wait for a while. I will go back to where I've just come from, and you stay here and keep your eyes fixed on it. I will come back dancing,' said Burrulupurrulu.

Off he ran, and came back dancing until he was in a suitable place. He hurried up, took aim, and the wives said to him, 'Wonderful husband, don't miss him with your spear. This is the only one we've got.'

'Be quiet,' Burrulupurrulu said. And he aimed his spear, and pointed it straight at the fleshy part, and said, 'This will go right into its fleshy part for us, women.' And he threw the spear . . . aim . . . fire, like that, and it pierced into the shark, right into his back. The spear pierced the shark's back right through and the spear went into the sand on the other side. The shark tossed and thrashed about.

Then Burrulupurrulu came up out of the water, and there on Gulkula hill he danced. And after that he went down to the beach and asked, 'Where is it?' And they replied, 'Not yet, husband, it is still thrashing around.'

So again he hurried off, and from a long way away he came back, dancing, and that was the end. The shark was throwing himself around, and then he died. And the wives said, 'That's the end, my husband, happy arms, happy elbows. He's lying there quietly.'

They went down to the shark, lifted it up, dragged it from the water, cut it up and put the flesh into piles. The right side of the shark was kneaded ready for eating, and there were separate piles of meat all over the place. Suddenly the remaining portion of the shark's body was frightened, and splashed into the water and swam up all the way to Nangalala where he died. He said, 'My tail will point towards the west, and my head in the other direction.' And he created the land of Nangalala, and went back. On the way he created some foods, only a few, because it was nearly morning. And he gave the places names as he went: Gawathana, Gununuwa, Maranydjiwuy, and Garulngur. The names from the shark are the genuine all-time names.

Mayngurrawuy, Milingimbi[15]

Of the numerous legends which explain the origins of the great rivers of Australia, perhaps the most remarkable is that which tells of the formation of the Murray River. The story of Ngurunderi follows the bends and turns of this mighty river, describing their formation in the Dreaming time by the mighty Ponde, the Murray cod fish, as he fled from his ancient pursuer.

FORMATION OF THE MURRAY RIVER

Ngurunderi

A central story of the Lake Alexandrina tribes is their myth of the making of the Murray River by the Ancestral Hero, Ngurunderi, when he was pursuing a gigantic Murray cod called Ponde, sometimes visualized as in human form. The epic chase commenced in the interior of New South Wales. Ngurunderi pursued Ponde down the river using lala or rafts to aid his progress, beaching them as he shifted from reach to reach of the river. These rafts were constructed from strips of red gum bark and provided a floating platform from which Ngurunderi could launch his spears. Whilst following Ponde, Ngurunderi came to Mannum or Kauwira. The giant fish, whilst endeavouring to escape his tormentor, kept cutting new reach after new reach into the river, thrashing and weaving from side to side as he cut the deep water channel. Suddenly, at Kauwira, the fish changed direction at the great bend in the river still known as 'Ponde'. Ponde continued his sinuous course, with Ngurunderi closely following behind, passing Maraum, a place name which incorporates a reference to the strong right arm of the hunter whose awesome spear launchings forced Ponde southward. Attacks by Ngaralta men kept both the fish and Ngurunderi hugging the eastern bank.

Overleaf: The great River Murray was formed as the hunter of Creation times chased the mighty Murray cod from New South Wales to Lake Alexandrina, the bends and reaches being formed as the fish thrashed along the channel. *photo R. Edwards*

The great hunter finally reached Kobathatang and hurled his spear, striking Ponde in the tail. The shock was so great that the fish darted straight ahead, cutting the long straight reach which extends to Peindjalang near the town of Tailem Bend.

Having failed to kill his fish, Ngurunderi and his two wives (who will be remembered from the Crow and Eagle story in Chapter 3) hastened along the straight stretch of river to Tailem Bend. Taking up a position on the top of the cliff where the centre of the town now stands, he aimed again at Ponde but failed again. Hastily launching his raft once more, he followed on downstream, passing Wellington as he tried to catch up with Ponde. However, the cod escaped him into the wide waters of Lake Alexandrina at Yeratang and here Ngurunderi set up camp. It was whilst camped here that he was disturbed by a being call Muldjewangk which broke holes in his net. He and his wives therefore were unable to catch any fish at all here so Ngurunderi shifted his main camp to warm sandy ground, on the eastern side of Lake Alexandrina, near the present town of Ashville. Here he hauled his rafts up onto the land and today they are represented as the twin summits of Mount Misery. They are called Lalangenggul, which means the two watercraft.

Maraure tribe, Darling River[16]

The mention of Muldjewangk, the strange creature which tore Ngurunderi's nets, is interesting and may relate to the being in the legends of the former Wellington people which was said to live in the river at the point where it entered the lake. It was thought to entice children into the river to drown them. A similar creature was recently mentioned by Henry Rankin of Point Macleay, on the shores of Lake Alexandrina.

The Muldjewangk

Up along the river the old people used to camp and they would tell the kids, 'Keep away, keep away from the river, especially when it's getting dark.'

A little boy was playing, and he was missed — they found his tracks to the edge of the river, and then the tracks stopped; something had grabbed him. So some of the men rubbed body fat all over themselves and took feathers in their mouths and dived into the river. They went down and down. They saw a big cave down there, and saw three Muldjewangk sitting around the little boy, the Muldjewangk are half men and half fish and are all covered in seaweed. The men started singing them and put them all to sleep, and then grabbed the little boy and took him up to his mother and father again.

The Muldjewangk is a big monster who moves around the lake, and has his home beneath steep cliffs on the eastern side, where the water is deep.

One day, a steamer was coming down the river with two barges full of grain behind, and then it suddenly stopped, though the paddle wheels were still going round. At the back of the barge there were the two big hands of Muldjewangk holding on. The captain got out his gun. 'Don't shoot,' said the old people, 'don't shoot him, just let the barges go.' But the captain went ahead and shot him and the Muldjewangk got cross and pulled the barges right down into the river. Old people said to the captain, 'You're going to suffer now.' And the captain got blisters all over his body, all weeping red and sore, and he took five or six months to die. We say, if you see a big lot of seaweed floating across lake, move out of the way, it's the Muldjewangk.

My kids, they swim in the lake over the hill there, and yesterday they found a huge footprint about three feet long. 'That's the Muldjewangk,' they scream and yell. 'That's right, baby,' I say to my daughter. 'You be careful, don't play around too much.' I tell them that, even though the monster isn't in the lake any more.[17]

The story of the formation of the Murray River is remarkable in that hostile tribes which lived along the far reaches of the Murray each had a similar version of the same Creation story. Language and therefore names differed, but the essential elements remained. The following version is from the Wotjobaluk in Victoria.

114

Totyerguil

Totyerguil was a mighty hunter. One day he left the Mallee scrub, which was his country, and camped with his family close to present-day Swan Hill. Soon his two wives, Gunewarra the black swans, had a meal ready for him, and while he was eating it his two sons went collecting wattle-gum of which they were very fond. When they arrived at a large waterhole they saw a huge fish basking in the sun close to the surface of the water. The two boys ran back to tell their father.

Totyerguil quickly made a canoe, and when near the sleeping fish threw a spear with all his might, which struck it on the back, the spear remaining stuck upright between its shoulders. The fish, who was Otchout the cod, awoke with a start, and rushing towards the banks of the waterhole commenced to form a channel by tearing up the ground and allowing the water to fill it up, so he could escape from his enemy.

Otchout did this so rapidly that Totyerguil was unable to keep pace with him and soon lost sight of him, although he kept on his trail by following the newly-made river. At dusk Otchout excavated a long wide billabong where he rested for the night. Totyerguil, however, did not rest, and coming upon the sleeping cod at daybreak next morning was able to throw a second spear which struck Otchout in a spot immediately behind the first, still protruding from the middle of his back. Otchout again ran off digging furiously, and once again escaped from his pursuer. That night he made another large billabong in which to rest, and there Totyerguil found him next morning and was able to wound him with a third spear, which struck the codfish just behind where the two former weapons were still implanted. This procedure was repeated over several days, until they reached the neighbourhood of where Murray Bridge in South Australia has since been built, and there Otchout made a very large and deep waterhole in which he hid. He has since gone to the sky, where he became the star Delphinus.

By this time, Totyerguil had thrown all his spears, which are now the spines projecting from the back of present-day cod. Not having any more spears, and being unable to find Otchout in the deep waterhole, he abandoned the chase and landed upon the bank. There he set his canoe on its end, and stuck his paddle-pole upright on the ground. The canoe became a huge gum tree, and the paddle-pole a Murray pine, both of which trees were later pointed out to the children of the tribe when the story of the making of the Murray River by Otchout the cod was told. Ever since that time canoes have always been made from gum-tree bark and paddle-poles from Murray pine branches.

Wotjobaluk tribe[18]

The two versions of the formation of the Murray River, of Ngurunderi from the Lake Alexandrina tribes and of Totyerguil from the Wotjobaluk people, show that although names and details may differ, the essential elements of great myths are carried from one people to another and remain intact. The great river Murray was formed as the hunter of Creation times chased the mighty Murray cod from New South Wales to Lake Alexandrina, the bends and reaches being formed as the fish thrashed along the channel.

PORT PHILLIP BAY

One story of the formation of Port Phillip Bay by the people of the Mornington Peninsula has been told in Chapter 1. Another version is given by the Kulin from the other side of the bay. According to Billi-billeri of the Kulin, Port Phillip Bay in Victoria was formed by the Yarra River which drained the vast waters previously locked in the mountains of the Woiwurong Kulin people.

The Yarra River and Port Phillip Bay

Once the water of the Yarra was locked in the mountains. This great expanse of water was called Moorool, or Great Water. It was so large that the Woiwurong people had very little hunting ground, although the tribes to the south had excellent hunting grounds on the lovely flat which is now Port Phillip Bay. Mo-yarra, the head man of the Woiwurong, decided to free the country of the water and cut a channel through the hills in a southerly direction to Western Port. However, only a little water followed him, and the path gradually closed up. Water again covered the land of the Woiwurong.

Some time later, the headman of the tribe was Bar-wool. He remembered Mo-yarra's attempt to free the land and knew that Mo-yarra still lived on the swamps beside Western Port (Koo-wee-rup). Each winter he saw the hilltops covered with the feather-down which Mo-yarra plucked from the waterbirds sheltering on the swamps.

Bar-wool decided to drain the land. He cut a channel up the valley with his stone axe. But he was stopped by Baw-baw, the mountain. He decided to go northwards, but was stopped by Donna Buang and his brothers. Then he went westwards, and cut through the hills to Warr-an-dyte. There he met Yan-yan, another Moiwurong, who was busily engaged in cutting a channel for the Plenty River in order to drain Morang, the place where he lived. They joined forces, and the waters of Moorool and Morang became Moo-rool-bark, 'the place where the wide waters were'. They continued their work, and reached the Heidelberg-Templestowe Flats, or Warringal, Dingo-jump-up, and there they rested while the waters formed another Moorool.

Bar-wool and Yan-yan again set to work, but this time they had to go much slower, because the ground was much harder, and they were using up too many stone axes. Between the Darebin and the Merri Creeks they cut a narrow, twisting track, looking for softer ground. At last they reached Port Phillip. The waters of Moorool and Morang rushed out. The country of the Woiwurong was freed from water, but the flats of Port Phillip were inundated and Port Phillip Bay was formed.[19]

THE FORMATION OF THE CLARENCE RIVER, NEW SOUTH WALES

In New South Wales, the Clarence River rises in the mountains near the Queensland border and enters the sea at Yamba. The three stories which follow together form the Aboriginal history of the making of the Clarence River by the wicked old woman of the Creation period, Dirrangun.

The Source of the Clarence River: Dirrangun at Tooloom

Some people say that Dirrangun is a witch, that she's mean and cunning and brings you all the mischief in the world. Others say that she's friendly. But she's a very old woman and she has long hair down to her knees.

Dirrangun had two married daughters and a son-in-law. This son-in-law was a Buloogan, a strong, handsome man. The daughters of the Dirrangun were his two wives. The daughters quarrelled with their mother and the Buloogan took the quarrel up and sided with his wives. They starved the old woman; they didn't pass her anything to eat and she became angry.

Dirrangun's camp was under a big fig tree at the waterfall which is the source of the Clarence River. There was a basin, a hollow in the rock, which contained their water. Dooloomi was the name of the pool, and it was the jurraveel or home of the spirit of the water. Tooloom now is the white man's name for this waterfall — Tooloom is the nearest he could get to saying Dooloomi.

While the son-in-law and his two wives were out hunting and gathering food, Dirrangun drained all the water out of the pool with a bark coolamon, or carrying dish. When the Buloogan and his two wives came home in the evening, there was no water. The two wives were running about all over the place looking for water, but there was no water. Dirragun had put leaves and bark over the empty basin hole in the rock so that the place was hidden. For two or three days the Buloogan and his wives could not get a drink of water and they became desperately thirsty.

Dirrangun was pretending to cry for them. Some people say that Dirrangun was sitting on this coolamon of water in her camp, hiding it, and that when the Buloogan found this out, he got angry and cried, 'Well, you're not going to have all the water! I'll let it out!' He thrust his spear into that coolamon and let it out.

Opposite: The Coorong area of South Australia once maintained a large Aboriginal population. Legends remain which tell of the formation of the waters in the Creation era. *photo R. Morrison*

Others say that when Dirrangun, the Buloogan and his two wives went to sleep, the Buloogan's two dogs, who were thirsty, found the water which Dirrangun had hidden in the coolamon. Two mountains nearby, called Dillalea and Kalloo-Guthun, are named after those two dogs. In the night the dogs returned to the camp of the Buloogan and stood over him. And the water dripped from their mouths. When the Buloogan felt this he woke up and followed the two dogs back to where Dirrangun was asleep with the hidden water.

When the Buloogan saw where the water was hidden, he was angry. He caused heavy rain to fall and the hollow rock-basin began to fill. The water rose and rose and backed up where the creek is now.

When the water began to rise Dirrangun climbed into the fig tree and made a platform in the boughs. But the water rose and swept her and the fig tree away and left a hollow beneath the cliffs where the waterfall is now. Dirrangun was holding on to the fig tree as she was swept away. She was swept over the second fall, which we call Ngalumbeh. At the bottom of this fall she was whirled around and round, still holding on to the fig tree, in a whirlpool for half a day.

The water was getting stronger and stronger. The Buloogan had cursed the water to make it unmanageable. It took her and the fig tree away down into the Clarence River. From time to time Dirrangun would sit in the torrent with her legs wide apart trying to block the water, but each time the flood would bear her away. Where the South River comes into the Clarence River, Dirrangun sat with her legs outspread. The water rose and went up and made the South River. There she sat until the flood rose and swept her and the fig tree on again.

Below Grafton, on the river, there is a fig tree growing. Many old men would see that fig tree and say, 'Oh, look! Dooloomi borrgun!' which means, 'That fig tree belongs to Tooloom!' Those old men would say, 'Dirrangun. She's away down there, but she belongs up there at Tooloom.' But Dirrangun is still in that fig tree below Grafton.

Eustan Williams, Githavul tribe[20]

The Murray cod escaped the hunter in the wide waters of Lake Alexandrina. *photo D. Conroy*

The Dams Dirrangun Made along the Clarence River

Somewhere in the mountains near Tooloom, in those forests of tall trees, somewhere in those mountains hidden by drifting mists, the old woman Dirrangun kept hidden her sacred spring. This old woman didn't want anyone to know where the water was. It was good water and she used to get it herself. But one day she was sick. And there was a young man called a Buloogan. He was a very well-built young man, he was handsome. She asked this Buloogan if he would go and get the water and sent him up to this secret spring. She had to direct him and tell where it was. So the Buloogan set off into the mountains to get some of the water in a bark coolamon.

When the Buloogan got to the water, he found that Dirrangun had dammed the water up. The Buloogan broke the dam and the water started to run away.

When Dirrangun saw the water coming, she started to try and dam the water. But the water began to come faster and wider. These mountains that you see here are the dams Dirrangun made to stop the water. But the water broke through them.

And at last the water came down and went into the sea, which we called in the language, Burraga. That's how this river, the Clarence, came to be here. Mount Ogilvie, that's one of the dams Dirrangun made. The gorge down below Baryulgil is the place of the last dam that Dirrangun made. But the water broke through.

When the water got down to Yamba, Dirrangun realized that she couldn't stop it, so she cursed it and made it salt so that no one could drink it.

Somewhere in the mouth of the Clarence is the last stand of Dirrangun as she tried to stop the water. She threw herself in front of the water to try and stop it, but the water just rushed over her and she was turned into stone.

Lucy Daly, Bunjalung tribe, Baryulgil[20]

Dirrangun and Her Family at the Mouth of the Clarence River at Yamba

A long time ago in the early days there was a tribe on this side of the river in Yamba and a family, just a family, at Iluka, straight across the river from here. The tribe from here was invited to go over the river and visit this family. And this old Dirrangun, she was a cranky old lady, she was the mother of this family.

And when the tribe from here went over to Iluka to have a day with this family, Dirrangun wouldn't offer them anything to eat, she was that cranky. She had a daughter-in-law and one son and a daughter. Everyone that went there found that she would never offer them anything to eat. This old woman was terrible, wicked and mean. Her son had two little boys, and the daughter died and the daughter-in-law died and left her there with the son and two grandsons. That's the old Dirrangun I'm talking about.

And then, they tell us that the sea was calm then, at that time. And the son made up his mind to go away with the two boys and leave his mother. So he got to work and made a canoe. When he had finished the canoe he took it down to the beach. He put one boy at the back of the canoe and one in front. Then he got in and started to paddle away.

The mother followed him to the beach and she didn't want the son to go. But he wouldn't stop, he took no notice of her. She sang out after they got a good bit out on the water in the canoe. She called out and told them not to leave her on her own.

She had a yam stick with her, and, when he didn't take any notice, she started to hit the water. And she started to corroboree, sticking the yam stick in the ground and cursing. She started to tell the waves and sea and the water to be rough, the wind to come and the water to rise. And she cried and coo-eed for them to come back, but they took no notice.

So she watched them until they got out of sight. The canoe was on its way to Ballina. And just when they turned the little canoe to go into Ballina, the waves came up and the canoe sank and went under with the two little boys and the father.

And today they say you can still go to Ballina and they can show you that canoe with the two boys, one in front and one at the back, and with the father holding onto the paddle in the middle. They were turned into rock.

Then, two or three years after, the Dirrangun jumped into the river and drowned herself. There you'll hear that roar of the sea, that noise. That's supposed to be Dirrangun looking for her son and two grandsons. You'll hear that sound at Eungarri and Shelly Beach and it works right back to Ballina. That's her under the water, she's turned into a big rock.

You might have heard of those white men blasting that stone, in the mouth of the river at Iluka. That's her. They can't touch it. They can't interfere with it. They tried, but they can't. The white people asked my father if it would be right, if they blew that stone up. My father said, 'No, if they did, all the sea water would rush in.' She's supposed to block it. That's the true thing that the old people told us.

My father, he used to get all us children and tell us. He said, 'Whenever you hear the roar of the sea, that's Dirrangun. She's looking for her son and two grandchildren.'

My father told the white people, 'Don't touch that rock.' The white people tried and it rained and rained and wouldn't allow any boat to go out to sea. They had to leave that stone and it's still there to this day.

Bella Laurie, Yeagirr tribe[20]

The last story by Bella Laurie is strongly reminiscent of the myth in Chapter 1 of the first people coming across the sea and arriving at Yamba.

THE RIVERS OF THE NORTH

The great river systems of western Arnhem Land comprise the two Alligator Rivers, the Liverpool and the Cadell Rivers. These spread across the land in a veinlike network of waterways and small tributaries. At times the mighty rivers carve a path through towering rock faces as they pass through the escarpment areas. In the Wet Season when the earth is dank and the sky overcast and when rain falls daily, the land teems with wildlife, the rivers swell and overflow forming vast swamps and billabongs in the low country. In this wild and remote area, Aboriginal hunters found an abundance of food and Aboriginal groups have undoubtedly lived in this area for 30,000 years. The extensive black soil plains which extend from the base of the escarpment with their waterholes and swamps provided a natural habitat for crocodiles, a wide variety of fish, notably the great barramundi, birds such as emu and waterfowl, and game including kangaroos and wallabies, possums, flying foxes, echidnas, snakes and goannas.

When movement across the plains became difficult in the Wet Season, families retreated to higher ground and frequently made camps in rock overhangs where they painted delicate ochre images of their own vision of nature and the universe. Innumerable paintings have survived to this day and provide us with a magnificent historical record of life in this part of Australia for tens of thousands of years. Some of these paintings depict the legendary Totemic Ancestors who are credited with forming these great waterways, the Rainbow Serpent from the Alligator Rivers, the Giant Crocodile from the Liverpool River and the Barramundi who, like the Murray cod, formed the bends and reaches in the sandstone gorges of the East Alligator River as he thrashed along its course in the Dreaming.

A Gunwinggu legend tells of the great Crocodile Ancestor who rose long ago inland behind the mountain ranges. He slowly made his way overland towards the sea, chewing the land as he went, and making deep furrows which filled with water to become the Liverpool River.

One of the stories told about Ngalyod, the Rainbow Serpent, is that when she assumed her serpent form and moved to the waterhole where she now lives in the Dry Season, the furrow filled with water and became the East Alligator River.

In Cape York the rivers which rise on the desert plateau of the Great Dividing Range include the Kennedy, Hann, Alice, King and Moorehead Rivers.[21] These radiate out and exit into the Gulf of Carpentaria. Long ago, as Aboriginal stories relate, during a feud between the snakes and the birds, the birds lit a fire in the Great Dividing Range to destroy the snakes. The fire destroyed the grass and foliage, leaving behind the arid plateau which exists today, and only a few snakes escaped. These burrowed from the range to the sea and in their wake the waters flowed, thus making the rivers.

Opposite: The rich soils and thick reeds of the swamp country provide a natural habitat for many species of birds and wild life. *photo D. Conroy*

FORMATION OF SPRINGS

One of the few stories which remain of the people who lived on the Adelaide Plains, the Kaurna, concerns the formation of the small coastal freshwater springs along the Fleurieu Peninsula.

Tjilbruke and the Coastal Springs

The springs which dot the coast of the Fleurieu Peninsula are believed to have been created in the Dreaming by the great Ancestral Hero, Tjilbruke. Tjilbruke rose out of the ground near Mount Hayfield. During winter, he lived in the scrub at the camp of two women named Lepuldawi and Watiriorn, which today appear in the hills as the two highest peaks. Tjilbruke travelled to the coast in the summer to fish and gather shellfish at Rapid Head. One day news came to Tjilbruke that his sister's son, Kulultuwi, had been killed near the Sturt River, at Marion. He travelled quickly to that place and found that the young boy had inadvertently killed an emu, his own totem. This meant that the boy had broken a very strict tribal taboo, and as a result he had been struck down right at the moment when he was taking the head of the emu from the fire.

The body of the dead youth was taken to a place near Brighton where, in accordance with ancient custom, it was being smoked and dried. When he arrived at the beach, Tjilbruke seized the body and, weeping and crying, took it back to a spring on the beach at Marino (today this is located on the Kingston Park Reserve) and here Tjilbruke completed the smoking process. Tjilbruke then gathered the body in his arms and carried it along the coast until he came to a spot near Hallett Cove, where he rested with his burden. Tjilbruke was overcome with grief and tears streamed down his face and fell onto the ground. At the point where the tears struck the ground, a spring of fresh water rose from the sand providing a permanent supply of water for successive generations of Aboriginal people.

Tjilbruke soon recovered sufficiently to continue his sad journey, but when he reached Port Noarlunga he broke into tears again, and yet again at Red Ochre Cove, and at both these places springs flowed from the soil where his tears fell.

Tjilbruke then went on to a place a few hundred yards south of the old Port Willunga jetty. The tide was out so he sat on the damp sand. But each time he rested, the thought of his young nephew caused grief to well up in him and his tears flowed again. To this day fresh water can be found by digging in the sand at this spot when the tide is low.

The old man carried the body onto the beach at Sellicks Hill, where he noticed a fine bay where sea salmon could be caught at night. He could not control himself and tears flowed down his face, bringing another permanent spring into existence. Tjilbruke's wearisome journey along the coast continued beyond Myponga to a spot just south of Carrickalinga Head where a small swamp marked one of his resting places. He then went to Kongaratingga where a small cave in the hillside provided him with a resting place. Before reaching the cave Tjilbruke sat down and cried, bringing forth another small spring. Tjilbruke travelled further south, along the coastal cliffs as far as Cape Jervis and from the cape he turned northwards, skirting the foreshore below the cliffs, eventually coming to another cave called Janarwing. He left Kulultuwi's body at the entrance while he walked into the darkness to find a suitable ledge where it could be left, as was the tradition. He put up sticks to form a platform and the remains were carried in and placed on this and abandoned.

Tjilbruke was so full of grief he did not want to return to the outside world, but continued to merge into the hill until he saw the sun shining through a high crevice. He climbed up and as he slipped through the crack in the rock near a swampy lagoon, he transformed himself into an ibis, and today Tjilbruke may still be seen on this lagoon catching fish.

Kaurna tribe[22]

The miraculous advent of freshwater springs is the subject of many legends which are well remembered by Aboriginal people today. These were important stories to tell the children as knowledge of the whereabouts of fresh water was essential in times of drought when small families were on the move across vast areas.

The following stories relate the formation of other springs throughout Australia by the Dreaming Ancestors in the distant past.

Knowledge of the whereabouts of freshwater springs has been essential to Aboriginal nomadic groups. Their miraculous advent is the subject of many legends. *photo P. Tweedie*

The Fresh Water at Raymanggirr

Raymanggirr is a place on the northern coast of Arnhem Land somewhere near Lake Evella. This story I'm telling you is about a spring at Raymanggirr.

The grandchildren of the old frill-necked lizard man were collecting honey. The frill-necked lizard heard, and stopped and listened. 'Aha! My grandchildren are collecting honey! He heard them chopping the tree to collect the wild sugarbag. 'That tree's going to fall down,' he said and so he ran to a rocky point in the sea and looked up at the land. He named that point Mayawalpalnga and then he ran on.

Then his grandchildren called to him: 'Come here, you dear old thing! You can have the top part of the honey in the tree, we'll have the bottom part.' And they ate the honey. The lizard was eating his over there when he got something stuck in his throat. When we cook the frill-necked lizard, we still find these splinters in his throat. And he ran off into the bush calling, 'A bit of the tree has stuck in my throat.' He ran down to the edge of the sea water, into where the lily roots are. And here, where the water runs into the sea, it is fresh. That old lizard man showed us where it is, and we can drink it today.

This is how the people collect it. They go down with a pannikin. When the tide's not full you can just collect it in a pannikin. But when the tide comes in and the spring is submerged, the water is collected in the mouth, sucked up into the mouth, and spat into a paperbark cup or pannikin. It's collected in the mouth. It is held in the mouth, carried over, and spat, and more is collected, and spat out, and more, and spat. Then it's carried to the camp and given to the people. 'Sorry, not much water! The tide's in. Too much salt water. We'll go back later when we can dip for water properly.'

If anyone objects to the spit, you can get a long hollow piece of wood like a bent didjeridu and the water will flow into it until it fills up. And another one, until that

123

one fills up. Then carefully lift out the wood, and carry it to the camp and put it down. The water just flows by itself. When the tide's out, it runs down the beach. At Raymanggirr

Manuwa, Milingimbi[23]

The Formation of Spring Waterholes in the Flinders Ranges

A family was walking from Curnamona to Barratta Springs. Because of dry weather there was no water and being so hot the family got thirsty. The old man told his family to walk along slowly toward Mount Victor while he went to Barratta Springs to wait for a kangaroo. He wanted to kill it and make a waterbag out of its skin to carry the water back to his family, which by this time would have been somewhere near Mount Victor.

At Barratta Springs, the old man waited for the kangaroo which was coming from Murnpeowie. As the kangaroo hopped along, the old man could hear the thumping sounds. The next stop the kangaroo made was at Pepegoona Spring, near Wooltana Station. From there, the kangaroo hopped on to Nurowi Springs and made water. There was no water there, so he hopped on to Emu Bore, which is now an artesian bore. From Emu Bore, the kangaroo hopped on to Limestone. He couldn't find any water there so he had a rest. The white ground at Limestone represents where the kangaroo rested. He then hopped to Glenwarrick Springs and from there he started hopping towards Barratta, but on his way he saw a big snake which now represents Tooths Knob Hill on the Martin's Well property. He got frightened so he went around towards Kemps Dam. There was no water there, so the only place he had to go was to Barratta Springs.

When he got there the old man killed him, got his skin and made it into a waterbag, filled it up with water and headed off towards Mount Victor to find his family. When he got to Mount Victor, he saw his family lying on the ground. They were dying, so he quickly poured water on them. As he poured the water on them it spread and formed a swamp or a kind of a lake. When he saw them moving and starting to come around, he jumped into the middle of the water and he saw his family turning into ducks. He disappeared into the sky and formed the Morning Star.

His family couldn't find him, so they looked into the sky and yelled out, 'Look up there! That's our father looking down at us.' That is how the springs were formed from Pepegoona Spring in the north down the eastern side of the Flinders Ranges to Barratta Springs.

Eileen McKenzie, Flinders Ranges[24]

The previous story bears a strong resemblance to the story in Chapter 2 of the formation of Lake Eyre, and the 'swamp or kind of lake' could well have been this lake.

Another legend from the Flinders Ranges tells of the giant Arkaroo who made the freshwater pools by drinking too much water.

Arkaroo's Dreamtime Journey

Back in the Aboriginal Dreamtime, a giant serpent known as Arkaroo, who was living in the main water pound in the high Gammon Ranges south-west of Arkaroola, slithered down to the plains to quench his thirst.

Arkaroo descended upon Lakes Frome and Callabonna and drank them both dry. The water was saline, and he became bloated. He dragged his heavily laden body back up towards the Gammons, and in doing so, he carved out the deep sinuous gorge that is now known as Arkaroola. On his way back he stopped at several places for a rest, and while doing so he formed springs and waterholes along the way. There are a few permanent ones around there now.

He dragged himself up into the Gammon Ranges, where he now sleeps safely in a hideaway at the Yacki Waterhole. Restlessly he sleeps on with his belly full of water, and whenever he turns the rumbling in his stomach sends out great noises

Opposite: In seemingly dry desert, central Australian Aboriginals dig for water at a site where the myths relate that water was created. *photo R. Edwards.*

The giant serpent Arkaroo formed the hills and
waterholes of the Flinders Ranges. *photo R. Edwards*

that can be heard from time to time to this day. The minor earthquakes and
rumblings have been recorded.

One of the most important waterholes left around these parts by the Arkaroo is
that of the Paralana Hot Springs. The Aboriginals of long ago found this spring
very convenient. They used to use it for domestic purposes, as well as bathe in it. It is
said to have cured minor aches and pains. This spring became hot when, back in the
old time, two young warriors fought for the love of a young girl. The victor, after
killing his opponent, plunged his fire stick murder weapon deep into the spring,
thus making it hot. Since then the water emerges only little below boiling point.

May Wilton[25]

CREATION OF SALT WATER

Many legends tell of the time when all the waters of the earth were fresh. A variety
of animal Ancestors, however, spoiled the water by urinating in it, and salt water
was therefore created. The belief that urinating Ancestors of the Dreaming created
the salt waters is held not only on the northern coast of Australia, but also in the
Kimberleys.

The Bush Cockroach Makes the Water Salt

This story I'm going to tell you belongs to the Gamalanga tribe. Off they went, the
lizard, the bush cockroach and the wallaby. Off they went, then they sat down. 'Let's
stay here.' And the wallaby had brought some fresh water in a paperbark basket.
There was fresh water everywhere — the water which is nowadays all salt. He
brought the fresh water and he hid it.

'Here we are! Now off you go, cockroach, and get some white clay. We're going
to paint each other,' said the lizard.

The fresh water which we drink is provided for us by the wallaby
and the salt water was made by the cockroach. *photo P. Tweedie*

'Who's first? You first, lizard, come here!' said the cockroach.

So the lizard was painted first — very nice. 'Okay now, it's my turn to paint you.'
So he painted the cockroach. He should have done it carefully, but he just splotched
and left it. Then he got up. The wallaby just watched them.

The cockroach looked at himself. 'Hey! I made a good job of painting you and
you did a horrible job on me. I think I'll urinate in your water, you might drink it.'
Off he went, urinating everywhere and all the water went salt.

The wallaby looked up and saw. 'Hey, stop urinating in my water! Up he
jumped and grabbed the paperbark cup, and hid it. He thought the cockroach
might have urinated in it.

So the fresh water which we drink is provided for us by the wallaby and the salt
water was made by the cockroach. That's the story.

Djan'palil, Milingimbi[26]

How Water Became Salt

A long time ago, when there was only fresh water, there wasn't any sea. When they
killed a turtle it urinated, and it became salt water. Then the wind started to blow
and the clouds started to gather together. Then it started to rain. It was getting
drier. The sun shone down and made the land hot. That's all.

Carol Puruntatameri, Bathurst Island[27]

The Aboriginals of the Kimberley district of Western Australia had a similar belief
about a giant serpent named Wonnaira who made all the rivers as he travelled
inland from the sea. The big waterholes along the river courses were places he
rested when he was tired. He camped for a long time at the shallow lake into which
the Sturt Creek empties, and when he urinated the water turned saline. The salt
water found in other lakes in that part of the country was believed to have been
brought there in the same way.

127

CHAPTER FIVE

The Seasons

My hut is nearing completion,
With forked sticks and roof like a sea-eagle's nest, with rails and door. . .
They are always there at that billabong, with the wide expanse of water . . .
It is almost ready. We make these huts all around, and north-east of Milingimbi.
Clouds banking along the horizon, passing north-eastward over the Crocodile Islands. . .
Thus they were making the huts. We saw their heaving chests and the rising clouds from the
*   west, small clouds rising and spreading,*
Saw their heaving chests, as black clouds came bringing a sheet of rain,
Sound of thunder, roaring of wind and rain. . .
I am making it for myself, with forked sticks and with rails. . .
Thunder leaving its noise for me, sound rolling along the bottom of the clouds,
Echoing on the billabong, across the wide expanse of water. . .
I am making my sea-eagle nest to float in the rising waters of the billabong.[1]

When the heavy, oppressive lull before the Wet Season finally breaks and torrential rain covers Arnhem Land, families retreat into their wet-weather huts on stilts likened in the song above to a sea-eagle's nest. The blinding flashes of lightning which shoot across the sky, and the deafening eruptions of the thunder are not however seen as manifestations of natural forces unrelated to man. To the east, the thunder is the voice of Jambuwal, the thunder man, and in the west the lightning bolts are the stone axes thrown by Namarrkon, the Spirit of Lightning. The Rainbow Serpent, the Turtle, the Great Dreaming Whale and the Lightning Snakes are all animals who are linked with thunder, rain, storm clouds and lightning in the sacred stories of many of the clans of the far north.[2]

The Wongar or Spirit animals who created the great storms with their thunder and lightning also gave rise to men and women of many clans in Arnhem Land today. The sound of the thunder is therefore heard as the voice of the Great Spirit and the rain clouds and lightning are seen as manifestations of his presence in the sky. Ceremonies may be held either to bring on storms and rain or to ask that they cease—and the requests, provided that the ritual is correct, are always heard.

LIGHTNING

NAMARRKON, THE LIGHTNING SPIRIT

Namarrkon is the Spirit of Lightning of the Gunwinggu of western Arnhem Land. He is often depicted in cave art and on bark paintings and is greatly feared. He causes severe tropical electrical storms, which tear through the countryside, causing damage everywhere, destroying camps and even killing people. Indeed it is widely held that the 'Marrkidjbu' or 'clever sorcerers' have the power to call on Namarrkon to strike a particular person whom they wish to have killed.

Namarrkon is always depicted with a circuit around him, which is sometimes interpreted as thunder clouds or lightning. Stone axes are attached to his elbows and knees and it is by hurling these with tremendous force that Namarrkon causes lightning to strike.

Opposite: When the thunder and rains of the Wet Season commence, the people of Arnhem Land build bark houses on stilts, likened in their song-poetry to sea-eagles' nests. *photo J. Isaacs*

Cave painting of Namarrkon, the Lightning Spirit. When angered, he hurls
the stone axes from his knees and forms lightning. *photo R. Edwards*

It is believed that if the sacred Dreaming site of Namarrkon is disturbed by man,
he will send a violent storm which will most definitely result in severe disruption of
the people's camps and may even cause death.

An incident which involved a wild buffalo serves as a reminder to the Gunwinggu of the power of Namarrkon and the necessity to preserve his sites from
trespassers.

About thirty miles east of Oenpelli there is a taboo dreaming site called Namarrkon
which was the camping place of this Dreamtime hero as he came towards Oenpelli
from the east. It is a sacred site, which is rarely approached by the Aboriginal people
who fear the wrath of the Lightning Spirit living there.

Once a buffalo was speared in the vicinity and the wounded animal ran towards
the taboo site and died in a nearby creek. The water was discoloured with the blood
of the dying animal, thus disturbing the site of the Spirit Being. Suddenly a violent
tropical electrical storm sprang up and the wind, rain, lightning and thunder
inflicted terrible damage, destroying camps and causing trees to fall. The storm
confirmed and strengthened traditional taboos and this site is still today one of the
most feared and respected sites in the area.[3]

THUNDER

JAMBUWAL, THE THUNDER MAN

Jambuwal is an important Ancestral Being of the Dhuwa moiety of north-eastern
Arnhem Land and has his own song cycle. He lived in the Creation time and his
home was in the rain clouds. Djankawu and his sisters saw him and sang about him
when they travelled in their canoe from Baralku to the mainland. He was a very
good fisherman, especially for rock cod, which he killed with his spear, larapan.

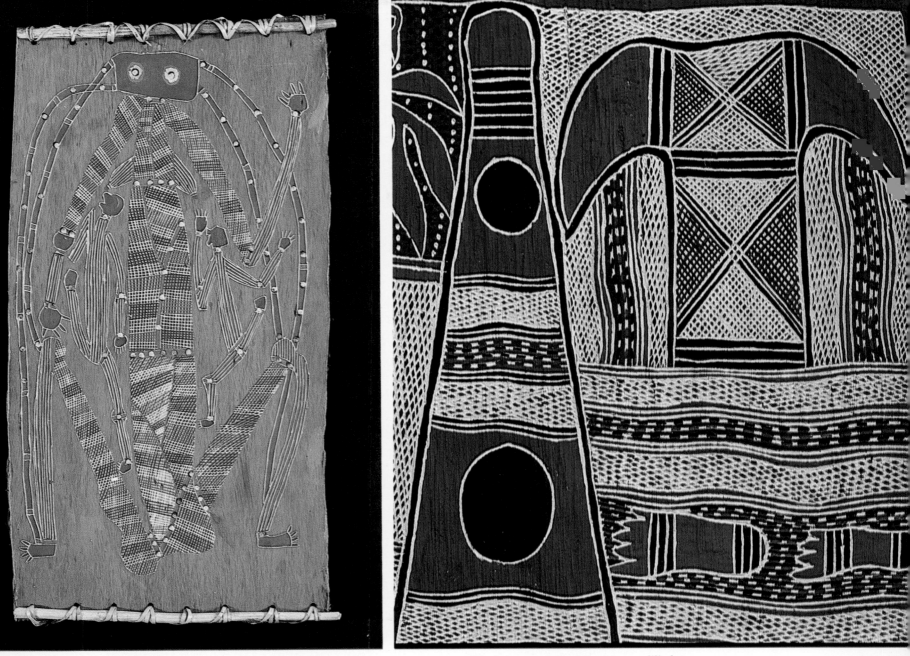

Bark painting of a female Spirit and her children
by George Djayhgurrnga of the Gunwinggu group
from western Arnhem Land. *photo J Steele*

Thunder symbol of the Manggalili clan.
Detail from larger work by Banapana
Maymuru of Yirrkala. *photo P. Tweedie*

One day, a Wongar spirit of the Creation time called Minggololo caught some rock cod; while the fish were cooking on the beach the Thunder Man was attracted by the smell, and coming down from his cloud he killed the offender with his spear to get the fish.

When Jambuwal walks in the water, he creates big waves which are dangerous to canoes.

He created a number of sacred places for himself. One of the major sites is in Riratjingu country at Mount Dundas, where he threw his double-ended club (thunderbolt) at Jalpawi Hill, breaking up the rock face into many fragments. The larger and smaller rocks, which are said to be Jambuwal's eyes, milirk, can still be seen there today. When he threw the milirk into the sky they formed into clouds. There are also some elongated boulders said to be the fragments of the bolt which broke when the Thunder Man struck the mountain. They symbolize the long yams, which are his food. Then he urinated from the sky, making rain all over the country, and the stains of his urine can still be seen today as yellow patterns on the cliff.

Wandjuk Marika, Yirrkala[4]

CLOUDS

The movements and patterns of the clouds, particularly the black clouds which herald the storms and lightning, are associated in the north with the great whale ancestor, Wuimiri of the Waramiri clan.

THE WHALE, WUIMIRI

In the Dreamtime, the Wongar time, when the great ancestors were roaming the earth, Wuramala, a man, went out into the sea in his canoe. He caught a giant whale but before he managed to capture him, the whale had sucked in a huge amount of

131

water and sprayed it into the sky in a fine mist which formed the clouds. These clouds are called Mangan and formed a triangular pattern still used in ceremonial designs today to represent the clouds formed by the spouting whale.

THE TURTLE, INIBUNGEI

The turtle, Inibungei, of the Manggalili people, also creates black rain clouds and strong winds and travels in company with the Lightning Snake in thunder clouds.

THE TURTLE AND SNAKE

A great Spirit Being of the Yirritja moiety of central Arnhem Land takes the form of a snake. The name of this snake cannot be spoken in everyday talk, only by the initiated inside the sacred ceremonial ground. When anyone sees one of this species, they refer to it by the general term for snake, 'Bapi'. This Spirit Being is said to make lightning with its tongue, clouds with its breath and rain with its spittle. This happens when it emerges from its home and stands erect in the sky. One of its Dreaming places is Lungkutja, the Birrkili homeland, which is thereby a 'dangerous' place.

The Turtle Spirit Ancestor called Guwarrtji travelled to Lungkutja in its Dreaming. Swimming through the tidal channels to the island he came to a reef near the island. Diving to the bottom looking for food, he scarred the rocks with his sacred marks. These became sacred rocks, Madayin, which means the power of the Dreaming Spirit.

He then rose to the surface over the reef, and looked to the north. Giant clouds stood up on the curving horizon as the sun was setting. He saw a rainbow of many colours and lifting his head, spoke to the northern monsoon.

On the other side of the sandbank, the snake had shed its skin, and lay shining in the sun. Guwarrtji the turtle was singing up the monsoon, Lungkurrma. Bapi the snake stood up and as the monsoons came closer, he stood higher on his tail. The clouds became black, heavy with rain. Rain and lightning cross-hatched the sky. When the storm finally passed, the sun glowed brilliant red against the fluffy white clouds. The snake and turtle still exist at their own places on either side of the sandbank at Lungkutja.

Mamalunhawuy, Milingimbi[5]

RAIN

The Wet Season of the north or the rains of the south may also be heralded by small birds.

BOUGOODOOGAHDAH THE RAINBIRD

Bougoodoogahdah was the old woman of the Dreamtime who lived with 400 dingos. She cared only for her dogs and each day they would prey upon Aboriginal hunters as they sought game in the nearby hills. She would entice young men as they were hunting to come with her and her dogs into the hills and then call out 'Fool 'em, fool 'em' and the dogs would quickly leap out, surround the men and attack them. This had continued for some time until a great many hunters were missed by their tribes. They began to suspect the old woman who lived alone and hunted with her dogs. So one day, some men hid in the scrub and watched what went on. They saw the dogs attack the hunters, but they also saw the old woman come in later and call them off, so they realized it had been her doing.

All the tribes then mustered together and decided to take vengence on the old woman. They collected their spears and nulla nullas and just as the dogs were about to attack a hunter, as before, they surrounded the woman and dogs and killed every dingo, as well as the old woman. The old woman lay where she had been killed but as the people were moving away, they heard a strange cry 'Bougoodoogahdah'. So they went back and beat her with their nulla nullas until all her bones were broken, yet still the cry persisted 'Bougoodoogahdah'.

One man crept up close and watched to see where the cry was coming from; he saw that from her heart, which was still beating, a little bird emerged crying 'Bougoodoogahdah'. This little bird runs on the plains even today calling out 'Bougoodoogahdäh'. The Aboriginals call it the Rainmaker, for if anyone steals it, it

Long-necked turtles. Detail of a bark painting by Bulun Bulun of Maningrida. *photo P. Tweedie*

In the Wet Season of the north, long-necked turtles are a favourite food of small family groups camped near the swollen billabongs. *photo P. Tweedie*

cries out incessantly until in answer the rain falls. When the country is stricken with drought, Aboriginal people look for one of these birds and finding it, chase it until it cries out 'Bougoodoogahdah'; as soon as they hear its cry, they know the rain will soon fall.[6]

RAINMAKING

The ability of Aboriginal people to communicate with the Spirits of rain and storms has fascinated many, and accounts of the unfailing results of rainmaking ceremonies and songs are common. Dick Roughsey, the Aboriginal writer and artist from Mornington Island, gave the following account of how the old men could make a flood.

In the old days, if it had been decided to make the flood to punish enemies of the Larumbanda, the boss of the ceremony would say, 'All right. But first we must make our wet-weather shelters on high ground at Dinglema' (a high sand ridge overlooking the island of Langu Narnji).

The houses are made from sticks, paperbark, spinifex grass and small branches. Firewood, food and water in big baler shells are stored in the houses.

When all is ready the chief flood-man says: 'We'll now make the flood. Tomorrow two men must go and get paperbark, rope, and two sticks to hold the clay. Then they must go to Mundoowa, to the special place to get the magic kial (white pipeclay).'

The two selected men go to Mundoowa, near the centre of Langu Narnji, dig the clay from the bank of a small creek there, and carry it in bark containers down to the coast at Binburragan Creek, and then round to Lil-lilta Point where the flood-sticks are made.

Overleaf: Black clouds herald storms and lightning. The whale sucked in a huge amount of water and sprayed it into the sky in a fine mist which formed the clouds. *photo P. Tweedie*

The sticks are about four feet long and two inches thick; the clay is made thoroughly wet and then packed around one end of the stick to form an oval mass about six inches thick and nine inches long. The clay is then wrapped in paperbark and tied up with string made from mudud, the beach hibiscus. This stick parcel is called a doolmidjal. If a very big flood is wanted, two of these flood-sticks are made.

When the doolmidjal is ready the men wait for low tide to expose a reef joining Langu Narnji to a small islet called Woonoonyea, about half a mile east off the coast. At low tide the men walk across to it and climb the northern outcrop, where they hide the doolmidjal in low bushes growing from cracks in the rough coralite rock. The men then return to Dinglema to await the very low tide which is necessary to expose the reef extending in an arc eastward from Woonoonyea to the special flood-making place more than half a mile out. Here there are five low archways in the coral reef.

When the very low tide arrives the two flood-men return to Woonoonyea and bring down the doolmidjal from its hiding place. They now mix more kial with water and paint white bands across their faces, bodies, arms and legs. These marks represent the white foam of breaking waves, or the teeth of the laughing sea, as my people say. At this time a good watch is kept to prevent surprise attack by people who may try and stop the flood-making ceremony from being performed.

Both men now walk east along the exposed reef carrying one or two doolmidjals. There are several narrow and deep channels on this, but they usually swim these and finally reach the flood-making place, called Bidjinyea-narwee, or Bad Small country, meaning a place where evil things are done.

The five archways are always under water and the chief flood-maker takes a doolmidjal, tears away some of the bark wrappings, and then dives down through the first archway, breaking off clay and spreading it through the water as he goes. He comes up for air and then dives down through the second archway. The clay turns the water white like boiling surf or floodwater.

While the swimmer dives and spreads his clay, his mate stands on a coral-head in waist-deep water and keeps calling out 'Wah, wah, wah,' in a loud voice. Usually only three of the archways are used, unless a very big flood is wanted. The old people say that a such a flood might cover all the land and drown everybody. When this part of the ceremony is over, the men return along the reef towards Woonoonyea until they reach a small sand cay called Gwa-argan.

Here the final part of the flood-making ceremony is carried out by both men. They come wading through shallow water to the beach and run up on the sand with arms outstretched, calling out, 'Wah, wah, wah! Tu tu tu tu tutu tu! Wah, wah, wah! Tu tu tu tu tu!' imitating the noise of a big sea. Still calling out, they lie down and roll over and over up the beach like big waves rolling up and crashing on the shore.

The men get up from the beach and with arms held out dance and high-step their way along the reef past Woonoonyea and on to Lil-lilta Point. As they go they call out, 'Wah, wah, wah. Now these people, our enemies, will die. All fish, dugong, turtle, sharks will die. The big flood will come and wash you up on the land. All things must die!'

After some days, if the flood was going on too long, the rain-men would sing this song:

Murri willi willi dureja	*Give us a clear place*
Gurrada walda dureja	*Make it shine again*
Murri willi willi dureja	
we ee e e e e e e!	
Walgu billi billi	*Sun come out*
Yarna birra birri	
Walgu billi billi	*Rainbow come out*
Yarna birra birri	
Munma goolya munma goolya	
Munma goolya munma goolya	
Wo o o o o o o o!	
Mungo gura buri	*Stars come out*
Gura gura boor bunoora	*Clouds go away*
Guramurra wuli dagurrabor budu	

136

Guramurra wuli dagurrabor budu
Wo o o o o o o o!
Yeeda birri go woona
Lilga bajee-jah   *Wind come up*
Birrilga woonda   *Only a little rain falls now.*
Lilga bajee-jah
Birrilga woonda
Wo o o o o ee ee ee ee!

Goobalathaldin, Mornington Island, Gulf of Carpentaria[7]

The next account is a unique record of the last of the nomadic people of the Simpson Desert. It tells of an occasion when Rib-Bone Billy made rain.

Ngadu-dagali the Rainmaker

Ngadu-dagali was a rainmaker. He came down to a place near the Herrgott Spring to make the rain come. He said, 'Take a heap of feathers matted together like kurdaitcha shoes, and put them onto the ground, make a nest.'

He put a rain-stone on the nest.

He chanted there for a long time; groups of men came and then went to bring back with them a host of others.

They put all that stuff, tents, tarpaulins, bags and blankets to make a temporary humpy, they put it there where the dam is, in the yard near the Herrgott Spring.

They made rain there, they sang there.

Then two men freshly painted themselves and decorated themselves with down feathers. They went down to the water, to the little lake, to that dam and they waded about in the water.

They sang, yes they sang there continually. They've been singing away, the main group, then those two came up, they had feathers in their hands. They showed the rainmakers' secret object. Well, they were making rain.

They sang, and they said to me: 'Come on, come over here! Take your clothes off and lie completely naked on top of the nest!' They broke up the rain-stone. I lay on top of this nest and they smashed this stone on my guts.

They smashed it to a powder in the end, and they sang and sang as they struck it. I got up out into the open, I went with no clothes on, we all went up into the open and stood on the open plain.

He got something, I don't know what else, and put it into the nest, and a piece of rain-stone lay there. I held two little pieces in my hands. They told me to throw them up and showed me: 'Look, they've become two little clouds!'

I had to get up on his neck, I sat on Ngadu-dagali's neck. And then a whole crowd of men came walking along carrying water, carrying buckets. They showered me with water.

'Stop, I'm cold' — but they took no notice. They poured water over the top of me, they went on throwing water over me.

Then it was all over, oh that nest — the old men took it and put it in some water that had been placed at the side, in some fresh water. They only took that part where the pieces of rain-stone were. They went down to the dam to throw the rest of the nest into the water, that was to become a cloud-mass. Then they went back home.

Where Murteen Khan's store now is, out in the open, is where they were camped. They went to the store (on the other side of the railway line). Mr Arnold was store-keeper then, and Mr Duggan. They (the store-people) said: 'Well, Bill, you been make'm rain?'

'Yes, he jump along might be two day.'

'Well, when he comes you get a bag of flour, sugar and half a bag of tea.'

'He come all right' — he was sure.

When it was well and truly pouring Mr Arnold was saying to some other Aboriginal man: 'Go back and tell that old man, tell Ngadu-dagali he should come and fetch his food.'

They went back, and he collected a huge quantity — there were 150 pounds of flour in a bag. He put it on his head and carried it back to his camp, pleased as punch.

Mick McLean Irinjili, Simpson Desert[8]

Yet another famous rainmaker, who could also cause drought, was also called Billy, 'Left-hand Billy' or Yangu. The events of the following story occurred over fifty years ago and are related by Walter Coulthard of the Flinders Ranges in South Australia.

LEFT-HAND BILLY

Mr McTaggart who owned Wooltana Station was a good station owner who tried to get people jobs, but once he made a mistake that he didn't forget about for a long, long time. He was quite a wealthy man and was involved in several stations. At the time of this story, before the First World War, there also lived an important Yura man called Left-hand Billy. He was known as 'Left-hand' (Yangu Watana) because he did most things like throwing his boomerangs with his left hand.

One day McTaggart came and shot Left-hand Billy's dogs and then said, 'Now, you bury them.' But Billy didn't do it so McTaggart had to send somebody down to bury the dead dogs. Left-hand Billy was very upset. He said 'All my dogs are dead. McTaggart, you'll be very sorry for what you have done, because in three months time it will be dry and your feed will die and in five or six months your sheep will be dying too. You'll see!'

'You can't say that! You can't make it be dry like that,' laughed McTaggart.

'Yes old man, you'll be sorry,' replied Left-hand Billy.

Well, after three months the dust was blowing, the winds got stronger and blew lots of feed away. It got drier and drier. There was dust every day, hot north winds blowing, blowing, blowing. The stock began to weaken and die.

'Hmm, hmm,' as McTaggart was often heard, 'Hmm, hmm, that old man might be killing my jumbucks after all.' Alf Beckman, the manager, could see the water going down, down. They were pumping all the time. Leaves were falling down from the trees. They started shifting thousands of stock, just getting them to Innaminka Creek where there was a bit of feed. Still no rain. Things were very serious: something had to be done.

'Hmm, hmm,' McTaggart said, 'I remember what that man said when I shot his dogs. I didn't believe him, but I'd better have a talk with him I think.' So he sent down his buggy to Left-hand Billy with a message to come up to the station house for a talk.

'No, go away.'

McTaggart sent the buggy back. 'No, he shot my dogs, he might shoot me too!

So McTaggart tried again and again. 'No.' 'No.' Once Left-hand Billy asked, 'Has he got any sheep?' 'No,' the messenger answered, 'They're mostly dead.' 'Hum, my dogs are dead too.'

McTaggart sent a message, 'I'll give you anything you want — tobacco, clothes, tea, sugar, beef. I'm sorry. Come up to my place.'

Left-hand Billy thought McTaggart had waited long enough. 'O.K., I'll come.'

He was welcomed inside, and Mrs McTaggart put a good tablecloth on the table and served nice food. They talked all day and looked after him well.

'Look Billy, I'm sorry about the dogs and if you made it go dry like this, I want you to make it rain. Things are really bad, even my horses are dying.'

'But why, why kill all my dogs?'

'Some dogs had killed some of my jumbucks so I had to kill them!'

'But some of my dogs were only little, they wouldn't do that.'

'Well, maybe I was wrong and I'm sorry, I won't do it again, and you can have anything here you want if you just come up and ask for it. Now can you make it rain?' pleaded McTaggart.

'Of course, I could make it rain tonight.'

'Well, will you?'

'All right, McTaggart, O.K., I think you learned your lesson.'

That night a big wind blew up, the rain clouds came and a big rain fell and fell, not just for the night but heavy rain for five days.

Then it was calm. The grass shot up and things began to get back to how they should be. McTaggart was thankful and kept to his promise that Left-hand Billy could come and ask for more rations any time.

'Well, McTaggart, I don't tell lies. I do the right thing. You'll have more rain, any time, so long as you don't shoot my dogs. I like my dogs. You know you did the wrong thing.'[9]

Opposite: In times of extreme drought Aboriginal sorcerers would invoke the power of the Spirits by performing ceremonies to bring storms and rain. *photo R. Edwards*

CHAPTER SIX

The Sun, Moon & Stars

In Aboriginal life where people sleep under the stars with little shelter, the night sky is enthralling and dominating, and the subject for innumerable myths. In the clear air of the inland and the tropical north, the stars shine with great brilliance and luminosity in the vast sky, unimpeded by the undulating landscape. Some Aboriginal people, particularly in the desert, are aware of nearly every star in the heavens, and most of these stars have stories associated with their origins.

All over Australia, it is believed that the stars and planets were once men, women and animals in Creation Times, who flew up to the sky as a result of some mishap on earth and took refuge there in their present form.

Generally Aboriginals see the sun as a woman and the moon as a man and when there is an eclipse of the sun, it means therefore that the sun woman is uniting with the moon man. Many stories about the origin of death are associated with the moon. He also dies, yet is reborn every month. The sky itself is often believed to be the home of the Spirits — thus in north-eastern Arnhem Land a shooting star is seen as a spirit canoe carrying the soul of a dead man to a new land.

Among the people of the Adelaide Plains, South Australia, the sky was believed to be a place similar to earth: the Milky Way being a large river flowing through the sky. The dark patches in the Milky Way are lagoons along the river.

In Victoria the people saw the sky as a solid vaulted cover over the flat circular disc of earth. Beyond the solid cover was a beautiful country with abundant food and water, where the spirits of the dead went to live. The Ancestral Beings and cult heroes, who also live in this land, can be seen from the earth as stars. The solid vault of the sky was believed to be propped up at the far edges of the earth. Myths recorded by Daisy Bates many years ago in the Great Australian Bight[1] tell how the sky was held up by a great tree, Warda, which had to be protected at all times so that the sky would not fall down.

Another myth from the same area relates how the earth and sky were once connected by a great totem board which acted as a track between the earth country and the sky country, whose people were interchangeable. A group of women travelling to the sky on a cold night lit a fire to keep warm and the great track was burnt in half, forever dividing the sky from the earth people.

BELIEFS ABOUT THE SUN AND THE MOON

The sun's rays touch us, warming our backs . . .
Rays like the parakeet – feathered string of our sacred poles!
Feathered string like our child! Red glow of the sun.
Rays warming our backs, like feathered string! Like feathered sacred poles!
That sun rises above us, burning our backs, going to the Place of the Sun.
It burns our backs, and it shines on the water at Lilildjang.
Its warm rays touch us, stretching to Arnhem Bay . . .
It leaves its home in the water, and rises, burning.
Warm rays touching our backs, touching our sacred poles!
Shining and making the mainland clear to see!
For us it shines on the sacred sandhills at Port Bradshaw.
Stretching out its rays, warming our backs, illuminating
the water holes at Arnhem Bay,
That sun, sending out its rays to Elcho Island,
Burning our backs.[2]

Opposite: The Sun is a woman who wanders across the sky spreading light and warmth. *photo P. Tweedie*

The sun is always a woman, and wanders across the sky spreading light and warmth, taking a long road in summer and a much shorter one in winter. The verses quoted above are spoken by Djankawu and his sisters as they feel the warm rays of Walu the sun on the coast of Arnhem Land. For the Djankawu, the sun is comforting, like a mother, and its rays show them the paths to follow on the mainland.

Two myths from Victoria give differing versions of the origin of the sun. The first is from the Wotjobaluk of northern Victoria, the second from the Murray River tribes.

The Origin of the Sun

Gnowee, the sun, was once a woman who lived upon the earth when it was dark all the time, and the people had to walk about with the aid of bark torches.

One day she left her little boy asleep while she went out to dig roots for food. Yams were scarce, and Gnowee wandered so far that she reached the end of the earth, and continuing her wanderings, passed under it and came up on the other side.

Not knowing where she was, as it was dark, she could not find her little boy anywhere. So she went into the sky carrying her great bark torch, and still wanders across it and then travels under the earth looking for him.

Wotjobaluk tribe[3]

The Origin of the Sun

In the old days no sun rays blessed the earth, and people groped about by the feeble light from the stars. At this time the members of the Kurwingie family, the emus, were entirely 'sky-birds'. They never landed upon the earth, but preferred to live in the clouds. One day a Kurwingie woman flew low upon the land, and she saw that the earth was inhabited by other beings, who, apparently, were having a much better time walking about than she was flying through the air with nowhere to go.

On another occasion, when flying low, she saw that a group of these beings were dancing, and she distinctly heard the sound of a sweet song being sung by one of them. The emu could not restrain herself any longer, and landed amongst them. After introducing herself to the rather surprised beings who, she learnt, were members of the Courtenie or Native Companion tribe, she told them that she wished to become a dweller upon earth, as it was a much more pleasant place to live, and that, if allowed, she would like to join them in their dance.

One of the native companions, a wicked woman, quickly hid her own wings behind her back, and told the emu that she would never be able to dance, run about, catch fish or frogs, or even live upon earth, because her huge wings were in the way. However, she said, if she were willing to have her wings cut off this would be possible. The emu readily agreed to the amputation, but no sooner was it done than the wicked Courtenie unfolded her wings, and flew off amidst great laughter, followed by the rest of her tribe. This is the reason emus cannot fly to this day.

A kookaburra perched upon a branch of a nearby tree, saw these proceedings and took up the laughter, and now his descendants laugh again whenever they think of the trick.

The wingless emu took some days to recover from the shock, but gradually accustomed herself to life upon earth; and having tasted many succulent plants and enjoyed the beauty of the landscape, she decided that the change had been for the best.

In due course the breeding season came around, and she built herself a great nest which she filled with eggs, and sitting herself upon them began her incubation period.

One day the wicked native companion, out for a walk with her newly hatched brood, happened to pass that way. When she saw the emu sitting on her eggs she hid the whole of her family except one, went up to her, and pretended great friendliness. The emu, who had become used to life upon earth, bore her no malice, and when Courtenie saw that she was perfectly happy with her lot she decided to play another trick on her. She told her how foolish she was to sit on so many eggs, and what a worry was entailed in raising a large family; she proudly displayed her one chick, and boasted of her great freedom in having only one to look after. She then suggested that the emu should break all her eggs except one, which the foolish

Kurwingie, the emu. The wicked native companion hurled her one remaining egg into the sky, where it ignited the firewood left by Gnawdenoorte and became the sun. *photo D. Marfleet*

Kurwingie did. With that the native companion called her brood from their hiding place, and laughing at the emu, marched off.

However, Gnawdenoorte, the Son of the Great Man, having seen what had happened, resolved to punish the wicked Courtenie. He caused her long and graceful neck, which was her most beautiful feature, but through which passed the untruths which did so much damage to the poor emu, to become crooked and full of wrinkles; and he changed her sweet voice into a harsh cry. Further, try as she might, she was only able to lay one, or at the most two eggs at each breeding season. These peculiarities are still in her present-day descendants.

The emu and the native companion did not meet again until the next breeding season, when once more the emu was sitting on her numerous eggs, and the native companion was followed by her lone chick. Courtenie approached Kurwingie with honeyed words; however the emu had learnt her lesson, and told her that she would have nothing more to do with her, and asked her to leave. When the native companion began using insulting remarks, she sprang from her nest, and made a determined rush towards her crooked-necked tormentor. Courtenie waited calmly for her approach, and when within a few feet she flapped her wings and vaulted lightly over the emu's back, alighting close to her nest, where she immediately started to smash the eggs. Kurwingie turned about, and again rushed at the native companion, but with no better results, since the latter again flapped her wings and sprang into the air, clutching the one remaining egg in her claw. While the emu was recovering from her rush she threw the egg with all her might into the air, hoping that it would smash when it fell. However, when the egg reached the sky it struck a large heap of wood which Gnawdenoorte, the Great Man's Son, had piled up there. The collision was so great that fire followed, and the whole world was flooded with light.

When Gnawdenoorte saw how much better the world was with light, he decided to kindle a new fire each day, which he has done to the present time.

Murray River tribes[3]

143

Walu the sun goes down into the sea every evening and
becomes Warrukay the great fish so that she can swim
under Munatha the earth and come back again to the
right place for morning. *photo P. Tweedie*

Just as some stories tell of a time when there was no light and no sun, the following
story from the north-west of Western Australia relates how darkness first came to
the earth.

Daughter sun, mother sun, and all the stars, were diving for waterlily bulbs.
Mother sun thought she would take a walk. She collected her walking sticks (the
sun's rays) and went out till she came to the cypress pine trees. She tried to go
through them but she was jammed between the pines and couldn't get through so
she turned back. Daughter sun said she would come. She got her walking sticks (her
rays). She was going to the pine trees. She put her walking sticks, the sun's beams,
through, and came through, then climbed up. While she was coming up the sky, a
rattlesnake saw her. He waited for her in the middle of the pines and when she came
closer, the rattlesnake sprang out and fought her. As they fought the rattlesnake bit
her all over. She hit him back with her walking sticks and she rolled around in pain.
She was rolling down low. She stood all her walking sticks up, then she rolled down
out of sight, and it was dark.

Elkin Umbagai, Mowanjum[4]

In Arnhem Land, Walu the sun goes down into the sea every evening and becomes
Warrukay the great fish so that she can swim under Munatha the earth and come
back again to the right place for morning.

The Sun and the Moon Always Change into Fish

This is a different story told by our ancestors. Okay in the afternoon when the sun
goes down, and goes in, well he becomes a fish and clears the way for the moon so

144

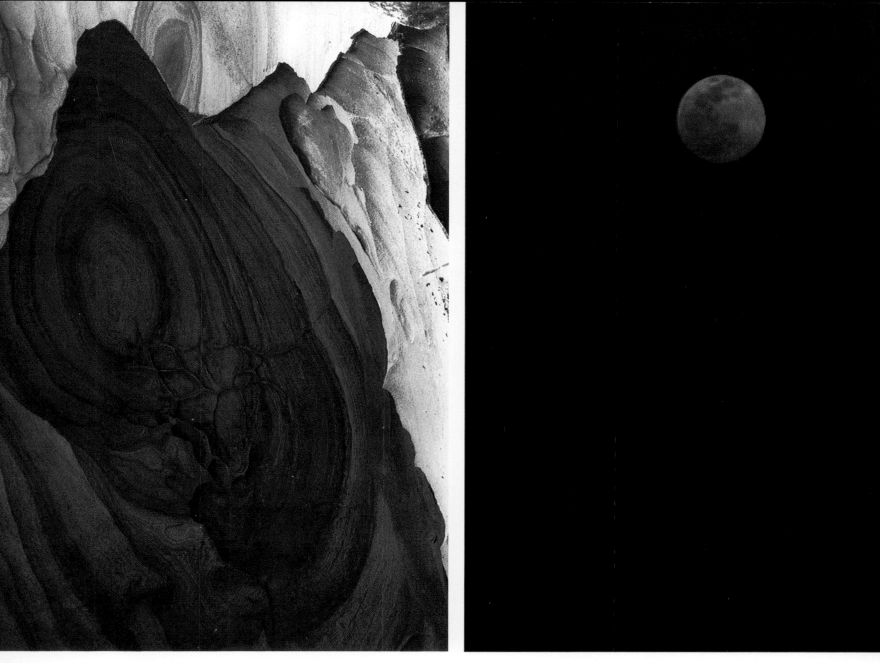

The sun's rays touched the rock.
photo B. Thompson

Staring at the moon may be dangerous. A woman may become pregnant or the moon might get angry. During the day he becomes a Juykal fish. *photo D. Conroy*

that he can come out. Now the moon will rise, and move across, and around sunrise, he will go in and become a fish. (This story was told by our ancestors.) So they both become fish. The sun becomes a Warrukay fish and the moon becomes a Juykal and so he rises in the morning and moves across and sets, and the moon rises. And they change back into the sun and the moon at the place where they rise every day. The sun rises in the morning and the moon rises at night. So they will change from fish into the sun and the moon. The old people used to tell this story. That's what our ancestors told us.

And that's the end of the story.

Djawa, Milingimbi[5].

In South Australia Meeka the moon was married to Ngangaru the sun, and they lived in a cave with all their family where the moon goes down. The moon always knew when it was going to rain, and made himself a shelter which is seen from earth as a halo around the moon. Ngangaru the sun was a good wife and went out to gather vegetable food every day, sending her warmth and rays across the land.

The moon is generally a more powerfully mysterious image in the myths than the sun, often being associated with the coming of death and pregnancy. Many stories reflect taboos against staring at the moon. Myths of the moon's origin vary; one from the Bagundji tribe of western New South Wales describes the moon as an old man whose nephew is jealous of the privileges of his full manhood.

Moon and his Nephew

Moon and his nephew were hunting emu. The nephew ably assisted Moon in capturing the bird and preparing it for cooking. When it was cooked he asked for a piece of meat, but was refused. His uncle said, 'Go away — eat pigface!' The boy did so and returned to camp but resented his uncle's actions and vowed revenge.

145

Moon came back with two or three emus and he and his wives ate emu meat. While the old man went away for a while, the women gave the boy a little piece of emu meat.

Next day, the boy and his uncle went out to hunt emu again. 'I feel ill,' said the boy and went further away. When he looked up he saw grubs in the nearby tree. He told moon, who came and climbed up the tree. Then the youth blew on the tree to make it grow tall. Having done this several times, he asked his uncle: 'What's up there?' 'It's the sky.' 'Grip it hard,' said the boy and then he made the tree go small again. That's how the Moon came to be in the sky.

The boy went back to the camp and told the wives of the moon he would be their husband, but although they slept with him they ridiculed and insulted him

George Dutton, Bagundji tribe[6]

The same legend about the moon is told in South Australia, with only a slight variation.

Namana (uncle) was a greedy man and whenever any young fellows caught anything he would tell them that they shouldn't eat it.

One day two of his nephews caught an emu, but he told them it was forbidden for them to eat it, and took it away from them.

Some time later the two nephews approached their namana and asked him to come out hunting. They all went up the creek and came to a large gum tree. They stopped. The two nephews called to their uncle saying, 'There's a lot of witchetty in this tree.' They asked him to pull some out.

Namana started from the bottom of the tree, collecting the grubs and throwing them down to his two wives who were also sisters and very young. The wives caught them and cooked them on the fire.

While namana was climbing further up the tree for more witchetty the older nephew blew on the tree to make it taller. The tree grew taller and taller until namana called out that he was getting dizzy. When the tree reached the sky they told namana to touch it. As soon as he reached out to get hold of it the nephews pulled the tree down fast, leaving their namana up in the sky. He called out to them but they just said, 'You stay up in the sky, you stop there, you can die and then come up again every month. We'll look after your wives.'

And so now namana is the moon (Vira), and they both took a wife.[7]

The beautiful story of Moon and his sister the Dugong is told in a lengthy song-cycle of north-eastern Arnhem Land. The cycle is called the 'Moon-bone', for the Moon when he was a man lived near the claypan of the Moonlight at the place of the Dugong by Arnhem Bay. When he died he went down into the sea where his bones became the nautilus shell. Ever since, the Moon repeats this death, casts away his bone, and is reborn.

The Moon and the Dugong

In the Dreaming period, the Moon lived with his sister the Dugong on the flat plains bordering Arnhem Land. During the Wet Season when the rains fell regularly this area of country was covered with water, and when the waters subsided vast claypans were left. There was one large claypan there which after the rains became a billabong. This was the claypan of the Moonlight; the Moon, after making it, lived there and later it became his reflection. The Moon and the Dugong collected lily and lotus roots every day. One day, however, as the Dugong was collecting them she was bitten by a leech. She returned to her brother and said:

'This place is too dangerous for me, the leeches are always biting me. I like this country, but the leeches spoil it for me. I am going out into the sea, where I will turn into a dugong.'

'And what shall I do?' asked the Moon.

'Why, Moon, you can stay in the sky; but first you must die.'

'But I'm not going to die like other people,' the Moon answered.

'Why do you not want to do that, brother?' asked the Dugong.

The horns of the Moon were bent down, sinking into the place
of the dugong, the moonlit claypan. *photo P. Tweedie*

'I want to die and come back alive again,' he told her.

'All right. But when I die, I won't come back and you can pick up my bones.'

'Well, I'm different,' the Moon said. 'When I die, I'm coming back. Every time I
get sick I'll grow very thin; then I'll follow you down to the sea, and I'll go with you a
long way out into that sea. And when I'm so thin that I'm only bones, I'll throw them
away into the sea and die. But after three days I'll get up again and become alive,
and gradually regain my strength and size by eating lily and lotus roots'.

'All right, brother,' the Dugong answered. 'You can stay in the sky, it is better for
you.'[8]

The song poetry itself expresses this myth as follows:

Now the New Moon is hanging, having cast away his bone:
Gradually he grows larger, taking on new bone and flesh.
Over there, far away, he has shed his bone: he shines on the place of the Lotus Root,
*   and the place of the Dugong,*
On the place of the Evening Star, of the Dugong's Tail, of the Moonlight claypan . . .
His old bone gone, now the New Moon grows larger;
Gradually growing, his new bone growing as well.
Over there, the horns of the old receding Moon bent down, sank into the place of
*   the Dugong:*
His horns were pointing towards the place of the Dugong.
Now the New Moon swells to fullness, his bone grown larger.
He looks on the water, hanging above it, at the place of the Lotus.
There he comes into sight, hanging above the sea, growing larger and older . . .
There far away he has come back, hanging over the clans near Milingimbi . . .
Hanging there in the sky, above those clans . . .
'Now I'm becoming a big moon, slowly regaining my roundness . . .
In the far distance the horns of the Moon bend down, above Milingimbi,
Hanging a long way off, above Milingimbi Creek . . .

147

Slowly the Moon Bone is growing, hanging there far away.
The bone is shining, the horns of the Moon bend down.
First the sickle Moon on the old Moon's shadow; slowly he grows,
And shining he hangs there at the place of the Evening Star . . .
Then far away he goes sinking down, to lose his bone in the sea;
Diving towards the water, he sinks down out of sight.
The old Moon dies to grow new again, to rise up out of the sea.[9]

The Moon and the Evening Star

On the billabong which covers the claypan in the Wet Season, the water lily and lotus lily bloom in profusion. These are symbols of the Evening Star which can be seen on clear nights when the moon is also shining. The Evening Star, as a lotus, lives in the Dreaming country of the Moon, it lives on the claypan which reflects the image of the Moon and in which he disappears at night.

Up and up soars the Evening Star, hanging there in the sky.
Men watch it, at the place of the Dugong and of the Clouds, and of the Evening Star,
A long way off, at the place of Mist, of Lilies and of the Dugong.
The Lotus, the Evening Star, hangs there on its long stalk, held by the Spirits.
It shines on that place of the Shade, on the Dugong place, and onto the Moonlight
    Claypan . . .
The Evening Star is shining, back towards Milingimbi, and over the Wulamba
    people . . .
Hanging there in the distance, towards the place of the Dugong,
The place of the Eggs, of the Tree-Limbs-Rubbing-Together, and of the Moonlight
    claypan . . .
Shining on its short stalk, the Evening Star, always there at the claypan, at the
    place of the Dugong . . .
There, far away, the long string hangs at the place of the Evening Star, the place
    of Lilies.
Away there at Milingimbi . . . at the place of the Full Moon,
Hanging above the head of that Wonguri tribesman:
The Evening Star goes down across the camp, among the white gum trees . . .
Far away, in those places near Milingimbi . . .
Goes down among the Ngurulwulu people, towards the camp and the gum trees,
At the place of the Crocodiles, and of the Evening Star, away towards Milingimbi . . .
The Evening Star is going down, the Lotus Flower on its stalk . . .
Going down among all those western clans . . .
It brushes the heads of the uncircumcised people . . .
Sinking down in the sky, that Evening Star, the Lotus . . .
Shining on to the foreheads of all those headmen . . .
On to the heads of all those Sandfly people . . .
It sinks there into the place of the white gum trees, at Milingimbi.[10]

Another story about the Moon from the opposite side of the Gulf of Carpentaria (north-western Queensland) tells how two brothers, the Moon and the Morning Star, created the landscape and how the Morning Star became the first woman.

The Moon and the Morning Star

Two young newly initiated men were travelling southwards from the north-east. They were brothers and had no wives, for as yet there were no women. As they travelled they were singing. They sang all night long as they lay on their backs:

I go up into the scrub	*You be cooking the while!*
To make a club	*Now in the moonlight*
You cook meanwhile!	*Let's dance and sing!*
I go up into the scrub	

At this time, long long ago, there were no rivers here so they made the rivers as they went along.

The elder brother made a stingray spear and speared stingray and they made a camp. Before this, no one had ever made a stingray-barbed spear, no one had ever

148

cooked or eaten stingray. They took the cooked fish from the ashes and broke it in two to share it, then they camped for the night. The full moon shone on them and all night long they lay there singing. The moon went down and the morning star rose.

At that time there was no sea. There was only a small creek lying along the sand beach and beyond it to the west there was only scrub. There was not enough room for everything. So they threw a boomerang out westwards. It went round in a circle, felling the scrub, and came back up again. In this way, they cut an opening in the scrub and cleared a space. The water followed them back up again.

On westwards they travelled; they kept throwing the boomerang and felling the scrub, and the tides followed behind them. Then they found a good shady spot and camped.

The elder brother pretended to go to sleep and the younger brother did the same, but while he was asleep his elder brother cut off his genitals and slit an opening there. He then squeezed him to make breasts, and so made the first woman.

The elder brother got up early the next day. The younger brother slowly sat up and gazed at himself. 'Ah! I'm a man no longer! What is this cut here? I've become a woman!' Then he saw his breasts: 'Who made me a woman? Last evening I was going about as a man!'

The elder brother said: 'You are my wife now!' and picked up his younger brother's spears and put them with his own. Then he shaped a yam stick for his wife. She stripped fibre from the wild fig tree, twisted it into twine and made a dilly bag. She went about picking up shells and putting them in her dilly bag. She also made a large grass basket to carry her yams in. The couple then went on westwards, the man throwing his boomerang, felling scrub.

They camped. The woman gathered firewood and made a fire. They lay there, the man singing. At daylight they went on out westwards.

At last they came to the end of their journey and stayed there together. The water was still following them, the tide was following them.

So now when you camp on the sand beach you see the boomerang (the new moon) that the moon threw before him as he travelled from the north-east out into the west, followed by the morning star — just as women today follow their husbands. Leaving their silver tracks behind them on the water, they take the tide out with them and bring it back up again full of fish; then they go down into the west and stay in their camp for a while.

And now the people of the sand beach remember the moon, and all the good things he brought them, as they dance and sing in the moonlight during the calm happy days and nights of the dry winter weather.

Munkan, western Cape York[11]

Staring at the moon is reputed to be most dangerous and the story which follows from north-western Western Australia, acts as a cautionary tale to the young.

Two children were lying down and looking up at the moon as it was rising. They lay side by side and watched the moon. As long as they were awake they just gazed up at the moon, and the moon got tired of being stared at, so it fell out of the sky onto the two children, and it splashed all over them and they were stuck together. They couldn't move. There are two rocks which represent these children stuck together somewhere in Worora territory.

Elkin Umbagai, Mowanjum[12]

In a similar story from Milingimbi, many people are killed by the moon.

The Moon killed some People

People were living at a place called Barrnyin — a man and his wife and children. They had been eating lily roots and now they were moving on to a new place.

'Where will we camp?'

'Here.'

149

So they built a shelter and a fire and when the older people lay down to sleep, there were four children left sitting and eating.

'Hey, let's look at the moon!' they said to themselves. The moon was out, and the children were sitting talking quite close to their parents. And they looked at the moon, and their parents said, 'Hey! Don't stare at the moon! He might kill us! He might come down from up there and kill us!'

But they said, 'Oh no! He wouldn't come down. No! He's way up there in the heavens. He won't come down here.'

The parents said to them, 'All right, but if you continue to stare at him, he will come down and kill us.'

The children stared at him. And they continued to do so until he came down, and killed them all. He came singing and dancing, "Mm — m, Mm — m, Mm — m, Mmmm, ga — a Yay!' and he chopped at the children and the old people until they were all dead.

At Ramangining, they still sing the same song that the moon sang. The old people told us about this, and also we saw the place where it happened, and the bones of the people.

Djawa, Milingimbi[13]

In all cultures, the moon is associated with pregnancy and childbirth. Daisy Bates was told that if women looked up at Meeka the moon in the sky, he would give children to them, whether they wanted them or not. Any woman who did not want to give birth to a child was very careful not to gaze at the moon.[14]

THE MILKY WAY

The Milky Way on a moonless cloudless night streams with a soft glow across the centre of the sky, and to the Aboriginals is invariably a river with many landmarks. The dark starless patches are also renowned in myths, as seen in this story from South Australia.

In Dreaming times long ago, Jooteetch the native cat and Wej the emu were husband and wife and lived together. One day when Jooteetch was out hunting, Wardu the wombat walked out of the trees and came to Wej's camp, where she was alone. He asked her to lie and make love with him and she consented. As the sun went down she said to Wardu, 'You must go now, for if Jooteetch finds you, he will kill us both.' Wardu got up, but he covered Wej all over with the precious red ochre used for ceremonies.

When Jooteetch returned, he asked Wej how she got the red ochre.

'Oh, I found it,' Wej told him. But Jooteetch had seen Wardu's tracks, and made Wej tell him the truth. Then Jooteetch said, 'Make a fire.'

When the fire was burning fiercely, he caught hold of Wej and flung her into it. But Wej flew out of the fire and went up, up to the sky, where she became the dark patch in the Milky Way, called Wej Mor.[15]

A myth from north-eastern Arnhem Land gives some idea of the complexity of legends associated with the myriad of stars in the Milky Way.

In the early Dreaming time when animals and men were all one people, Walik the crow and Bari pari the cat decided to build a fish trap on the edge of the sea.

The first day, Balin the barramundi fish was caught in it with some of his friends and relations.

Bari pari and Walik were very happy to find so many fish in the trap, but instead of spearing them straight away they made a dance ceremony to show how pleased they were.

Balin the barramundi called out to other warlike clans to come and help him, but when they came they killed and ate all the fish themselves, even the barramundi.

When the crow people and the cat people came back to the beach, they found only the big fish bones of Balin lying in the sand.

'We must fight these people, but first we must bury the bones of Balin for he was our friend and totem. We would not have really eaten the barramundi.' So they found a hollow pole and buried the fishbones in it, painted it and set it in the sand.

They caught up with their enemies and had a big fight, but there were too many, and the crows and cats found they were losing.

So Walik said to his people and Bari pari said to his people, 'Come!'

They picked up the pole with the fishbones and flew up to the dark night sky. There they found places to camp by the side of the river that runs across the sky. The shining path of Milnguya the Milky Way is really the twinkling of their many campfires, and the small spots of the cats. Many things may be seen along that river. Walik the crow is there, and the burial pole. Ying-arpiya the great crocodile also swims in the river of stars, and big stars mark the spines on his back, and the curve of his tail.[16]

THE SOUTHERN CROSS

The Southern Cross is one of the outstanding constellations of the southern sky. Because of its shape, it is associated in some stories with a foot. The desert nomads believe it is the footmark of the wedge-tailed eagle, Waluwara, while the pointer stars Alpha and Beta Centauri are the throwing stick of the eagle, and the coal-sack, his nest. A myth from the southern part of the continent explains the origin of the Southern Cross. In Victoria, the two great Ancestor figures, the Bram-bam-bult brothers, eventually become stars of the Southern Cross.[17]

In Dreaming times, Warragunna the eagle hawk was uncle to Jindabirrbirr the wagtail and Joogajooga the northern pigeon. The two boys helped their uncle find honey by attaching a tiny piece of white down to the back of a bee with a drop of blood and following the bee to its nest in a tree. Their uncle would climb the tree to get the honey but he always cheated his nephews and ate all the honey himself, throwing them down only the wax. So Warragunna grew fat and strong and the boys became thin and weak and always felt hungry.

The stars of the Milky Way. Detail of painting by
Banapana Maymuru from Yirrkala. *photo P. Tweedie*

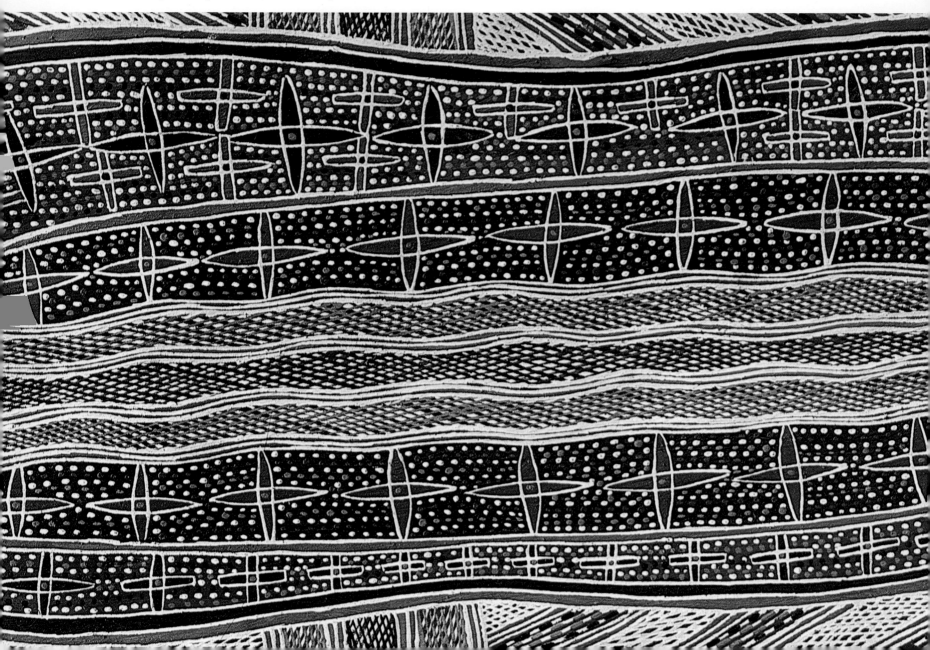

Orion and the Pleiades, a bark painting by Minimini of Groote Eylandt. To the people of Groote Eylandt, the major stars in the constellation of Orion are three fishermen, the Burum-burum-runja, and the Pleiades are their wives, the Wutarinja. In this painting the three stars in the T-shaped design (Orion's belt) are the fishermen and the other stars in the stem of the T (the sword of Orion) are the fish which they caught and their campfire. The incomplete circle above is the women's camp, a grass shelter in which the wives of the fishermen are seated (the Pleiades). This painting was collected by C. P. Mountford on the historic American-Australian Scientific Expedition to Arnhem Land in 1948 and is now housed in the Art Gallery of South Australia.

The nephews decided to hunt possums and lizards for a change. They skilfully tracked them down and then called Warragunna to kill them, which he did. However, he ate all the fat animals himself and gave the boys the thin ones, which had hardly a mouthful of flesh on them.

As Warragunna grew fatter, the nephews at last suspected he was cheating them.

They made a hole which looked just like a lizard's nest and put a sharp pointed stick firmly in the bottom of it. Next day they led their uncle to it and he stamped his foot down on the hole very hard and swiftly to kill the lizards. He cried out loudly with the pain and his foot swelled, and he became very sick.

The boys were glad he was in pain. But Warragunna called out to Koorduwain the sorcerer to help him, and he quickly came and pulled the stick out of his foot. As he did so, water came gushing out the hole in Warragunna's foot and made a great rushing river. Then Warragunna died, but his foot went up into the sky and can still be seen shining there as the Southern Cross.[18]

ORION AND THE PLEIADES

Many myths about the Pleiades or Seven Sisters have one common factor all over Australia: the Seven Sisters all spend much time running away from the unwelcome and usually illicit advances of a male, often associated with Orion. In New South Wales, the sisters are called the Mayi-mayi and are chased by a man Wurunna who succeeds in catching two of them by a trick and making them his wives, until they escape into the sky to become the Pleiades.[19] In eastern Arnhem Land, Pingal the moon lusts after the sisters and pursues them, but they manage to climb up to the sky, where they still flee from the moon. In the Kimberleys, the Seven Sisters are chased by the eagle hawk, the Southern Cross, and in a Dieri myth from Lake Eyre, the ancestor figure who tried to capture one of them was prevented by a great flood. It is therefore understandable that many myths about the Seven Sisters form an important part of women's ceremonies in the Western Desert region of Central Australia. This myth from Central Australia emphasizes these points.

After being in the sky some time, the Kunkarangkalpa (Pleiades) decided to come to earth and make a meal of the wild figs that grow at the base of the Walinynga Hill. They camped at various places near the hill and eventually took refuge in a cave. Some of the boulders now to be found in the cave are the Kunkarangkalpa women asleep, and the rocks outside the cave are the women warming themselves in the sun.

Nirunja, the man of Orion, followed the Kunkarangkalpa from the sky, and searched for them everywhere. He saw they were in the cave and, knowing they would escape if they saw him, he created an emu at the top of the Walinynga Hill to attract their attention, and made a thick screen of fig trees to hide his movements. He moved to where he could see the women asleep in the cave, and coming very close, tried to lie down with them. But the Kunkarangkalpa women forced their way through the end of the cave and escaped from a small hole, fleeing to the sky. Nirunja, disappointed in his desires, climbed to the top of Walinynga and continued his pursuit in the sky.[20]

The theme of pursuit does not exist in Arnhem Land, where Orion and the Pleiades are often fishermen and their wives, in separate canoes.

The following myth from north-eastern Arnhem Land gives the origin of the five stars in the Orion constellation.

In the early times there were three very good hunters, Birubiru, Jandirngala and Nuruwulping and in the Dry Season they spent many days fishing from their canoe called Julpan. Every day they only managed to catch kingfish, and as all three of them belonged to the kingfish totem, it was forbidden for them to eat this fish.

At last they became angry with the fish that kept getting caught, and were anxious because they had no food to take home to their children. One of the men said, 'I am going to take home any fish I catch from now on, whether they are my relations or not. No one should go hungry when there is food to be taken. That is what I think.' The others agreed, and they pulled in three more kingfish.

The sun saw what they were doing and called up a great storm to stop the men from breaking the Law. The clouds and sea and wind combined to make a great waterspout over the canoe. The nose of Julpan, the canoe, turned upwards, and flew round and round and up and up within the spinning column of water, with the three men still holding their fishing lines.

They went right up to the sky, Julpan the canoe, and the three friends, Birubiru, Jandirngala and Nuruwulping, forming the stars of Orion. The fish are the tiny stars below the canoe, trailing still on the string lines.[21]

SCORPIO

Another prominent constellation is that of Scorpio. A myth from Central Australia describes how these stars originated as two lovers who broke tribal law.

During an initiation ceremony in Creation times, a girl who was strongly attracted to the youth being circumcised concealed herself in a hole instead of returning to the women's camp as was the Law. At the end of the ceremony the youth was taken to rest by a fire and the camp became very quiet. When the girl thought everyone was asleep, she left her hiding place, crept up to the initiate and persuaded him to copulate with her.

However, as the penis of the youth was so swollen because of the rite of circumcision, they were unable to separate. Death was certain if they were discovered, so the girl took the youth in her arms and flew up to the sky.

Later, the guardians of the boy woke up to replenish the fire, and seeing the boy missing, searched the ground for tracks, which soon revealed what had happened. Looking up, they saw the two lovers travelling rapidly along the Milky Way.

The two men attempted to climb into the southern sky in pursuit but their feet kept slipping. They succeeded at last and strode along the Milky Way with great steps. (Paired stars in the Milky Way are their footprints.) The boomerang and throwing sticks that they threw at the couple also turned to stars. The second magnitude star, Shauld, in the tail of Scorpius is the elder guardian, and the star close by, the younger guardian. The boy and girl are the small paired stars to the right. The head ornament of the boy, which got knocked off in the flight, is the star cluster just below the constellation.[22]

Every bright star in the night sky has a myth to account for its origin. Two stars known to everyone, even those who do not regularly observe the sky, are the Morning Star, heralding dawn, and the red planet, Mars.

THE MORNING STAR

On the sea's surface the light from the Morning Star shines as we move,
Shining on the calmness of the sea.
Looking back I see its shine, an arc of light from the
Morning Star. The shine falls on our paddles, lighting our way.
We look back to the Morning Star and see its shine, looking back as we paddle.[23]

In north-eastern Arnhem Land[24] the people believe that when a man dies, his spirit is taken over the sea in a Spirit canoe, which travels early in the morning along the light that falls from Barnambirr, the Morning Star, and this string of light is called Jari.

The spirit goes to Baralku, an island beyond the sunrise, where it is welcomed by friends who have died before. When the spirit is well established in Baralku, he sends a message back to earth by the Morning Star, who in turn sends it on to his relations with one of her white birds.

The morning star, Barnambirr, is a shining light held in a mesh bag, and is tied to the island Baralku by Jari, her string of light. That is why Barnambirr can never rise high in the sky: she is held down by her string.

An account of the Morning Star from New South Wales is very different.

Mullyan the eagle hawk built himself and all his relations a nest at the top of a very high Yarran tree, where he lived apart from his tribe.

The eagle hawk was a cannibal and hunted men with an enormous spear, taking their bodies back to the tree to be cooked and eaten by himself and his women. Friends of the dead men determined to find out where they had disappeared to and managed to follow Mullyan's tracks right to the foot of the huge tree, but it was too tall and straight for them to climb.

The men decided to call on the Bibbees, famous climbers, to help them. The Bibbees went to the Yarran tree and started at once. There was only light enough that first night for them to see to reach a fork in the tree about half-way up, where they camped. In the morning they saw Mullyan fly off and climbed up to his camp. Hiding a smouldering stick in one corner of the camp, they went quietly down again.

The people below were pleased at the plan to burn out Mullyan and moved away from the tree in case it should fall.

When Mullyan came home, tired after an unsuccessful day hunting, he threw down his spear on the corner of his camp and suddenly the fire from below burnt through, and burnt up Mullyan and all his relations. Their charred bones fell to the ground, but Mullyan went to live in the sky as the Morning Star. On one side of the Morning Star is a little star which is his one arm (the other was burnt off in the fire); on the other side a larger star, which is Moodai the possum, his wife.[25]

MARS

The red planet, Mars, in a myth from Lake Alexandrina, was once a hero, Waijungari, who in one account was made by his mother out of red excrement and is always depicted as red in colour.

Story of Waijungari, who became the planet Mars
Nepele the great hunter was camped with his two wives near the lake. While the women were down by the water collecting freshwater mussels, they noticed Waijungari, a newly initiated man, drinking water through a reed stem. He was

The Morning Star. Detail of a bark painting by Binyinuway from Dipirringurr. *photo P. Tweedie*

The water lily is the symbol of a star; its stalk is the path of the star as it moves across the sky, the flower its bright glow. *photo P. Tweedie*

covered in red ochre from the ceremonies and so the water became reddish as he stood in it to drink.

The two women thought him very desirable. Waijungari, who had not seen them, walked back to his camp and the women followed and watched him. The older sister said, 'Stand over there, younger sister, and place your bag of mussels quietly down, so that he doesn't hear you. I'll stand here.' Then the two women imitated the noise of the emu.

Waijungari took up his spear: 'Ah, there is food for me!' and came softly out of his camp to stalk the bird. The two women seized hold of him by the penis and the elder sister said, 'This man belongs to us, hold him firmly.' Then Waijungari yielded and they lay down together as the sun set, covering themselves with kangaroo skin rugs.

Nepele began to be suspicious: 'Where are my two wives?' and he looked for their tracks. He found them all asleep together and seizing a firestick and some grass, placed them over the camp where they slept. He said to the fire, 'Burst into flame when you hear them snoring' — they snored and it ignited.

As the camp burnt they fled with their kangaroo skins full of water. The fire raged all around in the dry reedy country, and they dropped the skins one by one to try and quench it. At last they dived into the mud, covering themselves up to their teeth in water and mud while the reeds burnt around them. The fire slowly died down and they came out of the water, looking for a way to escape from Nepele.

Waijungari looked up at the sky. 'We will go up there.' So he untied one of his spears and speared the sky. The first spear fell back, but the second one held and the sky sagged down towards earth so that he was able to reach his spear. He climbed up into the sky. 'This is good ground — you two climb up with me.'

Then the women climbed up, and they all remained there in the sky as stars and Waijungari became the planet Mars.

Jaralde tribe, Lake Alexandrina[26]

CHAPTER SEVEN

The Cycle of Life

The Great Ancestors, as we have seen, created every rock and waterhole, every tree and boulder that now forms the face of Australia. When they changed their physical forms at the end of the great Creation era, some remained behind on the surface of the earth, some left their images painted in a cave, and many travelled to the other land in the sky where they watch over their descendants today. But before the Great Ancestors left the earth, they taught their descendants, the Aboriginal people, all that they needed to know to live in harmony with nature, its birds, plants and animals, and with each other. They left instructions which formed the basis of ceremonies by which young boys could become men, responsible leaders of the community well versed in the sacred Law. And they left sacred sites and objects full of their 'power', the essence of life itself, safely in the keeping of the old men. The responsibility for safeguarding these sites and the sacred objects connected to them has rested with these old men and their sons since time immemorial.

The complete explanation for traditional Aboriginal life is found in myths and legends. The laws contained in them condition social organization and behaviour, as well as ceremonial life. Not only therefore is the landscape full of meaning and significance as a result of the actions of totemic heroes in Creation times, but these ancestral beings laid down clear instructions governing the role of men and women, marriage laws, bearing and raising children, food hunting and gathering and distribution of food in the camp.

MEN AND WOMEN

In the legends of the Ancestors, a man might have more than one wife, but she had to be of the right tribal relationship to him; she could never, for example, be his tribal sister. A son-in-law in the Creation era was never permitted to speak to his mother-in-law or even approach her, and both men and women were expected to assume full responsibility for carrying out their duties in life. Whereas men were required to hunt and bring home meat for the family, it was the role of the women to gather vegetable food by digging for yams and tubers, gathering seeds and fruits and making seed damper or 'nardoo.' Along the coast, while the husband fished in his canoe or with his spear, the wives would gather shellfish, eggs and edible seaweed. These were the roles and responsibilities of men and women in the distant past and they remain the same today in traditional Aboriginal communities.

MARRIAGE RELATIONS

The laws against marriage or sexual relations between tribal brothers and sisters are strong and in the case of a breach of the law, punishment could be severe, even death. The following story from the Bunjellung tribe on the Clarence River area in New South Wales was collected early this century.

Karambil and the Seven Sisters

Seven sisters, who were called the Warweenggary and who were members of the Bunjellung tribe, once lived on the Clarence River in New South Wales. These girls were all very clever and inside their yam sticks they had secret charms which protected them from their enemies. Each day, while they were hunting carpet

Opposite: A 'Mimi' woman kneels, giving birth. One woman supports her from behind while another delivers the baby. *photo J. Steele*

snakes in the bush, they carried their yam sticks with them for protection. A young man named Karambil was very much in love with one of the girls and always followed them. The seven sisters tried to discourage his romantic inclinations, because they were all his tribal sisters and therefore any association with Karambil would be punished severely under tribal Law. Karambil however would not be deterred as he was obsessed with the beautiful young girl; one day, having hidden in the bush while the sisters were out walking, he came upon the young girl he desired most when she did not have her yam stick with her. He was therefore able to carry her off to his own camp.

The other Warweenggary sisters were furious when they found that she was missing and decided to punish Karambil for his crime. They journeyed far into the west where they found the winter and they sent back frost and exceptionally severe weather to the camp where Karambil and the girl were living. The girl did not feel the terrible cold because her sisters had managed to send her charmed yam stick to her by a secret messenger and she was therefore protected. Karambil however shivered and suffered severely and finally sent his wife back to her own people. The seven sisters then decided that they should not cause any more hardship to the remaining people in the tribe by the severe cold so they travelled far into the east, where they found the summer, and sent the warm rays of the sun back to melt the frost and ice.

The Warweenggary then left the earth altogether and travelled into the sky, where the constellation known as the Pleiades still represents their camp. They can be seen every summer and they bring with them pleasant warm weather, after which they gradually disappear towards the west.

After the departure of the Warweenggary, Karambil looked far and wide for another wife, this time determined to comply with the marriage rules of his people. He found a young woman who belonged to the Kooran section, a beautiful young girl whom he wished to marry. Unfortunately she was already married to another man named Bullabogabun, a great warrior. Although Karambil succeeded in seducing her and taking her away from her husband, when Bullabogabun discovered that his wife had eloped he followed Karambil in a great fury. In order to escape his pursuer, Karambil climbed a huge pine tree which grew near his camp and hid amongst the topmost branches. Bullabogabun, however, gathered all the wood he could find and piled it into a heap at the base of the tree. He set fire to the sticks and burnt the pine tree to cinders. As the flames reached high into the air Karambil was carried with them far into the sky, where he remains today near the Warweenggary as the star Alpha Tauri, and he now follows the sisters eternally, just as he did in his youth.[1]

The ultimate punishment for love between tribal brothers and sisters was death, and the following Tiwi story from Bathurst Island still acts as a cautionary tale to the young people.

Ikeiginni and Kuparunni

Ikeiginni was a young girl of the Dreaming who lived on Bathurst Island and happily went out to gather food with her mother. She collected sweet-tasting yams from the jungles and teredo worms from the mangroves. She gathered the fruit from the cycad palm trees and her mother taught her how to soak them in fresh water for three days until the poison was leached out. Ikeiginni played and laughed with all the young boys and girls every day.

Soon Ikeiginni reached puberty and in accordance with custom she was told that from then on she must not associate freely with her young tribal brothers — but she did not listen. She was already the sweetheart of a youth called Kuparunni who was her tribal brother. Foolishly, she continued to run about and go down to the lagoon to swim with him. Her father was shamed beyond his tolerance and decided to punish the two of them. He went out hunting with Kuparunni and told him to climb a tree for sugar-bag honey but instructed him when he was out on a branch to make cuts in the branch behind him. Kuparunni knew the branch could fall down,

Opposite: When Kuparunni was out on a branch his uncle told him to make cuts in the branch behind him. The branch fell and the young lovers were killed. *photo R. Edwards*

carrying him with it, and entreated his uncle to let him cut a different way, but to no avail. Just as Ikeiginni ran to the tree calling to Kuparunni to give her some honey also, the branch fell and both the young lovers were killed. Kuparunni changed into a frill-necked lizard who still lives on trees, hiding in shame from the tribespeople, and Ikeiginni became a black cockatoo who calls to her lover from the branches above.

Tiwi, Bathurst Island[2]

The story of the fate of Bamabama, the spirit man with huge genitals, who was always trying to have sex with his tribal sisters is well known in eastern Arnhem Land.

Long ago in mythical times lived a spirit man named Bamabama who was continually interested in sexual intercourse, usually with girls of a kin relationship forbidding such an act.

Bamabama was sent as messenger to a neighbouring camp to issue an invitation to a jadi (mortuary) ceremony. When he arrived there they selected three boys for him to take back. Bamabama challenged the boys to a race to a nearby lagoon. When they had finished he told them that they were rather slow and that he would like to see whether their sisters could do better. While the girls were running he watched them intently and chose the one he liked best to accompany him. When they reached the lagoon he said, 'I can see a fish, let us go and catch it.' They both waded into the water and caught many fish. Suddenly Bamabama cried out in pain, 'A fish has bitten my foot, it is hurting terribly.' This was only a trick to induce the girl to agree to set up camp as it was nearly sunset. He insisted that he was in such pain that he could not possibly continue on and ordered her to get some wood to make a fire and cook the fish. He also told her to bring sheets of stringybark to make two shelters, one for each of them.

Some time after they had retired to their respective shelters, he began to throw little stones on the roof of the girl's hut. As she grew more and more frightened he told her that the Spirits of her dead ancestors were trying to get her and that she had better join him in his own shelter so that he could protect her. After the girl had moved into his hut Bamabama made love to her. However, his penis was very big and in forcing himself upon her he killed her.

In the morning he wrapped the dead girl into sheets of paperbark and carried her to the camp. But before coming to the camp he hung the bundle in a tree. The mother asked him,'Where is my daughter?' He said, 'She is sick. She ran too much after bandicoot. I left her behind in that tree.' When the mother and the relatives found the dead girl they knew what had happened; they got very angry and began hitting Bamabama with fighting sticks. He ran away, picked up a fishing spear and killed a dog. Then he took another spear and threw it into ngadu (cycad nut damper which is ceremonial food) and broke it up. Only a crazy man kills dogs or destroys food. As the people could not catch Bamabama they made a big basket, a wargadja (sacred dillybag), and put it over him, tied it together and threw him into the lagoon. There Bamabama turned into a stone. The tide came up and covered all the camp and all the people changed into animals and birds. Now this is Law. The people are afraid this could happen again and the Law was made in those days that a man must not behave like Bamabama.

Narritjin Maymuru, Yirrkala[3]

MOTHER-IN-LAW AVOIDANCE

The pursuit of the Witulin Sisters by Waku the crow described in an earlier chapter[4] is an example of a most important myth about the rules of avoiding any contact, but particularly sexual relations, between mothers-in-law and sons-in-law or between others who were in this tribal relationship to each other. The crow pursued the sisters far and wide and when he sought to make them his wives they continually escaped, forcing him to wander on hopelessly lost.

The following Wotjobaluk myth from Victoria also points out the inevitable punishment for breaking this taboo.

160

The Bat and the Mother-in-Law

A bat once lived in the sandhill country. No one lived near him except the owl woman, who was his mother-in-law. Although it was forbidden for a son-in-law to speak to his mother-in-law, she had gradually made him break this rule, so that now they talked to each other. But they were not happy. The bat was sorry that he had broken the ancient custom of the tribe by speaking to her, and the owl woman was not happy because she desired him as her husband.

One day the bat told the woman to get the meat he had left hanging on a honeysuckle bush. She went and found it, but instead of bringing it home she ate every scrap of it. When she came back he asked her if she had brought the meat. She answered, 'No, since you will not be my husband.' He said no more about it but resolved to be rid of her. Later he said to her, 'Go and get some water.' The owl woman got the wooden bucket and started to go for the water in the waterhole; then she asked him, 'Where shall I get the water from?' The bat answered, 'Go further in,' and she went further in. He kept calling out, 'Further yet,' and the water reached her waist, then her neck, and still he said for her to go on. But when the water bubbled in her mouth she said, 'I will not go any further,' and began to return.

In the meantime, the bat had made an image of himself and had covered it with his rug. Then he hid in a tree. The owl woman came back to the camp and said to the image of the bat, 'Here is the water.' Receiving no reply she hit at it with her yam stick, and then she saw the deception. She looked for him everywhere, crying out, 'My husband, my husband, where are you?' At last she found him and they went back together to the camp. The bat decided on one final punishment to be rid of her.

Next morning they both went out and gathered yams. The bat cooked the yams and sent the owl woman for water. While she was away he pounded a lot of yams in a wooden bucket and kept them steaming hot. As soon as the owl woman was seated he stood up and told her to open her mouth. When she had done so he dropped the mass of burning hot yams into it, and so choked her to death.

This is the punishment she deserved for breaking the tribal Law.

Wotjobaluk tribe[5]

Sometimes the rules of mother-in-law avoidance, which forbade speaking or looking directly at her, might seem impractical in a very small family group. In these cases communication channels were established through the wife, the mother-in-law's daughter. Her son-in-law could speak to her 'through' her daughter. A myth which reinforces another practical solution to unavoidable contact is the following from the Kulin in Victoria.

The Bat and the Emu Maidens

Balayang the bat was miserable and uncomfortable because his wife had died. Now he had no one to dig up murnung, his favourite roots, or to gather yams and grubs for him, and since that was woman's work he could not do it himself.

The only person living near him was his mother-in-law, and to her, of course, he could not talk, as this was prohibited by tribal custom which could not be broken. Her husband had died, so she had no one to hunt game for her, and she could not ask her son-in-law to do it. Then she thought of a way. One day when Balayang was away from his camp she quickly carried a basket full of roots to it and left it there. When he returned he was pleased; he waited until she left her own camp and he took some game-flesh over to her. So they managed to help each other that way.

After a while Balayang felt very unhappy again, because he wanted a wife to keep him company and to talk to. His mother-in-law guessed what was troubling him, so she made magic. She went to a log lying on the ground and hit it with her yam stick. Two young emu maidens came out of the log. The old woman told them to go into the swamp. This they did, and swam about beating the surface of the water with their hands, making a noise like the drumming of an emu man.

Balayang heard this noise and taking up his spears, went to investigate. But when he peered through the scrub he saw the two maidens swimming about. He took the spear out of the spear-thrower and sat down where they could see him. So

Traditional stories teach the importance of marrying within the kinship laws.
Dhuwa marries Yirritja and Yirritja marries Dhuwa. *photo P. Tweedie*

they called out to him, 'Do we call you grandfather?' He said, 'No.' Then in turn
they called 'Father? Father's brother? Brother?' to which questions he said 'No.'
And the girls said, 'Then we call you husband,' and they went with him to his camp
as his wives.[6]

PROMISED HUSBANDS AND WIVES

In the selection of a wife, strict laws are followed. In north-eastern Arnhem Land,
the people are broadly divided into two halves, or moieties, called Dhuwa and
Yirritja. A Dhuwa must marry a Yirritja and vice versa. Old Djawa, the senior tribal
elder on Milingimbi, made these comments.

'The Guthin, or Balangarr, was a rat-woman and this promise was made by her.
She made a sensible promise: When you have a daughter you give her to your
gurrung* and your gurrung only. Not your brother or gathu or that would mean
Dhuwa marries Dhuwa and Yirritja marries Yirritja. That's not good. Dhuwa must
marry Yirritja.'[7]

It is common for young girls to be promised in marriage to older men, sometimes before they are born. Important men may acquire a number of wives, some of
them much younger than they are. Young girls are taught it is proper for them to go
to their older husbands without complaint, and many traditional stories teach this
by inference.

* Gurrung is a man in proper relationship to marry your husband's sister's daughter.

162

Nabinkulawa and his Young Wife

A man lived long ago who was called Nabinkulawa, and because he was a good hunter he was given a second wife, a young girl called Mirnaliwo. She was frightened of her husband and despite the pressure of her family refused to live with him. A number of years passed and Mirnaliwo became pregnant. Nabinkulawa knew the baby was not his as his young wife had a sweetheart. One day while they were all out looking for sugarbag it started to rain, so Nabinkulawa built two shelters — one for him and his first wife and the other for Mirnaliwo.

Nabinkulawa was a Marrkidjbu or 'clever man' with great powers and he wanted to kill Mirnaliwo because of her sweetheart. He went into the bush near the camp and made a Ngalyod, a Rainbow Serpent, and instructed it to go and kill his young wife. The Serpent was told to travel underground and to emerge inside Mirnaliwo's shelter and to eat her. The snake left Nabinkulawa and travelled underground to the shelter, where it surfaced and swallowed Mirnaliwo head first. It went back underground and travelled towards the sandstone country where it emerged inside a cave and vomited her onto the wall of the cave. Today she is a rock painting and is a warning to all young wives.

Gunwinggu, north-eastern Arnhem Land[8]

LOVE MAGIC

In Aboriginal society, as in any other since time began, lovers will attempt to find a way to meet despite the strictest regulations and controls which others place upon them. If at first the attraction is not felt by the loved one there are always the lengthy and beautiful love songs which will certainly capture the heart.

The seagull flaps its wings, flying along;
*   it is always there, in the west, at the place of the Red Egg . . .*
The voice of the seagull, its cry, drifts all over the country . . .
It circles low over the cabbage palm foliage . . .
Crying out, at the place of the fresh water,
The gull swoops low, skimming the water, at the wide expanse of billabong . . .
Keen beak probing, it searches for food, skimming the water . . .
Circling over the billabong grass, and the water-lilies . . .
Circling around, in search of the freshwater leech . . .
Always there in the west, the sound of its cry: at the place of the Red Egg . . .
This string is mine [says the seagull], at the place of the billabong . . .
String, short string, and a bird's head . . .
The keen eyes of the gull search for food in the night, as a lover looks for his sweetheart . . .
Flapping its wings, and crying out as it flies . . .[9]

This love song from Arnhem Land refers to the seagull searching for food as a lover looks for his sweetheart at night. The images in the poem refer to the practice of making wooden images of seagull's heads which are attached to feathered string. These are used in love-magic. The head would be laid before the desired woman and the string would be gently pulled along so that it seemed like a bird in flight. The beak was carved slightly open, and holding a leech or grub. The small creature in the beak symbolized the capture by the bird (the lover) of the food (his sweetheart).

The Djarada is a widely known technique of love magic, and has been described by Dick Roughsey of Mornington Island in the Gulf of Carpentaria.

Gidegal the Moon Man

When Gidegal the moon man was on earth he was a great lover of women. He was always after women and made many songs to make them fall in love with him. Gidegal made the big sacred ceremony of Djarada and left it to us so that a man could sing a woman to be his wife. It is still used today. My older brother Burrud, or Lindsay, is the biggest song-man of the Lardil. Men often get him to sing the Djarada songs to help them get the woman they want.

When Gidegal the moon man was on earth he was a great lover of women. *photo P. Tweedie*

When a man wants to marry a certain woman he calls on his close male relatives to help him. They go out in the bush to the sacred ground and get it ready. A big circle is cleared in the sand and smoothed off. In the centre an oval shape is painted on the ground using small balls of bird-down coloured with red ochre and white pipeclay. It has a red centre. This represents the woman's vagina.

A tall pole is stuck in the ground just in front of the oval. The pole is decorated with paint and feathers and represents a penis. Strings covered with white bird-down hang from the top of the pole to represent the seminal flow. Oval holes are dug on each side of the central symbol and their edges painted with red ochre feathers. These also represent vaginas. The men decorate their bodies with red and white paint and ochred bird-down. Each paints his own mulgri on his chest and arms. On their thighs they paint ovals which also represent women.

When everything is ready the Djarada man stands before the feathered pole with legs spread, knees bent and hands on thighs. His two relatives, perhaps grandfather and uncle, kneel over the holes at the side. They begin singing the cycle of love songs. As they sing they sway their hips back and forth in the rhythmical motions of love-making.

In the first song Gidegal sings his own body so that he'll be strong and attractive to the woman. Each song is sung several times before going on to the next. The songs do not have to be heard by the woman, she may be many miles away.

In the second song, Gidegal sings the woman so that she will begin to dream of him. He sings, 'Guraday Lardimah, Guraday Lardimah — Gura Binba Binba' (You will think sweet of me in your dreaming).

Opposite: Love magic cave painting in Arnhem Land. *photo R. Edwards*

165

He now sings, 'Bulgeery Rumana Mungeera Girano' (You will dream that I am making love to you). He sings a fourth song to make himself more attractive, and as he sings he rubs juice from the roots of a special bush over his body. The juice is mixed with goanna fat.

Gidegal sings a song so that the woman won't be able to stop looking at him. He sings again so that when the woman wakes next morning she will find herself wet as though from love-making. The last song describes the woman walking about next morning, knowing that she belongs to the man who sang in her dreams.

Gidegal sings all night and all next day, repeating the song cycle over and over. The songs make the Evening Star twinkle and the woman is again reminded of her lover. He sings the lightning flash and when she sleeps she dreams of the lightning and sees the form of her lover in the flash. Her heart is warm and glad.

The Djarada songs of Gidegal never fail. The woman can't help falling in love with the singer of Djarada, even if she didn't like him before.

Dick Roughsey, Mornington Island[10]

ROLE OF MEN AND WOMEN

The division of labour between men and women in everyday life is implicit in many myths which clearly describe the food gathering activities of women while the men hunt larger animals. Many myths overlap in the areas they deal with. Thus a myth about an ancestral hero may involve hunting lore, marriage customs, the role of men and women and their responsibilities to their kin as well as taboos surrounding food. The actions of the Ancestral Being himself therefore sets the eternal pattern for Aboriginal society.

Men had the aggressive role, the responsibility of spearing and capturing animals, or of fishing and of providing the meat for the family. Women were expected to gather vegetable foods and fruits, grind seeds, cook damper and dig for roots. Of course if small edible animals came past they were not forbidden to capture them, though it was often the young children, accompanying their mothers, who pursued small lizards and marsupials.

Women did not however hunt large animals and the following stories told to Kabbarli early this century by a small group of Aboriginal people at Ooldea, a camp at the edge of the Nullarbor Plain, tells of what befell certain women who hunted meat in the Dreaming times.

The Women who Hunted Meat

In Yamminga times, there was once a tribe of jandu (women) who used to live by themselves, at a place called Yardagurra, in the Great Australian Bight. Now it is the law of the tribe that men and women should live together, not separately, and that the men should hunt for wallee (meat) each day, while the women go out to gather mai (vegetable food). But these jandu did not observe the law: not only did they live by themselves, but they went out meat-hunting each day, armed with men's weapons: spears, spear-throwers, and hunting knives. Like men they stalked and speared the kangaroo, and hunted the emu across the plain.

Tchooroo the Great Snake, whose task it was to uphold the law, reproached these women for their way of life. 'You should not hunt for wallee,' he told them. 'That is men's work. You should collect mai. That is women's work and this is the hunting law.'

But the women did not take any notice of Tchooroo's words; they went on hunting for meat just as they had done before. When Tchooroo saw that they had not listened to his words, he became angry and turned all the jandu into jiddi joonoo (termites' nests). All the tall peaked jiddi joonoo which stand now at Yardagurra were once the meat-hunting jandu of Yamminga times, who were punished by Tchooroo the Great Snake because they broke the law of the tribe.[11]

Women were expected to provide as much variety as they could in the foods they gathered and to diligently search for vegetables, if necessary, far from the camp. Generosity was admired and selfishness deplored.

166

Joord-Joord (Shag) the Lazy Woman

In the long-ago Yamminga times, Joord-Joord was a jandu (woman) and she had two sons. Every day her sons went into the bush to hunt possum and other meat, and when they brought home their game, they always gave their mother as much as she could eat.

Joord-Joord should also have gone out each day to collect roots and berries and other vegetable food, and to look for bardi and small game such as lizards, for that was a woman's work. But she was fat and lazy, and every day, every day, she gave her two sons nothing but nyell-guru and ngar-ran (white ants and ants' eggs), which she could collect just outside their camp. She would go a short distance and fill her bin-jin (bark vessel) with these, because they were so easy to get. When her sons came home with the langoor or wallaby or goanna they had hunted, every day they saw only the same food in their mother's bin-jin: nyell-guru and ngar-ran. That was all their mother could be bothered to find for them. At last, they grew tired of eating ants and ants' eggs, and one day they threw all the contents of their mother's bin-jin on the fire. As they burned, the ants and the ants' eggs made a loud crackling noise.

'What do I hear burning? What is it?' Joord-Joord called out.

'Nothing,' her sons told her. 'It is nothing.'

And now, every time they came home and found nothing but ants and ants' eggs in Joord-Joord's bin-jin, they burned them.

One day they came home early, bringing fat langoor with them. They found their mother sifting and sifting the nyell-guru and the ngar-ran.

The eldest son said to his brother, 'Let us punish our mother, because she does not follow the Law of the tribe and bring us proper food. She gives us nothing but that no-good nyell-guru and ngar-ran, while we bring home good meat and always give her a fair share of it.'

When Joord-Joord looked up and saw her sons coming towards her, she guessed what was in their minds. 'They are going to punish me because I do not go out to collect proper food for them,' she thought. She seized her digging stick and began to hit her sons with it as soon as they drew near. Then each of her sons picked up fire sticks from the fire and hit their mother on the back. And that is why, when Joord-Joord the Shag became a bird, she had a black back. 'Joord-joord! Joord-joord!' she cries as she goes along.

Women should bring home proper vegetable food when their sons fetch good meat for them: that is the law of the tribe.[12]

The following stories, the first from the Central Desert and the second from Warburton/Kimberleys in Western Australia, are most revealing about the duties of wives to provide food for their husbands, the need to prepare it carefully and the potential for jealousy between wives should the husband favour one more than the other.

The Wanambis Punish their Wives

During the early days of Creation, two snake-brothers camped with their two wives at the mouth of the Piltadi Gorge at the eastern end of the Mann Ranges. Every morning the two wives of the snake-men walked to a spring nearby to gather food and especially to catch small marsupials, called Mitika, by smoking them from their burrows. They would gather spinifex grass into bunches, push it tightly into the mouth of a burrow, and set this on fire. When the blaze was strong enough, they inverted their wooden dishes and, cupping them over the hole and fire, beat them up and down to cause plenty of smoke. The animals inside would come to the entrance of their burrows to escape and be suffocated in the fumes.

Every night the two wives brought the animals back and threw them in a heap for the men to cook. The men were so well fed that after a while they did not bother to hunt any more and just sat around singing and making ceremonies. Their laziness enraged their wives and one day they rebelled and cooked and ate all the Mitikas themselves, providing nothing for their husbands.

The husbands were furious at the action of their wives; they travelled away from their camp underground some far distance and made another camp where they would not be affected by the smoke from the women's fires. They decided to change into Wanambis and to punish the women while in this form. Each day while the women were hunting, their husbands who were in the form of Wanambi snakes would make tracks and burrows across their path, enticing them after large game. But each day the women were able to catch only a small carpet snake which barely fed them. The women pursued the Wanambis until finally the Wanambis revealed themselves as giant serpents with manes and beards and devoured their wives.[13]

This story serves as a moral tale concerning the duties of wives to feed their husbands and also implies that wives should not resent the time men take with ceremonial matters.

Crow and White Cockatoo

The eagle had two wives, the crow and the white cockatoo. The crow would go and get termite-grubs and bring them back to camp. But as well as grubs, there would be bits of grass, leaves and dirt in the digging bowl. Not being skilful at yandying she would leave it and eat it anyhow, pebbles and all. But the eagle wouldn't eat the crow's termite-grubs.

However the white cockatoo would get termite-grubs and yandy them until there were no pebbles or leaves in the digging bowl — only grubs. The eagle would come and be very pleased to see them. He would get them and eat them all up.

The eagle would spear a kangaroo, bring it home and give the crow the back, the two rib sections, the bare arm bones and the two feet, all the poorest parts. But he would bring the best parts and give them to the white cockatoo.

So the two wives would eat their meat and go off again the next day for termite-grubs. The eagle went out, looked around, speared meat, brought it and gave it to them. But the crow couldn't give him her termite-grubs, for he would only eat what the white cockatoo brought and gave him.

'Why, he always leaves mine,' thought the crow. 'Right now I'm going to really give that white cockatoo a good hiding.' So when the husband went out hunting again the two wives were sitting in camp. The crow was picking up all the old bones and eating the meat off them. Then she made up her mind, hurried off and got a digging stick, and gave the white cockatoo a good hiding; then she left her. The white cockatoo just crawled away, being very sore from bruises on her shoulders, arms and legs.

The crow sat there until she saw the eagle come back from hunting. When he came and sat down, she went over and said to him, 'Listen. The white cockatoo has got a little baby boy. It's just like you. Truly it's just like its father.'

So he gave the meat to the crow. 'Take this and give it to her.' The crow said, 'I'll go and build a windbreak and light a fire.'

So the crow went over there and made out to cry like a baby. Then she ate all the meat and came back. Next morning she went again and pretended to give the white cockatoo meat and water. She would sit there and make out to laugh and laugh, then come back and say, 'The eagle's baby is a beautiful child.'

But the eagle was thinking, 'My wife wasn't having a baby. The crow is lying to me.' The next morning he went and, after having a drink, followed the tracks. He said to himself, 'Here are the tracks where the white cockatoo went. Why, she was so ill she had to crawl.'

So he came back and said to the crow, 'I'll go and look around for meat and come back.' Then the eagle followed the tracks, thinking, 'These tracks are old and faint.' But he kept on following and he saw the white cockatoo on the edge of the water, just going into it.

The eagle thought, 'What shall I do?' He went into the water and followed for a long time, but he couldn't catch her. The white cockatoo went right into the water and drowned. She died there in the deep water. Then the man sat down and cried for his wife.

On his way back home the eagle saw a bobtail lizard, killed it and brought it with him. Then, when he saw a rabbit burrow, he dragged the lizard around the opening of the burrow. He made it look as though a carpet snake had gone in there.

Then the eagle came home and saw the crow sitting there. He came up to her and said, 'Listen, I saw a place where a carpet snake has gone into a hole.' The crow was very pleased. They both had a drink, got up and went along until they saw where the carpet snake had gone in. So the crow started digging. She went on digging and digging and digging. Then the eagle lit some dry grass and quickly threw it down the hole after her, so that the crow died inside the hole. The fire burnt her right up.

The eagle went off and lived by himself.

Stanley West, Warburton[14]

The history of relations between men and women is fascinating but not always cordial. As many of the Creation stories have shown, women originally kept the sacred Law, they sometimes owned the sacred objects and kept them in their dilly bags, but at some point in the history of the Dreaming, their status was altered; the men stole the sacred Law and have retained the knowledge ever since. As in many societies of the world the women became the subject of jests by the men due to their garrulous nature — they were far too frivolous to be entrusted with the sacred matters of Law; they gossiped too much.

The Fights Caused by Bulangarr the Rat-Woman

Now I'm going to tell you about our custom of fighting in groups and who said we must always settle our disputes like this. This was in another time.

Who created this Law? Rat-woman. She was a terrible trouble maker. She went about telling stories to all the people about other people, and everyone used to fight because of her lies.

You can see what she is like from her tracks. First she makes one big hole, then she makes a lot of small ones leading from that big one. That tells you she has many conflicting ideas — she likes putting other people into trouble, and of course she gets into trouble herself.

As a result of all her mischief all the people had a ganygarr in the Wongar times, an all-in fight. The fought with many spears and when their spears broke up they turned into the leeches you can see today.

Djawa, Milingimbi[15]

The gossiping rats are the subject of songs from both the Wonguri-Mandjikai cycle of the Moon-Bone and the Rose River love song cycle.[16]

In most accounts of the history in the shift in relationships and roles, the women, however, remained unperturbed. The roles which became fixed in the Dreaming era, of men hunting and keeping the sacred Law and ceremonies and of women gathering food, grinding seeds and bearing children continued over the millennia to come. For the women had the most sacred gift of all. As the Djankawu Sisters said when their dilly bags were stolen containing their sacred 'rangga',

[Men can do the ceremonies] now, they can look after it. We can spend our time collecting bush foods for them, for it is not right that they should get that food as they have been doing. We have really lost nothing, for we remember it all, and we can let them have that small part. For aren't we still sacred, even if we have lost the bags? Haven't we still our uteri?[17]

THE BIRTH OF THE TRIBES

The angry Wandjinas sent a flood
And the water reached them all.

But in the waves,
One man, one woman,
Grabbed the tail of a kangaroo.

They clung to its tail as it swam
And it reached the rocks.
Here, on this side, they climbed up,
So that we were born,
So we go on being born.

Sam Woolgoodja[18]

Some of the great ceremonial cycles of the north have explained the birth of the first people long, long ago from their great Ancestral mothers: Waramurungundji in the west, and the Djankawu Sisters in the north-east. Another great Creator-Ancestress, Maralaitj, who came from the direction of Indonesia, gave birth to many tribes at various waterholes in the Gunwinggu country of western Arnhem Land. She gave each group their language and kinship group and finally moved to the end of the rainbow where she now remains forever.

Because of the sacredness of many aspects of the birth of the first people and the secrecy which surrounds the ceremonies recreating these Dreaming events today, the details cannot be revealed here. The sacred and secret ceremonies remain immensely important links to the Dreaming Ancestors, and their power can only be retained if the secrets are kept from unitiated men and from women.

Songs relating how the Djankawu Sisters gave birth to the progenitors of the North-eastern Arnhem Land people follow. These songs were originally collected and translated by Professor R. M. Berndt from Mawalan of Yirrkala over thirty years ago.[19]

Using the mauwulan *carefully,* waridj, *with hips swaying:*
We are not tired, walking along, but our hair is grey from foam,
From the foam splashing, at Bralgu, the Spirit Land, away over the rough sea.
Carefully, waridj, *we lift up our* rangga . . .
Yes indeed, all right, waridj Miralaidj: *you feel unwell?*
My body is tired from dragging the stick, waridj, *poking it in so carefully.*
Turn over the mouth of the mat, come closer up into it, waridj.
This is our place, at Banbaldji, at Bunawauwima,
Where we may sit and rest.
Yes, waridj, *indeed! We put it in here,* waridj, *put the* mauwulan *point into the left side of*
*   that mat . . .*
Our camp is in the middle.
But I feel unwell, waridj. *Indeed, I am full of people!*
In here are rangga-*people! Come, open the mouth of this 'mat'!*
This basket, which is a uterus!
Yes indeed, waridj Miralaidj. *You must help me, for you are my leader . . .*
That 'basket', waridj, *comes from the Place of the Mauwulan!*
Yes, that basket is drying from the foam which splashed it at Bralgu, the Spirit Land, across the
*   sea:*
All its feathers are shining, drying.
Quietly she opens her legs, only a little, opening that 'basket':
Our basket, with its feathered string and its pendants . . .
Our feathered strands, which were spread out carefully to dry in the sun's rays, at the Place of
*   the Mauwulan.*
The hot sun dried them, its rays looking down on them with scorching heat: thus we spread out
*   the feathered strings.*
Carefully lay out the feathered strings, leading to the Place of the Sun . . . !

The song tells of the birth of some of the first people. 'Those children are drying' and the lines which follow, mean that the children have emerged from the ngain-mira. They have been born, and are lying in the sun. 'She opens her legs, only a little: the sister has numerous children inside her, and if she opens her legs widely they might all rush out. So, little by little, at the stopping places along their journeys, the sisters give birth to all the different tribes, each with their own language and totems. As the children are born, wet with 'foam', they are placed in the warm rays of the mother sun to dry. The tribes throughout the north of Australia thus trace their descent from the great Ancestors.

CONCEPTION TOTEMS

In a personal and different way, however, each man and woman is linked spiritually with the Dreaming. Each person is connected to a totem object, animal, creature or

170

plant and is therefore the émbodiment of that totem in human form. Men and women are therefore not only the children of the great Ancestors, but sometimes the reincarnation of them. The pregnancy of a woman is always associated with a dream in which the father or mother 'finds' the child. Child spirit centres exist in many areas and women visit these places if they wish to have a child, or conversely, avoid them scrupulously if their family is large enough already.

The little story which follows was written by Buru Goonack of Mowanjum in north-western Australia to illustrate this relationship of a boy to his totem.

Bulunbud, the Grass

I was born out of a grass, because I am related to it. I feel that I was born out of a grass seed because I feel tossed to and fro all the time.

When the seed breaks out, then I pop out of the seed pod, but I am not a baby for my mother to carry around, I am already a man with a big future.

I was born: when I came I wasn't alone, my grandparents were there watching me, they greeted me too, and I greeted them. My parents had already died and I had only my grandparents. They gave me the name Bulunbud meaning, 'the grass'. It was only when I had grown up I found out what my name was.

One day late in the evening I asked my grandfather what the name meant. 'Well,' said the old man, 'you were called that because you were grass before you were born.' Then he told the story of how it happened.

'One day, before you were born, I was hunting and I heard this crying in the grass. I came back to your mother and told her. Your spirit was taken, then you were born, but now your parents are dead, and you are Bulunbud, the grass.'

Daisy Utemara, Mowanjum [20]

Birth of the Tribes. Segment from bark painting of the Djankawu story by Wandjuk Marika. *photo R. Edwards*

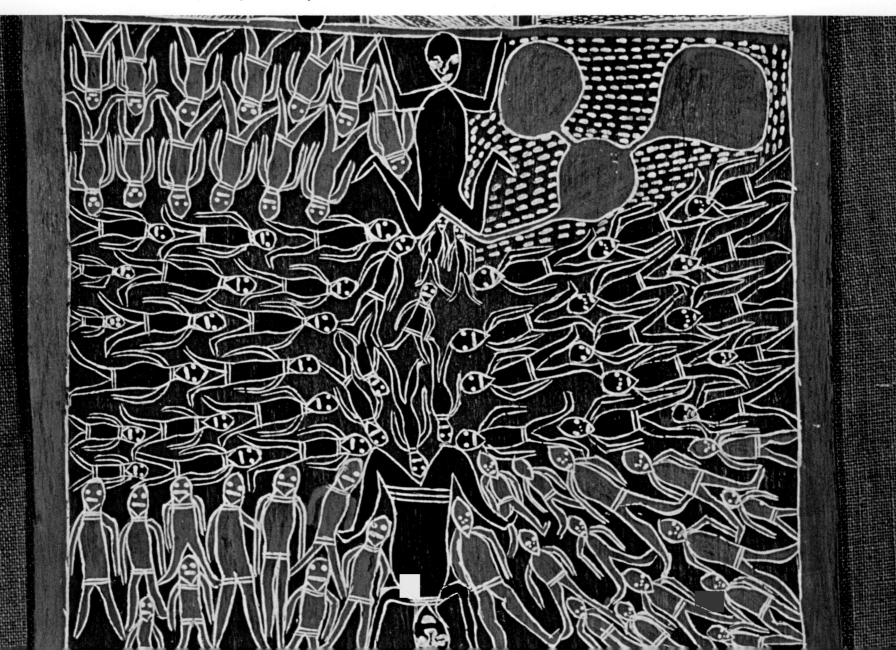

Every Aboriginal man and woman can tell the story of how his mother or father found or dreamt of his spirit totem. The people of Mowanjum have related their stories, and they are retold here by David Mowaljarli.[21]

Gertie Garndur

In the Dreamtime the fish used to go round and round, but one fish broke out and as he was flapping along he broke up the bank. That is how the Sale River, which Aboriginals call Pantijan, came to be. Now, the fish that had been making those rings became ring rocks. They still remain there, and that's where the Aboriginals used to go fishing. They used to poison the fish with poison roots.

At one time, when all the Aboriginals were living around that area, Gertie Garndur's father and mother happened to be living with them. One day, when they were fishing, a spirit child, who was Gertie, speared her father's eye and he cried out that a fish had speared his eye. Then he left the people fishing and went to lie down in the camp. The spirit child came into his dreams and said, 'Father, it was I who hit your eye and my name is Jarnanya, which means fish.'

Jarnanya (Gertie) was born in the Bugudu where Kunmunya airport now stands, in her country, the Prince Regent.

May Winani

Winani, May's spirit name, means the shadow of a Wandjina cliff, and also Wandjina's kidney; the shadow or reflection of the red cliff, that's what Winani means.

May's father and mother were living with all the Aboriginals at a place called Wundulle, which is the biggest spirit water. One day her father, while drinking, happened to see something like a shadow reflecting in the water. When he saw the reflection of the stone in the water he could see a child. He got a shock and looked back towards the rock, but suddenly she wasn't there. He knew then that it was a spirit child. Whenever parents, either the man or the woman, see a spirit child they don't tell anyone for a month, until the mother is pregnant.

When they had all gone home Winani's father dreamt the child came back and said, 'It's me, Daddy, the spirit child.' So Winani was born at the Prince Regent, near Pantijan. Her totem is bush bananas.

Eileen Legullnu

Legullnu, Eileen's name, means slippery rock. At one time all the Aboriginals were living near Windjina Gorge. In many good years, when good rain fell and trees and flowers blossomed, people came from everywhere. They liked to have their initiation times in those seasons.

In the Dreamtime the barramundi had swum in rings too, in the mouth of the Lenard River, but these barramundi decided to flap along to Windjina Gorge where the Aboriginals fish. One day, when the women were fishing, Eileen's mother threw in her fishing line and caught a spirit barramundi. While trying to catch the barramundi she slipped on the rocks and fell down.

The spirit children said to Eileen, 'You made your mother fall!' So Eileen said to her mother, 'Mother, it is me, Legullnu, your spirit child, that you caught on your line.'

Eileen Legullnu was then born at Kimberley Downs Station. Her totem is one of the Wandjina people, Gallulu, which means Rain God.

Jack Wherra

This story is from a long time ago, back in our Ancestors' time, at Kunmunya. Some spirits were digging the roots of the grape. They were digging, probably, about a mile deep and long, and as they were digging along they saw that they had no

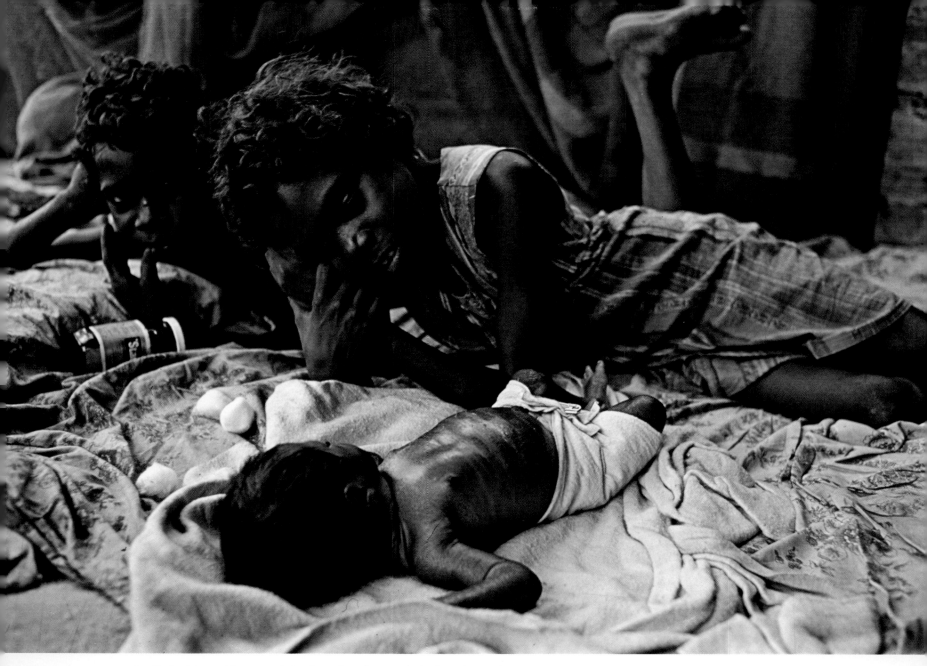

At Walkerbimerri in central Arnhem Land a new baby is welcomed
with wonder and love by his sister. *photo P. Tweedie*

seawater left. They dug the roots right to where the vines were, then they broke off
the roots. At the other end everybody pulled out the roots, which were nearly at the
edge of the sea. When they pulled the roots out the seawater rushed in about a mile
where the vine was, and that's where the sea stopped. That is how it became a
waterfall, starting from Kunmunya and going to where the grapevine was. It is
spirit water. These were spirits who dug the grape roots and we believe that these
grapevines give spirit children to parents.

Now it happened that when all the Aboriginals were living there Jack Wherra's
parents dug for grape roots and got plenty. They cooked them and peeled them,
and after they had eaten plenty of the roots they slept. His parents dreamt that a big
peeled grape root was lying down and at the end of the grape root they heard the
spirit child say, 'It is I, Jack Wherra.' They both kept it in mind until the mother
became pregnant.

Wherra, Jack's Aboriginal name, means peel. Jack was born at Camden Harbour, near Kure Bay. His tribe is called Beragrude, meaning hibiscus flower.

Windbag

There is a place, a huge mountain, called Jarmalawuru and this is the story of a
spirit goanna who crawled around everywhere. While she was crawling around, the
country became a plain, so the goanna decided to dig. She dug all night, digging the
hole, digging until the sun rose. Towards sunrise she came out and cracked the
earth open. Then she cried, 'I've been digging all night,' and stopped digging. This
happened where Napier Downs Station now stands.

When she went down again into the hole she left water. The name of that spring
is Dumbul, which means spring water.

Now, Windbag's family happened to be living near that mountain, around the spring. In the early hours of the morning an old lady awoke and saw the goanna. She woke all the other people and said, 'There is a goanna here, near our camp.' Windbag's father had two wives. The first wife said to the younger wife, 'Kill this goanna,' and the younger wife did so. It was a spirit goanna. When they cooked the goanna it didn't have any fat, only watery meat which had no taste in it.

After sleeping the next night, the first wife said to her husband, 'I have dreamt of a spirit child and I believe your second wife will have to be the mother of it.' The younger wife also dreamt of the child and in her dream the child said, 'It is me, Jarmalawuru, the spirit child of the goanna.' The young wife kept the dream in her mind until she became pregnant.

So Jarmalawuru was born in the Mount Barnett Ranges. His totem is Naru-Naru, which means the frog tribe.

The people of the Kimberleys tell their history and the story of their lives in language full of poetry. The Worora elder, Sam Woolgoodja, talks of how he came to know his child:

In its own Wunger* place
A spirit waits for birth –
"Today, I saw who the child really is" –
That is how a man
Learns to know his child.

As I looked at the water
of Bundaalunaa
She appeared to me:
I understood suddenly
The life in our baby –
Her name is Dragon Fly.[22]

Namaaraalee† made him,
No one else,
No one.
But not all things are straight
in this day.

A person's totem is like his other self. It cannot be killed or eaten by him, and will stay close to him in life, sometimes perhaps giving signs or warning of danger. Henry Rankin of Point Macleay in South Australia has related several instances in his own life when his totem warned him and gave him messages.

Ngaki – that means, how do you say it 'totem'.

My totem's the Cape Barren goose. Ngaki all the time gives us signs. One day my father went hunting for ducks and swans, while his brother was sick in Adelaide hospital. A pelican came and settled on dry land near him, and dropped one wing like it was broken. He looks at the bird, pulls back the hammer in the gun, then thinks, 'No, I won't shoot him, he's trying to tell me something.' Then the bird got up and flew straight to Adelaide. My father came home and said, 'Something's wrong up there with my brother,' and almost twenty minutes later the boss came down the path. 'You don't need to tell us,' said my father. 'We got the sign.' That was right, my brother had passed away, the boss was coming to tell us.

Another time, I saw my totem, the Cape Barren goose, coming down the path flapping and dragging his wings, then he turned and went to Adelaide. And I knew that my aunt, old Mildred Rankin, passed away in Adelaide hospital.

One time, my father and I went fishing near the Narrung Ferry, and we were coming along the reeds in the boat when the pelican, my father's totem, came right close up beside us. We put our guns up, click, click, no guns went off. Pelican flies down again, click, click, no guns went off. 'What the hell's wrong with that gun?' we say and put in new cartridges again, when pelican come near again, click, click, still no go off. Then horse and cart come up alongside on the land. 'What's up?' we say.

---

* Wunger (or Wongar) means Dreaming/spirit   †Namaaraalee is a Wandjina spirit

'Your sister is going to hospital, cut her leg very badly on a bit of glass while sliding down a bank, she's on that ferry now.' So the bird was trying to tell us.[23]

CHILDBIRTH

Childbirth itself is strictly the concern of the women. A camp is made apart from the rest of the community and the woman in labour is looked after by other women closely related to her.

The story which follows of the black snake man and his wife the dove gives a lovely account of the birth of a child to two Dreaming heroes from Cape York. The name calling procedure and the presentation of the baby to the father is still practised in these areas.

The Black Snake Man and his Wife, the Dove

The black snake and his wife, the dove, once lived by the river. Each day they gathered bush honey from the trees, laid it on tea-tree bark and carried it back to camp to eat. Some days the dove collected yams as well and her husband speared fish. They would either eat all their food at night in the camp, or wrap some up in tea-tree bark and carry it with them as they walked along the river to their next camp. One day as they prepared to travel further, the dove woman said, 'I'll sit here and rest, my husband, the child inside me is weighing me down heavily and will soon be born.'

Her husband told her to stay in the camp, and said he would go away to hunt until the baby came.

Dove woman knelt there, sitting on her heels, and cried, 'Ei! Ei! It's taking a long time, such a long time to be born . . . Now at last It's coming! As the baby's head emerged she cushioned it with her hands, then she called out, 'Ung-a! Ung-a! Now It's really born. Now It's born!' and she drew the tiny baby from her. Then the dove woman held the cord and said: 'I am alone, so I must hold the cord and call names for my baby myself. Who else is there to call for me?' and she called out names, one after the other. As she called 'Yumitya', her husband's name, the afterbirth came away, and she knew this was to be her son's name also.

Dove woman was very tired after the labour and, resting her little son on a soft cushion of paperbark, she lay down beside him and slept.

A little while later, her husband the black snake came back and made a camp a short distance away from her. He sat down and, not looking in his wife's direction, said aloud, 'I wonder what the baby is.' Because of the taboo surrounding childbirth and the flow of blood at birth, the wife spoke aloud as if to herself, 'It's a man-child.' Gently she put the baby to her breast and suckled it. For five days she rested there until the heavy bleeding stopped. Each day the husband, who could not approach her, left yams a little way off but within her reach. Neither of the parents could eat fish at this time.

The next day she said aloud, 'I've finished with it,' meaning that the red blood had stopped and she was therefore able to find her own food. When the blood flow had ceased altogether, after about eight days, she said to her husband, 'I have recovered and will bring the baby to you.'

Dove woman then gathered yams and small fish and filled her dilly bags to the top; she put on a woven string girdle and covered her face with clay and her body with ashes. She rubbed her baby's skin with black charcoal, putting just a smear of white clay on his nose, and then cut off his dry umbilical cord to give to her husband. Gathering her newborn baby in her arms, she proudly carried him to his father.

Black snake sat at his camp, and seeing the mother and child approaching, held out his arms to take his new baby. Black snake sat and dove came and knelt before him, giving the baby to him. Black snake gazed down at his child for some time, then fastened his navel cord around his neck. The parents paused a little and together looked at their baby son. Then dove woman laid her yams and fish before her husband and picking up her dilly bag rubbed it across her baby's mouth saying, 'Don't cry too much.' Then she laid it on his stomach saying, 'Don't run after others for food, come to us, your parents, and we will always keep together.'

Then husband and wife were reunited again. The wife made a fire and there they slept with their new boy-child.[24]

175

THE EARLY YEARS

From its first days in the arms of its mother through the years of early childhood, a child learns the right way to behave through the stories of the Dreaming. He already has his own totem, his family and clan, and his own Dreaming country, but he must be loved and cared for, and taught the rules of everyday behaviour daily as he is not yet a man.

As soon as a child can walk, his grandfather or grandmother may then sing to him gently, songs of the land and its animals, rocks and trees, and of its waterholes with their fish, snakes and turtles. The child learns many lessons of daily life listening to cautionary tales from the Dreaming.

In the Kimberley area, the Wuduu or 'laying of hands' on infants ensures they will walk strongly, grow tall, and observe the laws of the people. They will be independent and respected members of the community.

By the campfires, in the early morning and at dusk, it is still a common sight today, as it was centuries ago, to see a grandmother or grandfather stretch her hands over the fire and gently touch the young child on various parts of the body, quietly and lovingly talking to it as she does so.

Sam Woolgoodja speaks to his daughter:

Don't take.
"Wuduu, Wuduu":
At the fire I touch you –
I hand you the strength of Wuduu,
Don't let yourself be turned.
Here on your ankle
Here on your knee
Here on your thigh,
Stay strong.
Don't let your forehead swell
(wait, wait)
Don't say the words of the men,
Don't go begging, granddaughter.

. . .
he showed us the Wuduu that we make
for the little boys and girls:
The men who know still touch them
So each day they learn to grow.

Her two thighs, her two legs, her fingers –
The words are put there
that the Wandjinas gave us.
They said to keep on
And until today these words have lived.
The Wuduu touching will not stop,
It is our strength[25].

Namaaraalee is highest, he made it all,
We must keep those ways he pointed out.
Now that I have told you
We are walking to the place his body was
cradled.
He is in the sky.
This half moon we will go to him.

Daisy Utemara, who is also from the Kimberleys, explains the significance of touching each part of the child:

Now, the children had their lessons every day. Early morning and in the evening their grandmother and their mother warmed their hands and touched their forehead, eyes, nose, mouth, hands, and right down to their feet, which meant Wuduu, the warming of hands. When they touched the forehead, that meant to give; and the nose, not to go around to another person's fire; eyes, not to see evil things and not to love up with any strangers; mouth, not to use bad language; hands, not to steal what doesn't belong to you; and the feet, not to trespass on other people's land. Now the father told the children about the wunun, which meant the sharing with other people. The father and mother and grandmother told them about sharing everything — the last thing you have you must give.[26]

David Mowaljarli's account of the Wuduu explains the different instructions given to boys and girls:

Before the sun rises and before eating food, they press the warmth of fire to the little child's eyes with these instructions: 'Don't concentrate your gaze on the things of others. Don't depart from your father's ways; don't neglect your brother and uncle; don't neglect your neighbour.

As soon as a child can walk, his grandfather or grandmother may sing to him gently, songs of the land and its animals. He learns the first steps of the traditional dances. *photo P. Tweedie*

'You were not just born for me, you were born for the whole neighbourhood. They rejoiced when you were born, oh, you are a real man born to us,' they tell you, and they press your hands.

You might like adulterous ways so they press your genitals, if you do your testes might grow large.

To her, the young girl, they say, as they press her breasts, 'Don't sway about and don't concentrate on men with your gaze.' Then they press her pubic area. They say to them, only recognize one in-law, then become married.

Trouble, and accidents, occur when a kangaroo has a spear put through his buttocks and the spear breaks off and sticks out unexpectedly. 'I hit him with a stick,' they say, suddenly the kangaroo jumps and the spear takes off from the kangaroo and we are pierced, we get bumped onto the ground. We die.

Then there is no neighbour about to help us in the bush. That's the accident that might happen. Don't neglect your neighbour.[27]

Stories told to children from the Dreaming may simply enrich and enhance their knowledge of their environment and the animals around them, explaining how all the creatures took on their present form, or they may serve to explain the right way to behave, the respect due to elders or the need to share food.

A large body of oral literature of stories told to children deals with the responsibility of adults to care for children, and the necessity therefore for children to follow the advice and instructions of their parents carefully and to play close to the camp. Most Aboriginal communities instil the fear of evil spirits or devils in their children at an early age. These spirits often lurk in dark wooded areas, in caves, or at waterholes. They most frequently roam around at night but wayward children can be seized at any time. Mrs Elkin Umbagai's story of the Agula, the evil spirit or devil who eats children in the Kimberleys, is one such story.

During ceremonies the children are close observers, often imitating the dancing of the adults in small groups of their own at the side of the clearing. *photo S. Doring*

How the Agula Swallowed the Two Boys

One day a man took these two little boys out hunting. He was their Gundi. They both went out with him, then at a certain place he told the boys to wait while he hunted. They were both playing and at the same time they were expecting the man, but instead of the man coming it was this Agula. The two tried to run away and hide but he soon got hold of one first and swallowed him and then the other one. Then he walked away. It was time for their boss to come back now. He called out to them but there was no answer. He said, 'This is the place where I left them both and they should be around.'

When he came closer he could see the tracks where the two boys tried to run away and hide. He looked carefully on the ground to see whose tracks they were. Then he saw these funny tracks on the ground and he knew it was the Agula. This man started to take a short cut. When he came to the place where he thought Agula had crossed he could see the footprints. This he did for quite a while. At last he got right ahead of this Agula. He came across the path where he thought the devil would pass. He looked for footprints but he couldn't see any so he thought he'd hide and wait there. He waited. First of all he heard parrots screeching, then he said, 'Well, he's on his way.'

Then he heard a cockatoo screeching. He then knew that the devil was coming closer. After the cockatoo, very close he could hear a rock pigeon flutter. Then he hooked his spear with his spear-thrower. The devil came by closer. The man waited till he passed just a few yards away. Then he speared him through the head, then again he put another one into him. He didn't want to spear the body, he knew the two boys were in there. When the devil had fallen down the man cut the Agula open with a stone. He knocked out pieces from the rocks and cut him open with that. He took one of the boys out first. He found a nest of ants. Then he took the other boy out and put him on the same nest of ants, then those ants started nibbling at the

178

boys. When they felt the pricks from the ants they started wriggling. The man watched. The more they wriggled the more ants got on them and bit them. At last both opened their eyes and they saw their own friend, the boss. Then he asked them what had happened. They didn't know. All they knew, the Agula came towards them and he had swallowed them both. He then showed the boys this Agula. The two boys threw stones at the devil all day. When he took them out of the devil's tummy he rolled them both in the sand before he put them on the ants' nest. When they were awakened by the ants he made a fire, broke down bushes, green leaves, then smoked them both. They would have had a shock. They left the body of the devil there and he took the boys back to the camp where they were camping at the time, and they went and told the parents of the boys that they were swallowed by this Agula. It happened while the man was out hunting and they were both left at a certain place to wait for him. Since then they didn't leave children alone in the bush without adults. A group of men went back to have a look at the body of Agula. Not there, disappeared, that's how they knew he wasn't an ordinary man.[28]

A similar story told by the Kulin in Victoria contains a dual moral to both parents and children:

The Old Woman who Stole Children

Not far from where Mansfield now is, there lived a hideous old hag, all alone in the bush. She was wicked, and used to find and keep little boys and girls who wandered away from the camps.

In one of the Kulin camps some distance away from her there was a very nice little boy, so nice that he was everyone's favourite. Since everyone liked him, he thought he would be safe anywhere, so he went from one camp to the other all by himself. When he got there people would welcome him and give him pieces of

From its first days in the arms of its mother through the years of early childhood, a child learns the right way to behave through the stories of the Dreaming. *photo P. Tweedie*

possum to eat. But one day he disappeared, and no one knew where he was, until they remembered the wicked old woman who was always taking children. But she would not give him back, as she had hidden him underground.

In their distress, the Kulin went to Bunjil, the All-Father, and asked him to restore the little boy to them.

Bunjil was very sorry for them, and told Kowurn, the spiny ant-eater to go and find him. So Kowurn burrowed down under the old witch's camp and found the boy, who was not hurt but very frightened.

And Bunjil said to the Kulin, 'You must not let little children wander away from the camps.' And then he told the child, 'Let that be a lesson to you,' and he went back to his own camp which is in the sky.[29]

Every Aboriginal tribe has many such simple stories which are told at night around the campfire or at other times when they see a bird or animal which reminds them of a tale from the Dreaming. Most stories contain references to many facets of life woven into one simple narrative. The following children's story is told by the Wogait people, or 'Sand beach people' of western Arnhem Land and tells the fascinating story of the sea-mammal or dugong when she lived as a woman. Dugong have fascinated mankind since the earliest times, many researchers being convinced that the female dugong, which has breasts and suckles its young and which also carries its young on its back, gave rise to the early European sailors' legends of mermaids. To the Wogait people, however, the dugong is a woman, Mamanduru, a jealous woman who once stole the beautiful baby belonging to her friend, Moodja.

The following story warns against jealousy and deceit and incidentally teaches the young girls how children are conceived by their mothers when they wander near the 'baby-shades', the spirit centres of children.

The Dugong Woman Steals a Baby

A long time ago, two very good friends, one called Mamanduru and the other Moodja, were out gathering cockles on the mud-flats at a place called Dartpur, which is the Frog-dreaming stone a little out to sea from a well of fresh water on a mangrove and sandy beach called Binbinya.

Each one had a little baby which she carried on a clean sheet of paperbark under her arm, as the hunting women carry their bark dishes when out gathering yam and lily-bulbs.

Outwardly the two women seemed to be happy as they went their way, laughing and chanting the tribal songs, but that Mamanduru was very jealous of her friend Moodja. Moodja's baby was so pretty that everybody in the camp would come over to tickle it and to see it smile, but Mamanduru's baby was as ugly as old frogmouth the bird who sits all day on a tree.

Mamanduru and Moodja put their sleeping children under a nice shady hibiscus tree and when it was low tide they went out to gather cockles.

Mamanduru said to her friend: 'I've got plenty of cockles now; I'll go to the shady tree near the well to cook them ready for you to eat with that honey we cut from the tree . . .' But that rubbish one Mamanduru lied to her friend; she had only a little tucker in her bark carrying dish. All she did was to go back and steal that pretty little baby of Moodja's and go off into the bush.

Well! That Moodja woman came out of the mud flat with plenty of cockles and that poor thing cried and wept when she found out that her pretty baby had been stolen and the ugly one left behind in its place.

Moodja had a hard time following Mamanduru's tracks, she would constantly double back on her tracks and walk on stone and in water to cover up her foot tracks. She was a very cunning woman. But the mother kept going and at last found Mamanduru and her baby in a big clump of pandanus trees beside a big saltwater beach.

The two women then fought hard with fighting sticks. Mamanduru said that the pretty baby was hers, and Moodja got very angry and threw that poor ugly thing into a big pandanus tree, and straight away it changed into the mother of all the frogs that lives in prickly leaves.

180

Young children gradually learn the intricacies of traditional symbols as they watch their father Bulun Bulun depicting the stories of their clan Ancestors and their clan country. *photo P. Tweedie*

That baby frog made plenty other frogs in that tree, and these are friends of all the baby shades that belong to us black people. All together they sit down in pandanus trees and wait for a mother to go by, then they jump at them and go inside that mother's belly and when born they are proper children.

Well those two women fought with their wooden fighting sticks and that poor Moodja got hit on her knees with a stick and as the stick hit, her legs broke and she hopped off into the jungle like a wallaby, but before she changed into a wallaby she gave that Mamanduru a proper good beating with a fire stick that she picked up from the fire that Mamanduru was using to cook her cockles. That fire stick was covered in ashes and these went into Mamanduru's eyes so she ran blind-eyed into the salt water with Moodja's baby on her back. After that time wallabies keep in the scrub, dugong live in the sea, and frogs cry, cry, at night in trees. Dugong and wallaby give us tucker and frogs give us babies.

Wogait, western Arnhem Land[30]

The following two stories reflect on the punishments which still befall parents or grandparents if they harm the children in their care in any way. In the first story, told by Mrs Elkin Umbagai, the children were killed for foolishly making fun of their father. This was much too severe a punishment and as a consequence the mothers took revenge.

In the second story, from Cape York, northern Queensland, a wicked grandfather eats his grandchildren when the mothers are out gathering food. His punishment is harsh but just.

The Two Boys and Their Father

The two mothers went off and left the two children with their father. They made a bough shed and it was a fairly big one, and their father was making spear points.

Every time he chopped off a piece to make the edges it would go 'tick'. As he made a noise they'd say to their father, 'You are letting out the wind.' Every time he chipped off a piece they'd both say those words.

Dad didn't want to hear any more of this so he got his stick and hit them across the necks with it and killed them both, and he got paperbark and covered the bodies. He went on with his spear heads till finished, then rested. His two wives came back. They had little possums for the two children to play with. They wondered what had happened to the children because they didn't run to meet their two mothers. When they came to camp they asked the father. He said, 'Just look under the paperbark.'

So the two mothers lifted the paperbark and tried to wake them up, but the children didn't wake up and the mothers knew they were dead. They asked their husband what had happened. He said: 'Those children were making fun of me. You didn't teach them enough, how to behave.'

So they made a big fire and they roasted their yams and other roots, cooked up their meat — possums, bandicoots and goannas and snakes. They made sure he had a good meal. After having his tea he lay down. The two women made another fire, and while they were waiting for the second fire to settle down they both went and buried the two children.

The man was closing his eyes when the two women came back after burying the children. They both said, 'We will kill the man too.'

They got two flat sticks like boards and while the husband was lying down with his eyes closed the two women collected a lot of hot ashes with these flat boards and got the ashes and threw them over his face. He jumped around and cried with pain. They put more on all over his face, and they put more all over him until he died. Then they both ran off to their own people.

Elkin Umbagai, Mowanjum[31]

Left and below: Childhood is a time of games and joy, of exploration and discovery, as well as learning the right way to behave. *photos P. Tweedie*

The Wicked Father

Long, long ago before the coming of the white man, Nargeearr the Rainbow lived in his little Mijjaa, a few miles away from Dallachy Creek. He lived with his two daughters and two little grandsons. They were very happy for many years until Nargeearr became old and feeble and could go hunting no more. He depended on his two daughters to feed him, and as game grew scarce after one very dry season, they had to go further and further afield in search of food.

One day the little boys told their mothers that they were tired of walking and would stay at home that day with their grandfather. The sisters set off for Dallachy Creek, Dool urah, in the hope of finding some fish. It took them two days to find enough for the whole family, so on the second night they trudged wearily home with their burden, anticipating with joy the reunion with their little sons.

As the sisters approached the camp, they noticed that all was quiet and their boys were not to be seen. Their father lay asleep in a corner of the Mijjaa, and they woke him quickly and asked about the children. For a long time the father refused to speak, but at last the dreadful truth was told. The father had become desperately hungry and, thinking some accident had befallen his daughters, had killed and eaten the two infants.

The two sisters went away, distraught with grief. A great hatred welled up in their hearts and they began to plan his death. They waited until the sun was going down and crept up to the little grass Mijjaa. When they heard the sound of snoring coming from inside the humpy, Elder Sister took her fire stick and twirled it until the smoke curled up in the evening air. Then she set the dwelling on fire and she and Younger Sister ran away as fast as they could. When they looked back over their shoulders, they saw that their father had turned into a ball of fire which flew into the sky in a great arc. It rolled across the sky until it reached Gould Island, and then sank into the ocean, where they saw it no more.

Whenever we see the rainbow, we are reminded of the great punishment to the wicked father.[32]

PASSAGE TO ADULTHOOD

As the children grow stronger they must take a more active and responsible role daily in gathering food and providing for the family. Young girls learn to make their own woven string and twined pandanus carrying bags and young boys make spears for themselves, practising their aim on small animals. Miniature didjeridus with small mouth pieces are also made for the young boys so that they can start to learn the complex pattern of circular breathing required in order to master the rhythmic drone of the instrument. During ceremonies the children are close observers, often imitating the dancing of the adults in small groups of their own at the side of the clearing. The children in some Aboriginal desert groups also have their own play ceremonies which they hold away from the camp.

The Pitjantjatjara children or Tjitji have their own ceremonies today, held in the sandy scrub outside the small settlements. At these they dance, mime and sing some of the stories which particularly catch their imagination. One of these, Alkuwari and the Mamus (devils), is a favourite.

Alkuwari and the Mamus

A young boy called Windaru went hunting in the bush. When he returned home, however, his old grandmother Alkuwari sent him off from the camp, refusing him entrance. Young Windaru, in spite, set fire to her camp and killed her husband Karbama.

Now Alkuwari was a friend of the Mamus, the evil-spirit devils who lived far away in the north-west, and she called on them to avenge the death of her husband.

The Mamus appeared. They whined with a high-pitched nasal sound, and constantly giggled as if mad. The terrifying Mamus chased Windaru until, coming to a huge tree which reached from the land to the sky, he climbed it and hid on the constellation Orion. The Mamus also climbed up into the sky, but Windaru pushed their ladder down and the Mamus fell to earth and died instantly.

Pitjantjatjara, central Australia[33]

At puberty, childhood is over. Girls must take on the role of women in preparation for marriage. *photo S. Doring*

The Pitjantjatjara treasure their ceremonial life and encourage the children to perform play ceremonies. Since the children were babies at their mothers' breasts dozing during the nocturnal ceremonies, they have absorbed the sacred atmosphere of ceremonial life, and they bring this sense of ritual and importance to their own play. The children act out this myth of Alkuwari, some boys acting as singers. The girls sit perhaps a metre (yard) behind the boys and join in the rhythmic thumping of their thighs during the singing. Some actors participate as Mamus, blurting Mamu sounds and giggling in a high-pitched voice, improvising a variety of absurd movements. Stories of the Tjukurpa or Dreaming time which concern the antics of children and the events which took place as a result of some misdemeanour are favourites of young boys and girls.

As the children approach the age of puberty a more serious element is introduced into their training. The boys are approaching their time for manhood ceremonies and soon the girls begin to menstruate and their childhood is over. They will then be considered women, and in many tribes will go to their promised husband to take on the responsibilities of being a wife. Mrs Elkin Umbagai of Mowanjum tells the story of training a young boy before his initiation.

Training for Manhood

Often when a lad was at the age of twelve, his parents would send him along to his teachers. His teacher would be an elderly man and a bachelor, with whom the lad could live.

Each day he would go out to hunt with his teacher and to learn how to track and stalk. He would be asked to look up into the trees to find the honey bees' nest. When the honey bee hive was found, the boy had to climb up the tree and chop the branch down. As he climbed, he'd cut the trunk of the tree to make steps to guide him up.

When stalking, the lad would stand still and watch his teacher carefully as he aimed at the kangaroo, then speared it. After the kangaroo had been speared it would hop away, but almost ready to fall from the wound of the spear. The teacher would then ask the lad to do exactly the same as he did, to kill the wounded kangaroo while the animal rested. The lad then would spear it, which killed it this time. He then ran towards the fallen animal with a stick and beat it on the head to make sure it was dead.

The teacher showed him how to take its insides out and to get a small stick with a special point at one end, where they sharpened it, and poke the stick into the wound to close it up with a bit of its intestine which they tie round and round the stick. It was ready then to carry back to camp. The lad had to dig the hole in which the kangaroo had to be roasted. A big fire was made beside the hole.

At first the kangaroo was thrown onto the flaming fire to singe the hair off, then the feet were cut off, also the tail. When the fire died down, the kangaroo was put into the hole with hot ashes in it, then covered over with the rest of the hot coals.

While waiting for the kangaroo to cook, the teacher would tell the lad always to walk or stand in the direction the wind blew. He would tell him the names of all the trees, animals, birds, reptiles, flowers, grass, rocks and stones. He taught the lad all about nature. The rising and falling of the tides and of the four different seasons. He learnt his relationship to Mother Nature.

As the lad grows older, he is told about the initiation which will soon take place and how the lad must behave during the ceremony. He is told not to eat liver, the reason being that when the lad is being initiated, he will lose a lot of blood, and only after the initiation is over is he able to eat liver.

He is taught that the stars, birds and animals are his faithful friends and that he will always be guided by them. Throughout his lifetime, he keeps on studying about Mother Earth and Mother Nature.

Elkin Umbagai, Mowanjum[34]

Every boy must pass through initiation ceremonies which are at the heart of the ritual life of the tribe. A boy leaves his mother as a child and returns to camp a man. But as well as their function of making men of the tribe, these ceremonies, by recreating events of the Dreaming and carrying out the instructions of the totemic ancestors, link the present with the past and so recreate the eternal Dreaming. Ceremonies recreate the beginnings of Aboriginal society and explain its laws and customs. Initiates are instructed carefully in all aspects of the sacred Law and begin to understand the deeper significance of traditional beliefs and Law.

Jack Mirritji from Maningrida recalls here his own initiation.

Making a Young Man

When I was about fourteen years old, my father's youngest brother, at that time my second father, talked with several older people to arrange my initiation, a ceremony in which an Aboriginal boy is made a young man. He told the older men: 'Mirritji is old enough and it is time to teach him the way and beliefs of his father and his grandfather. He must learn by now about the important things of the Dreamtime so that he will start to know.'

And the older men agreed with my father's younger brother and they asked him what kind of Bunggul (ceremony) he would like for my initiation. He told them that he would like the Marndayala or dog dance and he discussed that with some other people who wanted to initiate two other young men as well. Everybody agreed with the Marndayala ceremony because in this Bunggul all people concerned could take part in it, no matter what their Dreaming was.

All these arrangements were made in a secret language and I couldn't understand it. I didn't understand either why so many people were coming to the camp and why they were all singing. They sang dead songs while the little kids were playing around. The two other boys and I were sitting at some distance from them.

Suddenly three men started to run in our direction. At the same time they threw spears in our direction just over our heads, and all kids were very frightened; we too

Ceremonies re-create the beginnings of Aboriginal society and
explain its laws and customs. *photo P. Tweedie*

of course. We did not know what was going to happen to us and we thought that the
three men were going to kill us. We started running too, in front of them, but finally
they caught us not far from the camp where all the other people sat down. When
they got us they said: 'We are not going to kill you, but we are going to make you
young men, so that you will become a man out of Aboriginal knowledge.'

But we were still very afraid because at that moment we didn't understand what
they were talking about. Besides we saw our parents crying and that made it all
worse. We started crying too.

The three men told us that from now on we were not allowed any more to talk or
to cry. We had to keep our mouths closed because from now on we just had to listen
to all the things the older people would teach us. And they told us a lot of things
about our Mardayin, our old time Law, things we didn't know before.

Then the men gave us dilly bags, very important ones, to wear around our necks
during the moments when they made us young men. Our heads were painted with
white clay (gamununggu), the symbol of mourning, because boys were about to die,
and men to be born.

The men brought us back to camp and we saw people making a big ring on the
ground. People with clapsticks were singing, while another man was playing the
didjeridu. We sat down and people dressed us up with armbands and pendants
around our necks, and nagas (loincloths), and belts of human hair painted black
and red. Then they painted our bodies all over and they told us not to talk to
anybody.

All people started dancing and this dancing and singing went on for the whole
night. When the sun brought her light back again the circumcision took place.

The two other young boys were made young men with razor blades, but I, as the
third one, was done with the blade of a stone spear. This was because the razor blade
was, after using twice, not sharp enough any more, but the blade of the stone spear
wasn't very sharp either. The other two boys had a much easier operation; it didn't

hurt them as much as in my case. We all lost some blood, which was running over our body. The women cried and yelled, making a sound like a black train.

During the operation the men put the very important dilly bags in our mouths, to prevent us from crying and shouting out while the operation was going on. If the women, who were dancing around the place where the ceremony took place, would hear us crying and yelling out, it would be a very bad thing. Also the man who was doing the circumcision would probably slip with his blade when we were moving and crying.

When everything was finished, we all had forgotten the pain and now we were very proud to be young men.

Afterwards the men who were involved in our young men business took us to the places where the old people sat down under the cool shade of some trees. They kept us teaching. They showed us how to use a little short bamboo pipe to drink water with until the wounds of the operation were healed. Till then it was not allowed to touch water with our hands.

The older people were a little unhappy that we had been initiated, because now we were allowed to have women, and they had to give us a promised wife.

Jack Mirritji, Maningrida[35]

David Mowaljarli describes the first dances of the pelicans and ducks of the Dreaming or in his language, Woungood times. Then there was no Law, no system of promising wives, no order in society. So the pelicans and ducks created a ceremony; they painted themselves beautifully and created many dances and songs.

The Pelicans and the Ducks

Nerrima has many swamps where they had their big dancing grounds; it is also a sacred place. There the pelicans painted themselves in black and white ochre and the ducks were painted in brown and yellow, and they sang all the sacred songs. Both the pelicans and the ducks knew they were beautiful as they sang and danced differently — going towards each other, running and leaping high as if they were going to fly again. They were so happy after creating sacred objects and songs.

They then passed it on to the new world, where the people of today now follow it. They shared and offered everything, and promises were made, and these people began their history.

After all this they went down to the lake and dipped in the water. And all became birds that could fly. That's how they got their feathers — from this clay paint.

For generation after generation different Laws were made for the people — they shared everything together and made promises to young girls for young and old men — for the days to come and the generations to follow on. To keep the Laws of their forefathers was one of the most important Laws.

The Aboriginal people began to make their own history after they went down to the sacred lake and placed their heads in the water and became birds such as the pelican or the duck, with feathers and the paint which is like a dye and cannot be rubbed off.

From the generations that followed, till today, the Aboriginal people held and still hold sacred ceremonies for the young boys as they become men, and carry on many other things.

The feathers of the birds are known to have been clay, as the Aboriginal people believed, and as is very true. To the Aboriginal people the birds are sacred, because they believe that the birds, such as the pelican and duck, made a history in the old times between themselves and the Aboriginal people.

David Mowaljarli, Mowanjum[36]

Initiation ceremonies are still carried out today in the central and western desert areas and in Arnhem Land. Boys are made men in ancient ceremonies practised for thousands of years throughout Australia. In the south-eastern areas, although traditions have faded, the sacred Bora grounds where Baiame taught the Kamilaroi and other tribes how to carry out the initiation Laws still remain. They remind us that although many tribes may have vanished, their spirits live on and the great

Opposite: Young men practise the rhythmic drone of the didjeridu on the banks of a billabong in Arnhem Land. *photo P. Tweedie*

spirit Baiame remains watching over his sacred areas, just as he did at the Bora ceremonies. At those great gatherings, a gigantic figure of Baiame was made with logs and soil, and a small figure was made some distance away to represent his wife. Initiates were led into the circular Bora ground and along a predetermined path to the next circular mound. The whirring voice of Dhurramulan roared through the trees and struck fear into the young boys' hearts as they faced their ordeal.

Although the Bora ceremonies marking the initiation of young boys are no longer practised in the south, in the northern areas they are kept alive by the old men. They tell us that these ceremonies must be continued or the sacred Law will not survive. The secrets will not be passed on to the uninitiated.

David Mowaljarli adds this message to his story of the pelicans and the ducks:

Through the generations that followed the initiation of young boys was carried out by the Aboriginal people — until nowadays and until forever. It will be the most sacred and valuable thing that ever happened to them — for always. For the young man of today it is a proud thing to say, 'I have been made a man and have been through the Law,' and to be the man of today and the man of the future as well as the past.

HUNTING AND FOOD GATHERING

As hunters and gatherers of food, Aboriginal communities have a great respect for the earth and its creatures and plants which provide them with sustenance. There are essential rules of behaviour in respect of hunting and gathering which ensure that the supply of food will not diminish from season to season, and that all members of the group will receive adequate nourishment. Violation of a totem animal may cause illness or death. Greed and selfishness are considered serious crimes and are severely punished.

In times of extreme hardship, also, cannibalism was known in Australia, but stories such as the following from Victoria acted as forceful deterrents.

The Cannibal Woman

There was an old woman who lived with two ferocious dogs in the mountain country. Her camp was near the track used by messengers going from one tribe to another. When a messenger appeared, she would offer him food and drink, and suggest that he camp there for the night. This offer was generally accepted, because the track was a difficult one, and the messengers were glad of good food. However, as soon as they were asleep her two dogs would set upon them and kill them.

When several men approached together she would keep the dogs quiet, and by her manner no one would suspect that she was a cannibal, which was the reason for the killings. She would cut the bodies up and cook them in the ordinary blackfellow oven.

At last two men were appointed by the tribes to solve the mystery of the missing messengers. They started off on the usual track, and before long saw the smoke of the old woman's fire. Soon they came upon her camp, and were well received. She asked them to camp there for the night, and gave them plenty to eat. They made their shelter ready, and arranged their rugs over logs to resemble sleeping men. They then hid and waited. Presently the old woman emerged with the two dogs, which she set on what she thought were the sleeping men. The men promptly speared the two dogs, and, now being sure of their facts, they speared the old woman also.[37]

This story is strongly reminiscent of the great legend of the cannibal woman of the Centre and her 400 dogs told in Chapter 5. The legend also extends to the Gulf of Carpentaria where the old woman Eelgin with the aid of her giant devil-dingo preyed upon her fellow man.[38] In all the myths the penalty for such violent anti-social behaviour was death.

WATER LILIES

Green, purple flowers
Hanging over the lily pads
Shining in the sunlight
Moving back back and fro,
Touching the water moving
roughly along the river.
Fish moving among the lily pads
Go up and down.
Lily roots stuck in the

Hard dark mud.
Waiting for somebody
To get them.
They are big round
Roots;
Like peanuts
Growing everywhere
In the deep
Rough river

Filled with the
Green smell of the
lily pads
and flowers.

Joyce Yikawidi
Courtesy Dhupuma College
photo P. Tweedie

The Totemic Ancestors instructed men in every aspect of daily life and by their actions showed the technique of hunting, of gathering seeds, fruit and roots and of preparing it and dividing it between the members of the community.

The Euro Brothers

The Euro Brother Ancestors of central Australia invented both the spear and the spear-thrower and are also responsible for the introduction of fire to the Bird Ancestors. The Bird men, Ntjirenkua, ate their food raw before the Euro Brothers taught them how to cook it.

Long ago in Creation times the Euro Brothers met the Bird men as they were hunting game. The Bird men were spearing their quarry with fragile sticks made from a small bush and bringing it back to camp raw. The Euro Brothers made long spears and strong spear-throwers from hardwood and gave these to the Bird men. They also taught them how to prepare a fire and cook the game in the hot coals. Then they showed the Bird men how to take the meat from the fire, place it on leaves and divide it into the appropriate portions, giving each man his share according to his status.

Aranda, central Australia[39]

191

HUNTING KANGAROOS

In the remote areas of western Arnhem Land dwell the mischievous 'Mimi' spirits. Although not great Creation beings, these small creatures are believed to have lived in this country before the Aboriginals and numerous ancient rock paintings testify to their extraordinary hunting abilities. They carry a range of weapons and can accurately spear a kangaroo from far away. It is thought that the Mimi taught the Aboriginal hunters their own skills, and this is the reason for their exceptional skill at hunting kangaroos today.

Stalking and killing a kangaroo or wallaby with spear and spear-thrower was an exercise in stealth, strength and precision as well as intelligence. All environmental factors had to be considered but particularly the direction of the wind. When a gentle breeze was blowing, the hunter walked into the face of the breeze so that his scent was blown behind him. The rustle of leaves and branches also disguised the sound of his bare feet on the ground should he accidentally tread on a twig or make a noise which would alarm his prey. One spear was held ready in the spear-thrower while replacements were carried in the other hand. If two men were hunting together and a kangaroo was sighted, one man would circle around the animal distracting its attention while the hunter advanced stealthily to within range, making use of all available camouflage as he went. One second he would be behind a tree, the next an anthill, then poised motionless he would merge with his surroundings. Standing completely still, legs apart, he would take aim and suddenly hurl the spear with enormous force into the body of the animal.

The kangaroo was carried by throwing it over the shoulder and holding it by the legs. Once back at camp the body was thrown down. The internal organs were often removed out in the bush, and before cooking its hind legs and forelegs were bent or broken and sometimes bound to its body. The animal was thrown unskinned onto

Below: Whilst gathering food for the family, women find a file snake, a favourite plaything before it reaches the campfire. *photo P. Tweedie*

Opposite: Both bush food and pandanus for weaving are gathered in handwoven dilly bags. *photo P. Tweedie*

the fire. Hot coals might be placed inside its belly to help cook the meat through. In the northern areas, an oven of coals may have been made to cover the animal. A paperbark and earthen mound over the coals would ensure that the meat was well cooked.

The meat was divided up into predetermined sections and each was given to particular members of the family according to custom and tradition. The old men received the softest and tastiest meat in deference to their status in the community.

One thing the hunter tried to avoid and dreaded he may accidentally do was to injure either his own totem or the totem of one of his close family members. There is a wealth of evidence in stories and mythology to alert him to the dangers of such a misadventure and the unhappy consequences.

The following story is told by Jack Mirritji of a kangaroo hunt he went on with his brother when still a young boy. The story explains how a young boy learns the technique of hunting, but ends with disaster and a lesson he was never to forget.

The Death of My Father

One day my brother Barayuwa and I went out hunting early in the morning round the hillside. Nearby there were cliffs and hills and springs running onto the flat valley. We stopped and painted our bodies with wet sand to make us look like the brown antbed, so the kangaroos could not see us as a black man, or smell us, or see the spears and run away from them.

So we followed the cliffs and hills, the springs and the flat valley. We walked to the side of the mountain, looked around the countryside and brother Barayuwa saw a big brown rock kangaroo (called in Jinang, Gandayala), lying down behind a tall shady gum tree in some long grass.

I did not see the kangaroo because I was only a small boy, about fourteen years old. My brother Barayuwa was much older than me. He was a big man who had seen about twenty-five Wet Seasons. He told me the kangaroo was there, and he said, 'Stop! The kangaroo is there, and you had better put your head down and bend your back low and follow behind me.'

We crouched down and crept up very quietly and slowly — left leg forward one step, right leg in the air, looking for a place on the ground that will make no noise. Barayuwa's right foot touched the ground and stopped.

He took his hooked woomera, and brushed the flies away because they could take his smell to the kangaroo who would run away from it. He said, with his hand, 'You had better stop. Devil-devil spirits make the kangaroo stand still. Do not frighten him because I am very close to him, and I want to kill him for my food.'

My brother Barayuwa turned round to me and he said with his right hand (the same hand which made the kangaroo stay still), 'You have to sit down very quietly and do not make any rattles.'

He took three steps and then he was behind a big shady tree. With his tongue he licked the point of the shovel-nosed spear. He pointed the spear towards the kanagaroo, and then threw it as hard as he could, to send it flying into the side of the kangaroo.

The kangaroo jumped up and down, and was fighting with my brother. He came running towards me and said, 'Now Mirritji, your turn to run after the kangaroo and kill him.'

While they were still fighting together, I ran after it and threw my little shovel-nosed spear at the back of the kangaroo. I hit it and it dropped down onto the ground.

Barayuwa jumped out of the way from the kangaroo and stood still, looking at me with a wild face. I was very happy and was running towards him saying, 'Brother, you are a good shot. Now we've got him — we've got that kangaroo.'

He said to me, 'You just missed me, you little rat. Fancy throwing a shovel-nosed spear like that! You're lucky I'm your elder brother. If you threw a spear at another man, he would throw it back at you. You dumb fool, you have a brain like a stone axe.' And I could not answer him. I just stood still and scratched my head. Barayuwa went to get a big stick to hit the kangaroo on the back of the neck and kill him.

Barayuwa gave me all the gear and the tools — two woomeras, two dilly bags, two fire sticks, one stone axe, one stone file, and five shovel-nosed spears — to carry, while he took the kangaroo down to the river to cook it.

While Barayuwa was walking through the bush on the scrublands carrying the heavy kangaroo, I asked him what the name of this kangaroo was. 'Was this one called Ngarrku, the plain wallaby?' I said to him, 'Wawa (brother), what is the name of this kangaroo?' He said to me that this was not Ngarrku the plain wallaby, this was Gandayala, the brown rock hill kangaroo. This was our mother's and our uncle's Dreaming totem.

I asked him again, 'Jaba (elder brother), if this is our mother's and uncle's Dreamtime totem, they might be dead now at the camp because we have killed this Gandayala.' Then Barayuwa got angry and said to me, 'Mirritji, I'm getting tired of you talking to me so much while I'm carrying this heavy kangaroo. You better shut up and let me go on.' Then I stopped talking and we walked quietly down to the river to cook the kangaroo.

When we arrived at the river, Barayuwa put the kangaroo on the ground and had a rest, after walking and carrying the heavy kangaroo so far. I gathered pine wood for the fire. First I made a pine wood platform fire, and put on it some small stones and some antbed. The kangaroo would cook much more quickly with the heat of the stones and antbed. While I gathered wood, Barayuwa rubbed the fire sticks together to light the fire under the pine wood platform, and it was soon burning the pine wood.

First we broke the two back legs of the kangaroo and pulled out the tendons to tie the legs together. Then we threw it on the platform fire to burn all the hair off the skin. Afterwards we put it on some leaves and grass so that the meat would not get in the sand. Then we cut open the belly and took out the heart and the liver. We threw the heart and the liver on the fire first so that we could eat them while the rest of the kangaroo was cooking. Then we dug a pit, put the hot ashes in it, and threw

The resources of the environment are adapted to provide all of life's needs, including bark from a tree to make a carrying dish. *photo R. Edwards*

To lighten the load, and to discard waste, the kangaroo
is cleaned before being carried home. *photo J. Isaacs*

the kangaroo on top. We opened the belly and put in some hot stones and antbed,
then covered the whole lot with paperbark and sand to keep the heat of the ashes
inside.

When the smoke started to come out all round and we could feel the heat with
our hands on top of the sand, the kangaroo was ready to eat. We removed the sand
and quickly ripped off the hot paperbark. Then I stood at one end and Barayuwa at
the other and we each took two legs and quickly lifted the kangaroo out of the pit. It
was then ready to eat.

When the sun was going down we left the river to go back to camp. It was dark
and I was frightened of the noises of the owls and the devil-birds who were talking
to us from the bush as I walked along behind Barayuwa.

My mother and father were not in the camp. Only our old grandmother and our
younger brothers and sisters were there. Meji (grandmother) cried when she saw us
with the kangaroo, because she knew that we were big enough to hunt for ourselves
like the grown-up people, and she was happy about that.

When she stopped crying, she told a lie. She told us that our mother and father
had gone to Milingimbi to exchange some of our mats, bags, net dilly bags, hooks,
spears, woomeras, boomerangs, bamboos, fire sticks, stone axes, ochres, digging
sticks and bark paintings for sugar, rice, tea, tobacco, jam, potatoes and flour. They
didn't know what money was, and they wanted to buy only good things.

Barayuwa told grandmother and all the kids to get the kangaroo that was
hanging in the tree. Grannie went to pick it up, but all the kids were not very happy
like they had been at other times when we had brought home a kangaroo. They just
sat there and stared at us with sadness in their eyes and worrying hearts for our
father. Barayuwa asked what was wrong with all the kids.

We thought that Grannie was telling us a lie about our father and mother going
to Milingimbi. Then one of the kids came and said that our father had passed away

late that evening, when we had been only a mile or so from the camp. Father had gone to lie asleep beneath the Gurrugurru, the wooden bush shelter, where he died.

Jack Mirritji, Maningrida[40]

The women, as well as the men, follow the pattern of the Ancestral Spirits as they gather the foods available in their environment. An unusual example of this occurred on Groote Eylandt, off the east coast of Arnhem Land, where long ago there once lived a group of Spirit Women called the Wuradilagu. These women lived together amongst the trees and were seldom seen as they covered themselves with paperbark whenever there was a possibility of being observed. The Wuradilagu women set the pattern for the life of the Groote Eylandt women until relatively recent times and early visitors to the island seldom saw evidence of the women but heard their singing and soft calls in the bush. Under cover of darkness the women would meet their husbands or lovers, but in daylight they covered their heads with paperbark if they were forced to come into the open to collect food or water.[41]

BUSH FOOD

Aboriginal people over the centuries learnt to adapt to the changes in climate and vegetation of the Australian continent and to obtain a rich, varied and nutritious supply of food from their environment.

The daily life of hunting and preparing food, bringing it back at dusk and excitedly gathering round to share in the meal, the rest afterwards followed by soft

One of the favourite foods of the Arnhem Land people is the beautiful purple water lily. When the flower dies it forms a dense knob of seeds which the women grind between stones, form into a dough and bake in the ashes of the fire. The flower itself, its stalk and its bulb are all eaten. The long stems stretch from the mud on the bed of the billabong to the surface of the water and these taste a little like celery. The water lily bulbs are gathered after the flowers have died; they lie undetected in the rich mud, and groups of women search for them as prized delicacies. In muddy water the women feel with their toes in the soft mud until they find them, but in clear billabongs on hot days they prefer to dive in and feel with their hands. These highly nutritious chestnut-like vegetables are then roasted in the fire. *photo P. Tweedie*

The bush of Arnhem Land provides a variety of fruits and
berries for Aboriginal families. *photo P. Tweedie*

chatter until sleep came under the stars; the sounds of the bush and the love of
tribal land: these are remembered with regret and longing by many Aboriginal
people throughout Australia, as they speak of the traditional life of their youth.

Jack Mirritji describes below his early years of hunting and gathering food in
central Arnhem Land.

In this story, I'd like to tell something about the good food we take from the bush.

Aboriginal people in Arnhem Land eat a fruit called Gampila. It grows on a
creeper. The fruit is dark blue and its stem and leaves are light green. The fruit
tastes like wine. The honey bee collects the nectar from the flower of this plant. It
takes it to its hives among the rocks or in a tree, either in the tree tops, at its roots, or
at the end of a broken branch. The honey formed from the nectar of the Gampila
flower tastes like syrup.

Another good food found in these hives consists of the eggs of the honey bee.
Though the honey bees sting people who break into their hives, the stings are
usually not painful enough to drive the people away. In order to find the hives of
the honey bee, Aboriginal people use the following methods: they cut a hole in the
bark of a particular tree whose freshly cut wood attracts the honey bees. When the
bees come, the people attach the 'cord' of a spider's web to the tail of the bee. When
the bee is released the white 'cord' is easy to see, and the bee can be followed to its
hive. The men bring their dilly bags to fill with the food from the hives. They use a
stone axe to cut into the beehive. These stone axes are not easy to use.

For many years Aboriginals have been using brown antbeds for food. The
brown ants build their nests against trees. They make them about four feet high.
When Aboriginal women are looking for food, they can easily find these antbeds
anywhere on the mainland and often they find an anteater at the same time. The
women collect pieces of the antbed and take these home to their families. The

198

antbeds taste like the meat of the coconut. The anteater and the pieces of the antbed are eaten together in the same way as fish and chips are eaten.

White clay can also be eaten, as well as being used for painting. This white clay is mainly found in wet ground, but sometimes it can be found in dry soil. When eaten, white clay tastes similar to dry milk powder, and like milk powder it can be mixed with water. Then it is used for painting. People of the North Australian centres still eat white clay just as people of the olden times did.

The mangrove tree worm can also be eaten. This worm is about a foot long and about half an inch wide. It has a blunt tail with a 'lid' similar to an army cap and many sharp teeth. They eat wood from the mangrove trees. The worm can be found in dead or living trees. Before eating them, you have to cut off the head and the tail. Then the insides can be sucked out and swallowed. There are two others and the biggest one must be boiled. When eaten raw, it causes a sore throat. The smaller one is the 'father' of the sandfly and a Dreaming of the Aboriginals belonging to the Yirritja moiety. The dance of the mangrove tree worm is still danced today.

These are just a few examples of the bush food we eat.

Another time when I was still living at Japirdijapin many Wet Seasons ago, I went with my father to get sugarbag (wild honey). He used to climb on top of the trees and look for the bees going into or coming out of the cutting where the sugarbag is. He would make a cradle out of paperbark to get the honey syrup. We also used grass for drinking water dew and we tasted the honey syrup which is like sugar. It is too strong and sour when you drink it straight so you have to drink it with water dew. It makes you thirsty if you drink it straight so you have to mix it with water like Balanda do with rum or whisky.

In the Dry Season we walked to the inland away from the coast. All the waterholes and billabongs were dry and people from the islands like Milingimbi, who were visiting relatives in the inland, were dying for water, but we and other hill

The long-necked turtle will feed a small family. In the Dry Season the turtles submerge in the swamps and are found by the women by feeling carefully in the mud with their feet. *photo P. Tweedie*

Preparing the giant barramundi for cooking. *photo R. Edwards*

country people knew how to get water from the paperbark tree. These trees stand near the billabongs or swamps. When we cut the flat part of the tree all countrymen can drink the water juice coming out of the tree. It is salty water, not very delicious, but when you are dying for water you are too glad to drink it. In Jinang we call it tree water (Maraka, paperbark water). When we were camping near a beach, river or dried out billabong during the Dry Season, we knew another way of getting water. That is by making a hole with a digging stick near these places. It takes a long time to dig a hole deep enough for the water, and the first water will be dirty. But after a while it will become cleaner and it is all right for drinking. However, it still tastes strong.

In the Wet Season there is plenty of water and you can drink fresh water at every place.

Jack Mirritji, Maningrida[42]

Daisy Utemara of the Kimberleys, whose life today has taken her further away from the traditional way of life of her childhood, remembers those early years with some regret, as does Thomas Murray of the Pitjantjatjara.

The Country Where I Lived Before

I went hunting and I roamed the beautiful country. I went here and there, I did not worry about anything or anybody, I just lived in this beautiful country that was mine. In the early mornings I woke up to see the sun. I straightened my spears and my woomera. I warmed them over the fire and I started to walk. I watched every step wherever I went and when I killed a kangaroo I carried it back to my camp and cooked it and shared it with my family and my relatives. When the sun was setting I said to myself, 'Tomorrow is another day,' and I slept and dreamed about the future.

Sometimes I have bad dreams and sometimes I have good dreams and one day I dreamt a dream that I was going to be pushed out of this land and my people were going to be shot. I said that is only a dream and it will never happen and so I tried to forget it and go about my hunting and looking for kangaroo and other things.

I did that, year after year, months after months. When the rain came I slept in the cave and when I was lying down I could see the paintings of all kinds of animals and in the middle was the Wandjina. I was proud of it and I smiled and when the rain was finished I walked on the wet ground and made my foot prints on it and my thoughts came back to me again about the dreams I had. When I was standing near the river and watching the fishes swimming and the freshwater turtles and the crocodiles; that's my food I said. I looked up and saw the mountains and I wanted to climb them and look over, and I did. I was happy.

When I went hunting for kangaroos I never stood where the wind blew, otherwise the animal would smell my perspiration, so I would walk from the other direction. I not only watched for the kangaroo but kept an eye out for any signs of danger. I thought to myself if the grass was ready to be burnt for the kangaroo; yes, it was ready. I called all the men to come with me and burn the grass. Two men each side of the grass took long sticks. They both went each side and burnt the grass. It was very thick and there were lots of kangaroos in the midst of it. While the other men waited and waited until the two men met themselves from each side. The blazing fire and smoke came and drove the kangaroos straight up to the men who were waiting and they killed them but some of them escaped. This was my life which I lived.

Daisy Utemara, Mowanjum[43]

A Description of Life Before Contact with the White Man

This story is about the early days, when men and women used to be naked with no clothes. They used to kill and eat meat, kangaroo as well as goanna and emu. After sitting around a bit, they went and pitched camp at another waterhole, then they went to a claypan and ate around there, returning after a while to the waterhole. When they saw smoke rising from another camp in the distance, they met up with other people and stayed on with that company, before moving off again. While staying at a waterhole, they might see a messenger come into view from another camp.

The blazing fire and the smoke drove the kangaroos straight up to the men who were waiting. *photo P. Tweedie*

Boyun hunting wild fowl near his bush home at Walkerbimerri, central Arnhem Land. *photo P. Tweedie*

The people would grind up seeds for food and put it in wooden bowls. The women prepared the seed by rubbing it in their hands to free the husk, so that the seed fell out. They then poured the seed on hard antbed and lit a small fire to burn off the waste, hitting and pounding the seed with a stone and then winnowing it in the air. Gathering it up they put it in a bowl, tipping out the rubbish. In the afternoon they would grind the seed on a smooth flat stone, and when the sun set they cooked it, mixing it with water and spooning it out onto the fire with their hands. When it was put in the hot ashes, the cake spread and while it was cooking the children played some distance away.

When the food was ready, the children came to get it. Their mother and father painted the child's abdomen first, smeared his nose with food so that the seeds would not fall on the ground, and then gave him the cake. The seed remained on the bushes for some time and the women continued to prepare and cook it. If it rained and became hard to find the seeds, they went to another place.

While they stayed there they might see a man bring a pre-initiate into the camp, and they would meet up with other people, going backwards and forwards between several camps. Not having the white man's food they ate only seed and meat.

While they were living like this, they saw white men coming with camels and they met up with them and stayed together. The white men gave them food and after tasting and eating the flour they thought: 'What is this like that we are eating?' They soon forgot about flour on returning to their normal life. Sometimes they followed the camels at a distance, watching them.

One day they saw that Mr Wade had come, and they followed him to Warburton, and stayed there. When they returned to the bush for dingo scalps, they ate wild fruits and finished them all up. When the water ran out in the bush, those at the settlement stayed on, and other people from the north came down to eat the wild fruits. After staying in the bush for a while, eating seeds and kangaroo, they went

201

back to the settlement, and increased in numbers. Nobody remained in the bush and those people who came from the north have disappeared. But others are still living in the far north, many more naked people with no clothes.

Thomas Murray, Pitjantjatjara tribe[44]

SHARING FOOD AND WATER

In Aboriginal communities where the roles were clearly divided, one man or woman may, depending on the result of the day's hunt, bring home the bulk of the day's food for the small group camped together. The absolute necessity for people to share their food and not eat alone has therefore been an obvious and most important rule of life since the Creation era. Greed and selfishness are intolerable and over-indulgence, as with other characteristics which threaten the hunting-gathering society, meets with dire punishments elaborated upon in many myths.

The Aboriginal people live in a relationship of mutual dependence with their environment. The land offers them life and nourishment but in turn, the people must ensure the continual reproduction of animal species by performing increase ceremonies and protecting sacred sites.

In Central Australia songs are sung at increase ceremonies for a tall iltjota grass from which oily seeds are obtained for making into bread. Similarly, at a group of rocks which represent the metamorphosis of heaps of native oranges gathered in the Tjukurpa times by the native orange Ancestress of the Aranda people, these verses are sung:

In great clusters the fruits are hanging down;
Gleaming a rich yellow, the fruits are hanging down.
Gleaming a deep gold, the fruits are hanging down;
Gleaming a rich yellow, the fruits are hanging down.[45]

While the songs are sung the rocks are gently cleared of grass and weeds and dusted with sprigs from nearby bushes. By these methods the men ensure that there will be an abundance of seeds, grasses and of fruit as well as animals.

The resources of the land were indirectly conserved by only taking food which could be consumed immediately and not tolerating waste. Some myths also give the basis for the practice of re-planting portions of yams and other root vegetables to ensure a continual supply. The habit of leaving a little of the tuber in the ground is still maintained on Bathurst Island and throughout Arnhem Land. Among the Tiwi on Bathurst Island it was the practice to put some of the yam root back in the ground to placate the yam spirit and incidentally provide for the next season. Young children learn these principles as part of everyday life, from the older women as they gather, and prepare food.

Jalna, an old woman of the Waddaman tribe, while cooking seed bread on the campfire, told her listening children: 'When you dig up yam, you must all time leave little bit end of that yam in ground . . . if dig it all out, then that food spirit will get real angry and won't let any more yam grow in that place.'

Another story which reflects the unconscious need to conserve natural resources and ensure the continued reproduction of the species was told by Ngulwua of the Finness River on the edge of the Timor Sea in northern Australia.

Windjedda and the Wild Goose Eggs

When the wild geese gather in hundreds on the swamp-plains across the north to make their nests amongst the reeds along the banks amongst the mangroves, the tribespeople gather to feast on the eggs which are easily gathered. Each day the families go out to collect the eggs and feast on them at night. When the chicks grow big in the shell, however, it is time to cease collecting them. The laying season is nearly over and taboos are then enforced. No young men were entitled to collect or eat the eggs, only the very old men were permitted to do so. The young were now expected to hunt other foods.

A desert family rests in their brush shelter. These shady dwellings are perfectly designed for desert conditions: the warm sand provides a soft floor and the air is able to circulate freely within the shaded canopy. *photo R. Edwards*

The young Windjedda, it was said, was born greedy. Some say his mother ate too many rich foods when he was in her body, others that he grew two stomachs when he was given water whilst still drinking milk from his mother's breast. Windjedda was so hungry for goose eggs that he broke the taboo and was overcome by a huge tide. He is now a blue heron that constantly seeks food at the edge of the shore.

Ngulwua, Finness River[47]

The danger of greed and not sharing food is apparent in the following story from Yirrkala, north-eastern Arnhem Land.

Djirid and Damala

Two Ancestral Beings, Djirid the kingfisher and Damala the eagle hawk were preparing for a fishing trip. The small son of Djirid was looking for crabs and fish at the water's edge. He caught many and in his hunger and eagerness quickly made a fire and cooked them. His father and Damala asked him for some but he refused and ate all the food himself.

The two older men were silently furious, and when they had returned from their fishing did not give any of their catch to the young boy. The boy pleaded and cried out for food and began to scatter himself strangely. As he did so his body sprouted feathers and he changed into a kingfisher. The two men also changed into birds and followed the small boy into the sky.[48]

Similar stories are common throughout Australia. Frill-necked lizard turned on long-necked tortoise because he gobbled up all the prized fat from everything they caught.

203

The Gunwinggu also have a cautionary legend which tells of the fate of the greedy fisherman. This man continually caught far more than his family required. The foolish hunter was finally entwined in the suffocating arms of an octopus and drowned.

Kath Walker, the Aboriginal conservationist/environmentalist and poet remarks in her book *Stradbroke Dreamtime*,

'Today, when the white man's food is eaten so widely by Aborigines, the tribe no longer hunts the dugong. They believe that to hunt dugong when their bellies are full would be to act against the natural law of 'kill to eat'. They believe that the Good Spirit would punish them severely if they killed dugong out of greed and that the Good Spirit might take one of the tribespeople to even the score.'[49]

The story of Kurburu the koala from the Kulin tribe of Victoria provides another lesson — water must be conserved. Hoarding or stealing it will meet with violence or death.

Kurburu, the Koala

The Kulin were all gathered together to feast on Gurring, the gum which exudes from wattle trees. They had already mixed it with water in their tarnuks, the wooden bowls, when Kurburu the koala came by. When he saw the gum in the tarnuks he asked the Kulin for some. But they were too busy to take any notice of him, and when he asked again they told him, 'Go up the tree and get some for yourself, you lazy fellow.' This made Kurburu very angry, and when the people had gone to get more gum he took the tarnuks full of water and put them on top of a young gum tree. When he had made himself comfortable on the fork of a tree with all the tarnuks around him he said to the tree, 'Grow up quickly', and straight away the tree began to grow until it was bigger and higher than any other tree.

When the Kulin returned they could not see their tarnuks anywhere. At last someone looked up and saw Kurburu sitting in the fork of a very high tree with all the tarnuks around him. The Kulin were very angry, and shouted, 'What are you doing up there with our tarnuks? Bring them down again.' But Kurburu only sat and said nothing. By and by one of the men took his stone axe and began climbing the tree. With his axe he chopped notches on the trunk to get his big toe in and was getting high up when Kurburu looked down. Seeing the man he said, 'Hullo, what are you coming up here for?' and the man answered: 'I am coming to kill you for stealing our tarnuks.'

Kurburu said nothing in reply, but picked up a tarnuk full of water and threw it at the man, so that he fell off the tree and was killed. Another man went up and also was knocked down, and another, and another, and still another followed, but they were all knocked down by Kurburu.

At the foot of the tree the Kulin were very sad, they lamented for the death of their young men, and cut their heads in sorrow until the blood ran out of their wounds.

A wind sprang up and carried the smell of the dead to where Bunjil, the All-father, was sitting in his camp. He got up, took his spears, and walked along sniffing the air until he came to the place where the Kulin were mourning their dead, at the foot of the tree. He looked up the tree and saw Kurburu sitting in the fork of the tree with the tarnuks all around him. Bunjil called to him, 'Give me a drink of water, I am thirsty,' and Kurburu answered, 'Come up here and get it.' Bunjil was very angry, because everyone had to obey him. So he called for two of his young men to come to him.

When they arrived he took them to the tree where Kurburu sat looking about him, and said to them, pointing to another tree close by: 'Come and practise. Climb this tree one on each side, and when I say "look out" bend to one side so that the tarnuk which Kurburu throws will pass under your arm without harming you.' The two young men practised as Bunjil had told them to, and while they were doing so they saw some sugar-ants travelling up and down the tree to their nests which were on the tree. Since the young men were very fond of Bunjil they took some of the larvae from the nest for him to eat. That is how the Kulin learnt to eat sugar-ant larvae.

When the young men got close to him Kurburu the Koala grew
frightened and moved higher up the tree. *photo R. Edwards*

When they had practised enough they went up Kurburu's tree. They went up,
one on each side, until they got past the notches that the Kulin had made. Then
Kurburu, hearing their chopping, looked down from the fork and saw them
coming. He took a tarnuk and threw it at one of them. But he bent to one side, and
the tarnuk passed underneath his arm. The same thing happened each time a
tarnuk was thrown. When the young men got close to him, Kurburu was
frightened, and moved higher up the tree, leaving the tarnuks behind. The two
young men quenched their thirst, and then went up and killed Kurburu. Then
Bunjil ordered his young men to come down and to bring the tarnuks, which they
did, and he gave them back to the Kulin; he also told them always, in the future, to
cook koalas with their skin on, and never to remove the skin at any time. Further, he
told them to break the koalas' legs before cooking them, so that they would not be
able to climb up a tree and take their tarnuks with them.

Kulin tribe[50]

Food must not only be conserved and shared, it was also to be respected, as is made
clear in the following story of the origin of Lake Bannister as told by Kabbarli or
Daisy Bates.

The Spirit Kangaroo and the Bush Mice

In Yamminga times, a group of Yungar, the people who lived in those far-off days,
made a big camp at Dowingerup, in the south-west of the land. It was a good place,
with plenty of water and food for all the Yungar as well as the animals and birds with
whom they shared the land.

Now all these Yungar were protected by a great Janga Yonggar, a spirit
kangaroo which lived in a cave nearby and watched to see that the men, women and
children of the tribe kept the Laws. And the special meat food of the tribe was

kangaroo, because the Janga Yonggar was their elder brother and their totem. The tribesmen knew that they must obey the hunting Law and eat only the full-grown kangaroos, for the little kangaroos were as their own children. If they had eaten the young kangaroos, then the Janga Yonggar would have punished them by taking away all their kangaroo meat food. There was another Law that the Yungar must obey, too, and it was this: they must never mock the kangaroo, or imitate its hopping and leaping.

Every day the hunters of the tribe brought home the meat food: turkeys, possums, and other creatures as well as kangaroos. Every day the women gathered roots, grubs, fruits and lizards. There were many children in the camp. The girls would go food gathering with the women, who showed them how to find roots and grubs and small creatures with the digging stick. The boys would go with the hunters on short journeys and learn how to stalk and spear the meat food, how to throw the boomerang and use the hunting knife. When the hunters went on long journeys, however, they left the boys in the camp, to be looked after by the demmangur, the old men and women whose hunting and food-gathering days were over.

One day, the hunters prepared for a journey that would take them a long way from the camp. They told the boys that they must stay with the demmangur. 'Do not go away from the camp,' they warned their sons. 'Be content to play about the cooking fires, for the old people cannot follow you into the bush to bring you back.'

The girls thought the boys were lucky to be able to play all day while they had to help with the food gathering, as they always did.

The hunters set out. The boys went with them a little way from the camp, and then they were told to go back quickly to the old people. As the boys followed the way that led back to the camp, one of them said, 'Look! Here are tracks of karnding

Bark painting of Karrbarda the long yam by Anchor Barbbura Wurrkgidj of Oenpelli. The yam is similar to the sweet potato and has a long branching tuber with vine-like foliage. *photo Aboriginal Arts Board*

Bark painting of barramundi by Johnny Rarrkgal Djokiba of Oenpelli. The rivers of the north teem with giant barramundi, much favoured by Aboriginal fishermen. *photo Aboriginal Arts Board*

— bush mice. Let us pretend they are kangaroos, and hunt them and cook them for meat.'

All the boys thought this was a good idea; they forgot the Law of the Janga Yonggar, which forbade them to mock the kangaroo or use it in their games. So they played their hunting game; they found a nest of baby mice, which they speared with hard, stiff rushes; and they carried the dead mice back to the camp on their backs, just as the hunters used to bring home the kangaroos. When they came near the cooking fires, the old people saw how the boys pretended the dead mice were kangaroos. 'Do not mock your own meat food,' they said. 'It is forbidden.' But the boys just laughed and went on with their game. They cooked the little mice and divided them among themselves, just as the hunters used to divide the kangaroo meat. Then they ate their portions, and stuck out their stomachs as though they had enjoyed a great feast, and afterwards lay down to sleep.

Meanwhile, the full-grown mice, who had been away from the nest seeking food for their young, came back to find their babies gone. They called and called to their children, but heard no answer, no answer. They looked about and saw the boys' tracks and followed them, still crying for their young ones. Soon the mice reached the place where the boys had cooked and eaten their babies, and they found nothing left but their bones.

'The boys have killed and eaten our babies, and pretended they were kangaroos!' wailed the mice. 'They have mocked the Janga Yonggar. Let us go to his cave and tell him.'

Sadly and sorrowfully, weeping and wailing, they went to the cave where the Janga Yonggar lived. The Janga Yonggar came out to see what had happened, and when he heard about the game the boys had played, he was very angry. He strode up and down, up and down, biting his beard and spitting it out again in his rage that the boys had mocked him. Then he said, 'I cannot punish the boys, for their fathers are Yonggar Borungur — my brothers — and they are my own children. But I will go to the Janga Woggal, the spirit snake, to tell him what has happened, and he shall punish them.'

Small edible snails are collected and placed on paperbark before cooking. *photo P. Tweedie*

So the Janga Yonggar went to the Janga Woggal, and he said, 'You must punish the boys, for they should not mock me. If they are not punished, then in time the Yungar will stop obeying any of the hunting Laws.'

The Janga Woggal shared the anger of the Janga Yonggar, and promised to punish the boys. He went with the Janga Yonggar and the sorrowing mice to the camp of the Yungar. And here the Janga Woggal lifted up the ground under the camp on his great back, and upset all the shelters where the old people and children and dogs were sitting. The whole of that place was turned upside-down. And then the Janga Woggal made a great lake appear in that place where the camp had been, and all the Yungar were drowned. The Janga Woggal drowned the boys because they had broken the Law of the tribe, and he drowned the old people because they had not taught the Law properly. So Dowingerup Gabbi was made, and it still stands today. It is known as Lake Bannister.

And now, when the Yungar sit down by Dowingerup Gabbi, if they look down into the water, they may see, far below, the shadows of the trees and bushes and the shelters of the Yungar whose boys mocked the Janga Yonggar.[51]

FOOD TABOOS

In the story of Djankawu from north-eastern Arnhem Land (see Chapter 2) the two sisters inserted their digging stick or Djuda into the ground and placed the sacred emblems beneath the soil, making wells and causing sacred trees to grow.

They sang as they went along:

Put in more djuda roots, rangga, making a well . . .
They stand with shining feathers quietly, solemnly, as we call the invocations . . .
Carefully, dragging along the mud and the grass!
Come, we put in these djuda, making a well:
Let them dry in the hot rays of the burning sun . . .
Drying their damp feathered strings in the heat, feathered strings like yam creepers . . .[52]

Elsewhere in Arnhem Land, also, sacred yams grew as the result of similar actions by the great Ancestors. If women gathering food inadvertently dug up any of these 'sacred' yams, misfortune would follow. The sacred emblems buried by the ancestral heroes resembled the yam tuber in form, the feathered string attached to them being likened to the vine-like foliage of the yam. Women are not permitted to see these emblems and the story of the penalties of digging up 'sacred' yams may be seen as an allegory about the danger of unwittingly looking at a sacred rangga or emblem.

The Sacred Yam

A long time ago two women, Dangawukpuy and Gawutjumu, were camped in the region called Djawal'ngur. This is my own country, and I am the elder in charge of that country and its ceremony.

Dangawukpuy spoke thus: 'Hey! Sister, let's go and hunt for yams.'
Gawutjumu replied: 'Where will we hunt?'
And Dangawukpuy answered, 'Over there at that place in Djawal'ngur.'
Off they went. When they reached a certain place, Dangawukpuy saw the leaves of a yam, which is a totem of the Djambarrpuyngu people, called Gulaka. She cried out, 'Look, these leaves belong to a "big" piece of food.' Gawutjumu said, 'Truly, sister; let's dig!' And dig they did. They thrust their yam sticks, called dhona, into the ground. Immediately they both died. Because that Gulaka from this place is dangerous.

All their clanspeople started looking for those two women. They couldn't find them although they were dead in the jungle. They looked and looked, but nothing. They saw the hole in the jungle where those two dug out the yam. 'Maybe this hole is the clue; they took a dangerous "yam" and it killed them.' Thus they spoke.

If people take the 'small' yam, that's okay. But if they take the 'big' yam from this spot inside the jungle, then they will die. Because those two women dug up a sacred rangga object buried in the jungle. Only the old men can see this. So it killed them. Everyone cried and cried for those two women.

Manuwa, Milingimbi[53]

The Sea Monster and the Girls Who Ate the Wild Fruit

Off went two girls for wild honey. They got their dilly bags and an axe and off they went. As they walked, they kept looking out for honey. Some they ate and some they put into their dilly bags.

Down they went to the beach and put their dilly bags on the sand. But they hadn't washed their hands and they had been eating the wild fruit called munydjutj. They sat for a while, then the older sister said, 'Let's go and gather oysters.' They hung up their dilly bags on a tree and walked down to the water.

They gathered oysters there, knocking them off the rocks. Then the younger sister turned and saw an island. 'Look! There are some more on that island,' she said. 'Let's swim over. We'll wade through the water.' One stayed on the mainland getting oysters, and the other went to the island where the totemic monster was. She was eating oysters and the monster opened its eyes and was watching her. All the time while she was getting the oysters, the monster was watching her.

The tide was getting higher and higher. The girl who had swum to the island looked over her shoulder and said to herself, 'Oh! Oh! It's a long way to the shore, isn't it?' Higher and higher came the tide, until the monster was submerged. Then he took her away. She called out, 'Help! Help! Help! Sister, help!' But the monster took the sisters under the water far away to the place where he lived. He had only been warming himself in the sun before; it was his favourite place.

Back in the camp lots of people were looking for the two girls. They searched and searched, then one suggested to the others, 'Maybe a Totemic Ancestor ate them yesterday.' This is what he said to the people who were there, ready to fight whoever may have taken the girls. The dilly bags were still hanging where the two girls had put them.

The people kept on searching. They searched and searched, until it was time for sleep. They slept until daybreak, then followed the girls' footprints, and eventually found only their dilly bags, hanging on the tree. They said to each other, 'The Totemic Ancestor from that place probably came to them yesterday.'

We believe that if a person eats the fruit munydjutj and a totemic sea serpent smells the odour, he becomes very angry, either killing the person concerned or making him sick, or sometimes causing thunderstorms and a great deal of lightning.

Lunepupuy, Milingimbi[54]

Accounts of the dangers of hunters trespassing in sacred areas, or areas where Totemic Ancestors are resting, vary across the continent. In some the Ancestral Spirit himself of the plant or animal is inadvertently angered if a sacred yam, fruit, fish or animal is caught or injured.

The Spearing of the Sacred Clam

Long ago in the Dreaming time, a hunter called Inetina was spearing fish; as he walked between the coral pools he heard a voice calling to him. He saw an open clam shell and the voice said from within, 'You stabbed my shell as you passed. Are you a woman to be so careless?' Inetina was insulted and, quickly picking up a large stone, hurled it at the clam. But the clam was the Great Ancestral Clam himself and as it was crushed and died a great red cloud rose and covered the land. It was a cloud of sickness which spread and caused everyone to die where they were — in their camps and out in the bush. Their bones lay white over the land like pieces of coral.

Iwaidja, western Arnhem Land[55]

Extremely important taboos are placed on eating certain foods, sometimes even touching food, at various times in a person's life. On Bathurst Island amongst the Tiwi, the immediate relatives of a deceased person are decreed Pukumani or taboo, and may not touch food until certain mortuary ceremonies are completed. They must be hand fed by people who are not Pukumani. Similarly menstruating women, whose blood flow is known to pollute water and anger Rainbow Serpents, are separated from the community and restrictions on their handling food enforced. For the young boy initiate also, strong taboos concerning foods exist and the following legend from Cape York acted as a strong deterrent to young initiates tempted to touch forbidden food.

The Rainbow Serpent and the Young Initiate

Long ago, a young initiate and a small boy went out hunting. He called to the small boy, 'Oi! Boy, let's go hunting.' They walked and walked until finally the initiate found a possum. He cried, 'Bring an axe, there is an animal here, let's cut it out.' He cut the tree and poked the animal with a stick. Then quickly seizing the possum with his hand, he pulled it out and killed it. The little boy said, 'It is bad food, you have just come out from the initiation ceremony (Monka), we must not eat it.' The older boy replied, 'That does not matter, you and I will eat anything, I am hungry.' The boy spoke again, 'But you are just out from the Monka.' The initiate put his hand in and pulled out another possum by the tail, killed it, and threw it down. He poked his stick in repeatedly, each time pulling out a possum. He poked the stick in again, but this time water gushed out. 'Ah! Water is coming out from the tree and here is a fish! Bring me my spear. I will spear it,' he said and speared the fish. Suddenly the singing of the Rainbow Serpent was heard. He tried to run this way, but it was no good, the water followed him. The water flowed out and the boy tried to run away, but the Rainbow Serpent ate him.

The small boy went back to his father. He arrived there and his father asked him, 'Where is your elder brother?' 'He is not here; a snake has eaten him.' His father said, 'Let us all go and look for him.' They went and searched.

The boy cried: 'There is the place where my elder brother was eaten!' They dug and found him. The father put his hand in to pull him out. The Takobi cried, 'It is I, Father.' But he was a long way away. The father said, 'Let us go and dig in another place.' His mother was there crying for her child. They dug in another place and found a hole. The father felt with his hand again. 'I am here, Father,' but it was only his ghost. He took the searchers a long way. His father said, 'Let us dig again.' They dug and dug and dug, but they only found deep water. Then the father said, 'We must leave him.' They all cried a ritual cry for the dead, for the lost boy.

The Rainbow Serpent remains at that place to this day.[56]

Opposite: Bark painting of Gurrumirringu the Ancestral hunter by Malangi. One of the most important parts of the Manharrngu clan (Liyagalawumirri tribe) mortuary rites ceremony tells the story of the mighty hunter Gurrumirringu, who was killed by a poisonous snake.

Gurrumirringu was a great Ancestral hunter who was known throughout the land for his skill at tracking game. One day, after a successful hunting trip and heavily laden with his catch, he set off back to his camp. Now not far from where he lived was a billabong where, unknown to him, an evil spirit had taken the form of a tree and lurking beneath its roots was the poisonous snake Dharapa. The evil spirit tree wished to kill the hunter and enticed the weary Gurrumirringu to come and rest beneath its shade. Being hungry as well as tired, he made a small fire and prepared to cook himself a meal. Suddenly the angry snake Dharapa emerged from the roots of the evil spirit tree and inflicted a fatal bite.

Story courtesy Ramangining Craft Centre. *photo P. Tweedie*

CHAPTER EIGHT

Death and the Spirit World

DEATH

In any society the death of an individual comes as a threat to the whole fabric of life. Amongst Aboriginals, however, death is seen as inevitable only in the very old. Death of a healthy man or woman must have been caused by the evil magic and sorcery of some enemy of the dead person. Natural causes of death are seldom admitted except in the case of very young babies and very old people whose death causes little disruption to the pattern of society. But when an adolescent or a person in the prime of life dies there is a sense of great loss and the whole camp goes into deep mourning. Sorcery must be suspected as the cause of the untimely death and must be revenged. Sorcery pervades Aboriginal life, even though few people in any group would admit to practising sorcery. In some areas a sorcerer is able, by means of his powerful magic, to extract some vital organ, fat or blood from his victim, leaving no external mark. He then revives the man, allowing him to return to camp as if normal, but in two or three days he dies.

Another method found in Cape York and in the northern Kimberleys is to make an image of the person out of straw and imitate on it the form of death desired. Sometimes the image was painted on rock or bark showing spears protruding from a vital part of the body. The most feared type of sorcery, however, is 'singing' or pointing a bone, stone or stick believed to be powerfully imbued with magic, in the direction of the victim. Very careful precautions are taken in handling such dangerous powers; a ritual stance is taken up with the sun or moon behind the sorcerer, and the chant sung incorporating the victim's name. Once a man knows he has been 'sung' he loses all desire to live and death becomes inevitable. Magic is held in enormous dread as it activates supernatural powers from the Dreamtime which cannot be controlled by man. The victim feels he has been castigated by his society for some crime, and believes himself that the verdict must be just and he must die.

Once sorcery is suspected, an inquest must be held to determine the identity of the sorcerer and exact retribution from him or his relatives. A common method of finding the sorcerer is to look at the cleared ground of the grave; a hole in the smooth dust could indicate the direction of the country of the murderer, or even insect tracks could reveal the whereabouts of the murderer. A careful consideration of all the facts is given by the fully-initiated men of the tribe. Sometimes the corpse itself is interrogated. As questions are asked about possible murderers the spirit of the dead man is believed to cause the corpse to jerk around at the correct name. Once the murderer has been established, a settlement is reached with the dead man's relations to determine the price to be paid, or the punishment to be exacted. If the dead man has seriously broken some taboo or law, very little retribution is asked for. A frequent way of taking revenge is for the dead man's kin to secretly perform sorcery on the murderer or his relations, which is intended eventually to cause a death.

The investigation into sorcery after a death is a way of directing the angry and confused emotions aroused by sudden death. Death has to be understood personally in the context of Aboriginal life, where a man's whole life is a network of personal relationships with men, animals and the land, and sorcery provides the framework. Death has to be caused by some man personally antagonistic to the dead man, not by the impersonal forces of nature.

Opposite: Hollow log burial coffin. Detail of a bark painting by Bungawuy from Ramangining. Some time after burial the bones of the deceased are ceremonially dug up and placed in a hollow log which has been painted with clan totems. *photo P. Tweedie*

Even with the advent of Western medicine, although the European explanation of death might be superficially accepted, the people still look beyond that and attempt to discover who caused the death. In Carnarvon, Western Australia, a man who was drunk fell off the back of a truck and was killed. Two years previously this man had been involved in a fight with another man over a woman. The other man took a rifle and while trying to shoot the first man accidentally shot and killed the latter's uncle (his mother's brother). The second man was convicted of manslaughter and jailed, but the Aboriginals regarded the first man as being to blame for the death. This man was told that he would have to 'go through the Law' (be initiated) and be subjected to certain tribal punishments, but he successfully evaded these. When it was learnt that he had fallen off the truck, some of the older men declared that he had finally been punished by the spirit of his dead uncle, which had lain in wait for an opportunity to take his life and had pushed him off the truck.[1]

THE ORIGIN OF DEATH

In myths about the first occurrence of death in Creation times eternal life is possible for man, but it is rejected because of some mistake, or bad choice, or trick. Very often the moon is implicated, as he waxes and then wanes almost to nothing, but revives again. He offers this way of life to the other creatures, including man, but through some mistake or misadventure, man chooses death.

A simple story from the Wotjobaluk in Victoria relates this unfortunate incident.

Why Men Die

When all animals were like men, Mityan the Moon was a man also. His magic was very powerful and when people died he would say, 'You get up again' and they came back to life. But there was an old man who was his enemy, and whose magic proved stronger than Mityan's although he had no power over Mityan himself. He caused death to be final and since that time people no longer have come to life again, with the exception of Mityan. For when he died he went to the sky and comes back to life each month.[2]

In a Nullarbor Plain story collected very early this century Meeka the Moon descends to earth and meets Yonggar the Kangaroo.

Moon asked Kangaroo, 'What happens to you when you die?' The Kangaroo tried to delay his answer so that he would hear about the Moon first, and he pursed his mouth, spat reflectively, and turned his head from side to side. Then he nibbled some grass while he waited for Meeka to speak again. But the moon was cunning and began to tickle Yonggar to get him to answer. Finally the Kangaroo said, 'When I die I go nowhere, and my bones turn white as they lie on the ground, and the grass grows over them and covers them up.' Then Meeka laughed and said, 'I die, I die, I sit up again; I die, I die, I sit up again.' If the moon had spoken first all the people would have come alive again like Meeka the Moon.[3]

The same belief is held at the other end of the continent, in north-eastern Arnhem Land. Here the Moon talks to the Parrot Fish.

Death Comes to Man

In Wongar times, Moon said to the Parrot Fish, 'I am going to die, but I won't be finished, for I am going to be alive and come back.'

Parrot Fish said, 'You are no good. What do you want to die and live again for?'

Moon said, 'What about you?'

Parrot fish said, 'Me? I'll die, but I won't come back, and you can pick up my bones.'

'Well, it doesn't matter about you,' said Moon. 'When I die I want to come back. Every time I get sick and get more sick and get thinner and thinner until only my bones are left, then I'll die, but I'll come back again.' The Moon then got sick and wasted away until he had died, then came back again.

214

As the Tiwi Pukumani ceremony commences, participants paint their faces and bodies in elaborate geometric designs which link the people to their Ancestors of the Dreaming. *photos R. Edwards*

Overleaf: Cave where the bones of the dead are at rest. The placement of the bones in a cave marks the final stage in mortuary ceremonies which may last intermittently for years after the person's death. Here the chambers also house spirit figures painted in white clay. *photo R. Edwards*

Parrot Fish said, 'I won't be that way. When I die, when man dies, we'll stay dead. You come back, but that is wrong.' The Parrot Fish died and never came back, but the Moon, ever since those Wongar days, has been well and fat, then become ill and wasted away until he was dead, but he always comes back again and grows to full size.

When the Moon had had this conversation with Parrot Fish he had wanted Parrot Fish to be like him. He had said, 'Come on and become alive again like me. I can fix you so that you will come alive again.' 'No,' said Parrot Fish, 'I want to die and stay dead.' This is what makes man stay dead and never come back to life. The Parrot Fish was a silly fool.[4]

On the Nullarbor Plain the people told a story to Daisy Bates over fifty years ago of a sacred spear of death which brought Death into the world and which hurtles across the Plain seeking victims.

The Spear of Death

In the far-off Yamminga times, so long ago that death was not yet known to the yoongar, the men and women of the earth, an old man and woman lived at Ngangalup with their only son. Each day the old man went out hunting for food. One morning he stalked an emu across the plain, and when he came near it he cast his spear. But the spear missed the emu and flew far, far away, and so the old man lost his quarry, and thought he had lost the spear, too.

But as he looked into the distance, shading his eyes with one hand, to see where his spear had gone, he suddenly beheld it returning at full speed, and coming straight towards him. He dodged the spear as it reached him, only to find that it turned and came towards him again; and when he dodged it a second time, once more it threatened him, so that he had to keep dodging it again and again; and each time he hoped that it would go away and leave him alone. He knew that if he misjudged the direction of the spear by only a fraction, it would go straight through his body and kill him.

After a while the old man grew very tired with this continual dodging of the spear; then his son came running to him, and when the young man saw what was happening, he said, 'Let me take your place, father, for you are growing very tired.'

Although he was exhausted, the old man replied, 'No, my son. You might be speared, for you are not so experienced in the arts of hunting as I am.'

'Let me take your place for only a little while, so that you can rest,' the boy pleaded.

At last the old man agreed to let his son take his place, and while he rested beneath a tree, the young man began to dodge the tireless spear as it came hissing towards him again and again. Alas, the son was not as experienced as the father in judging direction and distance; he let the spear come too close to him, and it pierced his body and he died.

The old man and woman, full of grief, buried their son in the ground, and soon afterwards they went to live in another place. If the boy had not been speared, then for ever afterwards all the yoongar would have been able to dodge any spear that was thrown at them, and moreover they would never have known death at all.

After the death of the boy the Law of the tribe decreed that the place where he was killed by the spear must always be strewn with fresh blackboy rushes by any of the yoongar who passed that way; any old rushes that lay there must first be removed before the fresh ones were put down. And if anyone neglected this Law, then in a short while he would die.[5]

Tiwi Pukumani ceremony in progress on Melville Island. Several different ceremonies are held before the culminating ritual around the grave posts. *photo R. Edwards*

Women were also blamed for the advent of death. Daisy Bates recorded a story about a giant totem board linking earth and sky by which men and women could travel to the sky and have eternal life. One day the women who were travelling along this totemic track made camp and inadvertently burnt the sacred board, severing the connection, and so death came into the world.[6]

Amongst the Tiwi the two main causes of death, the actions of the moon and the foolishness of women, are brought together in their story of the coming of Death — the story of Purukupali. On Bathurst and Melville Islands the main ceremonies of the Tiwi people centre around elaborate funerary rituals. These were first celebrated after the death of Purukupali, the first man to die on earth, who decreed that death would from that time be the fate of man. His death was caused by his unfaithful wife Bima, who loved Tjapara the moon. Bima left her baby in the hot sun while she went into the bush with Tjapara the moon; the baby died and in anguish Purukupali said that all men should die as a result.

Purukupali

Long ago Purukupali lived at that country we call Jangarnti. His little son, whose name was Djinini, he became sick. He became sick. Then Purukupali looked after his son, but he became really ill and it went right through him. Purukupali said to Waijai his wife, the curlew (long ago Waijai — when she was a woman — well her name was Bima. Bima was her name, Waijai the woman, Purukupali's wife) 'I'm going hunting for our food, because we are hungry.' So Waijai went hunting too, taking her small son with her. Then Tjapara sneaked up there and those two met. They met, Tjapara and Waijai, Bima. They met, and those two were sitting on the grass, Waijai and Tjapara. She did not watch her little son but went with Tjapara. And the baby boy died in the hot sun.

The Pukumani participants leave the village and walk to the dead man's tribal country where the giant posts have been erected, and where the body will be buried. *photo D. Conroy*

Purukupali came back and found the baby dead, that little boy, his son, dead. 'Alas, my dear wife, your son is no more,' he kept saying. Then 'Oh!' she kept calling. 'Kwai! Kwai! Your son is dead,' he kept calling. Then she came and kept on calling like a curlew, 'Waijai! Waijai! Waijai!'

Then Tjapara came as well. 'Give me the boy,' Tjapara said. 'No,' said Purukupali. 'Give me the boy.' 'No.' 'Give me the boy. In three days I shall make him well.' 'No. I shan't give him to you. Now that my son is dead we shall all follow him. We shall all have to follow my son. No one will ever come back. Everyone will die.'

Purukupali made that Law. He was a hard man in what he said. He grabbed his throwing sticks — his forked throwing sticks. Purukupali. He and his brother started fighting. Tjapara too had some forked throwing sticks, and fought and fought and fought and fought until at last Purukupali hit Tjapara in the eye and Purukupali won the fight. He kept hitting him with his fighting stick. Purukupali won the fight. Then — Tjuri, tjuri, tjuri, tjuri tjuri, tjuri, tjuri. He went up into the sky, to that place in the sky that our Ancestors long ago called Jungupi.

Then Purukupali grabbed his son Djinini and said, 'We shall have to go to Tjipampunumi. We shall have to go to Tjipampunumi. No one will ever come back. From now on everyone will die.' And he kept on stamping his foot so that he made some pits with his foot. He has left his mark there. Purukupali took the dead body of his son and walked into the sea. The sea rose to his middle. The water kept on rising and he kept on stamping his foot. Now here, now here, now here — and then the sea took him. The sea took Purukupali and it took that baby. Then only the sea remained. Waijai came running to the sea shore crying with grief, 'Waijai, Waijai, Waijai, my son, my son, my son, my son.' She cried for a while. Then it was over. She was still.

'Waijai' means curlew, and Bima became the wailing bird calling out her dead baby. The place where Purukupali walked into the sea with his dead son is now a whirlpool. Tjapara the moon rose into the sky, where he is reincarnated every month. And the marks of his battle with Purukupali can be seen on the full moon's face even today.

Foxy Tipimwuti, Bathurst Island[7]

Amongst the Aranda people of central Australia, the cry of the curlew reminds the people of the wails of mourners, as it does the Tiwi. For the desert people death is the final catastrophe in which man is destroyed, although his spirit lingers on to haunt his relatives. Once, long ago, a curlew man had the chance to rise from the dead but his efforts were thwarted by the magpie.

The Curlews and Magpie

Long ago, male and female curlews emerged from beneath the rocks of the earth. But the first curlew man was too quick to emerge, and because he followed too closely behind the women the curlew sorcerers were angered and caused his death; and then he was buried. However he did not remain buried under the earth, but began to rise immediately. First his head, then his neck became visible, but as he struggled his shoulders got stuck and he was caught in the ground, unable to fully rise from the grave. The magpie watching hurled a spear into the curlew's neck and trampling him back into the grave said, 'Remain rooted down firmly for all time; do not attempt to rise again; stay for ever in the grave.' But for the magpie the dead curlew would have been able to return to life, and if he had done so death would never have been final; all men would have had the chance to rise to life again.[8]

The man who told this myth added briefly that, but for the cruelty of the Urbura, the dead man would have grown up into life a second time; and if he had been allowed to rise all men who died since that day, would have risen again after death in the same manner. But the Urbura had finally crushed the unfortunate curlew man, and stamped his head down a second time into the grave: 'And now all of us die, and are annihilated forever; and there is no resurrection for us . . . Today, the piercing shrieks of the curlews still ring out over the dim plains in the chill night air; the mournful bass notes of the night owl respond to them from a hollow gum-branch

The massive ironwood Pukumani sculptures are in place on the beach. Each is elaborately painted in earth colours in readiness for the climax of the Tiwi mortuary ceremonies. *photo D. Conroy*

somewhere in the darkness; the men are reminded again of that first tragedy which ordained that the dead should henceforth rise no more.'[8]

SPIRITS AND BURIAL

As David Mowaljarli has explained, a man's spirit exists before birth,[9] in its totemic birthplace, and this spirit will leave him and continue to exist after his death. When a man dies, his true spirit must therefore be hastened to its proper resting place, the place of its totemic origin. If the spirit remains around the camp it will harass and frighten his relations and therefore all precautions are taken to keep this wayward spirit out in the bush with the other spirits of the dead. In northern Australia, and even as far south as northern New South Wales, the patches of rainforest jungle which sporadically occur amongst the drier, more open eucalypt forests are much feared and avoided as haunts of spirits. On Bathurst Island, for example, such dense patches of rainforest are only entered by many people together and at the brightest time of day, and even then only to dig a particularly favoured yam.

In order to diminish the attraction of his familiar surroundings to the dead man, his body may be treated with bitter-smelling smoke and the limbs broken and tied to prevent his spirit re-animating his body. In some areas the widow or mother of the dead person may become ceremonially dumb for several years, never uttering a word during the whole time of mourning, or the spirit might be encouraged to return. The tracks of the dead person are swept away and his camp abandoned and avoided. Favourite places where he sat down are marked and avoided also. His name is never mentioned, and even words with a similar sound are not used.[10]

Once a man dies his mourning relatives are placed in a dilemma, wanting him back, but fearful of his spirit remaining amongst them. Every effort is made to persuade the spirit that it is best for him to leave the camp.

221

This conflict is expressed in a myth from the Kandyu who inhabited the head of the Archer River in north Queensland. The story describes the desperation of a grieving man trying to make his dead brother return to the grave. In the dance-dramatization of the myth a man imitates Polpol the Hero-Ancestor of the house-fly clan as he sits up in his grave, his eyes outlined with circles of white clay to emphasize their size, just like the fly's protruberant eyes. The story is told here by Jimmy Corporal.

The Fly's Spirit

Polpol the house-fly and Wauwudyumo 'the fly that sits down in a wet place', were once brothers, going about as men. One day, Polpol the house-fly grew sick and died. In preparation for burial, Wauwudyumo dug a hole in the ground and at the bottom of the hole he laid bark. He laid bark on top of the body and buried his brother facing west. Then Wauwudyumo cried for the dead man and stamped his feet on the ground. He beat his hands together, holding them up in front of his face, beating out the rhythm, as flies do when they rub their forefeet together and lift their legs. He cried and sang for the dead:

> Alas! Alas! For me, the younger brother!
> Me, the younger brother!
> Alas! Alas! Alas! Alas!
> Alas! For me, the younger brother!
> My older brother has left me all alone!
> Alas! Alas! Alas! Alas!
> Me, the younger brother!
> He has left me all alone!

Suddenly, Polpol the house-fly spirit left the dead and came out from the grave. Polpol came up to the ground where his younger brother was crying for the dead.

During the Pukumani ceremony a bark basket painted with traditional designs is inverted over a post. One of the mourners waits beside the basket and the mortuary post before the ceremony commences. *photo R. Edwards*

Then Wauwudyumo, sensing something was wrong, stopped and listened — he heard a stick snap! Then he admonished Polpol: 'Go back! You must not come up! You must go back! This ground is forbidden!' Polpol the house-fly's ghost reluctantly went back. He sat down with his back against a tree, turning his back on Wauwudyumo, and sang a mournful song:

> *I shall be hungry by and by!*
> *A man am I!*
> *I don't want to go back to the grave!*

Wauwudyumo remained firm and he again told his brother's spirit:

> *Back you must go! This place is forbidden!*

As Polpol slowly retreated he put his head out of the ground and cried, singing, one more time:

> *By and by I shall be hungry!*
> *A man am I!*

Then he went into the grave, never to return.[11]

Amongst Aboriginal people today throughout the continent, the belief in spirits of the dead coming back to haunt the living is still very strong. Henry Rankin from Point Macleay in South Australia speaks here of his own experiences.

Often people who are dead come back, they jog you or poke you to warn you of something. You look around; nobody's there. 'What are you mucking around for?' you say, and then they go. My mother told me never to be frightened of spirits, if you see one in the room, just talk to him quietly.

I saw my mother once, two years or so after she died. I had really bad pain in my neck — I went to sleep, and then I heard a voice. I woke up and looked , and there was my mother standing by the bed with her dog, dressed in a beautiful white gown, with a beautiful glow all round her. I was kicking my wife with my left leg but she didn't wake up. 'What's the matter?' says my mother. 'There's a bad pain in my neck,' I say. 'I'll rub it for you,' says my mother, 'you go to sleep.' I feel a hand on my neck and I go to sleep. Next morning I wake up and there's no pain.[12]

FUNERARY CEREMONIES

In northern Australia the ceremonies for the dead are very protracted, and may even extend for years after the actual burial. These brilliant and dramatic rituals originated in Creation times and closely follow the first ceremony for the first death.

Not only do the funerary songs and dances send the spirit of the dead to the spirit world away from the world of the living, but they also celebrate the relationship that the living have to the plants and animals of the natural world around them, and comfortingly re-affirm the unity of man and nature after the disruption and sadness of death.

In the Kimberley area the following myth tells of the death of the native cat Ancestor and the origin of the funerary customs.

Native Cat and Black-Headed Python

In the Dreamtime the native cat and the black-headed python lived as man and wife. The native cat was the husband and the python was the wife.

One day the husband decided to take his wife to his father's country. 'Come, my wife, we will find a place to live,' he said and then they began their travels. They travelled all day till noon, then the husband paused and said: 'I think we have to make a camp somewhere where there is some water and I have to hunt for some kangaroos before it gets too dark.' 'All right,' said the Python. 'Bring back a roo for our tea, and I will look around for some wild honey and other food.' So they both went out hunting and returned at sunset. 'I have killed a roo, what have you got?' 'I got wild honey and some roots,' said the wife. 'When we finish eating we can go to sleep.' They finished eating and then they went to bed.

223

They travelled next morning, they travelled for a while until they came to this huge mountain. 'Well,' said the cat, 'that is the place we are going to live. When we come a bit closer, you will love this place. This country is my father's land and when he died, he gave me this land.' 'Now we can settle down,' said his wife. 'We will live in the cave and you can put everything in there.' 'All right,' said the python. So they settled in. 'You and I will go hunting further down on the river bank; I will leave you there and I will hunt for kangaroo.' Then they went on their way and hunted and lived on the land for a long time.

Then one day the cat became very sick; he had boils all over his body. 'Dear wife,' he said, 'I am not feeling well; I think I'd better lie down.' His wife made him lie down and then she looked after him.

She hunted all day long and got food whenever she could. When it got cool in the afternoon, she would return to her husband. The black-headed python looked after him, she got paperbark, put it in water and rubbed her husband with it, but this still did not cure him. 'Well, I must make a stone wall and he can lie there if anything happens,' said the python.

Then she began to make the stone wall. Right around she put stones, and she put paperbark in it for her husband to sleep on; when she had finished she laid her old husband down. Then she cried and cried. 'What shall I do?' she kept saying to herself, 'who is going to look after me?' Late in the night he died. She covered him with paperbark and left him on the stone platform.

The wife then left. She went into another land but before she went away she cut off her hair and she covered herself with charcoal until her head was black. She left everything behind except for her charcoal; then she went on her way.

She came to this other country. When she came a little closer she cried out aloud. The people saw her and saw that she was the black-headed python; they all began to ask her things: 'What is the matter, where is your husband?' She said her husband had died, she showed them her head, where she had cut off her hair. Then the people cried because she had lost her husband. Then she had to make camp far away from the others, because she was a widow and that was the custom.

Three days passed since the death of her husband. Then something happened. The native cat came to life, he rubbed his eyes and said to himself, 'Where am I? Where is my wife? I have died and I came to life again, I am so happy.' He then said that he must go and look for his wife. He followed her footprints until he came near to the place where she stayed.

When he came near, his wife saw him and screamed out to him, 'Aieee, aiee, where are you?'

'I am alive again, I am happy to see you.'

'Here is the dead man,' the people said. 'We are all happy to see you.'

'Where is my wife?' he said. 'I want to see her.'

'Here I am,' said the python. 'Why did you come back again? Go back to the dead. I have already cut my hair and I have rubbed charcoal all over me, I am black and that represents death. Go back to the dead please.'

'I thought you were going to be happy. I died and then came back to life again. Oh my dear wife, truly I have to go back to the tomb.'

'Yes, you can go back to your tomb and die and stay there. You know I have done all those things to let people know that I am a widow.'

'All right, my wife, I will do that.' The native cat then went back and died.

The Aboriginals believe that when the husband dies the wife has to rub her body with charcoal and cut off all her hair. When she is a widow she must follow all this because it is the custom; if she doesn't then she too will be killed.

Daisy Utemara, Mowanjum[13]

The story of the Native Cat and the Python is the origin of the custom of laying the corpse on a platform of stone, as well as of the duties of widows. The story also reflects the universal fear of the re-entry of the spirit of the dead into the world of the living and the need to perform the ceremonies correctly to ensure the spirit will not bother anyone.

Funeral ceremonies are most elaborate and drawn out among the Tiwi people

Opposite: When the ceremony is over the grave posts are left to the elements. *photo R. Edwards*

Mourners surround the posts performing elaborate dances throughout the day. *photo D. Conroy*

on Bathurst and Melville Islands. Here the rituals for prominent men continue for years and are by far the most dominant theme in the ceremonial life of these exuberant people. The ceremonies include dances and songs about every aspect of life, not only the tragedy of death, and are performed with great dramatic flair and colour. Men and women participate equally, although men take the leading role in organization of the ritual.

When a man dies those who are closely related to him cannot participate in the preparations for the funeral ceremony and are said to be in a taboo state of 'pukumani'. They are isolated and cannot touch food. The dead person's name also becomes taboo and cannot be spoken. The more distant relatives set about employing people to make beautifully carved and decorated grave posts and bark baskets.

According to ancient tradition the first pukumani or funeral ceremony originated in Creation times when Purukupali organized the first funeral rites for his dead son, Djinini.

The First Pukumani Ceremony

When he found his son Djinini was dead, Purukupali called out, 'Go, all of you! You must go and make grave posts. Go and make grave posts! First there will be a preliminary dance — a little dance, when everyone claps, then when you have finished, when you have cleared the ground, come and tell me.' Then they danced. Pamatikimi, Purukupali's other wife, and then the dead baby's mother Bima danced. Then she sat down. But first the bereaved Purukupali stretched out his arms, for he was a big man and not young. He was a big man. First he sat down, then he danced. The woman Pamatikimi danced as well. Our mothers were big. Bima (Waijai) as well, Waijai danced. They were Purukupali's wives.

The first 'little' dance is held within a month of the death, and the big, main

226

At dusk the Pukumani ceremony ceases and the mourners rest in preparation
for the climax the next morning. *photo D. Conroy*

ceremony some time later. Faces are intricately painted for hours before the dance
begins, and ornaments put on. The director of the dance lights a fire and everyone
dances in the smoke, so that the dead man's spirit will not recognize the dancers by
their smell.

'When we dance, we start when the sun is up high. We put dots on our faces. We
take hair belts, white cockatoo feather headdresses, false beards, dingo hair cres-
cents, goose feather balls, cane armlets and fibre armlets.'

'Let's go! We're going now,' the headman says, 'Oi! Children! We're going now.'
He makes a little fire.

'You,' he says. 'You, you first!' They dance around the fire there as the headman
stamps his foot shouting, 'Ai! Oi!'

'Oau!' they all shout, and they all throw their spears and cry. They clap their
buttocks. 'Oi!' they shout. The headman sings a song to chase away the spirits.
Everyone dances and then they finish.

They sleep that night and then next morning they eat a little possum, wallaby or
mashed zamia palm nuts. Then they dance again. When the dancing and singing is
finished the headman says, 'Take the grave posts over there to the grave.' 'Ai!' they
answer. 'That's all. All right, let's go.' Five men dance, shouting, 'Ah! Ah! Ah! Ah!
Ah! Ah!' they shout. Then they cry. One woman calls out, 'Alas for him my brother!'
Another woman calls out, 'Alas for him my uncle!' Another woman calls out, 'Alas
for him my father, my father!' The widow too — 'Alas for him my husband! Alas for
him my husband! Alas for him my husband!'

Then the ceremony is finished and the posts are left in the bush.

Allie Miller, Melville Island[14]

The Tiwi mortuary ceremonies are unique in Australia; only on Bathurst and
Melville Islands did the great Purukupali instruct the people to carve the beautiful

227

hardwood burial poles. Elsewhere in Arnhem Land the people were taught by their Ancestors to place the bones of the deceased in hollow logs, but before that they sing his spirit to its resting place and paint the clan designs on his chest.

While a man is dying in the north-eastern areas of Arnhem Land all his relatives gather around and sing to him, to instruct his soul what to do when it leaves his body. The singing makes the dying man 'think of his totem and his clan country and he wants his spirit to go straight to that place when he dies' as one man described it. When he is dead the singing continues: 'If we didn't sing he might go bad because evil ghosts might catch him and take him out to the jungle country where they live. It is better that his Ancestors come and get him, and take him straight to his clan country where his totem came from.'[15]

When he is dead, his relatives all cut themselves to show their grief, and paint a beautiful and intricate abstract design representing his clan country on his body so that the Ancestors can see which totem the man belonged to, and carry the spirit straight there.

Many different songs are sung in the mortuary ceremonies, all directed towards helping the soul of the dead man on its journey and purifying the living. Many of the ceremonies connect the land and sea. The sea cycle describes the movement of the tide and sea coming up to land, through tidal rivers, into small creeks and lakes. The land cycle tells of the clouds gathering in the high country and the rain falling into creeks, the creeks running into rivers, and the great rainy-season flood going out to sea. Various animals, birds and fish are brought into the songs which express the intimate relationship of man to his environment.

The Morning Star ceremony is also an important eastern Arnhem Land mortuary rite. As the pale Morning Star first appears in the early dawn, Aboriginal people are reminded of the journey their spirits must make when they die. Each morning the Morning Star is let out on a long string from its home on the island of Baralku where the spirits live, and when the spirit leaves the body of a dead man, it follows the Morning Star back to its resting place at Baralku. The following story tells of the visit of a man to the island of the dead, the home of Barnumbir.

Barnumbir, the Morning Star

The east wind brought a yam leaf to Yaolngura, a Kalpri man. He looked at the leaf, realizing that it came from the country of Barnumbir, the Morning Star, and decided to go there. Making a bark canoe, he filled it with shells containing water and lily bulbs to eat, and set off on his long journey to follow the yam.

He paddled for many days, and eventually reached a small island where he ate sea birds' eggs. After another four days in the canoe he came at last to the land, the land where the sun comes up and from where the Evening Star comes out. He rubbed sweat from his armpits over himself to make him strong, and also on his spear-thrower with the human hair fringe.

The ghosts on the island recognized him as a friend and he started to walk across the huge island of the dead. The ghosts were so thickly packed together that there was no room for them to stand on the island. They whispered as he passed, 'Ah, that is Yaolngura,' and gave him yams. He sang for them, a song about the canoe journey to their island, which is still sung today in Dhuwa mourning ceremonies.

One old ghost gave him three young wives, and then Yaolngura said, 'I want to see your Morning Star, I want to see how you make it.' At last he persuaded the old woman Marlumbu who controls the star, to show it to him, where she had it hidden in her baskets. When he gave it back to her she turned it loose, for it was early morning, and it flew away like a kite, while the old woman held the string it was attached to. On the island of the ghosts there is a tremendously high pandanus tree, and Barnumbir flies up there first to see the ocean. The old woman held the rope with one hand and pulled more string out of the basket with the other, crying out her commands to the Morning Star to go to various places and bring daylight. The Morning Star flew from Melville Island, the English Company Island, and over Buckingham Bay to Elcho Island, the whirr of its wings like the sound from the flight of a quail. Old Marlumbu heard the string sing out which meant daylight was coming. The ghosts sang out, 'Pull in the rope!' so she pulled Barnumbir back as though she had caught a very big shark, and hid the Morning Star in her basket again.

228

In a final frantic display of emotion and distress the Pukumani ceremony reaches its climax as the mourners crowd around the grave posts, wailing and beating their heads as they farewell the deceased. *photo D. Conroy*

Then Yaolngura said: 'I'm going back to my own country now, to get my wives and children and bring them here.' He exchanged presents with the head ghost on the island, and set off in his canoe. The ghost women who had been his wives cried. 'Don't worry,' he said, 'I'll be back.'

He paddled for many days, and at last, with his canoe full of yams and porpoise and other food from the island of the dead, he arrived one morning as his children were playing on the beach. They cried out, 'Father!' and his wives came down to meet him. This man had come back from the island of the dead as a true human being, not a ghost. He fed all of his children and wives on the porpoise and yams and they went to sleep. He made a camp by himself at sundown, and asked one of his wives to come with him. He wanted to make love to his wife, but because of his trip to the land of the dead he broke his back. When his wife moved she thought he was sleeping, but she looked at his eyes and he was dead. All his wives and children started wailing.

What had killed him was those three ghost wives of his, who had stolen his spirit before he left, because they liked him. When he slept with his real wife, his soul went back to the waiting ghost women.[16]

The mortuary ceremonies are completed in stages over many months and then the bones are delivered into the custody of the man's mother who keeps them until a hollow log is made. This is a log coffin which has been previously hollowed out by termites and which is then painted with ritual clan designs. It frequently is painted with eyes at the top, the eyes of the spirit of the deceased, and after a final farewell, both the log and the bones within are left to the elements.

If the spirits stray from their path to their totemic country or the island of the dead, the white cockatoos alone will see them and give a piercing cry of warning. Their cry screams out across Arnhem Land today as they continue to warn the living of the presence of the spirits in the bush.

229

Listening to the cry of the white cockatoo
Listening to the call that he gives as he flies
The call of the white cockatoo flying through the trees
Looking for a place to land
We hear his cries (but do not see him)
White cockatoo looking for a place to land
Now we see him and he sees us
The white cockatoo sitting in a tree calls in alarm
The white cockatoo flies away
Where are you, white cockatoo?
This way and that way we hear your sound
And now we see him again, he's landed in another tree
White cockatoo.[17]

THE SPIRIT WORLD

Beliefs about life after death vary throughout the continent. In eastern Australia the spirits of the dead return to their sky home, where the Totemic Ancestors have gone before them, whereas in most areas of northern Australia the spirit returns to its pre-existent spirit home which may be an island or a totemic centre.

The Walbiri people of the central desert believe that the spirit of a man comes from Tjukurpa, or the eternal Dreamtime, and must eventually return there. Secret caves contain hidden 'Dreaming' stones which are storehouses of disembodied spirits who may enter a woman again and so be reborn. After death the spirit returns to the cave and remains there until the same process is repeated, but this time the spirit becomes a child of the opposite sex to its previous reincarnation.[18]

In other parts of central Australia, however, among the Aranda for example, the spirit of the dead man finally perishes when it reaches the island of the dead, where it is destroyed by a violent electrical storm. In many areas of Australia the dead live much as the living do, with their own camps and family life. Beliefs in the island of the dead where this takes place are prevalent. Myths from South Australia and Arnhem Land respectively give some idea of the complexity of attitudes to life after death. The first, from South Australia, concerns Kangaroo Island, the home of the spirits of the dead.

Nar-oong-owie, the Sacred Island

Ngurunderi was a great Ancestral figure of the southern tribes in South Australia, who established Tribal Laws. After death, the spirits of men follow his ancient travel paths to the island of Nar-oong-owie (Kangaroo Island) and thence to Ngurunderi's home in the sky.

Long ago, Ngurunderi's two wives ran away from him, and he was forced to follow them. He pursued them and as he did so he crossed Lake Albert and went along the beach to Cape Jervis. When he arrived there he saw his wives wading half-way across the shallow channel which divided Nar-oong-owie from the mainland.

He was determined to punish his wives, and angrily ordered the water to rise up and drown them. With a terrific rush the waters roared and the women were carried back towards the mainland. Although they tried frantically to swim against the tidal wave they were powerless to do so, and were drowned. Their bodies turned to stone and are seen as two rocks off the coast of Cape Jervis, called The Pages or the Two Sisters.

Ngurunderi dived into the water and swam out towards the island. As it was a hot day he wanted shade so he made a she-oak tree which is said to be the largest in Australia. He lay down in the shade and tried to sleep but could not for as every breeze blew he heard the wailing of his drowning wives. Finding he could get no rest, he walked to the end of the island and threw his spear out into the sea. Immediately a reef of rocks appeared. He then threw away all his other weapons and departed to his home in the skies, where those who have kept the Laws he gave the tribes will some day join him.

Cave painting of inverted sorcery figure, Cape York. *photo J. Isaacs*

To this day anyone who tries to sleep under a she-oak tree will hear the wailing that Ngurunderi heard beneath the giant tree on Kangaroo Island, the sacred island of the spirits of the dead.[19]

In north-eastern Arnhem Land the mokuys, or Spirits of the dead, also go across the sea to their island homes. Djawa of Milingimbi tells this story of the journeys of the Spirits when men die.

This is the story which my father told me and which his father told him. The Yirritja mokuy (spirit) goes to a place called Yumaynga which is the place of the Macassan people. That is where the coconuts come from and the mokuys float on coconuts to get there. The Dhuwa mokuy goes to a place called Baralku, floating on driftwood. Baralku is an everlasting place where the mokuys dance and wait for the newly dead to arrive.

When the new mokuy arrives on the beach the other ones poke him in the ribs to make him laugh. When he laughs with his mouth open they can look and see that one of his teeth has been knocked out in the initiation rite. They tell him which narrow path to take, and where he will be able to find fresh water. He gets a nice welcome and can join with the others. The mokuy who has not had a tooth knocked out tries to hide this by not opening his mouth to laugh, but he is discovered and must go to be with all the other mokuys who have not gone through this particular rite. Thus the one mokuy sitting in the middle separates the mokuys as they arrive, into the ones who have been initiated and the ones who have not.

Djawa, Milingimbi[20]

231

In central Australia and the Nullarbor Plain area two brothers judge the dead and take them up to the sky country. Two spirit beings, the Kungara brothers, made their home in the greater and lesser Magellan Clouds. When a man dies, the Kungara brothers watch from the sky and will punish or reward them according to their past behaviour. They come to earth as the man is about to die, and sit themselves near the camp of the dying man, waiting for his soul to leave his body. If the dying man has been honest, kindly and generous, the elder Kungara will prevent his brother from taking the spirit of the dead man. If the man has been previously mean and quarrelsome the younger Kungara will be allowed to take the spirit to his camp fire in the sky, and eat it.[21]

Among the Willilambi people in the Great Australian Bight is another version of the same myth. It was believed that two great spirit beings, Badhu-Wudha, the right-handed one, and Kurulba, the left-handed one, wandered the land in Creation times, punishing wrong actions. Eventually they went up to the sky as stars, looking like long white clouds. Whenever a Willilambi old man died, Badhu-Wudha would stretch out his right hand and take him up, and whenever a Willilambi woman or child died, Kurulba would reach down for them with his left hand.[22]

Another much more horrible creature who is believed to capture a man's spirit is Wulgaru, from the Katherine River area of the Northern Territory.

How Djarapa Made Wulgaru

In the Creation times long ago on the Katherine River, all people lived together happily. One day, however, an old man named Djarapa tried to make a man from magic songs sung over pieces of wood roughly shaped like the limbs of a man. Knee

The spirits inhabit darkest parts of rainforests, dark rock recesses, caves and waterholes. *photo B. Thompson*

In the rock shelters of Arnhem Land are ancient red ochre paintings of 'Mimi' spirits running, dancing and hunting. These were in fact painted by the 'Mimis' themselves. *photos P. Tweedie*

and arm joints were formed of round river stones, stuck together with red-ochred wax. He painted ears, nose and eyes on the image, chanting a magic song which had been taught him by a powerful medicine man. All day and night he chanted until he was hoarse, and at last in despair he gathered up his weapons and went on his way.

As he walked along Djarapa heard a loud clanking sound like the crashing of many trees behind him, and looking around he saw the terrible monster of wood and stone shambling along, its arms beating the air and bringing down trees, its knee and arm joints creaking. Trembling with fear, Djarapa noticed that the wooden man was only following him by sight, so he hid, and watched the monster shamble past him through a lagoon and into the jungle. That is how the devil Wulgaru came to the Waddaman people because of Djarapa's foolishness. It wanders around in the dense scrub, the self-appointed judge of the dead, punishing those who have broken Tribal Law, and still searching for the man Djarapa who first created it in the Dreaming.

Waddaman, Katherine River[23]

An Aboriginal stockman from this area once met Wulgaru and his terror is evoked in the account which follows.

Mahlindji's Ride with Wulgaru

Mahlindji the stockman had been following cattle tracks, when suddenly he saw the tracks of a large goanna disappearing under a bush. Dismounting and pulling back the bush, he saw to his amazement and horror the face of the evil one, Wulgaru, gazing up at him from the red earth. Mahlindji remembered how Wulgaru was reputed to take on strange forms to trap travellers and he became very frightened.

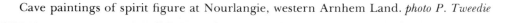

Cave paintings of spirit figure at Nourlangie, western Arnhem Land. *photo P. Tweedie*

He rode quickly towards the distant homestead. Those who had looked on the face of Wulgaru were believed to die soon after, as the evil one followed them until they looked around and then he snatched them away from the land of the living.

Mahlindji could tell by his horse's behaviour that some fearful thing was following them, and he sang the Emu Song to make his horse faster. The sun seemed to be sinking very quickly, so Mahlindji also sang a song to the Sun Woman to hold her fire stick higher in the sky. Then he came to the dense scrub where the dead are placed high on platforms of branches. In terror Mahlindji looked over his shoulder to see Wulgaru actually riding behind him on his own horse, beckoning to the spirits of the dead to come and assist him.

Mahlindji drove his spurs into his horse and rushed through the dark trees, calling on his totems. Everywhere he could hear a soft swishing noise like bat wings. Suddenly he was knocked to the ground. Trembling with terror he climbed up to one of the burial platforms and lay down with the dead man under his bark sheet. He heard the spirits lifting up the bark as he lay there feigning death, and he heard their soft voices saying, 'there are two . . .' Mahlindji felt by the swaying of the platform that he was being lifted up high and peering out from the bark shroud he saw a vast plain thronged with innumerable ghosts. As he watched their songmen started singing and clapping and he saw men from every tribe. The ghosts streamed towards a large cave, and he saw faces of his dead relatives, calling out to him to come and join them in the land of the dead.

As Mahlindji found himself right inside the painted cave, and saw the cave niches crammed with the bones and skulls of the dead; he realized he was in his clan's ritual burial cave and in the presence of Wulgaru who judges the souls of the dead. He was pressed forward by the crowd of ghosts until he was close to the dreadful Wulgaru. Wulgaru recognized him as a live man among the dead immediately, and the dogs beside him began to growl. In a flash Mahlindji turned and raced down the sky road, the ghosts pursuing him, angry at his intrusion. The dead are all equal and have no country of their own. They cannot bear a live man to visit the spirit land.

As one ghost reached out to catch him, Mahlindji called out to his Dreaming Totem, and straight away a big lightning flash came out of the sky like a snake, and after that he knew nothing. He awoke at dawn beneath the dead tree he had climbed the night before, and following the tracks of his horse, found a group of his people who had been searching for him. They were aghast at his story, and thought him very lucky to have survived such a night, after looking on the face of Wulgaru.

Waddaman, Katherine River[24]

SPIRIT BEINGS

The presence of spirits of the dead pervades certain parts of the landscape, and to an Aboriginal the bush is thick with all manner of spirits, not only the spirits of the dead. They inhabit dark recesses, deep caves and waterholes. Some were evoked principally to frighten children into obedience and to keep them close to the camp at night, but a great many others fell into a separate class. They were not human or animal but a separate class of indestructible being whose power was very strong. In Arnhem Land the mimi spirits and Namorodo spirits (described in Chapter 9) fall into this group, and in Cape York the Quinkans still dwell in bush caves.

In south-eastern Australia the tribes believed in an enormous variety of powerful spirit beings; the Myndie, previously mentioned as the giant snake of the south-east, was greatly feared. Myndie was very very long and very thick. According to the Wotjobaluk he moved only under orders from Bunjil, the All-Father. Any man who went to his territory of the Mallee in Victoria would die, and all the disease epidemics were attributed to him.

Horrific female spirits captured men and dragged them into their lair where they were devoured. One of these was Netto-gurrk. She, however, had a daughter who was much more pleasant, preferring to sleep with her mother's victims and then let them go.

In the south-east there was also a group of tiny spirits similar to the mimi of Arnhem Land. These were the net-nets, mischievous 'little people' who live in the

stony rises near Lake Condah where they make their homes in the caves. One was seen as late as 1932 by a local Aboriginal. He related an incident when he shot a rabbit, only to see a net-net run off with his catch. The net-net was very hairy and small with claws instead of finger and toe nails.[25]

Ngarangs were a group of spirit beings feared by the Kulin. They had long flowing hair and beards and long hairy arms and lived in the large swellings in the roots of some of the huge gum trees of south-eastern Australia, gnarled and lumped with age. They dragged their human victims here at night to eat them.

Baginis were female spirits who looked like pretty girls although they had sharp claws on their hands and feet. They fastened these into their male captives and forced them to make love. They soon tired of their captives, however, and let them go.

Supernatural creatures such as those mentioned above were known throughout Australia. We have verbal descriptions of their appearance and their disposition from Aboriginal story-tellers, but much more can be learnt about the spirit world of Aboriginal Australia by looking at the visual history, the ancient carvings and paintings throughout the continent which have depicted the world of man and his imagination for centuries.

Opposite: Painted wooden sculptures of 'Mimi' spirits by Guningbal, central Arnhem Land. *photo P. Tweedie*

CHAPTER NINE

Designs from the Dreaming

Red, the sacred colour of the red-ochre ceremonies of the desert heart, the blood shed on the earth by Marindi the dog of the Creation times who died when he fought the gecko lizard in the Flinders Ranges of South Australia. White, the pure white sacred pipeclay kept by the giant kangaroos and smeared over the body and face of Wirroowaa of the Lachlan River when he summoned the Great Spirit to the aid of his people. Yellow, the stains on the cliffs of the coast of Arnhem Land, the sacred colour of the Yirritja moiety of north-east Arnhem Land. And black, the charcoal left from thousands of campfires of the Ancestors of the Dreaming. These are the colours of the earth; the colours which have been here since the Creation era and which Aboriginals have used continually since then to paint on their bodies, their sacred objects and carvings, and to cover numerous caves, rockfaces and sheets of stringybark with designs shown to them by the Ancestors and telling the stories of Creation. The two divisions of the tribes of north-eastern Arnhem Land, the Yirritja and the Dhuwa, have divided the four colours between them as decreed by the great Ancestors; the Dhuwa own red and white while the Yirritja own yellow and black. The colours were traded from one group to another just as the sacred red ochre of the Flinders Ranges was sought by tribes hundreds of miles to the north.

The following story of the formation of red ochre by the dingo's blood was known by many tribes, including the Kooyiannie, Dieri, the Wonkonguru, the Ngameni and the Yaurorka.

Creation of Red Ochre from the Dingo's Blood

In the distant past, a gecko lizard named Adno-artina lived in a valley in the Flinders Ranges. Every day he would climb a peak and sing aloud so that everyone could hear him, 'Come out and fight. Come out and fight.' His challenge echoed along the valley daily until a large dog, Marindi, heard him and grew angry. He bounded up the dry creek-bed of the valley and yelled, 'I have come, I have come.' Adno-artina saw the challenger. He saw his enormous body and the white tip of his tail. He saw his numerous pointed teeth and decided on a plan which would give him the advantage over his ferocious rival. 'I will fight you later,' he said.

Marindi replied, 'We will fight later — you will make a feast for my pups,' and he curled up and slept at the base of the rock.

Adno-artina the gecko lizard was at his best at dark and so when the sun went down he stood up and issued his challenge to fight again. But to ensure he would not lose the advantage through fear of Marindi's size, he first tied a string spun from hair around the root of his tail so that his courage would be kept in and not run down his tail.

Marindi leapt up and tried to catch Adno-artina by the back of the neck to shake the life out of him, but the lizard ran in beneath his jaw, seized the dog by the throat and hung on. Marindi tried desperately to shake off the gecko but his sharp teeth only sank in deeper and suddenly the red blood spurted out. The blood formed a deep red scar on the high bank of the valley which to this day forms a deposit of red iron oxide.[2]

Opposite: Paintings on the body have preserved clan symbols from the Dreaming for centuries. *photo P. Tweedie*

photos above, below and opposite P. Tweedie

They are rubbing hard lumps of red ochre against the stones . . .
Chipping off fragments, pounding and grinding them into ochre-paint:
The sound of the scraping drifts across the country, into the place of the Snake . . .
They are sitting there, pounding red ochre,
Those spirits, people of southern clans . . .
Sound lifting into the air, from their pounding and scraping![1]

The designs in all Aboriginal paintings have particular meanings which have their roots in the legends of the Creation era. These designs have preserved the magnificently rich oral literature of Aboriginal people over successive centuries through the interpretation by generations of artists in paintings on the body, on bark and on stone.

In an Aboriginal community. painting the traditional designs on bark is only one aspect of the whole creative process. The desire to give visual and material expression to religious beliefs and myths concerning the travels and activities of the great Ancestral Spirits finds an outlet in many art forms. The same designs that appear on bark are also painted on the chests, arms and legs of ceremonial participants, on hollow logs used as coffins, and on carved wooden totemic animals. Animal emblems and symbolic geometric sculptures are also created in the form of intricate three-dimensional fibre constructions, usually made of bunched paper-bark wrapped in hand-spun string painted with natural clays and ochres.

What is most important to the Aboriginal artist is the inherent forces of the image and designs he is recreating — whether he paints on flesh or bark, or adds the finishing feathers and paint to an emu rangga or totem. He is conscious as he works of the spiritual presence and power of the Ancestral Being whose story is being told. The abstract cross-hatched body designs, each symbolic of a certain area or natural feature, are in fact believed to have been first designed by the Great Ancestors themselves.

241

Red ochre paintings on rock have survived for centuries.
Cave painting of Quinkan spirits and dingo, Cape York.
photo J. Isaacs

Luma Luma, the legendary giant who figures prominently in the Mardayan ceremonies of the Gunwinggu of Oenpelli, cut criss-cross patterns into his flesh and these are reproduced today as ritual body paintings and designs on bark paintings. Similarly Marwai, a legendary Ancestor of Western Arnhem Land, was believed to be a great artist of Creation times.

Marwai, the Master Painter

One great Ancestor, Marwai, was believed to have been the master painter, the keeper and distributor of designs amongst some groups in western Arnhem Land. He travelled about the country carrying chips of the ochre colours in his dilly bag which he hung from his neck. As he wandered, he rested at various caves and rock shelters in the Arnhem Land escarpment area and here he took out his ochres. He ground them on a flat stone until they formed a fine powder and then he mixed them with water to a paste. He painted some of the cave paintings which may still be seen today.

Marwai taught the people he met on his travels how to paint his designs; these designs were then handed down amongst the Aboriginal people for generations and are still incorporated in body painting designs. The great Gunwinggu painter Yirawala, whose major works are now kept in the Australian National Gallery, believed his own skills to have been derived from Marwai and he painted several 'portraits' of the master painter.[3]

Opposite: Bark painting of Luma Luma by Yirawala. *photo J. Steele*

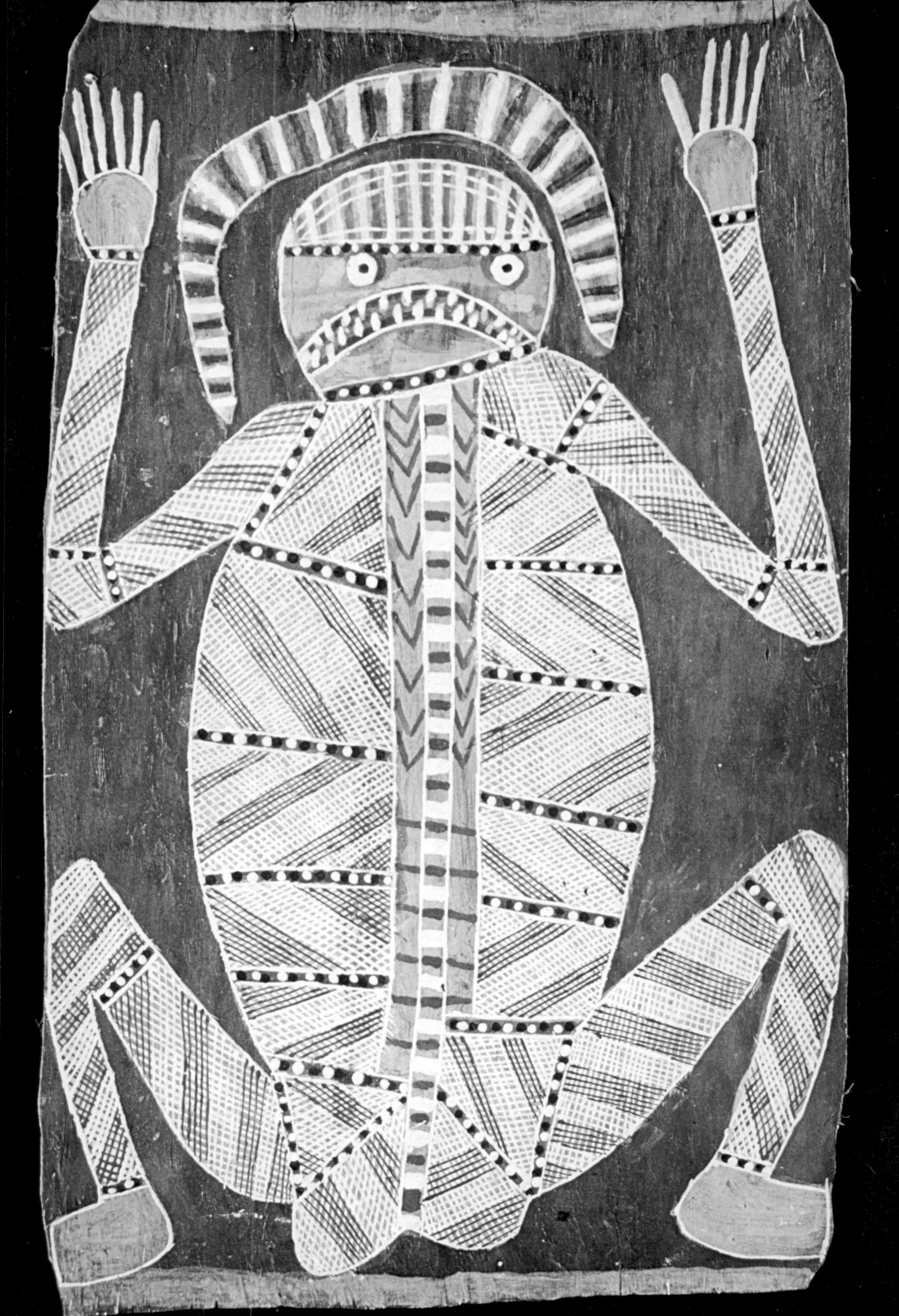

Luma Luma Gives the Sacred Designs to the Gunwinggu

Amongst the Gunwinggu and some other groups of western Arnhem Land, the giant Ancestor Luma Luma is credited with the ancient revelation of the designs now painted on the chests of dancers during ceremonies. These ochre designs comprise many fine criss-crossed lines forming an intricate pattern which covers the torso of male dancers. Each segment of the paintings represents an area of the man's tribal country.

Luma Luma was a giant Ancestor who came from over the sea, somewhere in the direction of Indonesia. He travelled far across the land and caused jealousy and resentment amongst the people by his selfish actions. Luma Luma was finally speared by the tribesmen, but before he died he showed them the sacred designs. He took a stone knife and carefully cut into his chest in a fine pattern of lines, revealing these as the designs which should be used in ceremonies. Luma Luma was allowed to return to the sea where he had come from, but the people, having learnt the dances and paintings from Luma Luma, continue to practise them today.[3]

Like Luma Luma the whale, the sacred whale of the Girrkirr clan of central Arnhem Land also gave the people their designs. The whale is the most important totem of the Girrkirr, and according to one of the clan, Birrkili, the great Dreaming Whale came from the east and as it came it formed rainbows in its spout which glowed against the giant black clouds of the monsoons approaching from the north. The whale arrived at the beach at Gurrumiya on the coast near Milingimbi but was suddenly caught in the shallows by the receding tide. The whale died there and made its great Dreaming site at Gurrumiya. When the tribes gathered at the beach and saw the decaying body of the whale they knew the diamond designs they saw on its back, and the patterns in the sky, had been given to them to use as their own

Bark painting of kangaroo by Yiwun Yiwun from Oenpelli. Some X-ray features are shown in the design. *photo J. Steele*

Bark painting by Weimangar of Benamarrka Ganora. Abstract totemic painting of crayfish from the clan country of the artist. *photo J. Steele*

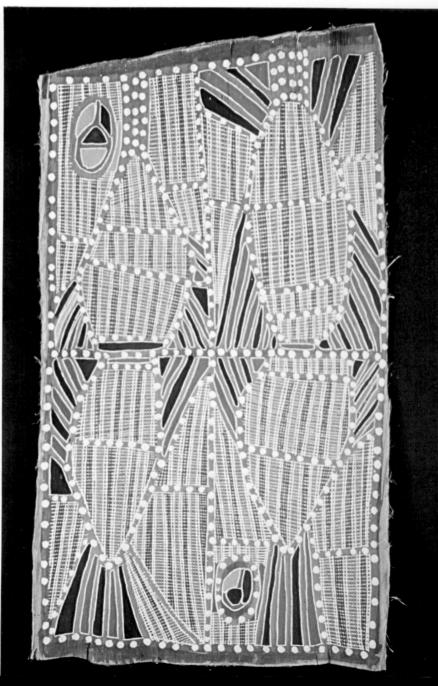

sacred emblems. The designs and colours used by the Birrkili today symbolize clouds, the rainbow and the great whale. To this day, whales seasonally beach themselves at Gurrumiya, and nowhere else.[4]

Further to the east, the great Laindjung, the Yirritja counterpart for the Djankawu ancestors of the Dhuwa moiety, was himself responsible for giving the Yirritja people all their sacred designs.

Laindjung Gives the Designs to the Yirritja

Laindjung came to the people from the sea and taught them their sacred rituals, songs and customs and named the totem animals. One day while a fisherman was standing at the edge of the sea, a figure rose from the waves. It was Laindjung, come to teach the people the sacred Law. His body rose from the water and as it did the white foam from the waves and the salt spray from the sea dried on his chest forming a beautiful honeycomb-like pattern of diamond shapes. His beard was white and bands of feathers hung from his forehead and upper arms. He carried a sacred yam rangga as his digging stick and told the fisherman he would give all his sacred knowledge to the people.

The diamond designs Laindjung bore on his chest from the foam and salt are today painted on the chests of Yirritja dancers at rituals and ceremonies. They are remembered carefully from generation to generation, and the story of Laindjung is told in episodes on sheets of bark—visual representations of the sacred Dreaming stories.[5]

The Dhuwa moiety also trace their intricate sacred patterns to their Creation Ancestors. When Djankawu and the sisters arrived on the coast at Yelangbara one of the first things they saw was the intricate patterns that Djunda the goanna had

Mandarrg's camp. One of the finest artists in Arnhem Land paints his barramundi design on bark with his family around him. *photo P. Tweedie*

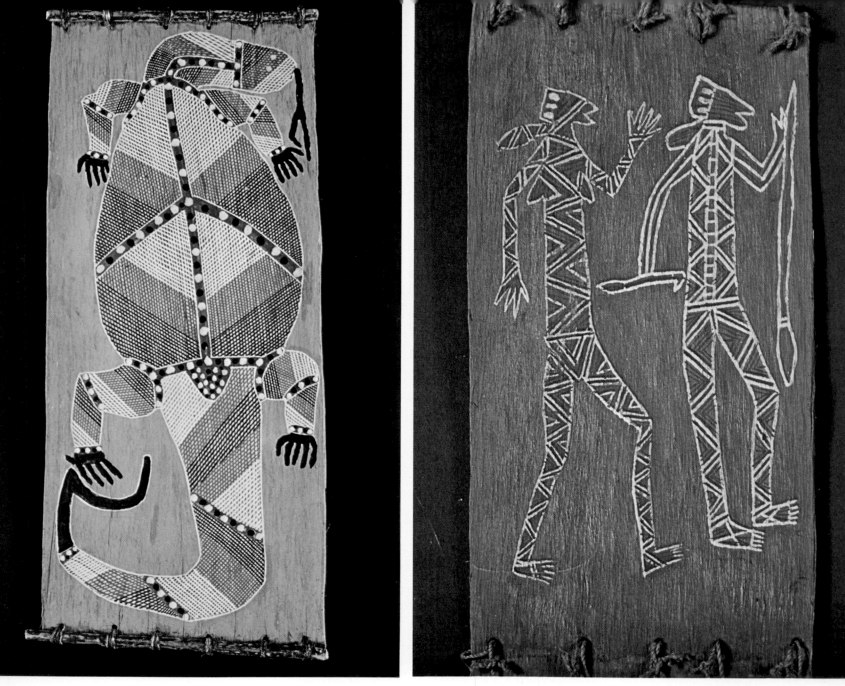

Bark painting of a goanna by Naroldol, Gunwinggu, western Arnhem Land. *photo J. Steele*

Bark painting by Bloocha, Rembarrnga group. An old man and woman are hunting when they see a black kangaroo and decree it as a totem. *photo J. Steele*

made as he ran across the sandhills.[6] These designs are repeated today in paintings that concern the travels of Djankawu. Similarly, reeds formed a beautiful pattern on Minala the long-necked tortoise of the Dreaming, as they flowed over her back as she swam amongst them in the freshwater billabongs. The patterns of reeds and the little air bubbles that formed on her have been repeated in paintings for generations.

PAINTINGS ON BARK

In the preceding selections from the enormous body of Aboriginal oral literature, the story of the Creation of the continent and the settlement of Australia by the Aboriginal people has emerged through sacred myths, legends and songs. In the northern areas, we also find today a vast source of visual records of this history in the form of Aboriginal paintings, and more specifically bark paintings.

All Aboriginal tribes who built their shelters with slabs of bark over a wooden framework painted on the inside of the shelter. The subject matter for the oldest of these paintings which still survive was taken from their immediate environment and depicts the everyday events of life. Paintings show animals such as kangaroos, birds, fish and reptiles in the surrounding country, and hunting scenes of stalking and spearing animals, fishing and gathering bush foods. Rituals of dance are also shown as well as evil spirits, the subject of so many legends. Today Aboriginal painters prepare rectangular sheets of bark on which to paint, as bark shelters are used only in some small outstations, though even in these an occasional painting is found on the interior of the bark wall.

These bark paintings are not however done only for pleasure; those which depict sacred symbols and designs fulfil important functions during traditional ceremonies. In eastern Arnhem Land they are kept in store houses and exhibited to

Dancers paint their bodies before taking part in ceremonies. *photo P. Tweedie*

initiates to explain the rituals, and in western Arnhem Land they are also used as illustrations of the sacred legends and stand in rows on the ceremonial grounds.

The relationship of the Aboriginal people to their land and the necessity for the performance of increase ceremonies in order to ensure the procreation of the species and cycle of life in nature has been explained in legend. The act of painting the animal, bird, fish and plant species on bark is also important in their continued reproduction.

Many bark paintings, particularly the sacred paintings, are replicas of body paintings used at important rituals. These often symbolically represent the person's clan country and its rocks, rivers, grass, clouds, trees and waterholes. The symbolism is sometimes obscure, yet when the story is told the painting glows with ancient meaning to the onlooker. Other paintings, much more graphic, are less sacred and show the animals, plants and figures in the non-symbolic physical form.

A man may have his clan's designs painted on his body many times in his lifetime, first at his initiation and finally at death. As a favour, and as a gesture of friendship, two men may agree to paint their own designs on each other's bodies as a deep honour and the care and precision with which this is done is noticeable. Splotchy, careless painting is not approved of and this is reinforced in myths throughout Australia. A Milingimbi story in Chapter 4 about the lizard and the cockroach who painted each other, one beautifully and one carelessly, and the trouble that ensued is echoed in the following story from the Central Desert.

Nintaka the Perentie, and Milbili the Goanna

During the earliest times the two great reptiles of the desert, the perentie and the goanna, agreed to decorate each other for a ceremony. Nintaka the perentie was a

247

fine artist and took great care with his work. He painted fine lines and dots over the body and tail of the goanna. When the ochre on his back had dried he turned over and Nintaka, using the thinnest of brushes, painted extremely fine lines on his belly.

Then it was Milbili's turn to paint Nintaka. The designs on his own body had taken some time to paint and the time for the ceremony was near. Milbili grew impatient and hurriedly painted Nintaka with crude splashes of yellow dots which he applied with pieces of rolled-up bark.

When the goanna had finished Nintaka asked how he looked. Milbili lied and said the designs looked beautiful and Nintaka therefore walked over to the ceremonial ground feeling proud of his appearance. As he walked, however, he passed a waterhole and bending down to drink saw his splotched appearance. Nintaka was furious and rushed to attack the goanna for his deceit, but Milbili escaped by climbing to the top of a high gum tree.

Nintaka cursed the goanna and said that from now on he must live in the branches of trees and take shelter in their hollow trunks, while he would use the rocks as his home and shelter. Even today the two reptiles keep to separate habitats and their designs remain on their bodies. The goanna is a beautiful lizard with a delicate lace-like pattern on its back while the perentie's dark brown skin is covered with large yellow dots and irregular lines.

Pitjantjatjara, central Australia[7]

The appreciation by Aboriginals of beautiful designs which are carefully executed is clear in the previous story. All men in Aboriginal society are artists. The following legend, however is unusual. It tells of a young gifted artist who, because at first he would not learn how to hunt, run, sing and dance—preferring only to paint—was forced to leave his people. His acceptance back into the tribe later was due to his gift to them of most valued earth ochre colours, and his status of artist was accepted thenceforth. The legend indicates that amongst Aboriginal people there is certainly

Milbili the Goanna (*left*) and Nintaka the Perentie (*right*). Milbili hurriedly painted Nintaka with crude splashes of paint, whereas Nintaka applied a delicate design of fine lines to Milbili. *photos D. Roff*

recognition, if reluctant, of the 'artistic temperament', in this case tolerated finally because the artist had assisted the community with the gift of beautiful ochres which they needed for their ceremonial preparations.

The Boy Who Drew

There was a young boy growing with the people who kept drawing pictures when he should have been learning how to hunt and learning how to sing and dance. He would not learn any of these things, but spent his days drawing in the sand and drawing with ochre on rocks. The old men grew angry because they needed the ochre to trade to the coast for salt, so they forbade the boy to use any more ochre.

So the boy cut his finger and used the red blood to draw pictures on trees; and the old men forbade him to cut himself. So the boy peeled the bark from a tree and with a sharp piece of rock he drew a picture on the bark; but the tree died, so the old men forbade him to take bark from the trees. He found a smooth patch of sand and drew a picture in the sand, but one of the old men walked over his picture and ruined it. So the boy left the people and walked into the hills.

He walked for three days and was far into the hills when he came to a small cave in a hillside, and the walls of the cave were covered with drawings that were better than any that he had ever made. He lived in the cave for a year, looking at the drawings and learning how they had been made, and he knew then that he could draw pictures like those on the walls of the cave. So he walked back through the hills and returned to the people, but as he walked he found a large patch of ochre with red, yellow, white and brown ochre, and he placed some of each colour on a flat piece of rock and carried them back to his people.

The old men welcomed him, for they could no longer find any ochre, and they asked him to draw them a picture with the ochre he had brought; and the boy drew a picture that was so beautiful that the old men said that he might use all the ochre he needed and might draw wherever he wished and whenever he wished.[8]

Rock engraving of turtle, Dampier, north-western Australia. *photo R. Morrison*

ART OF THE EARLIEST PEOPLE

The earliest artistic records of Aboriginal people are believed to be the 'Macaroni' markings deep below the Nullarbor Plain, in the dark innermost reaches of the Koonalda Cave. The markings appear to have been made by fingers drawn across the limestone surface of the cave wall. Other lines appear to intersect some of the finger markings and in one place a figure is almost discernible. In other parts of the cave, man's most ancient and universal design, the concentric circle, is just visible. The art cannot tell us a great deal about the civilization of that time, but it does give a visual record not only of Aboriginal habitation, but of the beginnings of art in this country, the beginnings of the need for human aesthetic expression. The etchings most probably had a religious meaning. As the cave could only be reached in the dark with the aid of torches, the laborious process of making the carvings must have been strongly motivated. The motivation of these ancient artists is lost in time, but although we do not have the key to interpret the most ancient art of this continent, an enormous body of designs engraved on rocks and painted on caves of more recent origin provides a fascinating visual record of the history of man and the unique culture which evolved on this continent.

ROCK ENGRAVINGS

Engravings into the surface of rocks are by far the most widespread works of ancient Aboriginal art. These extend over the whole continent except for Victoria and a small region of New South Wales. Ranging from isolated carvings to huge galleries on expanses of flat rock, these engravings include some of the oldest works of art in the world. The subjects range enormously. They frequently cover all animals of the environment in which they are found as well as large images of totemic Ancestors and Spirit figures. Many of the larger galleries are situated close to areas used by local tribes as ceremonial grounds, in particular Mootwingie north-east of Broken Hill in New South Wales, and Sturts Meadows also in New South Wales. At Mootwingie, for centuries before white men came to the area, images were carved in the rock surface on top of a huge boulder overlooking the ceremonial ground; and at Sturts Meadows literally thousands of subjects are shown in the rock gallery of scattered boulders along a small dry river bed. Birds, animals, human figures and their tracks, boomerangs, concentric circles and other abstract symbols are all shown.

Aboriginals today do not carve on stone and say the carvings which surround them are the work of Dreaming Ancestors, or people who lived long, long ago. But the areas where the huge Ancestor carvings are found, in particular the Hawkesbury River area of New South Wales where carvings of Ancestral figures of men up to 4 metres (12 feet) in length have been found, are places where the oral traditions of the local Aboriginal people did not survive the advent of white man. We are therefore left to wonder and surmise whether the giant figure is of Baiame the Great Spirit or another Creation hero from the legends of the area. The inhabitants of the Hawkesbury sandstone area may have gone, but their spirits and the spirits of their Great Ancestors live on in the bush at these awesome sites.

The power of some sites in south-eastern Australia depicting rock engravings of large Ancestors can be felt by tradition-oriented Aboriginal visitors from other areas. Recently Wandjuk Marika, a Riratjingu elder from Yirrkala and at that time Chairman of the Aboriginal Arts Board, visited one important carving of a large figure on the Colo River, New South Wales. He had been asked to inspect it for damage and make recommendations for preservation. He had not visited the impressive sandstone ridge before. Here the large figure of a man with legs and arms outstretched lies alone on a flat rock on top of the sheer cliff. Between the legs of the carved figure is a deep rock hole usually full of rainwater.

Wandjuk looked down at the figure and then quietly, shaking a little, moved off over the ridge and into the bush by himself. The rest of the party joined him later, to find him standing at a most unusual formation of weathered rock, tears streaming down his face. He said:

'This is what I was looking for. We didn't know what happened to that one. He left my country and travelled south. We knew he travelled south, then nothing. Now I know this is where he came. These rocks are the same as one place in my country. He is here. He is talking to me.'

Rock engraving from the Cleland Hills, central Australia. The very old design is unique in this area and appears to be a heart-shaped face with staring eyes. *photo R. Edwards*

Overleaf: 'Mimi' figures painted on a rock face near Cannon Hill, Arnhem Land. These are some of the finest and most elegant of Aboriginal rock paintings. *photo P. Tweedie*

The party camped overnight a few miles away and that night Wandjuk woke frequently, calling out loudly into the darkness. The next morning we found him quietly singing to himself, uncommunicative, subdued. But by the afternoon he was his old self, relaxed and talkative and willing to share his experience. He said he had been visited by a Spirit who was surprised to see him there because no Aboriginals had lived there for many years. The Spirit taught him a song, a song about the great Ancestor who had been carved on the rock. 'Na-Na-Warwee ah-Na-Warwee-ah,' he sang again quietly.

ROCK PAINTINGS

The beautiful and vast galleries of Australian rock paintings reveal more about the way of life of successive generations of Aboriginal people than any other form of Aboriginal visual art. It is possible, for example, to study the most ancient mono-chrome paintings of Arnhem Land and discern a range of hunting spears, weapons and utensils as well as ceremonial regalia which are not used by Aboriginals today. The positioning of subjects and their size in proportion to others may also serve as pointers to archaeologists and prehistorians in discerning cultural change.

While scientists maintain that the paintings of the spidery Mimi figures of Arnhem Land and the Bradshaw figures of the Kimberleys are the earliest paintings by Aboriginal inhabitants of Australia, the Aboriginal people themselves reveal that they were in fact created by the Spirits themselves; they were not done by human beings.

ART FROM THE WORLD OF THE SPIRIT

THE ART OF THE 'MIMI'

The finest and most elegant of Aboriginal rock paintings are the 'Mimi' figures. These are painted almost exclusively in red ochre and range in tone from pale red

251

to darkest brown. They are very fine in line and depict figures in motion, hunting, spearing a kangaroo, running and dancing. Sometimes they wear elaborate head-dresses and carry a multitude of weapons or they may appear completely un-adorned. Anthropomorphic 'Mimis' are also common. These frequently have the head of an animal, particularly a kangaroo, and the body of a human. The lines of the figures are very fluid and all are moving; their bodies bend and stretch as they hurl a spear or leap across a rock face. These old paintings are seldom superim-posed with newer paintings and large friezes of running and dancing figures can be found throughout the escarpment area of western Arnhem Land.

'Mimi' animal motifs include a variety of kangaroos and wallabies, turtles, fish, echidna, flying foxes, crocodiles and snakes. The thin serpents may wind for up to 3 metres (10 feet) across the rock face.

One of the main themes of the mythology of the Gunwinggu and neighbouring tribes centres on the mischievous thin 'Mimi' spirits which inhabit the rock crevices and bush of western Arnhem Land. Ancient red ochre paintings have been closely identified by Aboriginals as being paintings of 'Mimis' and by 'Mimis'. As the Mimis were believed to be exceptionally skilled spirit hunters who existed in this area before man and who eventually taught the Aboriginals how to spear a kangaroo, these paintings would seem to fit the image created.

The paintings also testify to weapons in Arnhem Land which have not been used there for centuries. All spears in the north are thrown with a spear-thrower; however the 'Mimis' are shown throwing a variety of unusual spears by hand. They also hold boomerangs, not seen in Arnhem Land for centuries. One of the most interesting paintings historically is of a Thylacine or Tasmanian Tiger. These animals, which became extinct on the mainland of Australia about 11,000 years ago, survived only in Tasmania, the last one dying in Tasmania in the nineteenth century. Unless it had entered the mythology of the area it is unlikely that the Thylacine would have been painted very long after it had disappeared; this leaves us with the conclusion that the Thylacine painting and other 'Mimi' paintings may

At certain sacred cave sites and rock shelters throughout Australia the great Ancestors themselves came to rest. Here they changed into their spirit form and 'they put themselves on rock', leaving their painted image behind. *photos R. Edwards*

Aboriginal tribes who built their shelters with slabs of bark over a wooden framework painted on the inside of the shelter. In the remote outstations of Arnhem Land today small family groups continue this practice. *photo J. Isaacs*

be at least 11,000 years old. Archaeological findings at Oenpelli in fact date many paintings to possibly 20,000 years ago.

The question of precise age of the art may be left unanswered; these galleries undoubtedly provide Australia with a beautiful and tangible record of successive occupation of an area of this continent which must rate as one of the great cultural heritages of mankind.

TOTEMIC BEINGS

The unity of man and nature, of a man and his totem, is expressed in numerous cave paintings in images full of imagination and life. Yams take on human characteristics, people have kangaroo heads, and animals have breasts or limbs like humans. By understanding the myths which explain this relationship of people to all things in their physical world, their essential oneness, these paintings seem logical and understandable. Without that insight their significance is lost. Nevertheless as paintings they are beautiful and fascinating interpretations of anthropomorphic and zoomorphic beings of the Dreaming.

When Mandarg and Spider Murulumi of central Arnhem Land gazed at these ancient paintings an old story was brought to mind.

Nagorgo the Father Separates the Men from the Animals

In the beginning, a long time ago, the creatures of the world did not have their present shape. One day Ngundid the snake, Mulili the catfish, Galaba the kangaroo and all other beings gathered in the country of the Rembarrnga people. From Maningrida way came Nagorgo, the Father, and his son Mulnanjini. They looked at all the creatures and said, 'You are not proper people and not proper animals. We must change this.' Then they made a ceremony which is still performed today. They lit a fire with their fire sticks which quickly spread until it engulfed all the beings and

255

Above: Rock painting, Delamere Station, Northern Territory. Painting associated with rainmaking ceremonies. *photo R. Edwards*

Below: Rock painting of Ancestral figure, El Sharana. *photo R. Edwards*

Above: Rock painting of a female
spirit figure, El Sharana.
photo R. Edwards

Below: Rock paintings, El Sharana. Spirit figure and
kangaroos superimposed on previous paintings indicate
the antiquity of Aboriginal designs. *photo R. Edwards*

Abraded grooves, one of the earliest forms of art on the continent, from the Lightning Brothers site, Northern Territory. The grooves represent falling rain. *photo R. Edwards*

scorched the earth and rocks. When the fire subsided all the creatures found that animals and humans had lost their strange features and looked as they do now.[9]

EVIL SPIRITS

As well as the benevolent 'Mimi', the evil Namorodo devils also dwell in the bush of western Arnhem Land at night and appear as ochre paintings on cave walls. Their bodies are very thin, only flesh held together by sinews. Their thick hair flows from their heads and their pointed jaws contain rows of interlocking teeth. Instead of fingers and toes they have long claws and they fly through the air at night making whistling noises. If a whistling noise is heard at night everyone must stand motionless or the Namorodo will shoot off one of its claws into the victim.

THE GREAT SPIRIT ANCESTORS

At certain sacred cave sites and rock shelters throughout Australia the great Ancestors themselves came to rest. Here they changed into their spirit form, or as the Gunwinggu say, became djang, and they 'put themselves on rock,' leaving their painted image behind. Such sacred Ancestral paintings include the great Wandjinas of the north-west, the serpent soul of the Walbiri in central Australia, the staring Quinkan figures of Cape York and in Arnhem Land the Lightning Spirit and the Rainbow Serpent.

Paintings of the Great Ancestors have been reverently retouched and given new life by successive Aboriginal artists and these powerful images are seldom superimposed with other designs but stare down from the rock shelters as striking images from the Dreaming. The power of the Spirit Ancestor dwells also at these sites and care must be taken when approaching them. The visitor must call out his name well in advance so that the Spirit will not be taken unaware. If Namarrkon or the Wandjina are angered they may send tropical storms or cyclones. So indeed might the Rainbow Serpent, or he might travel underground and devour the offender.

Rock engraving at Dampier, north-western Australia.
A thin spirit figure with outstretched arms is superimposed
on a broader, older figure. *photo R. Morrison*

Rock engraving of a large bird with
its eggs, and a crab, Dampier.
photo R. Morrison

The Quinkans will also attack by flying through the air and hitting their victims on the back with the stone axes they bear on their elbows and knees. These sites of Ancestral Spirit paintings are however also sources of spiritual strength for Aboriginal people today, places where they can draw some of the spiritual power from the Dreaming to bear on their daily life.

CONTINUITY OF ABORIGINAL DESIGNS

Today few Aboriginal artists paint on the walls of rock shelters. They prefer instead to continue their ageless design themes on bark. The rock galleries throughout Australia remain however as a source of the most varied and wonderful paintings of the environment and its creatures by generations of artists.

The most famous of these paintings were originally termed 'X-ray' art, because they show the internal organs of the animal as well as its outward shape. The Aboriginal artists painted both internal and external features of their subjects. Many of these paintings of huge barramundi, of kangaroos, echidna, long-necked turtles and other animals were painted as 'hunting' paintings to evoke the presence of the animal painted and thereby ensure a successful hunt. Others were painted by jealous husbands as sorcery figures, to inflict punishment on unfaithful wives. These figures would be inverted and have barbs or spears in the body, depending on the punishment envisaged by the sorcerer. Scenes of love and sex might be painted by a man as he sang the magical love-songs thereby enticing a young girl to be his lover.

In Arnhem Land today, many Aboriginal family groups have moved away from government settlements and missions back to their tribal lands in an attempt to live their traditional way of life in their own country. Here the rituals and ceremonies connected with the sacred sites of their Ancestors play a significant role in their lives. As an important part of maintaining the continuity with the past, many people are also finding renewed interest in expressing their beliefs through bark paintings.

259

CHAPTER TEN

The Visitors

Aboriginal people lived on this continent of Australia for many thousands of years, gradually adapting their way of life to the changing environment. There was a great deal of contact between different Aboriginal groups, exchanges and trading, and spread of ritual and mythology. Although the land of Australia remained the domain of Aboriginals alone for up to 40,000 years before European invasion, the Europeans were not the first aliens to sail to the shores of this vast country. The songs and stories of northern Arnhem Land and the coast of north-western Australia record the frequent contact of coastal Aboriginals with people from Malaya and Indonesia for centuries before the arrival of the pale-skinned balanda, the Europeans.

THE BAIINI

The people who appear to have come first are the mysterious Baiini who arrived by sailing ship. They came a very long time ago; some believe they were here in the Creation era as both Djankawu and Laindjung came across them on their travels. The great Djankawu and his sisters met the Baiini and exchanged goods with them, in particular some beautiful feathered string. Djankawu found the Baiini's spoon when they left, which was charcoal black from stirring trepang cooking fires and said, 'Ah, this is a good colour, I'll have this for my own,' and he used the black to paint sacred designs.[1] The great Laindjung also came in touch with the Baiini for it is said, he ate the rice which they grew for their own use.

The Baiini came to the coast before the Macassans in *lolperu* or sailing ships. They came as families, men, women and children, and built on the shores of Arnhem Land houses made of stone and ironbark. The women were beautiful, with lighter skin than the Aboriginals, and wore coloured sarongs of many patterns as they went about their daily work. They planted rice in both Warramiri country and Gumaidj country. This rice is called *birida* or husked rice, and was called *luda* by the Baiini. The womenfolk were very busy working in their camp or in the ricefields. They were often weaving at their looms which they brought with them in their sailing ships. They knew the secret of making cloth but never taught this to the Aboriginal people. Their cloths were woven on these primitive looms with yarn dyed in large pots with beautiful colours. The designs on this cloth were the same as on carved figures of the Baiini which have been made by the Yirritja people of Yirrkala. The old Baiina name for this cloth was *jalajal*, while the Macassans called it *liba*. The Europeans call it *dumala*. The design, which was used in many combinations and variations, was called *darabu* and comprised a pattern of coloured triangles.

The Baiini women are spoken of in many Yirritja songs, planting rice, cooking, weaving, dyeing, fishing, making armbands and necklets, stitching the sails for their boats and caring for their families. The men fished and hunted with harpoons and traps as Aboriginals do today, but are not remembered as well as the womenfolk whose attractiveness is still evoked in the use by Aboriginals of a personal name such as Karambal, 'the buttocks of a Baiini woman, like the stern of one of their boats'.

Traces of the Baiini remain along the coast of north-eastern Arnhem Land and the islands near by, from Blue Mud Bay to Elcho Island. There are rocks that are

Opposite: A Macassan well surrounded by tamarind trees at Milingimbi. The trees grew from the tamarind seeds which the visiting Macassans used to flavour their food. *photo J. Isaacs*

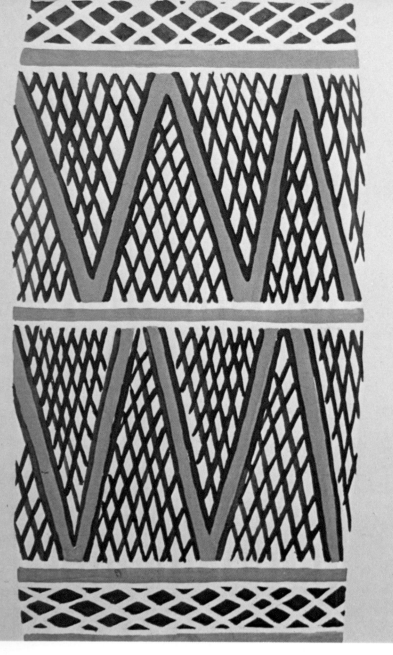

The designs on the cloth worn by the Baiini women formed a pattern of coloured triangles; these are repeated on carved wooden figures made in Arnhem Land by Aboriginal people. This design was painted by Diana Conroy from a Macassan figure in the South Australian Museum.

Carved wuramu figure by Mambur from Elcho Island represents a Macassan prau captain Deinmanga, and the overall design is the cloth he wore. R. M. Berndt collection, Anthropology Museum, University of Western Australia.

wrecked Baiini boats, others which are anchors and various places which are named after incidents involving them in the past.

A waterhole near Trial Bay represents a Baiini woman's vagina, commemorating the fact that she had sexual intercourse there. At Jamanga Island, near Cape Wilberforce, a large rock is symbolic of a boat that the Baiini pulled up on the shore. And at Duldji on the mainland, not far from Pobassoo Island, is the boijama tree shade where a group of Baiini rested, while a nearby rock in the sea is their anchor. Maranggauwa, near the Cato River in Arnhem Bay, is the place of a Baiini's spirit; a moving rock symbolizes his material substance. At Jikari, a 'movable' island, which appears to move up and down with the tide from the mouth of the river, is a Baiini boat. And nearby at Guramura, also in Arnhem Bay, are the remains of a large Baiini settlement, later superimposed by Macassans and Japanese, where gardens were planted with rice. At Balboi, near Trial Bay, Baiini planted 'coconuts', which today are paperbark trees. Near Maindjalnga, not far from Cape Arnhem, grows a 'whistling' tree under which Baiini rested from their work of trepanging. And at Banalbi, near Yirrkala, they were frightened by the Spirit Being called Thunder Man.[2]

Before the Baiini left Australia, they looked into the distance and saw smoke rising in the sky from the direction of the Celebes. Their headman decided to go to that land over the sea and leave the coast of Arnhem Land to the Aboriginals. The words of Rraying from Milingimbi when she tells of the departure of the Macassans or Indonesians (who came later, as we shall see) are strangely reminiscent of the stories of the departure of the Baiini.

Macassan and Dog Give Each Other Fire

This story which I am going to tell is about a Macassan. A long time ago, a man came

Bark painting of Macassan women weaving, by artist from Yirrkala. The artist's father saw these women weaving when he visited Macassar with trepangers last century, and he related his experiences to his son. Painting in the collection of the Art Gallery of South Australia.

to the mainland to us, and he was a Macassan man. He came quickly in his prau to the place called Bambal;* he landed. He went ashore and he made a house for himself. And the uprights which he drove into the ground were bamboo, and he planted food, he planted rice (*berratha*). He poured it out all over the ground, into holes which he had dug. He worked, and finished everything, the home and the garden, and he sat down.

Well, he sat there, and a dog came to him, and they were talking together. This is what they said to each other; this is what the white man (Macassan) said to him: 'There, I've given you some matches.' And the dog turned around, and the man said again, 'Here, these matches are for you.' And the dog replied, 'Those are yours! I call my fire sticks duttji.' Here he was talking about fire sticks, the little sticks we use, he was talking about duttji. He (the Macassan) sat there, and he saw smoke in the sky, above his home which was called Naninynga. At his own place there was fire burning. And he cried, 'Oh . . . h! My place, Murrunydjura, Guwalilnga, Dhangarrpura, is there fire there? I'm going back to the sea, to return to my own home.' And he pulled out all the uprights of his home; he pulled them out, threw them down, that was it. And he went off, he returned to his own place. So he pulled out the post of his house, and the holes are still there, and the rice turned into shell middens. Those shell middens which are quite high.[3]

When the Baiini left in their sailing boats their rice plantations fell into ruin and finally disappeared, but today a type of grass grows in place of those ricefields which is a food source for the Aboriginal people. The roots of these grasses or bulrushes are eaten and it is said the food came from the Baiini.

*Bämbal is about 8 kilometres (5 miles) from Galiwinku (or Elcho Island).

THE MACASSANS

Wati katika wata bili bata:wu wata wa:lisa
kwata wa:la taritari sa:m misa
kapalanggu kwatajlo ki matanuna sita:la
ki mai so:lor ke ta:wula palo e ka:
pulu e ma: paripari kanana bandaya
nurumbarumba ana'bi:lja ka'lo:d
boradini sowul de duku masala bada
pi:ya

Mawalan

This is a Macassan song that my father Mawalan knew and I knew it too. It's about the mast of their boat. Every time they left they used to pull the mast from the boat and put it on the deck. After that they took up the anchor and sang the song before they went out to sea again, back to their own country.[4]

I thought I had lost that song, forgotten some of it. But now I have found it again and I am happy. I can teach it to my son Mawalan.

Wandjuk Marika, Yirrkala

The story of the Macassans is an important part of the Aboriginal history of northern Australia. The seasonal visits of these Indonesian fishermen in their sailing praus, and their relations with the Aboriginal people over several centuries before Europeans came, are now a part of Aboriginal history recorded in song cycles of eastern Arnhem Land.

Since at least 1650, Macassan or Indonesian fishermen from the Celebes (modern Sulawesi) visited northern Australian coastal waters. They arrived in their sailing vessels, each normally of about 25 tonnes, called praus, fishing from the dugout canoes which they brought with them for trepang or bêche-de-mer, the sea slug which abounds in the shallow waters around the Arnhem Land and Gulf of Carpentaria coast. They sought the help of Aboriginal men to collect, cook, dry and smoke the trepang, which was then transported back to the trading port of Macassar. From there the cured trepang was shipped to China, where it was a highly prized ingredient in Chinese food. The Macassans also traded with the Aboriginals for tortoise and pearl shell.

The Macassans, unlike the legendary Baiini, did not bring their women with them and, although there are stories of young boys in the crews, these were not the children of the men in charge. They travelled in groups of thirty to sixty praus, each with possibly thirty men on board, and would arrive on the Australian coast in December each year, stay for the Wet Season, and return to Macassar four or five months later.

A variety of different races from Indonesia made the trip south during this phase of trade and contact with the land they called *Marege*. The Macassans or Mankasarau from the southern Celebes were the most numerous, but the Bugis, a distinctly different group of sailors and traders from the Celebes, also came south. The two groups are separated clearly in Aboriginal memories due to the difference in their praus. The bow of the Bugi ship was bent down and had an eye painted on either side so that it could see its way clearly through the waters to its destination. The bow of the Macassan prau pointed upwards.

The praus used by the Macassans are accurately recorded by Aboriginal artists on rock shelters and in bark paintings. The paintings at Marnggala cave on Groote Eylandt give a detailed visual account by Aboriginal artists of the different kinds of praus which landed on the shores of Groote Eylandt. Most are shown with crew on board, arms raised, working hard. The Macassans were Muslim and each fleet carried with it at least one man who acted as the prayer-man, calling out each day the religious chants towards the west. Stories relate how he climbed the mast of the prau as it was leaving and sent his chant echoing into the distant waters. Some paintings show men up the mast and most praus are laden with food and provisions for the sojourn on Australian shores. They carried in each prau several dugout canoes and many containers of food and rice. The paintings depicting them are in cross-section, the interior cargo shown in plan form. Huge metal boiling pots were also brought with them in which to prepare the trepang.

The following excerpts from songs are part of the long Baiini-Macassan cycle which is sung at mortuary rituals in north-eastern Arnhem Land.

The Prau's Rigging

It hangs down, that rigging, like falling rain.
They were looking at the rigging, hanging down from the cross-bar, from the top of the
mast . . .
They looked at the rigging,
ropes dangling downward . . .
Looked at it, hanging down from the cross-bar, from the mast, like falling rain . . .
On top of the cross-bar, hanging down to the deck, the sail at the mast . . .

The Prau Sails

It ran fast, that boat, swaying and splashing through the water,
Nose rising and falling, diving, cleaving the water.
That boat, heeling over, following the . . . sail
And slanting the mast, the main mast . . .

The Wind in the Sails

A fish has swallowed a hook: (they) haul in a kingfish, throwing it down . . .
Sails flapping, drifting along, that ship with its sails,
Going along, crying, whistling through the rigging and mast blocks . . .
Sound of singing from the mast top, and from the mast blocks,
East wind whistling and crying . . .[5]

The praus used by the Macassans were accurately recorded by Aboriginal artists on rock shelters and in bark paintings. Bark painting by Nandabada of Groote Eylandt. *photo J. Steele*

Rock painting of a paduwakang or trading prau which visited Australia in the mid-nineteenth century. *photo R. Edwards*

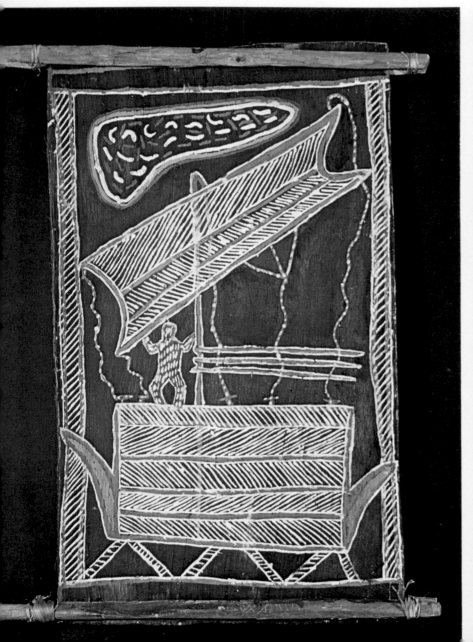

Stories like the one which follows from north-eastern Arnhem Land tell of the cordial relations which were easily established with the newcomers and how it was thought by some that they might be the Baiini returned.

Two Macassan praus were sighted coming into Port Bradshaw. Most of the Aborigines hurriedly scattered further inland, while others hid in the thick growth of the coastal jungles watching their approach. But two young boys were, for some reason, unaware of all this excitement; and they went out to spear fish in the mangrove swamps. In the meantime the praus anchored in the tidal creek at Daneia, and two Macassan boys left the boat to collect shellfish. While they were breaking open clam-shells the two Aborigines heard the noise. Stealthily they came creeping up through the foliage, and watched them.

'Who are they?' they wondered, gesturing to each other. 'They're not any of our people.' Then they looked past the two Macassan boys and saw the two praus. 'Maybe they belong to that old story from a long time ago. It might be Baiini come back.' So they drew closer and watched the two strangers.

After a while the two Macassan boys looked round and saw the Aborigines. They said nothing at first, just watched them. Then they all began to speak, but neither party could understand the other. Finally the Macassans made hand-signs, indicating that the other two should come with them to see their 'father'. As they came close to the Macassan camp they heard singing, and saw these visitors dancing in two groups, separated as in the moiety division of the Aborigines. It is said that these people always dance and sing before they begin their work of collecting trepang. The two Macassan boys signed to their companions to hide behind a large tree, while they went to tell their 'father' and see what he had to say.

The two Macassan boys met their 'father' and said to him, 'We've found something there. It looks as if we found a bird (meaning that they had seen something strange).' The 'father' got up, and taking his knife came with another Macassan over to the tree where the two Aborigines were hiding. They grabbed the boys' arms and held them tightly, examining them thoroughly all over. Then they took them over to the main camp, where crowds of Macassan men and youths surged around them, chattering excitedly. Then the two Macassan men who had seized the boys gave them food, and taught them to smoke tobacco in the long Malay pipe. Later on, they were allowed to return to their own camp.

They told the other Aborigines how kindly they had been treated, and so many of them from far and near came to camp at this place near the Macassans, and watch what they were doing. The two boys themselves went to work for the visitors, and gradually learnt their language. In this way a number of Aborigines began to understand what these Macassans said, and an increasing number worked for them. At the same time, the Macassans learnt some of the native dialects. Dainasi was the name of the two Macassan boys' 'father', and the captains of the two praus were Guramola and Wonadjei respectively.

Gumatj clan, Yirrkala[6]

Similar incidents are recalled all along the Arnhem Land coast. The trade which began was amicable and soon trepanging settlements were widely established. The Macassans built their platform houses on bamboo stilts and made steeply-pointed roofs of woven coconut palm leaves which they had brought with them.

The Visitors

. . . The roof lies finished; it rises high, with sloping sides.
Triangular in front view, the roof of the house is finished.
It is good, our house, our camp . . .
They lie within, the [Macassan] leaders, Wonadjewa, Gurumulnga'wa,
Daiungba, Gaiilng'wa.

It is finished, with its door of coconut leaves and bamboo . . .[7]

Opposite: A Macassan trepang processing site. In the centre is a hut on stilts surrounded by trepang boiling pots, the ashes from curing fires, a spoon, bottles of grog, a bamboo length, an axe and various knives. This remarkable crayon drawing recollecting a Macassan site was made by Mawulan of Yirrkala for Professor R. M. Berndt in 1947. R. M. Berndt collection, Department of Anthropology, University of Western Australia.

In time they planted coconut palms and bamboo and these materials became available to them on subsequent trips. The bamboo remains today, but the coconut palms have gone. The settlements began to have the appearance of a small Indonesian village but with an absence of women and children.

The camps were usually by the seashore, near to good drinking water, natural springs or wells and mangrove trees, which were used as fuel for drying and smoking the trepang. They kept chickens and occasionally brought cats with them. These places are now marked by beautiful large spreading tamarind trees, which have grown over the years from the seeds in the fruit pods used to flavour their food. Lines of stones each about 14 metres (15 yards) long were used to support the boiling pots and behind that was the bamboo smoke house. As the shellfish were collected daily the remains were heaped together and huge shell middens remain today close to the tamarind trees in many Macassan sites.

While they were camped on the shores of Arnhem Land the Macassans not only fished and worked to cure the trepang, but they made knives, sewed the sails of their vessels and made a simple form of pottery. Aboriginal people helped to make the pots, but this skill, like rice-growing, was never practised after the Macassans left. It was unnecessary work. Pots were not needed by the Aboriginals when light baskets and bark containers carried goods just as efficiently, and the open fire or roasting pit cooked their food well. They were quite superfluous. These Macassan pots, shards of which can be found at Macassan sites right along the coast of Arnhem Land, particularly at Yelangbara, were apparently made from local clays mixed with termite-mound substance. These materials were broken down when dry, then slaked in water. The excess water was then slowly driven off by the sun, and the resulting clay kneaded to make it workable. A simple wheel may have been used as well as a primitive kiln structure rather than an open fire to fire the pots, dishes and bowls. These vessels were mainly used for cooking and eating rice and for storing water.

The beautiful poems which follow are from the lengthy Baiini-Macassan song-cycles and speak of the 'clean food', the white rice boiling in the ant-hill clay pots.

Cooking rice on the fire; pouring it into a pot from a bag.
Pouring rice from a bag: rice, rice, for food . . .
Rice with its husk, pouring it there into earthen pots:
Into pots of ant-hill earth . . .
White, clean food, clean rice . . .
Removing its husk and pouring it into pots: making it clean.
Rice from that bag; food from those rice-filled bags . . .
Rice sticking in lumps, white scum on the boiling water.
Rice with its stems and husks . . .
Food poured from that bag and into the termite-mound pot . . .
Pouring water, washing, cleaning the rice, removing the stems.

Food boiling slowly in that earthen pot:
Bubbling with steam, boiling there itself.
Whiteness in that earthen pot, in those ant-hill earthen pots . . .
Slowly boiling, and bubbling with steam.
See the white scum, see the clean rice . . .
Rice from those bags, from those bags . . .
White scum, clean rice; clean food in that earthen pot.
Whiteness in that pot: rice, cleaned from stems, husks . . .
Food bubbling noisily there in that cauldron . . .
Boiling and bubbling with steam, water boiling away till the rice is ready . . .[8]

The making of metal knives also influenced and interested the Aboriginals and other songs from the same series describe the process in detail. Today swords and knives are produced as part of ceremonies related to the Macassans. The knives or *banuwana* were of several different types, a long knife was a *barang*, a kris *djaking* and a sword *djili*. These words have been retained, as have many different words describing the parts of the praus.

Cigarettes and tobacco were used by the Macassans and the long-handled pipe was another introduction of that time. By far the most important introduction of the Macassans was, however, their sturdy dugout canoe. Previously the Aboriginals had constructed simple bark canoes by stripping the curved bark from large trees, fastening it at either end, and bracing the concave interior with sticks. These could not stand voyages in heavy seas, whereas the dugout allowed the coastal people to fish in rougher seas for large turtle and dugong as well as visit the outer islands.

Many Aboriginals were employed in the trepanging industry, both on shore and on the praus. Some were taken back to Macassar and stayed there until the close of the industry. Many returned home the next season to tell of fascinating sights and experiences on their voyages. Djaladjari, a Wonguri man, when still a boy in about 1895, made the return journey to Macassar and told his story in detail in 1947 on Elcho Island.

Djaladjari's Voyage to Indonesia

I first saw the Macassans when I was a little boy living at Cape Wilberforce: I was with my father then, and he could speak Malay. We went on board a prau while it was anchored at Baraku . . . Later on I went with my father, and we worked for the Macassans at Pupabaidju (near Trial Bay), but there wasn't much trepang; so we moved on to Cape Shield, at Limbadjaua. Then we went to Woodah Island, or Deimundu as they called it, working at trepanging. I was about nine or ten when we came to Port Langdon (Djarakbi), on Groote Eylandt. Jadjung was the captain of that boat; his mate was Dandruwung, or Deindjadi as we called him, and the name of the prau was Kandu'ulang.

From Djarakbi we went back to Libabandria, Melville Bay. We worked there under Deindjadi, but didn't take much trepang because we already had a lot from Groote. The south-east winds were beginning to blow; we put up our sails and went on to Daitjnguru, the English Company Islands. We anchored in the Malay Road at the mouth of the Cape Wilberforce passage, then went on and anchored again at Djelalabu, in the Cadell Straits. Next day we went on to Dakarma, Elcho Island; and at the spring near where the Mission station is now we took on board a good supply of fresh water.

That same night we went straight on to Marungga Island, in the Crocodile Islands group, and then on to Manggarlta, Goulburn Island. We anchored at Wiala (Wyalla, on the South Island). Next day we continued along the coast to Darudja, half-way between Goulburn Island and Malay Bay. There was a white man there, Alfred Brown, who had some bullocks near Port Essington: he sold the hides and horns to the Macassans. This man could talk trade-Macassan and one of the Aboriginal dialects; we traded tortoise-shell with him for drink, and bought calico and food.

Then we left Brown behind, and went on through Bowen Straits to the next bay, Limbumitera, or Blue Mud Bay (between Port Essington and Cape Don). Here the Macassans used mangrove bark to 'colour' the trepang they had collected, making it better for selling in Macassar. When this was done they stored it away on board the praus, and weighed anchor. There were three boats in our lot, although there were many others as well.

I was on Jadjung's prau, where Deindjadi was mate; and now, as we were ready to go, the captain of the other two boats, named Wonabadi, began to argue with my boss. Deindjadi didn't want to take me to Macassar, but Wonabadi did. The two of them argued and shouted and threatened each other with knives. At last they decided that Deindjadi would pay me off, as I was to leave him and go with Wonabadi. So my old boss gave me a bag of rice, some *djunggalul* (mixed coconut and sugar), *kalagu* (three bunches of coconuts), white and blue striped calico, some Macassan 'starch' for calico (possibly soap), a knife with a curved handle, and a coconut-leaf basket of tobacco. I left his prau and went on to Wonabadi's, which was called Batadjowa. Jadjung, the captain on my old boat, came with me, leaving Deindjadi, who had been the mate before, to be captain there . . .

We spread our sails and went north-westwards, going outside and above Djowadjowa, Melville Island . . . On our way through the sea we came to Djadja Island, but didn't stop for water . . . At last we came to Leti Island, where we dropped anchor; and here we loaded more stores and fresh food that Wonabadi, our boss, had bought with trepang. It was on Leti that we saw *balanda* for the first time . . . We walked about the town with its houses, just the same as Darwin, and there were coconut trees too.

After about two days we left the port, and sailed to Danangigi Island. There were more houses there, and the people were the same as those at Leti; there were people from Java there too. We stopped there one day, and weighed anchor that night; we sailed on fast through a smooth sea, and saw no land until we came to Lant'djau Island. We passed this place, and then Jitara Island . . . We passed Keidjiri Island, too, without stopping.

Then we came to the big island of Madada, and to another called Laga, and further on to Bandei. From there by climbing to the top of the mast we could see Danagigi (Tanakeke Island, south of Macassar), called by the same name as the one we had passed before. This is the land of the Macassar men. Our prau swung around and came to Kalugubudu, a smaller island covered with coconuts (*kalugu* means 'coconut'), then we went on to Panumbunga, and passed by to anchor at Kambu'malagu. The town of Macassar was before us . . .

. . . When we reached Kambu'malagu, the port of the Macassans, the big *bunggauwa* 'boss' named Karei ('King') Deintumbo Buga came down to the wharf. He brought with him *djura* paper, which had on it many *darabu* marks (writing), and on this he wrote down what my boss Wonabadi told him about our cargo. Then Wonabadi said to him 'I've got some boys here' — referring to my companions and to myself.

'All right,' Deintumbo replied. 'I'll take all these men, and they can come to my place to sleep and have food.' He gave us money, and we went with him.

Near where I stayed several countrymen of mine (Aborigines) were living. There was Jamaduda from the English Company Islands, who had come to Macassar as a small boy. He had worked there, and never returned home. When I saw him he was a grown man: he had married a Macassan woman, and had four sons and four daughters. Then there was Gadari, a Wonguri-Mandjikai man from Arnhem Bay; he had come as a young man, worked there, and married a Macassan woman. When I met him he was middle aged and had a lot of children there, but I heard afterwards that he had died. He had been married to an Aboriginal woman before he had left the Australian mainland, and Duda is his son; but he didn't return to his wife. I saw Birindjauwi, too; he was still unmarried when I left Macassar. I met a Ngeimil man, and many others as well. In the old days, before I went there, young unmarried men who came with the praus would often get married to Macassan women and stop there; but usually the married men return home next season with the trading fleets. Sometimes young Aboriginal girls went to Macassar, too, but most of them stayed there to marry Indonesians or to work about the town.

Well, the next day we came down to the prau from Deintumbo's place, and unloaded the trepang. When Wonabadi had sold it all he paid the crew, and they were able to buy clothes, axes, tobacco and grog. We had a good time, and a lot of drink, and slept with some Macassan girls . . .

We saw so many things that it is hard to remember them now. There were the *balanda* white men, with horses and carts and big houses and strange looking clothes. But we also saw the *wuramu* 'Crook Men', just like those we sing about in the Macassan Song Cycle. These people came down from the mountains behind Macassar, from Bamundju and from the country of Stingkibadu: they used to come down to rob the townspeople, and set fire to the houses . . .

At last some of the Macassans and *balanda* caught these *wuramu* and put them in gaol at Kantaru, where the *wubada* policemen killed them. But the leaders of the *wuramu* were never caught.

Well, at Kambu'malagu there were stone houses, where the *bunggauwa* lived (the 'bosses', or the *balanda* Europeans). The prau captain Jadjung lived at Kambu'tumbu, and Deintumbo at Kambu'basi . . . Bunggasinga's place was at Kambu'kalasu, and the Chinamen lived at Kambu'djinga. At Kambu'maleiju a number of Malays and Macassans lived under a headman called Dara; at Kambu'biru was the Madi *bunggauwa*, who was a 'Macassan'; and at Kambu'guda, on the plain country near the lily swamps, lived Pupadjin, a Macassan prau headman who had

Opposite: Malangi of Ramangining. Long-stemmed pipes introduced into Arnhem Land by the Macassans have been used by Aboriginal people ever since. *photo P. Tweedie*

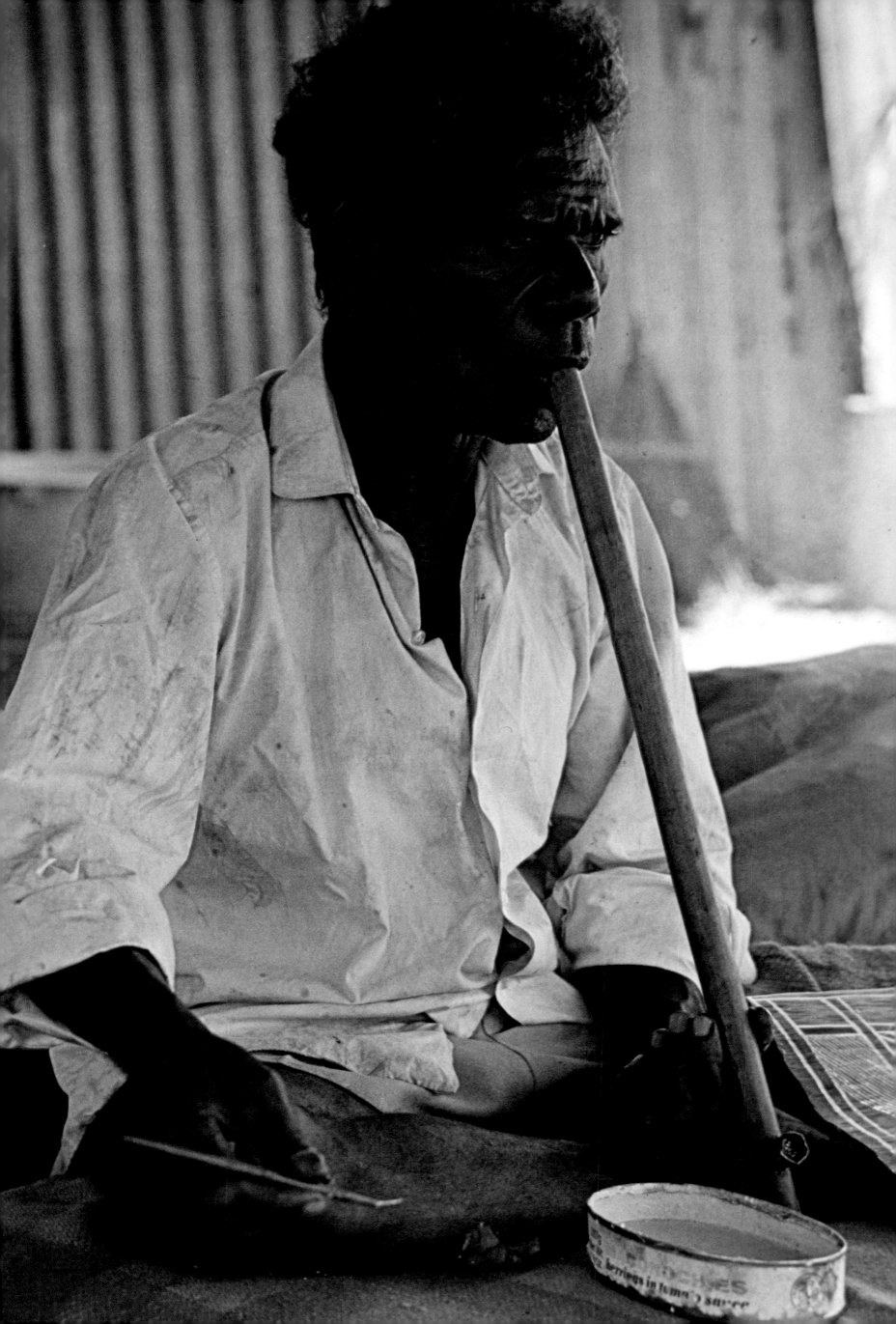

been to the English Company Islands. Mitjindi, another Macassan *bunggauwa*, was at Limbu'timbarun or Limbu'katuwung, and there were others at Wara. At Ranguwa were the *urarangu bunggauwa* (possibly a derivation of the Malay word *orang*, a person); these people lived not far from the beach. At Kambu'dadi, a flat place, there was a lily swamp like those back in our country, with a creek along which people used to sit; these were mostly Kupang (Koepang) people mixed with 'Japanese'. There were too many people, and I couldn't see them all. They had *bimbi* (nannygoats), *didung* (buffaloes), *djangadjanga* (fowls) and plenty of *paiauwul* (eggs).

Near Macassar we went to the small island of Leiileii (Leileiia), where they grow rice in large gardens, to the island of Gundingari where there are more gardens, and to Djamaluna Island with its gardens and large water tanks.

I went with the praus from Macassar, to visit the islands to the west and north-west; and we saw Putalambu, the 'mainland' as we called it, which is a long way north-west of Macassar. Here we saw the Babuwa people, who looked like 'half-castes', making calico. In our journeys we went to Bandei (or Banda Island) not far from the Aru Islands, and to Manggarei, north-west of Macassar, where there is plenty of tobacco. But then we came back to Macassar.

I stopped there for one *mauwudu* (translated as 'Christmas'), and one day my boss told us to start work. There were big tanks, in which we boiled syrup; and when this was ready we poured it into lengths of hollow bamboo, which we loaded on board. We put in stores of other goods and food-stuffs too, like rice, coconuts, *wadji* (rice and coconut in syrup), *daribu* rice biscuits, bananas, *djungalul* (rice soaked in water and dried in the sun, not the same as sweet coconut *djunggalul*), white sugar, *kula* (dark sugar), *djakuldjakul* (black and white grain, possibly sago), *santang* (like damper bread), peanuts, *dibuwang* (rather like taro), *lamikaiju* (a variety of potato), *djindulul* (meat balls in flour batter), mangoes, tamarinds, pumpkins, and *birali* (wheat or barley). When all these things were loaded on the praus, we weighed anchor, and returned the same way that we had come. And at last we reached the mainland of Australia . . .

Djaladjari, Elcho Island[9]

This account gives a detailed description not only of the route to Macassar, but also of the bartering practice between Aboriginals and Macassans, the reaction of an Aboriginal visiting a foreign place for the first time and also the cargoes carried on return to Australia. Such visits are a well-remembered part of north Australian folklore. Djaladjari mentions he saw the Babuwa people 'making calico' or weaving. Housed in the South Australian Art Gallery is an historic painting of this theme by the Gumaitj artist Mungurawi of Yirrkala. He has depicted Macassan women at their looms as described to him by his father who made visits to Sulawesi during trepanging times. His father, Mungurawi said, complained of the incessant noise the women made beating the cloth on the loom.

At Milingimbi in the Crocodile Islands a large beautiful arc of beach is sheltered by numerous huge shady tamarind trees. Dugout canoes on the shore remind all who visit the Aboriginal community there that the Macassans also came here for centuries before. About 400 metres (a quarter of a mile) inland from the beach lies the deep well called locally 'the Macassan well', ringed by tamarinds, its high banks a series of overgrown shell middens.

Stories of the Macassans are easily recalled by the Aboriginal people here. Dhawadanygulili tells the story of how the trepang were collected.

The Macassans Used to Collect Trepang

They lit the fire, that fire for the trepang, and it burnt all the time. Some of them went for trepang, they used to gather them all over there, and load them into their boats. Then they would cut the fins off, and make off for the camp.

The ones in the bush had been sitting there, and they would see the boat coming with the trepang. So they would get the fires going; light the fires there, and there, and there, and there. The boat would go up to the shore and the people would go

Macassan settlements along the shores of Melville Bay, north-eastern Arnhem Land. The crayon drawing on brown paper was made by Mawulan from Yirrkala for Professor R. M. Berndt in 1947 and depicts Melville Bay as though seen from above. Trepang processing sites are visible as well as the distinctive Macassan praus. R. M. Berndt collection, Department of Anthropology, University of Western Australia.

down and see. An unusual sight all those trepang lying in the sun on the deck. Poor things.

And again they went and dropped the anchor, and went diving for trepang, taking hooks with them and lines too. So they would dive, and string them up, the trepang. Whole ones, alive, until there were a lot, and they would drag them, and lift them into the big boat. Back at camp they would drag them off the boat, break off the hook. Then those trepang all drop down into the big fire. And they would be cut up little. And like that put out to dry in the sun until dry and hard. And the ones which had been laid out to dry first and were now ready would be put into bags. They took them down to the boats and the first boat would go back, carrying the sea food.

Dhawadanygulili, Milingimbi[10]

273

Many stories remembered about Macassan-Aboriginal relations reveal the closeness of the association. Aboriginal workers were given Macassan names, and these are frequently used in the stories. But relations with these visitors were not wholly cordial and tales are told of fighting and spearing. The Macassans, who had no women with them, no doubt frequently bartered for Aboriginal women, and, although this was not altogether frowned upon by the Aboriginals, reciprocal responsibilities were often not observed, resulting in vengeance and fighting. The following story tells of an event which happened on Elcho Island.

How a Macassan Boy Saved the Lives of Djilipa and Daymarrupa

I'm going to tell you a story about two men, my forebears, from Garriyak. There was at Wurrpan a man from Howard Island whose name in the Macassan language was Bunggathuwa, and his Aboriginal name was Djambirripa. He was sitting at Wurrpan, and his sacred net was hanging at Wurrpan. Well, the Macassans came, and landed at Wurrpan and a Macassan man came and cut up the net. When Djambarripa saw that his net had been cut up he sent the word for revenge. 'Why did you cut up my net? That net I called my mother? I will send for help to get revenge.' So many fighters came to Wurrpan, and they speared the Macassan.

Now, two of our people, Daymarrupa and Djilipa, were at Galiwinku. During the fighting a young Macassan boy had run and hidden in the jungle; he had walked from Wurrpan. Well, Daymarrupa and Djilipa found him at Galiwinku, which is about fifteen miles from Wurrpan, and they looked after him.

Some time after that, many Macassans arrived at Galiwinku, so the two men sent the Macassan boy down the beach to meet them. The Macassans saw him, and went to meet him, so he told them his story. The two men Daymarrupa and Djilipa, after sending the boy to his people, were sitting in the jungle, hiding, while he was telling his story: 'No, there are no longer any of us here! We're all finished. Buygathuwa, their leader, speared our people at Wurrpan, and there are none of us left.'

Then Macassan fighters arrived by boat, by boat, by boat, by boat, by boat, blocking up the whole of the beach at Galiwinku. Out came our two people Daymarrupa and Djilipa and the enemies rushed forward to stab them. The two men ran into the jungle at Nurruwurrunhana and the boy ran too, following them. The Macassans raced after them. The two Yolngu (Aboriginals) stopped, and ran again. And the Macassans kept chasing them. They ran until they reached Nalumara where they stopped. Now the Macassans surrounded them, and drew out their knives, but the young Macassan spoke up: 'No! These two people have been at Galiwinku all the time.' The Macassans would have speared them, those people of ours, but the Macassan child saved their lives. So they all returned together. And at the beach the Macassans gave the two Yolngu men lots of presents, knives and calico and lots of other things — we don't know the names of them all.

One Aboriginal saw them, and said, 'Hey, these two men think they're really important.' His home is quite close to Galiwinku. His Yolngu name was Wulumbur, his Macassan name was Djawala. And he looked at those two men, our forebears, and said, 'These young men, my sister's children, are really making themselves important. I'll hurry over to them.' So he came out of the jungle, and hurried over, ran down the beach, into a canoe and paddled. Off he paddled until he reached the big boat.

On the deck of the boat there were two men, one on either side, and as he climbed up into the boat, they stuck two knives into him and killed him. They threw him into the water where he floated and probably died.

Our forebears went back to the beach. And after that they may have stayed at Elcho or they might have gone somewhere else. This story is about our forebears, and their footprints are still at Galiwinku. That's all.

Banhdharrawuy, Milingimbi[11]

Alcohol was freely used in the latter part of the Macassan period and in many parts of the coast the lure of this fire water caused some disturbances. The Indonesians, although Muslim, drank freely and the humorous side of their antics is told in a short song from Groote Eylandt describing Damadarra, the master of a prau, swimming in the sea while drunk.

He swam to the open sea to collect trepang	*He was shining*
He went on swimming	*He went down to the bottom of the water*
A wave washed over his head	*He smoothed back his hair*
All the crew were there	*He couldn't see clearly through the water*
He was wet all over	*He was still swimming*
He was still swimming	*He was swimming carrying the soap*
He wore a turban	*He was smelling of soap*
He swam with his head down	*He was still smelling*
He dived head first	*He was still smelling.*[12]
From the deep sea	

The lifestyle of the Indonesian visitors was, it would seem, quite compatible with that of the Aboriginals. There were many features of their behaviour that found immediate understanding, in particular some of their religious customs. The Macassans proclaimed certain rocks on the coast to be sacred, *bapali.* they called them *Karei*, signifying kingship, and placed on them their offerings of food, goods and money to the spirits of the sea.

When the praus passed these rocks they would slacken their sails and send a canoe to the rocks to place an offering. The Aboriginals respected this idea as close to their own beliefs and would not touch the goods left. The ceremonies performed by the Macassans included the one they carried out before beginning the season's work and ritual mortuary ceremonies. The latter have inspired some aspects of the Wuramu ceremonies of the Yirritja moiety people today.

The Wuramu figure carved today may have been introduced by Aboriginals who had visited Macassar, or they may have seen them in Macassan burial rites on the Australian mainland. This Wuramu is a 'crook', a 'collection' or 'stealing' man. He has been identified at times with Dutch customs officials who came down to the wharf to collect their dues from the Macassan trepang fleets when they arrived from the northern Australian coast.

But sometimes, as in Djaladjari's tale, the original *wuramu* people are said to have been 'wild' natives from the hills who came down to the Indonesian villages on plundering expeditions. They robbed the houses, murdered those who opposed them, and set fire to huts and dwellings while their inmates were asleep. Some Aboriginals say that these pillaging Wuramu were the spirits of dead Macassans.

In funeral ceremonies derived from Macassan contact the Wuramu posts were placed on the grave while singing took place. Before this, however, the man who made a post, in company with his friends, takes it to each of the surrounding camps. All the food, tobacco, cloth or goods lying about is collected and becomes his property, in payment for his services; and it is for this reason that the figure is termed the 'collection man'.

The Wuramu belong to the Yirritja moiety, and especially to certain clans who are said to have come first into contact with visiting groups. Aboriginal Wuramu ceremonies take place in daylight in the camp. At a certain point in the Macassan song cycles, the figure is carried through the camp. Everyone knows what this means and they run to hide any loose belongings that are scattered around. Their clothing, weapons, food and tobacco will be seized by the Wuramu if it is not hidden. The Wuramu party moves through the camp collecting all they can. The loot is placed in a heap with the Wuramu in the centre, and when the songs are ended the belongings are distributed to the participants.

Contact and trading with the Macassans continued for several centuries. Just how long has never been determined. For the Aboriginals of the north it was a very long time indeed, long enough for their abandoned or wrecked praus to turn to rock, and their anchors or dugout canoes to become rocks and landmarks as well. Macassan footprints indented in the rocky outcrops are pointed out today.

The Macassans left behind many aspects of their language, as well as practical objects which expanded the technology of the Aboriginals — the dugout canoe, harpoons and metal weapons and, better known, the long Macassan pipe. The practice of erecting a memorial to the dead in the form of a flag can be seen in settlements on the north-eastern corner of Arnhem Land. This has come from the act of setting up the mast in readiness for the departure of Macassan praus and symbolizes the idea of the departure of the spirit.

The Macassans themselves finally departed for the last time towards the end of the nineteenth century, when they were prohibited by the Europeans from visiting the coast. Djawa, one of the most senior ceremonial leaders at Milingimbi, tells this story of when the Macassans came for the last time.

The Macassans Came for the Last Time

I'm going to tell the story about a long time ago when the Macassan men used to come here. The last time he came, the Macassan man said, 'Hey, I'm finished with your place here. I'm going back to Yumaynga.* And I'm finished with this place because the Marrigi, they are making trouble for me.' Marrigi means balanda; Balanda is European or Marrigi. 'He always chases me in my boat. He tries to force me back to my own country. He makes trouble for me from this big land here,' he said. And his name was Gatjing, Gatjing Munanga. We were fishing, my uncle Ngapipi and I. And he came across from the other side of the water from Gulman, to Walmu, the point of Howard Island.† He came in a canoe, and met my uncle and I. And he said, 'Hey, who is this child?' He was asking my uncle. And uncle said, 'Little brother.' 'And what's little brother's name? Has he got a name?' 'It's Djawa.' 'Has he got a Macassan name?' 'No.' 'His Macassan name is to be Mangalay. Over where I come from, there is a place called Mangalay.' Then, 'And his mother and father, where are they?' 'Over there hunting. And little brother and I are waiting here for them, his mother and father.' 'Well, when they come back, his mother and father, you will tell them his name. Tell them my name, Gatjing. I, Gatjing, named him Mangalay. Garra Mangalay is a place far away, and you will tell them that I am going away for ever, and I'm not coming back.' That's what Gatjing said, Gatjing the Macassan. And that's your story.

Djawa, Milingimbi[13]

The depth of the Macassan influence on Aboriginal culture can be seen in the symbolism used in mortuary ceremonies. A song about a Macassan ship's mast is sung and two men pick up the dead body and move it up and down as though they were lifting a mast. The meaning of this was described as follows:

Macassan man sang out when he raised a mast and when he did that all of us Yolngu men ran from our camps to see him go because all of us knew then that the Macassan was ready to go away. Some people would say, 'What's the matter with those Macassans, what are they doing?' And other people would say, 'Oh! they are going to another place because their mast is standing straight.' This is all the same as that dead man because he is ready to go away. We people say the same thing about him: 'What is the matter with him?' and it is like that dead man saying back: 'I am standing up straight now, I am going away. I want to go over that sundown way, my grandfather is there.'[15]

The corpse is carried as though it were a mast to the grave, where it is buried. Soon after this, a grave post is put up, and a mast of Macassan design is erected over the grave. The male relatives of the dead man paint themselves in his totemic design and sing the sacred songs of his clan. Putting up the mast symbolizes the final departure of the dead man, and the flags waving in the breeze farewell the spirit of the dead man on its journey to Badu, just as the Macassan flags fluttering on the masts of their praus signified their departure from the shores of Arnhem Land.

THE BADU ISLANDERS

'Come on, we'll paddle along,' the Spirits are saying.
Kiloru, Duriduri, Duradjini, Babaiyili, Wuramala, Kamali all go paddling along.
They take that long-nosed canoe . . . and paddle along through the water.
Standing, they pole with the paddle, pushing the water,
With arms flexed, paddling. The wet paddle gleams in the sun.
The canoe prow cleaves the water; the paddle is rhythmically dipping.
The paddle keeps moving; the sound of pushing the water . . .
To the Islands of Badu, past the Wessels to Badu, to the land of the Badu Gumaitj . . .
Up to the Islands of Badu . . .
The flattened end of the paddle moves, dipping, pushing the water . . .

276   *Yumaynga is a name for the Macassans' homeland — or any place where white people come from.
† Howard Island is about 30 kilometres (20 miles) east of Milingimbi.

The Macassan praus raised their sails as they left the shores of Arnhem Land. Today flags used in dances in north-eastern Arnhem Land symbolize departure. *photo P. Tweedie*

Towards New Guinea, to the Islands of Badu, past the top of Wessels.
Standing, paddling from side to side, just like the moving clouds;
The large yellow clouds, that form and reform in the distance, like the movement of
  paddling . . .
From the canoes of those Spirits — Karmali, Duriduri, Duradjini.
We saw the clouds, far out at sea . . . a long way out on the water.
Standing, with arms flexed and paddling from side to side . . .
Far out, in those Spirits' canoes — Duradjini, Duriduri, Kiloru, Wuramala;
Canoes belonging to Spirits, belonging to Babaiyili . . .
The paddle dips into the water, and sends the canoe splashing forward . . .[14]

This song comes from the Yirritja moiety Badu song cycle and is about the spirits of the dead as they paddle along to their ultimate home in the islands of Badu, a collective name for the Torres Straits Islands. The songs of Badu complete the cycle of north-eastern Arnhem Land songs telling of alien visitors, travels to their lands and the ultimate travels of the spirits after death, which encompass the Baiini, the Macassan and Badu stories.

The routes of some voyages of the Macassans took their praus along the southern coast of Papua and to the Torres Straits Islands. Aboriginals on these praus returned home with stories of what they had seen: villages amongst coconut palms, beaches that fringe islands with coral reefs and freshwater streams, dancing, the building of huts and details of food and varieties of fish.

Every year, at the end of the Wet Season when the monsoons are finishing, the winds change, and along the coast of eastern Arnhem Land a great amount of sea debris is washed ashore: coconuts, hundreds of them, pieces of driftwood and sometimes broken canoes are washed up onto the beaches. These canoes, some of them carved on the prow and sides, and the coconuts are thought to be gifts from across the sea, and the story of the spirit home beyond the horizon and the gifts they send back to the land of the living is told in the story of Badu.

277

CHAPTER ELEVEN

The Invaders

On the hot coast of northern Australia many Aboriginals had celebrated the approach of the matting sails of the Macassar-men, for they were merely summer birds of passage. But on the east coast the white sails of the English ships were a symbol of a gale which in the following hundred years would slowly cross the continent, blowing out the flames of countless campfires, covering with drift-sand the grinding stones and fishing nets, silencing the sounds of hundreds of languages, and stripping the ancient Aboriginal names from nearly every valley and headland.

Geoffrey Blainey[1]

Following the discovery of the eastern coast of Australia by Captain James Cook in the *Endeavour* in 1770, it was some eighteen years later that a fleet of eleven ships under the command of Captain Arthur Phillip arrived in the same waters of Botany Bay carrying their human cargo of prisoners, to begin a new British colony on the continent of the Aboriginals. No doubt some of the older men who lived on the shores of the bay could remember the first encounter with Cook — but this time the experience was much more startling and overwhelming.

In those first nine days, thirteen ships entered the quiet waters of the bay, the eleven English ships of Captain Phillip and two French ships commanded by the Comte de La Perouse. The English ships contained hundreds of seamen, soldiers and civilians as well as more than 700 convicts crammed below decks.

A mass of people such as this must have been far greater than any of the Aboriginals had seen before — like a swarm of massing ants carrying fire sticks. The menace of those magic fire sticks would have already been incorporated into the camp stories from the musket shot fired earlier by Captain Cook's party, and so they kept their distance for a few days, watching the movements of these strange men. Their uniforms and guns must have given them the appearance of beings with extended bodies and lumpy heads if one can judge from the evidence of cave art in other areas. In Arnhem Land and in Cape York Aboriginal artists have left a visual testimony of their reactions to the first sightings of white men in hats, carrying guns and riding horses.

Phillip moved his base from Botany Bay to Port Jackson at the end of those first few days, and the little English settlement which then began on the shores of Sydney Harbour in January 1788 had reverberations which spread across the continent in a wave which at first seemed only a low volcanic rumble but which gradually gathered momentum to become a violent eruption. Sickness and disease advanced before the path of spreading European penetration as whole Aboriginal tribes died from European diseases such as smallpox. As efforts were made to settle and farm a land whose climate and people seemed unwilling to co-operate, frustrations mounted and plunder and barbarious behaviour resulted. The history of the first 150 years of European settlement is one of forced dispossession, savagery and inhumanity to a people who had lived on the continent in harmony with their Ancestors, observing the Laws of the Great Spirits and receiving in return a peaceful and bountiful life.

In the early days of European settlement Aboriginal canoes could be seen every night on the still waters of Botany Bay, each carrying a fisherman burning a small fire on the floor of the canoe for light and warmth. But the numbers of canoes slowly dwindled, the fires no longer shone like fireflies on the waters, and today little can be traced of these ancient tribes of the Sydney area who were the first to

Opposite: When the fleet of eleven ships under Captain Phillip arrived in the waters of Botany Bay no doubt the sight was startling and overwhelming for the coastal Aboriginal people watching from the shores. *photo H. Herbert*

experience the holocaust. Phillip had noted before leaving his home country:

'I shall think it a great point if I can proceed in this business without having any dispute with the natives, a few of which I shall endeavour to persuade to settle near us, and who I mean to furnish with everything that can tend to civilize them, and to give them a high opinion of their new guests.'[2]

Captain Phillip's superior idealism before leaving England, and his view of the colonists as being 'guests' of the indigenous inhabitants, did not remain evident for long after the establishment of the penal settlement. Although Phillip forbade the molesting or killing of Aboriginals, it was not long before violence erupted. The people of the Gweagal, Wanngal and Cammeraygal tribes of the southern shores of Port Jackson tired of the strange visitors usurping their coastal hunting grounds. Following an encounter with Aboriginals in which one convict was killed and a soldier and several convicts went missing, Phillip, remaining idealistic, ordered his men to capture some of the Aboriginals. He wanted to teach them that they had much to learn from the English and show them they would be treated well. In turn he hoped to find out himself the reasons for Aboriginal anger and attacks on the settlement.

A man named Arbanoo was the first captive who, so the records of these first settlers state, was 'thoughtful, placable and gentle . . . but impatient of indignity, and allowed no superiority on our part. If the slightest insult were offered him he would return it with interest.'[3] Arbanoo's opinions went unrecorded, and so also apparently did the reasons for the Aboriginal attacks on the settlement. Captain Phillip and his small group of soldiers seemed never to realize that they might have overstayed their welcome as guests.

At the end of Phillip's four years as Governor, the settlement had expanded to Parramatta, fifteen miles from Sydney, where a small farming community was established at Rose Hill. It is almost inevitable that as the newcomers penetrated the bushland areas around the coast and to the west of the port, they would have crossed the paths of the Dreaming Ancestors; they may have come close to burial grounds, sacred rocks or trees and other sites of immense importance to the Aboriginal people. These would have gone unnoticed by the white men — to their eyes the sacred shrines of the Aboriginal people would have appeared invisible. Perhaps, inadvertently, some of the great Dreaming sites were desecrated by the men who were attacked at Botany Bay in the first uprising — we will never know. But if an analogy can be made with almost every other area of the continent where Europeans have wandered undirected through the remote landscape, the sacred sites of local Aboriginals would certainly have been at risk.

Captain Arthur Phillip returned to England with another captive Aboriginal somewhat more famous than his predecessor, Arbanoo. He was Bennelong, the tragic subject of European artists as he stands smiling in his velvet jacket and breeches on his way to meet the King of England, accompanied by his fellow countryman, Imeerawanyee. The two men waited more than a year in London longing to return to the shores of their homeland; they shivered in the cold bunks of an unheated ship in the London docks waiting to return to the land of their people — away from the crowds of white people whose overbearing interest and indulgence had waned and which had been replaced by apathy, amusement and embarrassment.

Imeerawanyee died from the cold before the ship departed, but finally Bennelong found that the sails were filled with wind and he was on his way home. For a short time after he returned he adopted the foppish manners of the English society he had observed. Dressed in a powdered wig, jacket, cravat, breeches, stockings and shoes, he lectured people against their nakedness. He was mocked in return and in a short time he became an outcast, wandering in a limbo between two worlds.

Another individual Aboriginal man who was singled out by early white colonists received rather different treatment, this time on the other side of the continent. He was Yagan of the Bibbulmun tribe, who once dwelt along the Swan River around what is now Perth. The Bibbulmun initially welcomed the white men, believing them to be the spirits of their dead coming back from their journey across the sea to the spirit land.

A friendship of mutual trust and respect was established between the Governor of the colony, Captain Stirling, and Yagan, a natural leader of his people. Yagan

Aboriginal people recorded their reactions to the first European settlers they saw by painting their images in rock shelters. *Above:* A man on horseback travels with a group of laden donkeys. *Below:* New images of a man in a hat and another on a horse are painted along with an emu over layers of older paintings. *photos R. Edwards*

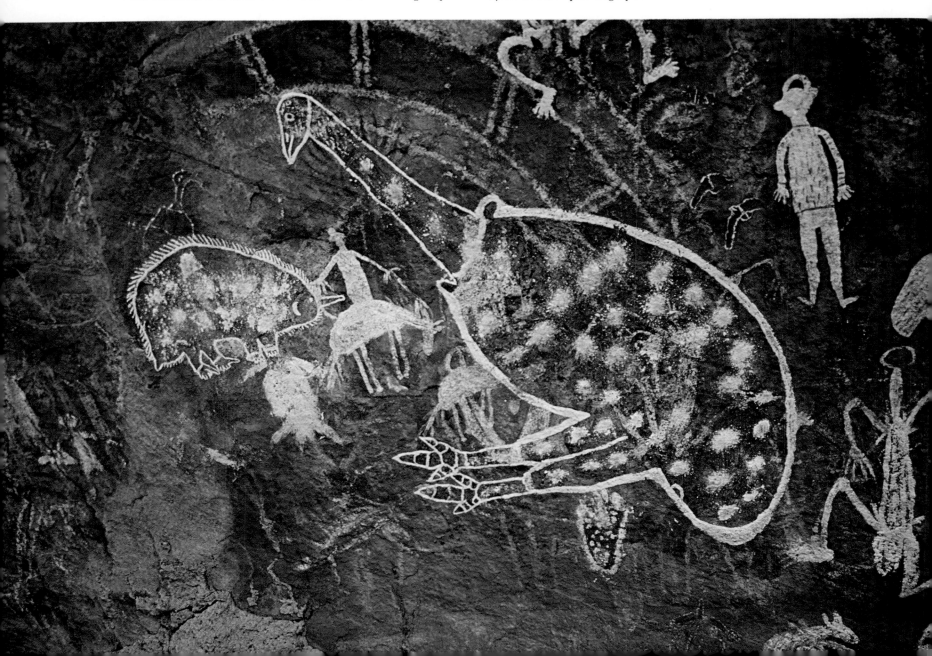

tried to reconcile the two opposing civilizations but found it extremely difficult to make the newcomers recognize the justice of his Tribal Law that paid back the shooting of an Aboriginal with the spearing of a white man. Yagan eventually became an outlaw with a price of £30 on his head and was finally shot by two young avaricious white friends while pretending to hunt kangaroos with him.

It has become a much repeated mistake of historians of this era to state that the Aboriginals put up little resistance to the invasion of their lands. Certainly there were no large-scale wars like those the American Indians and New Zealand Maoris waged in defence of their territory. This pattern of behaviour simply did not exist in Aboriginal culture. The Aboriginals did, however, systematically retaliate to the best of their abilities to the rape of their women, the annexation of their land and the violation of their sacred sites, but the battle was more like modern guerilla warfare, with sporadic attacks over a wide area. It was a battle waged across the nation by men who fought with spear and stone weapons against a civilization that had been through a massive industrial revolution, who had recently invented steam propulsion, and who fought with the aid of horses, guns and blades of steel.

THE FIRST ENCOUNTERS WITH WHITE MEN

The picture of the first encounters of Aboriginals with Europeans has been seen so far through the written history and art of the invaders. The images created were of the primitive natives as seen by the civilized man. The views of the Aboriginals as they gazed at the small boats coming to the eastern shores were not recorded. On other coasts of Australia, however, the reactions of the tribes who beheld these men for the first time has become a part of oral history and their descendants can relate today the story of the coming of the white man.

Contact with the Invaders

Aboriginal people from many places came to live near the seaside. They were all relatives. They went out to sea on the raft which they called Billilum and the women hunted for sugarbags, yams and berries and also gathered up shells and oysters. The men made long sticks, and made them sharp, so they could kill turtle or fish with them, while the women gathered poison leaves and roots to kill the fish.

But one day when the men went out for turtle eggs and other things, out on the sea they could see something moving. They wondered what it was, moving and coming towards them, so they gathered themselves all together and watched the thing. They saw people moving inside it, and they were white.

'What are they?' the Aboriginals thought, and others replied that they were Agula, devils. So they quickly told their wives and children to hide in the caves far away from the seaside. Quickly they gathered up their children and dogs and went up to the caves and left the men to see what they really were. Some of the natives yelled out, 'Kill the white Agula! See if they've got blood in them.' And so it happened. That's how the war started. They fought against one another, they killed some white people, and the white people killed the Aboriginals too. The Aboriginals found out that they were really humans, but they still didn't win. Then the white people took their land and the Dreaming times were forgotten. And so no more hunting for free food and the water they used to drink out of the rivers and gullies and springs; today and tomorrow were finished.

Daisy Utemara, Mowanjum[4]

As mentioned, the vision of the white men as spirits was also held by the Bibbulmun of the Swan River area of Western Australia, and it has also been recorded in the very north of Australia in Cape York.[5] In Arnhem Land the conflict came quickly, largely as a result of the cattle raising industry, and memories of relatively recent incidents are quickly aroused.

The White Man Who Came to Worral

A boat came, yes, a long time ago. It came, landed, and someone got out. He was looking around. 'This is a good place for me, I'll make myself a house and some

Rock painting of a giant horse alongside other traditional paintings
of animals and Quinkan spirits, Cape York. *photo J. Isaacs*

food.' So he got to work, cut down some bushes, dug a hole for water, and planted
food for himself.

And he just sat there, there at the place called Worral. Then two Aboriginal
women came into the house. He looked at them and decided to keep them. Other
people saw the two and started passing the story around. It wasn't too long that they
waited, then went to get him. They hit him and beat him until he was quite weak,
took the two women, and went off home.

But the story was taken to Yumaynga (where the white men live) by Dorrng and
Dawidi, 'Come with us, someone's been fighting one of your white people, come
with us.' So they went, and caught the men who had done it, and tied them up. And
went, and put them in jail. And there they sat, a long time, right until their hair
turned white, and they came back here. And they saw me — quite grown up.

Yanyba, Milingimbi[6]

Fighting over Cattle

The white men came from over there, in the bush. One of the important Aboriginal
men said, 'What have you come here for? You will go back. You have got white skin.
This place belongs to the Yolngu who have brown skin, and you are not going to
come here, this is not the proper place for you to go wandering around in. You want
to take the mainland. You will go back. You are white; only the brown people will
carry on meeting each other in this place.' That's what the important Aboriginal
man said a long time ago.

Good. 'Hey, there's lots of them coming to Murwangi. What are we going to do?
We are going to spear them.'

Overleaf: Rock painting which shows white men and their guns. White men were
frequently depicted with their hats on as though these were extensions of the body.
photo R. Edwards

283

Well, they brought the cattle with them. They brought cattle that wandered just anywhere, they went to Gattji, Dhamala, Yathalamara, to Warrklili, Ramangining, to Djapititjapin, to where there was water, even as far up as Dhabila. And the Aboriginals said: 'Let's go and spear the cattle. We'll steal them and spear them,' like that.

Good, so the Europeans tried to build a yard, but there were too many cattle, so they just spread out and wandered all over the place. To where there was food, to this place, this place, this place, this place and this place they went.

So the Europeans said: 'Let's use the horses. We'll take a tour around the place and see what's going on.' And the only cattle they saw were dead ones and Aboriginal footprints leading to and fro. And they thought to themselves: 'Where are these people who have been stealing and spearing our cattle? Why are they spearing them?' One of them said that, and then they went back to tell the boss. 'Hey! those Yolngu are stealing the Buliki all over the place, their antbed cooking places are scattered everywhere. What are we going to do?'

'We're going to kill them all,' that's what the boss said, 'because they're big thieves, and we'll kill them!' he said.

Good, so off they went from their cattle, looking for a fight. But when they found them they said to the Yolngu: 'When we first got here, we said we would teach you how to build houses: we will teach you. But you won't steal any more of these cattle.'

And the old Yolngu man said: 'No, no, you're simply not staying here at all. We are going to drive you off. We will repel you and spear you. You, and your horses too for good measure, and the cattle, and we'll steal them and spear them. We're starting a big battle so we can all spear each other backwards and forwards all of us, everyone. We Yolngu people are angry now. You carry guns and kill us with one hand. But we are a lot of people and the lot of us can kill you white people.'

Djawa, Milingimbi[7]

A Stockman Shooting at Dhawulmurr and Birriwun

They were sleeping, then morning. 'Hey, uncle, let's go hunting for witchetty grubs. We will dig for them at Mirrinyubirri and eat them,' said Birriwun. 'Let's go, nephew,' said Dhawulmurr. Off they went down to the billabong, sat down and started digging with their sticks; one young child was also with them. They were digging, then they heard the sound of horses' hoofs.

Birriwun turned around and said, 'Hey! Here come some stockmen, uncle!' And Dhawulmurr said to the young child, 'I will cover you up, boy, with lilies. Stay lying down. Don't get up,' that's what he said to him.

The stockman came closer and closer; the two men had brought a bunch of spears. The Aboriginals, two of them, the stockman by himself. Closer he came, and aimed his gun at them. 'Just watch, uncle. Don't spoil everything by jumping down, just don't do anything; we'll just stand and watch him, wait and see whether or not he's going to shoot at us. When he does we'll dive down.'

The stockman aimed his gun and fired at them, like that. And they threw themselves down, so he missed. Then they got their spears, aimed, *rarr* and missed, like that. Soon the stockman's bullets were all gone.

'You tease him with an emu dance, I'll do a stick insect dance.' So they did that, and fighting as well, all the time until they both got into the water. The white man's bullets were all gone. He just stood there, the two Aboriginals swimming. They got out on the other side and picked up the small boy who had been watching all the time. One of the men broke the bulrushes, aimed the spear, *datj*, and speared the stockman's horse right on the nose. The horse spluttered and reared and shot off, blood streaming from its nose. And the uncle and nephew picked up the child, and went off home.

Yanyba, Milingimbi[8]

VIOLENCE

In general, as the white men pushed further into the continent, taking over land for farming and cattle raising, the Aboriginal population was decimated. Violent atrocities were committed. Arsenic was mixed with their flour or inserted into the carcass of a sheep given to Aboriginals for food, and numerous instances of large-scale slaughter have been recorded. Bill Reid, a respected leader of the Aboriginal community of Bourke, tells of an incident still remembered in outback New South Wales when a hundred Aboriginal people were told to assemble in the cattle corral. They obediently did so, expecting some distribution of rations to take place. Instead they were surrounded and shot, one by one, in cold blood. The Aboriginal people of course retaliated to these outrages in many areas, but their toll was much greater and much more significant as whole tribes and languages vanished one by one along the coast of Australia.

In Tasmania the white invasion and occupation was complete and the whole Aboriginal population was systematically annihilated. A few children survived to be secretly reared as stockmen on the mainland, but the survivors of the 'Black Line' led an isolated and heart-rending existence in forced exile in a small white-supervised community on Flinders Island where they died one by one. Today a small stone church marks the spot on a cliff where the last of the Tasmanians sat in their Victorian costumes looking over the sea towards Tasmania.

Massacres were common on the mainland as well, and in the arid Birdsville Track area a few revealing Aboriginal accounts of these murders have been recorded. The massacres described by Ben Murray took place in the Birdsville area in the 1890s. The Wangganguru tribe were gradually coming out of the desert at this time as the cattle properties increasingly encroached on their hunting grounds. The hungry Wangganguru resorted to stealing cattle for food and as a result major massacres occurred in retaliation at Koonchera Point and Nappamanna Station. In the latter case, the Aboriginals had killed a man who had raped one of their women.

Desolate beach in Tasmania. Here the white invasion and occupation was complete. *photo G. & J. Eadie*

The Massacre

This story is from that old man Ngadu-dagali — his name means that he spears you in the ribs. A whole lot of people from up there killed a bullock and they were planning to go a long way off with the pieces of cooked meat and to stay away. They thought the white fellows wouldn't see the track and wouldn't find out where they had cooked it, so they cooked it in a very deep pit that they had dug, they made a fire and they covered it up really well. It was right on a cattle-pad, and the other cattle followed that pad. Yes, they left that ground looking all right and those cattle went back on that pad to the water, and they trampled all over the pad on top of the fire pit, but they left the bullock cooking inside.

Very early in the morning they came back and pulled it out. Then they covered it all up again nicely so that the white fellows would just see the bare tracks and wonder 'Why did they pull firewood around?' They pulled out the cooked meat saying, 'Cover up this pit, get some fresh soil and cover it up quickly.' Then they made a rough windbreak and made a fire in the middle, to make out that they'd been camping there. The other cattle came back again on their usual track over the top of the buried firepit. The white fellows came past looking around and said in English, 'They've been camping here — blackfellows' camp here. They must have killed the bullock, but where did they kill him?' They couldn't see, couldn't even see blood. They did not see any blood nor the track of the particular bullock that was killed. 'Where did they kill it?'

They never found one group of these people who travelled morn and noon and went on and on walking till they had gone far, far away from that place, still carrying some meat with them. But another group only went a certain distance; they reckoned that was far enough. One young couple, Ngadu-dagali and his wife, remained quite close, oh, the young woman did not follow her husband quickly into the lignum swamp to hide, she just stayed sitting on top of a sandhill. When the white fellows came they looked into her bag: 'Hey, there's meat in here! This is the one, mate, she's got a bullock chunk of meat here! That's one of them that killed it, give her a bullet!'

They killed her, they ripped her open with a bullet. Old man Ngadu-dagali stayed down in the lignum, he stayed there and heard the crack of the rifle. 'It's true what's happened to me, they've just killed my wife,' he said. Then he waited until they went away at last and until they had moved a long way off. Then he got up and quickly went up to see that young woman lying there dead on top of the sandhill. Oh yes, he buried her there. He buried her quickly and left following the track of the other people and said, 'Alas, they killed her just like that, I'm bereaved! They killed her just like that! Those white fellows are ready to kill anyone anywhere!' That's how he spoke to them.

So the people went on to a different creek, but it might still have belonged to the same owner because the white fellows caught sight of them out in the open plain near the creek and saw that there was meat there. Those people hadn't gone far enough, they were still quite close really. Then the white fellows killed them all, twenty of them, as many as all my fingers and all my toes. The white fellows chased them around on the plain to find out if there was meat there. They shot them all, even the pitiful little babies. But Ngadu-dagali dropped out of sight and crouched in the debris that floodwaters sweep against the butts of trees in creekbeds. He heard them being shot; he heard them crying out. At last, he came out quickly to have a look: 'It's true, even after they had gone onto the far side of the last creek, they are all dead now,' he cried. The other people, those who had gone far away in the first place, finally all went right away, and so did he. Then they left that country altogether.

Ben Murray[9]

The Aboriginal instinct for survival and adaptation was very strong, however. Communities of part-Aboriginals developed in many areas of Australia where the tribes had broken down and these perpetuated the links with the Dreaming past and continued to follow the way of life of the Ancestors. Many of the stories in this collection from south-eastern Australia have been preserved in the legends of these descendants.

THE SPREAD OF DISEASE

The river areas of the south-east, the Murray, Murrumbidgee and Darling, were heavily populated when Europeans arrived. These river bank people were amongst the first to suffer the devastating results of epidemics. Smallpox was one of the main killers and it is not surprising to learn that the Wotjobaluk, the large tribe on the River Murray, believed that one of their great Spirit Beings could spread smallpox at will. He was Myndie,[10] the giant serpent who was under the control of Bunjil the eagle hawk. The ravages which smallpox wrought on these Aboriginal groups were attributed not to the whites, but to the wrath of the great Myndie. Any man going into Myndie's country would surely die from a disease called Manola Myndie, the dust of Myndie. The scars left on survivors of the disease were called Lillipook Myndie, the scales of Myndie. The punishment of disease handed out by Myndie was thought to be the result of some violation of the sacred Law — and the white settlers were soon seen by the Aboriginals to be the cause.

Towards the end of 1840, several hundred Aboriginals were captured and imprisoned in Victoria by the military. Assistant Protector of the Aboriginals, Parker, has recorded [11] that the neighbouring Aboriginal tribes were attempting retaliation by sorcery. They sought to rouse the wrath of Myndie against the usurpers and cause sores, dysentery and death. Two people died and several others died later.

THE VENGEANCE OF THE SPIRIT ANCESTORS

The wrath which the Great Ancestors felt at the intrusion of the newcomers and the desecration of important sites has been felt throughout the Australian continent. Outbreaks of sickness, floods and destructive storms are frequently attributed by Aboriginal people to the anger of the Spirits. The wanderings of escaped convicts through the wilderness of the Colo River, north-west of Sydney, could well have brought them to one of the sacred caves where the Great Spirit himself dwelt. The flood which swelled the Colo River and formed a major flood of the Hawkesbury River in 1795 destroying the early settlers' crops was probably seen as inevitable punishment by the watching tribesmen of the surrounding hills. These feelings continue today. Cyclone Tracy, which reduced the city of Darwin to a heap of corrugated iron and debris at Christmas 1974, is spoken of by the Aboriginal people of the north as the result of the wrath of the great Beings who control the forces of nature.

One story prevalent in Darwin shortly after the terrifying cyclonic attack was that it was vengeance for the destruction of sacred sites by mining ventures; another Aboriginal version appeared in the journal *Identity* and attributed the holocaust to Jambuwal, the Thunder Man.

Jambuwal must have been really angry. I have never before heard his voice so loud or felt the earth tremble and quiver like a beaten snake. He seemed to be trying to blow the sea from its bed, to roll it over the town and the white men. The roof of the gaol flew away, and the walls slid down around us like a rotten fence . . .

After the night of the storm even the whites must have learned that Jambuwal is stronger than any of us, that to harm him or his people is to risk his anger. The white man may have guns, and dynamite to blast the rocks, but Jambuwal is the mightiest of all.[12]

While in the employment of Europeans, from time to time Aboriginal people have been forced to act against their better judgement in relation to sacred sites. A recent incident at Halls Creek is an example of the suffering this can induce. An Aboriginal bulldozer operator was asked by an ignorant foreman to level a sacred waterhole area. He protested, but was forced to do it. That afternoon he ran amuck with the bulldozer, 'mad in the head' as his relatives said, and tried to replace all the earth he had disturbed. He was placed in gaol over the weekend. Although his wife pleaded that he was ill, no help came and he died before the weekend was over. It rained from the time he touched the sacred site until his death.

YESTERDAY, TODAY AND TOMORROW

The Aboriginal people of Victoria believed that the sky was held up by props at the edges of the earth. The eastern prop was in the charge of an old man of the plains. Berak, the last of the Yarra River people, said that when he was a boy 'news' came to his people that this prop was rotting. The people were filled with anxiety and, in a frantic bid to save the sky from crashing, sent all manner of gifts to the old man to encourage him to repair it.[13] As Maddock has observed,[14] at a time when the whole fibre of Aboriginal society was under attack, when disease and loss of country had depressed the people beyond their tolerance, it is logical that their whole cosmos would crumble and that doubts would arise about the well-being of their universe.

The story of the inhumanity of the white administrators to Aboriginal families and the callous disregard for natural love between Aboriginal parents and children is long and has been told often. Children were wrenched from their parents and brought up in white institutions. Part-Aboriginal children, an embarrassment to the local white men, were rounded up and taken to remote settlements, never to see their parents again. Wally Guma, of Derby in Western Australia, has written his own story of his tragic childhood and it is reproduced here in full.

The First Settlers

The beautiful bush was my home. I enjoyed everything that was in it. I climbed the rocks and the hills, I swam in the waters where the rivers flowed, but how old I was I don't know. As I was playing hide and seek with the other children all of a sudden I heard a banging noise which stunned my ears. It was late in the afternoon. When I looked over to the camp my people were rushing like mad and I ran across to help my mother. We ran to the rocks but it was too late. We were surrounded by the white settlers.

My mother held my hand tight as we came close to the white men. We all sat down packed close to each other. Quiet, never make a sound. The white men bravely standing with their guns. They talked with their language which my people and I didn't understand. We only nodded our heads. Mother still held me tight. She put her arms around me. We all slept in one place and wondered what was going to happen to us when the morning came. My people slept with their eyes open, their thoughts far away. And there wasn't a dog left to bark. They were all shot dead. Dogs that were loved by my people like children. When the morning came my people were up already waiting to see what was to be done with them. The white settlers came forward and counted the children including me. I watched them with eyes wide open. I was frightened, trembling with fear, and my mother half choking, tears rolling down her cheeks, was saying truly she's going to let me go. Yes it is true, the white settlers are going to take me away. Then I was free from my mother's hands. I stood with the other children. We all lined up and I could see my mother whispering to the other mothers. I don't know what was she saying.

Now all the men and women lined up and the white settlers put chains around their wrists and they shot a fire gun to make us move. We children had two white men looking after us while they had seven. They drove us like bullocks, little bit by little. I could understand how these white settlers were taking us. None of my people understood English. They were bush men. That's what they called us. And as we were all walking we could see our beautiful hills and mountains, rivers and valleys; we crossed them and on the plains we made footprints. Even the kangaroos were frightened of us. We just watched with our eyes; that's the meat we should be sharing amongst us, I thought in my mind. Every time I looked back to my people I could see my loving mother in chains and thoughts came into my mind, what are these white settlers going to do with us? Are they taking us to a nice place? And once again I looked back to my mother and she smiled at me as if she was saying, son, you are missing your lessons. Every morning and afternoon I would stand near the fire and feel her warm hand touching me from my forehead, eyes, nose, mouth, hands, right down to my feet and the back of my body. I was missing it all.

Opposite: Sunset against baobab trees, north-western Australia. *photo R. Edwards*

And at last we came to the big river and the white settlers told us to sit down for a moment. And they gave us some food and showed us how to cook flour and tea. We enjoyed the white man's food. It was good and they really were kind to us or they were just pretending? What were they going to do? I didn't know. We children played around but our people were still in chains. Every now and then I would come to my mother and sit beside her and she would put her arms around me, and then I would go off again to play. The sun was setting and it was cool. The white people shouted at us to come; we couldn't understand what they wanted so one white man walked away and waved to us as if he was saying come here. So we all went towards him and he showed us to pick up a few sticks and bits of wood and we carried them back to where the others were. We made a pile of it and then they lit a match and made a big fire to cook some damper and boil tea and one of the settlers went hunting for kangaroo. He shot one and carried it back to the place where we were and they quickly cut it up and put the meat on the coals and gave us some to eat. When the night time came we, all the children, slept with our parents. I was very happy being with my mother again. And when the morning was coming we were separated from our people. There we had three white people that took us away and when our mothers and fathers and the other people saw this they started to cry, yelled out for us, and I started to cry too and I said, 'Mother when will I see you?' And she cried out in a loud voice and called my name and said, 'Guma, come back, my only son,' but I couldn't run, I only waved my hand to her and again I could hear her calling, saying, 'Guma, Guma, come back,' and I tightened my teeth with panic. I was only a boy but I understood everything. And when we were out of sight I could hear my mother's voice ringing in my ears, saying, 'Guma, come back,' and feel her hands clutching on to mine and I thought this was the end. But then we all went around the hill. There was a settlement with white people and also my colour, which made me happy, and we came closer, we came to a big wide gate and one of them opened it and then we all went in. All the people ran to us and welcomed us. They were my colour that went before us, but our parents went to another settlement. And the next day the white people gave us some clothes and there was a lady that looked after us. And then I went to school with the other children and first of all the teacher asked me how old I was and I said I don't know. Well I was bigger than the others; the teacher guessed and said I was seven. I learnt a lot while I was in school. Not like my tribal ways, it was different. I ate my meals at the table and said my prayers before I ate and washed my hands. Is that all I have to learn from the white people, is that all? But when I finish school will I face another task when I go back to my people? Every morning I attend school and I always think of my people.

I didn't have much education but why I was in the prison as a lad was because of the people was fighting with the white people. I couldn't remember how long I stayed in the prison. I was happy, I enjoyed everything because I didn't really understand what was happening. They asked me some questions. I answered them very slowly. I understood a little bit. I left all the other children at the Mission home. I am the only one that was separated.

The police troopers took me away to the big city. I was in Fremantle jail, that was my home. I almost grew up there. The place was surrounded with walls and wires. It wasn't a cave that I used to sleep under when the night time came. On my bed I always thought of my mother. I used to say in my mind, how is she getting on? And I still heard her voice saying, Guma my son where are you, where they have taken you? Are you coming back to me? And in my mind I would say, I'll come when I am free, and I said this again and again. I left my parents when I was seven years old and I didn't see my mother go. She died when I was still in Fremantle but I still hear her voice wherever I go now.

The time was coming when I was being released. The white men wanted to send me home, which they did. When I came back home I came on a big ship. I was so happy. I was a fully grown man now. And I was in Broome. I waited there until the boat from Kunmunya Mission arrived at Broome to collect cargo. When I saw the people I couldn't know them and they told me their names and we all cried for one another. And once again I was back with my people, for the first time since I was taken away when I was a child. And when I came to Kunmunya all the rest of the people told me my parents had both died which made me sad and lonely. But I still had uncles and aunties and also I have a sister. Just we two of us. When I settled down I found a job carrying wood and watering the garden every morning but this job wasn't enough for me. I wanted to carve, make snakes and shields and other things, and also I am a painter. I paint Wandjinas on bark, but I didn't have the right things to carve and paint with. Now when I am in Derby I have everything. I can carve and paint. I am an artist. I am a pensioner as well.

Wally Guma, Mowanjum[15]

Aboriginal people today who remember the life of their past grow sad as they think of the countryside where they grew up. Yet there is an acceptance. The invaders are here to stay.

The Europeans came and took my land. Nothing was left for me, only the black ground. I haven't got a real home that is nice which I should be proud of just like the caves. Inside there were beautiful paintings and the rivers and hills and the mountains I used to walk and when the rain fell and after it had gone I could smell the sweet scent of the bush. I miss everything, the kangaroos, goannas, lizards, snakes and freshwater turtles and the sea turtles, also the crocodiles and the turtle eggs and roots and yams and waterlilies. And here I am living with the white man's food. I must work hard and earn money. It's not like where I used to hunt for my food and be free. That is the way life is now.

Daisy Utemara, Mowanjum[16]

When an Aboriginal doesn't work he doesn't get paid; he has to stay hungry or get food from his relatives. The Aboriginal must stand up and work for his living; no more free food from the bush. He must face the new life, send his children to schools and live at a high standard, as white people do. But he mustn't forget his Tribal Laws, he must teach his children his Laws and the white man's laws too.

Daisy Utemara, Mowanjum[17]

Meat and eggs of the bush. The Aboriginal hunter is cooking the goanna in a hot earth oven. Aboriginal people in many areas are returning to their tribal lands to renew their traditional life. *photo R. Edwards*

It is fitting that the final words in the saga of the Aboriginal people's own history of the Australian continent should come from one of the greatest orators. His words are strong. The white invaders are like snakes whose venom has had its effect. Yet he is full of hope for the future of the Aboriginal people.

My People

A race of people who rose with the sun,
As strong as the sun they had laws,
Traditions co-existing with nature.

The cycle of the sun is likened to the life of man;
The snake is said to bite when the sun is at its most powerful zenith.
The snake has already bitten.

When the snake bites the sun,
The clan, the man, the sun,
Must sink cooling to its inevitable settings,
Yet, it is said, the sun will rise again.[18]

Opposite: Wayerpuy, child of the Arnhem Land bush country. 'Yet, it is said, the sun will rise again.' *photo P. Tweedie*

294

NOTES

CHAPTER 1: *The Arrival of the First Australians*

1 R. H. Mathews: *Folklore of the Australian Aborigines.* Hennessy, Harper & Co., 1899.
2 Roland Robinson: *The Man Who Sold His Dreaming.* Rigby, 1977.
3 T. G. H. Strehlow: *Aranda Traditions.* Melbourne University Press, 1947.
4 Roland Robinson: *Aboriginal Myths and Legends.* Sun Books, 1968.
5 Roland Robinson: ibid.
6 R. H. Mathews: *Ethnological Notes on the Aboriginal Tribes of N.S.W. and Victoria.* P. W. White, 1905.
7 Peter Dargin: *Aboriginal Fisheries of the Darling–Barwon Rivers.* Brewarrina Historical Society, 1976.
8 W. Ramsay Smith: *Myths and Legends of the Australian Aborigines.* Harrap, 1930.
9 R. H. Mathews: *Ethnological Notes on the Aboriginal Tribes of N.S.W. and Victoria.* P. W. White, 1905.
10 C. W. Peck: *Australian Legends: Tales Handed Down from the Remotest Times by the Autochthonous Inhabitants of Our Land.* Lothian, 1933.
11 L. Fison and A. W. Howitt: *Kamilaroi and Kurnai.* Robertson, 1880.
12 Hugh McCrae (ed.): *Georgiana's Journal, Melbourne 1841-1865.* Angus & Robertson, 1934.
13 Roland Robinson: *Aboriginal Myths and Legends.* Sun Books, 1968.
14 Roland Robinson: *The Man Who Sold His Dreaming.* Rigby, 1977.
15 C. W. Peck: *Australian Legends.* Lothian, 1933.

CHAPTER 2: *The Creation Era*

1 C. P. Mountford: *Ayers Rock.* Angus & Robertson, 1965.
2 Records of a seminar held at Ernabella, November 1971. Pitjantjatjara men, Government officials and representatives of the Presbyterian Board of Missions met to discuss Aboriginal development programs in the north-west of South Australia. Recorded and translated by Rev. W. H. Edwards. Transcribed by Andy Tjilari of Fregon.
3 Records of seminar at Ernabella, November 1971.
4 C. P. Mountford: *Ayers Rock.* Angus & Robertson, 1965.
5 C. P. Mountford: *Nomads of the Australian Desert.* Rigby, 1976.
6 C. P. Mountford: ibid.
7 A. P. Elkin: *The Australian Aborigines.* Angus & Robertson, 1961.
8 W. Ramsay Smith: *Myths and Legends of the Australian Aborigines.* Harrap, 1930.
9 K. Langloh Parker: *Australian Legendary Tales.* The Bodley Head, 1978.
10 Peter Dargin: *Aboriginal Fisheries of the Darling–Barwon Rivers.* Brewarrina Historical Society, 1976.
11 R. H. Mathews: *Ethnological Notes on the Aboriginal Tribes of N.S.W. and Victoria.* P. W. White, 1905.
12 K. Langloh Parker: *Australian Legendary Tales.* The Bodley Head, 1978.
13 R. H. Mathews: *Ethnological Notes on the Aboriginal Tribes of N.S.W. and Victoria.* P. W. White, 1905.
14 Aldo Massola: *Bunjil's Cave: Myths, Legends and Superstitions of the Aboriginals of South East Australia.* Lansdowne Press, 1968.
15 Sir W. B. Spencer: *Native Tribes of the Northern Territory of Australia.* Macmillan, 1914.
16 R. M. Berndt and C. H. Berndt: *Sexual Behaviour in Western Arnhem Land.* Viking Fund Publications in Anthropology, No. 16, New York, 1951, pp. 110-14. Story adapted from a myth concerning this mythic woman appearing in this book.
17 Douglass Baglin and Roland Robinson: *The Australian Aboriginal in Colour.* A. H. & A. W. Reed, 1968.
18 As told by Lurmak and Mangiju in R. M. Berndt and C. H. Berndt: *Sexual Behaviour in Western Arnhem Land.* Viking Fund Publications in Anthropology, No. 16, New York, 1951. pp. 110-14.
19 Aboriginal Arts Board: *Oenpelli Bark Painting.* Ure Smith, 1979.

20 E. J. Brandl: *Australian Aboriginal Paintings in Western and Central Arnhem Land.* Australian Institute of Aboriginal Studies, 1973.
21 I. Crawford: *The Art of the Wandjina.* Oxford University Press, 1968.
22 I. Crawford: ibid.
23 R. H. Mathews: *Ethnological Notes on the Aboriginal Tribes of N.S.W. and Victoria.* P. W. White, 1905.
24 C. P. Mountford: 'Rainbow Serpent Myths of Australia' in I. R. Buchler and K. J. Maddock (eds.) *The Rainbow Serpent: a Chromatic Piece.* The Hague and Paris, Mouton, 1978.
25 C. P. Mountford: ibid.
26 C. P. Mountford: ibid.
27 Sir George Grey: *Expeditions of Discovery*, Vol. 1. London, Boone, 1841.
28 M. E. Lofgren: *Patterns of Life: the Story of the Aboriginal People of Western Australia.* Western Australian Museum, Information Series No. 6.
29 I. Crawford: *The Art of the Wandjina.* Oxford University Press, 1968.
30 I. Crawford: ibid.
31 I. Crawford: ibid.
32 Sam Woolgoodja: *Lalai Dreamtime.* Rendered into poetry by Andrew Huntley, Poetry Australia, No. 58, 1976.
33 I. Crawford: *The Art of the Wandjina.* Oxford University Press, 1968.
34 W. L. Warner: *A Black Civilization: a Social Study of an Australian Tribe*, revised ed. Harper Bros., 1958. This version of the Wawilak story, collected by W. L. Warner, has been modified by Wandjuk Marika of Yirrkala.
35 R. M. Berndt: *Djanggawul.* Routledge & Kegan Paul, London, and Cheshire, Melbourne, 1952.
36 H. M. Groger-Wurm: *Australian Aboriginal Bark Paintings and Their Mythological Interpretation*, Vol. 1, Eastern Arnhem Land, Australian Aboriginal Studies No. 30. Australian Institute of Aboriginal Studies, 1973. Story appearing in above edited by Gawerin of Yirrkala.
37 C. J. Henry: *Girroo Gurrll, the First Surveyor and Other Aboriginal Legends.* Smith and Paterson, 1967.
38 Donald F. Thompson: 'The Hero Cult, Initiation and Totemism on Cape York', *Journal of the Royal Anthropological Institute*, Vol. LXIII, 1933.

CHAPTER 3: *The Great Journeys*

1 Tribal Lecturers from the Centre for Aboriginal Studies in Music: *Inma Nyi: Nyi.* Centre for Aboriginal Studies in Music, University of Adelaide, 1979. Reproduced with the permission of the Iwantja Community Council.
2 C. P. Mountford: *Nomads of the Australian Desert.* Rigby, 1975.
3 Story associated with ground painting. Translation J. Wilson, Papunya.
4 N. B. Tindale: 'Eagle and Crow Myths of the Maraure Tribe, Lower Darling River, N.S.W.', *Records of the South Australian Museum*, Vol. 6, No. 3, 1939.
5 Aldo Massola: *Bunjil's Cave: Myths, Legends and Superstitions of the Aborigines of South East Australia.* Lansdowne Press, 1968.

CHAPTER 4: *Earth, Fire and Water*

1 *Yura*, Adnjamathanha Trainees Newsletter, Vol. 1, No. 4, 1977.
2 R. H. Mathews: *Ethnological Notes on the Aboriginal Tribes of N.S.W. and Victoria.* P. W. White, 1905.
3 *Yura*, Adnjamathanha Trainees Newsletter, Vol. 1, No. 7, 1978.
4 Aldo Massola: *Bunjil's Cave: Myths, Legends and Superstitions of the Aborigines of South East Australia.* Landsowne Press, 1968.
5 K. Maddock: 'Myths of the Acquisition of Fire in Northern and Eastern Australia' in R. M. Berndt (ed.) *Australian Aboriginal Anthropology.* University of W.A. Press, 1970.
6 K. Maddock: ibid.
7 K. Maddock: ibid.

8 K. Maddock: ibid.
9 K. Maddock: ibid.
10 C. P. Mountford: *Nomads of the Australian Desert*. Rigby, 1976.
11 Daisy Bates: *Tales Told to Kabbarli: Aboriginal Legends collected by Daisy Bates*, retold by Barbara Ker Wilson. Angus & Robertson, 1972.
12 Aldo Massola: *Bunjil's Cave: Myths, Legends and Superstitions of the Aborigines of South East Australia*. Lansdowne Press, 1968.
13 Sylvia Hallam: *Fire and Hearth*, Australian Aboriginal Studies No. 58. Australian Institute of Aboriginal Studies, 1975.
14 Story told in Chapter 3, The Great Journeys.
15 Storyteller: Mayngurrawuy, translated by Michael Christie. ©Milingimbi Literature Centre 1979.
16 N. B. Tindale: 'Eagle and Crow Myths of the Maraure Tribe, Lower Darling River, N.S.W.', *Records of the South Australian Museum*, Vol. 6, No. 3, 1939.
17 Recorded by Diana Conroy at Point Macleay, South Australia, 1979.
18 Aldo Massola: *Bunjil's Cave: Myths, Legends and Superstitions of the Aborigines of South East Australia*. Lansdowne Press, 1968.
19 Aldo Massola: ibid.
20 Roland Robinson: *The Man Who Sold His Dreaming*. Rigby, 1977.
21 Percy Tresize: *Rock Art of South-East Cape York*, Australian Aboriginal Studies No. 24. Australian Institute of Aboriginal Studies, 1975.
22 Robert Edwards: *The Kaurna People of the Adelaide Plains*. South Australian Museum, 1972.
23 Storyteller Manuwa, edited by Matjarra, translated by Michael Christie. ©Milingimbi Literature Centre 1979.
24 *Yura*, Adnjamathanha Trainees Newsletter, Vol. 1, No. 11, 1978. Storyteller Eileen McKenzie, written by Des Coulthard.
25 *Yura*, Adnjamathanha Trainees Newsletter, Vol. 2, No. 3, 1978. Storyteller May Wilton.
26 Storyteller Djan'palil, edited by Matjarra, translated by Michael Christie. ©Milingimbi Literature Centre 1979.
27 *Ngirramini Ngini Parlingarri: Tiwi*. School of Australian Linguistics, Batchelor, Northern Territory, 1976.

CHAPTER 5: *The Seasons*

1 R. M. Berndt: *Love Songs of Arnhem Land*, extract from Song 2, Goulburn Island Cycle. Nelson, 1976.
2 R. M. Berndt: ibid, Song 20, Goulburn Island Cycle.
3 Story about Namarrkon site and buffalo, compiled from information provided by Aboriginal Arts Board, published in *Oenpelli Bark Painting*. Ure Smith, 1979.
4 H. M. Groger-Wurm: *Australian Aboriginal Bark Paintings and Their Mythological interpretation*, Vol. 1, Eastern Arnhem Land. Australian Aboriginal Studies No. 30. Australian Institute of Aboriginal Studies, 1973. Story appearing in above edited by Wandjuk Marika, Yirrkala.
5 Storyteller Mamalunhawuy, Milingimbi, English rendering by Ian Ferguson. ©Milingimbi Arts & Crafts 1979.
6 K. Langloh Parker: *Australian Legendary Tales*. The Bodley Head, 1978.
7 Dick Roughsey: *Moon and Rainbow: the Autobiography of an Aboriginal*. A. H. & A. W. Reed, 1971.
8 Luise Hercus: 'Tales of Ngadu-dagali (Rib-Bone Billy)', *Aboriginal History*, Vol. 1, No. 1, 1977. Related by Ben Murray and Mick McLean Irinjili, translated by Luise Hercus.
9 *Yura*, Adnjamathanha Trainees Newsletter, Vol. 1, No. 8, 1978.

CHAPTER 6: *Sun, Moon and Stars*

1 Daisy Bates: *Tales Told to Kabbarli: Aboriginal Legends collected by Daisy Bates*, retold by Barbara Ker Wilson. Angus & Robertson, 1972.
2 R. M. Berndt: *Djanggawul*, extract from Song 24. Routledge & Kegan Paul, London, and Cheshire, Melbourne, 1952.
3 Aldo Massola: *Bunjil's Cave: Myths, Legends and Superstitions of the Aborigines of South East Australia*. Lansdowne Press, 1968.
4 Peter Lucich: *Children's Stories from the Worora*, Australian Aboriginal Studies No. 18. Australian Institute of Aboriginal Studies, 1969.

5 Storyteller Djawa, translated by Michael Christie. ©Milingimbi Literature Centre 1979.
6 L. R. Hiatt (ed.): *Australian Aboriginal Mythology*, Social Anthropology Series No. 9; Australian Aboriginal Studies No. 50. Australian Institute of Aboriginal Studies, 1975.
7 *Yura*, Adnjamathanha Trainees Newsletter, Vol. 1, No. 10, 1978. Written by Christine Wilton, told by May Wilton.
8 R. M. Berndt: 'A Wonguri-Mandjikai Song Cycle of the Moon-Bone', *Oceania*, Vol. XIX, No. 1, 1948, p. 19.
9 R. M. Berndt: ibid, Song 12, p. 19.
10 R. M. Berndt: ibid, Song 13.
11 Ursula McConnel: *Myths of the Munkan*. Melbourne University Press, 1957.
12 Peter Lucich: *Children's Stories from the Worora*. Australian Institute of Aboriginal Studies, 1969.
13 Storyteller Djawa, translated by Michael Christie. ©Milingimbi Literature Centre 1979.
14 Daisy Bates: *Tales Told to Kabbarli: Aboriginal Legends collected by Daisy Bates*, retold by Barbara Ker Wilson. Angus & Robertson, 1972.
15 Daisy Bates: ibid.
16 Ann Wells: *Skies of Arnhem Land*. Angus & Robertson, 1964.
17 Daisy Bates: *Tales Told to Kabbarli: Aboriginal Legends collected by Daisy Bates*, retold by Barbara Ker Wilson. Angus & Robertson, 1972.
18 Aldo Massola: *Bunjil's Cave: Myths, Legends and Superstitions of the Aborigines of South East Australia*. Lansdowne Press, 1968.
19 K. Langloh Parker: *Australian Legendary Tales*. The Bodley Head, 1978.
20 C. P. Mountford: *Nomads of the Australian Desert*. Rigby, 1976.
21 Ann Wells: *Skies of Arnhem Land*. Angus & Robertson, 1964.
22 C. P. Mountford: *Nomads of the Australian Desert*. Rigby, 1976.
23 R. M. Berndt: *Djanggawul*, extract from Song 1. Routledge & Kegan Paul, London, and Cheshire, Melbourne, 1952.
24 K. Langloh Parker: *Australian Legendary Tales*. The Bodley Head, 1978.
25 N. B. Tindale: 'Legend of Waijungari, Jaralde Tribe, Lake Alexandrina', *Records of the South Australian Museum*, Vol. 12, No. 5, 1935.

CHAPTER 7: *The Cycle of Life*

1 R. H. Mathews: *Folklore of the Australian Aborigines*. Hennessy, Harper & Co., Sydney, 1899.
2 Bill Harney: *Tales from the Aborigines*. Rigby, 1976.
3 H. M. Groger-Wurm: *Australian Aboriginal Bark Paintings and Their Mythological Interpretation*, Vol. 1, Eastern Arnhem Land. Australian Institute of Aboriginal Studies, 1973.
4 Described in Chapter 3, The Great Journeys.
5 Aldo Massola: *Bunjil's Cave: Myths, Legends and Superstitions of the Aborigines of South East Australia*. Lansdowne Press, 1968.
6 Aldo Massola: ibid.
7 Storyteller Djawa, translated by Michael Christie. ©Milingimbi Literature Centre 1979.
8 Aboriginal Arts Board: *Oenpelli Bark Painting*. Ure Smith, 1979.
9 R. M. Berndt: *Love Songs of Arnhem Land*, Song 26, Goulburn Island Cycle. Nelson, 1976.
10 Dick Roughsey: *Moon and Rainbow: the Autobiography of an Aboriginal*. A. H. & A. W. Reed, 1971.
11 Daisy Bates: *Tales Told to Kabbarli: Aboriginal Legends collected by Daisy Bates*, retold by Barbara Ker Wilson. Angus & Robertson, 1972.
12 Daisy Bates: ibid.
13 C. P. Mountford: *Nomads of the Australian Desert*. Rigby, 1976.
14 *Tjuma: Stories from the Western Desert*, storyteller Stanley West, story writer Nancy Kanytjurri Fox, translated by Amee Glass. Aboriginal Arts Board, 1979.
15 Storyteller Djawa, translated by Matjarra and Michael Christie. ©Milingimbi Literature Centre 1979.
16 R. M. Berndt: 'A Wonguri-Mandjikai Song Cycle of the Moon-Bone', Song 5, *Oceania*, Vol XIX, No. 1, 1948; and R. M. Berndt: *Love Songs of Arnhem Land*. Nelson, 1976.
17 R. M. Berndt: *Djanggawul*, p. 40. Routledge & Kegan Paul, London, and Cheshire, Melbourne, 1952.

18 Sam Woolgoodja: *Lalai Dreamtime*. Rendered into poetry by Andrew Huntley, Poetry Australia, No. 58, 1976.

19 R. M. Berndt: *Djanggawul*, extract from Song 59. Routledge & Kegan Paul, London, and Cheshire, Melbourne, 1952.

20 Storyteller Daisy Utemara, Mowanjum, Western Australia.

21 Storyteller David Mowaljarli, Mowanjum, Western Australia.

22 Sam Woolgoodja: *Lalai Dreamtime*. Rendered into poetry by Andrew Huntley, Poetry Australia, No. 58, 1976.

23 Storyteller Henry Rankin, Point Macleay, South Australia, recorded by Diana Conroy.

24 Ursula McConnel: *Myths of the Munkan*. Melbourne University Press, 1957.

25 Sam Woolgoodja: *Lalai Dreamtime*. Rendered into poetry by Andrew Huntley, Poetry Australia, No. 58, 1976.

26 Storyteller Daisy Utemara, Mowanjum, Western Australia.

27 Storyteller David Mowaljarli, Mowanjum, Western Australia.

28 Peter Lucich: *Children's Stories from the Worora*. Australian Institute of Aboriginal Studies, 1969.

29 Aldo Massola: *Bunjil's Cave: Myths, Legends and Superstitions of the Aborigines of South East Australia*. Lansdowne Press, 1968.

30 Bill Harney: *Tales from the Aborigines*. Rigby, 1976.

31 Peter Lucich: *Children's Stories from the Worora*. Australian Institute of Aboriginal Studies, 1969.

32 C. J. Henry: *Girroo Gurll, the First Surveyor and Other Aboriginal Legends*. Smith & Paterson, 1967.

33 Margaret Kartomi: 'Tjitji Inma at Yalata', in *From Earlier Fleets: Hemisphere – An Aboriginal Anthology*, 1978.

34 Storyteller Elkin Umbagai, Mowanjum, Western Australia.

35 Jack Mirritji: *My People's Life: an Aboriginal's Own Story*. Milingimbi Literature Centre, 1976.

36 Storyteller David Mowaljarli, Mowanjum, Western Australia.

37 Aldo Massola: *Bunjil's Cave: Myths, Legends and Superstitions of the Aborigines of South East Australia*. Lansdowne Press, 1968.

38 Dick Roughsey: *The Giant Devil-Dingo*. Collins, 1973.

39 T. G. H. Strehlow: *Aranda Traditions*. Melbourne University Press, 1974.

40 Jack Mirritji, *My People's Life*. Milingimbi Literature Centre, 1976.

41 R. M. Berndt: 'The Wuradilagu Song Cycle of Northeastern Arnhem Land', Song 3, in *The Anthropologist Looks at Myth* (compiled by M. Jacobs; J. Greenway ed.). University of Texas Press, Austin, for the American Folklore Society, 1966, p. 211.

42 Jack Mirritji: *My People's Life*. Milingimbi Literature Centre, 1976.

43 Storyteller Daisy Utemara, Mowanjum, Western Australia.

44 A. Glass and D. Hackett: *Pitjantjatjara Texts*. Australian Aboriginal Studies No. 19; Linguistic Set No. 7. Australian Institute of Aboriginal Studies, 1969.

45 T. G. H. Strehlow: *Songs of Central Australia*. Angus & Robertson, 1971.

46 Bill Harney: *Tales from the Aborigines*. Rigby, 1976.

47 Bill Harney: ibid.

48 H. M. Groger-Wurm: *Australian Aboriginal Bark Paintings and Their Mythological Interpretation*, Vol. 1, Eastern Arnhem Land. Australian Institute of Aboriginal Studies, 1973.

49 Kath Walker: *Stradbroke Dreamtime*. Angus & Robertson, 1973.

50 Aldo Massola: *Bunjil's Cave: Myths, Legends and Superstitions of the Aborigines of South East Australia*. Lansdowne Press, 1968.

51 Daisy Bates: *Tales Told to Kabbarli: Aboriginal Legends collected by Daisy Bates*, retold by Barbara Ker Wilson. Angus & Robertson, 1972.

52 R. M. Berndt: *Djanggawul*, extract from Song 134. Routledge & Kegan Paul, London, and Cheshire, Melbourne, 1952.

53 Storyteller Manuwa, translated by Michael Christie. ©Milingimbi Literature Centre 1979.

54 Storyteller Lunepupuy, translated by B. M. Lowe. ©Milingimbi Literature Centre 1979.

55 Bill Harney: *Tales from the Aborigines*. Rigby, 1976.

56 D. F. Thompson: 'The Hero Cult, Initiation and Totemism on Cape York', *Journal of the Royal Anthropological Institute*, Vol. LXIII, 1933.

CHAPTER 8: *Death and the Spirit World*

1 Dennis Gray: 'Aboriginal Mortuary Practices in Carnarvon', *Oceania*, Vol. XLVII, No. 2, 1976.

2 Aldo Massola: *Bunjil's Cave: Myths, Legends and Superstitions of the Aborigines of South East Australia*. Lansdowne Press, 1968.

3 Daisy Bates: *Tales Told to Kabbarli: Aboriginal Legends collected by Daisy Bates*, retold by Barbara Ker Wilson. Angus & Robertson, 1972.

4 W. Lloyd Warner: *A Black Civilization*, rev. ed. Harper & Bros., 1958.

5 Daisy Bates: *Tales Told to Kabbarli: Aboriginal Legends collected by Daisy Bates*, retold by Barbara Ker Wilson. Angus & Robertson, 1972.

6 Daisy Bates: ibid. See Chapter 6, The Sun, Moon and Stars.

7 C. R. Osborne: *The Tiwi Language*. Australian Institute of Aboriginal Studies, 1974. Corrected and edited by Dorothy Tipimwuti, his wife.

8 T. G. H. Strehlow: *Aranda Traditions*. Melbourne University Press, 1947.

9 David Mowaljarli in Chapter 7, Birth of the Tribes.

10 L. Reece: 'Wailbri Beliefs', *Newsletter of the Institute of Human Ideas on Ultimate Reality and Meaning*, Vol. 1, No. 1, 1922, pp. 18-22.

11 Ursula McConnel: *Myths of the Munkan*. Melbourne University Press, 1957.

12 Storyteller Henry Rankin, Point Macleay, South Australia, recorded by Diana Conroy.

13 Storyteller Daisy Utemara, Mowanjum, Western Australia.

14 C. R. Osborne: *The Tiwi Language*. Australian Institute of Aboriginal Studies, 1974. Storyteller Allie Miller, Melville Island.

15 W. Lloyd Warner: *A Black Civilization*, rev. ed. Harper & Bros., 1958.

16 W. Lloyd Warner: ibid.

17 Traditional song from the film 'Madarrpa Funeral at Gurrkawuy' made by Ian Dunlop for Film Australia. Song translated by Howard Morphy.

18 L. Reece: 'Wailbri Beliefs', *Newsletter of the Institute of Human Ideas on Ultimate Reality and Meaning*, Vol. 1, No. 1, 1922.

19 K. Langloh Parker: *Australian Legendary Tales*. The Bodley Head, 1978.

20 Storyteller Djawa, translated by Michael Christie. ©Milingimbi Literature Centre 1979.

21 C. P. Mountford: *Nomads of the Australian Desert*. Rigby, 1976.

22 Daisy Bates: *Tales Told to Kabbarli: Aboriginal Legends collected by Daisy Bates*, retold by Barbara Ker Wilson. Angus & Robertson, 1972.

23 Bill Harney: *Tales from the Aborigines*. Rigby, 1976.

24 Bill Harney: ibid.

25 Aldo Massola: *Bunjil's Cave: Myths, Legends and Superstitions of the Aborigines of South East Australia*. Lansdowne Press, 1968.

CHAPTER 9: *Designs from the Dreaming*

1 R. M. Berndt: *Love Songs of Arnhem Land*, extract from Song 3, Rose River Cycle. Nelson, 1976.

2 G. Horne & G. Aiston: *Savage Life in Central Australia*. Macmillan, 1924.

3 L. A. Allen: *Time Before Morning*. Rigby, 1975.

4 Story from Milingimbi by Birrkili clan, told by Ian Ferguson.

5 H. M. Groger-Wurm: *Australian Aboriginal Bark Paintings and Their Mythological Interpretation*, Vol. 1, Eastern Arnhem Land. Australian Institute of Aboriginal Studies, 1973. Story appearing in above edited by Gawerin of Yirrkala.

6 R. M. Berndt: *Djanggawul*. Routledge & Kegan Paul, London, and Cheshire, Melbourne, 1952.

7 C. P. Mountford: *Nomads of the Australian Desert*. Rigby, 1976.

8 'The Boy Who Drew', *Aboriginal and Islander Identity*, Vol. 3, No. 4, October 1977.

9 E. J. Brandl: *Australian Aboriginal Paintings in Western and Central Arnhem Land: Temporal Sequences and Elements of Style in Cadell River and Deaf Adder Creek Art*. Australian Institute of Aboriginal Studies, 1973.

CHAPTER 10: *The Visitors*

1 R. M. Berndt: *Djanggawul*. Routledge & Kegan Paul, London, and Cheshire, Melbourne, 1952.
2 R. M. Berndt and C. H. Berndt: *Arnhem Land: Its History and Its People*. Cheshire, 1954. p.37.
3 Storyteller Rraying, translated by Michael Christie. ©Milingimbi Literature Centre 1979.
4 A. M. Moyle: *Songs from the Northern Territory*. Australian Institute of Aboriginal Studies, 1974.
5 R. M. Berndt: 'External Influences on the Aboriginal', *Hemisphere*, Vol. 9, No. 3, 1965, pp 2-9.
6 R. M. Berndt and C. H. Berndt: *Arnhem Land: Its History and Its People*. Cheshire, 1954, pp 41-2.
7 R. M. Berndt: 'External Influences on the Aboriginal', *Hemisphere*, Vol. 9, No. 3, 1965, pp 2-9.
8 Two songs from R. M. and C. H. Berndt: 'The Discovery of Pottery in North-Eastern Arnhem Land', *Journal of the Royal Anthropological Institute*, Vol. LXXVII, 1947 (published 1951), pp. 135-6.
9 R. M. Berndt and C. H. Berndt: *Arnhem Land: Its History and Its People*. Cheshire, 1954, pp. 51-4, 56-8.
10 Storyteller Dhawadanygulili, transcribed by Matjarra, translated by Michael Christie. ©Milingimbi Literature Centre 1979.
11 Storyteller Banhdharrawuy, translated by Michael Christie. ©Milingimbi Literature Centre 1979.
12 C. C. Macknight: *The Voyage to Marege: Macassan Trepangers in Northern Australia*. Melbourne University Press, 1976.
13 Storyteller Djawa, translated by Michael Christie. ©Milingimbi Literature Centre 1979.
14 Material from R. M. Berndt: 'Badu, Island of Spirits', *Oceania*, Vol. XIX, No. 2, 1948, p. 98.
15 W. Lloyd Warner: *A Black Civilization*, rev. ed. Harper & Bros., 1958.

CHAPTER 11: *The Invaders*

1 G. Blainey: *Triumph of the Nomads: a History of Ancient Australia*. Macmillan, 1975.
2 W. H. Stanner: 'The History of Indifference Thus Begins', *Aboriginal History*, Vol. 1, No. 1, 1977.
3 Tench, Watkin: 'A Complete Account of the Settlement at Port Jackson' in Fitzhardinge, L. F. (ed.) *Sydney's First Four Years*. Sydney, 1961.
4 Storyteller Daisy Utemara, Mowanjum, Western Australia.
5 C. J. Henry: *Girroo Gurll, the First Surveyor and Other Aboriginal Legends*. Smith & Paterson, 1967.
6 Storyteller Yanyba, transcribed by Matjarra, translated by Michael Christie. ©Milingimbi Literature Centre 1979.
7 Storyteller Djawa, transcribed by Gularrbanga, translated by Michael Christie. ©Milingimbi Literature Centre 1979.
8 Storyteller Yanyba, transcribed by Matjarra, translated by Michael Christie. ©Milingimbi Literature Centre 1979.
9 L. Hercus: 'Tales of Ngadu-dagali (Rib-Bone Billy)', *Aboriginal History*, Vol. 1, No. 1, 1977. Related by Ben Murray, collected and translated by Luise Hercus.
10 Described in Chapter 2.
11 Aldo Massola: *Bunjil's Cave: Myths, Legends and Superstitions of the Aborigines of South East Australia*. Lansdowne Press, 1968.
12 Anonymous Aboriginal writer: 'Jambawal the Thunder Man', *Aboriginal and Islander Identity*, Vol. 1-2, No. 6, October 1975.
13 Aldo Massola: *Bunjil's Cave: Myths, Legends and Superstitions of the Aborigines of South East Australia*. Lansdowne Press, 1968.
14 K. Maddock: *The Australian Aborigines: a Portrait of their Society*. Penguin Books, 1975.
15 Storyteller Wally Guma, Mowanjum, Western Australia.
16/17 Condensed from 'The Country Where I Lived Before' and 'Dream Times', storyteller Daisy Utemara, Mowanjum, Western Australia.
18 Speaker Albert Barunga: recorded by Michael Edols.

COPYRIGHT ACKNOWLEDGEMENTS

For permission to quote from previously published material we thank the following:

The Editor, *Aboriginal History*, for 'Tales of Ngadu-dagali (Rib-Bone Billy)' by Luise Hercus; Aboriginal Publications Foundation Inc. for 'The Boy Who Drew' from *Aboriginal and Islander Identity;* Angus & Robertson Ltd for *Tales Told to Kabbarli* by Daisy Bates, retold by Barbara Ker Wilson, and for *Stradbroke Dreamtime* by Kath Walker; Barrenggwa and Professor Campbell Macknight for *The Voyage to Marege* (Melbourne University Press); Professor R. M. Berndt for 'A Wonguri-Mandjikai Song Cycle of the Moon-Bone' (*Oceania*), for 'Badu, Island of the Spirits' (*Oceania*), for 'External Influences on the Aboriginal' (*Hemisphere*), for *Love Songs of Arnhem Land* (Cheshire), for 'The Wuradilagu Song Cycle of Northeastern Arnhem Land' in *The Anthropologist Looks at Myth* (Univ. of Texas Press), for *Djanggawul* (Cheshire); R.M. and C. H. Berndt for 'The Discovery of Pottery in North-Eastern Arnhem Land' (*J. Royal Anthropological Institute*), for *Sexual Behaviour in Western Arnhem Land* (Viking Fund Publications in Anthropology), and for *Arnhem Land, Its History and Its People* (Cheshire); the Brewarrina Historical Society for *Aboriginal Fisheries of the Darling-Barwon Rivers* by Peter Dargin; Dhupuma College and Joyce Yikawidi for the poem 'Waterlilies'; Harper & Row for *A Black Civilization* by W. Lloyd Warner; C. J. Henry and Kemp Place Investments Pty Ltd for *Girroo Gurrll the First Surveyor and Other Legends;*

Lansdowne Press for *Bunjil's Cave* by Aldo Massola; the Macmillan Company of Australia Pty Ltd for *Triumph of the Nomads* by G. Blainey; Melbourne University Press for *Myths of the Munkan* by Ursula McConnel and for *The Voyage to Marege* by Campbell Macknight; estate of the late C. P. Mountford for *Nomads of the Australian Desert* (Rigby); Thomas Nelson Australia Pty Ltd for *Love Songs of Arnhem Land* by R. M. Berndt; the Editor, *Oceania*, University of Sydney, for 'Aboriginal Mortuary Practices in Carnarvon' by Dennis Gray; A.H. & A. W. Reed for *Moon and Rainbow* by Dick Roughsey and for *The Australian Aboriginal in Colour* by R. Robinson and D. Baglin; Rigby Ltd for *The Man Who Sold His Dreaming* by R. Robinson; Sun Books for *Aboriginal Myths and Legends* by R. Robinson; the Tiwi School of Australian Linguistics and Carol Puruntatameri for *Ngirramini Ngini Parlingarri;* the Trustees, Western Australian Museum, for *Patterns of Life* by M. E. Lofgren; University of Western Australia Press for 'Fire Myths' by K. Maddock in *Australian Aboriginal Anthropology;* the Editor, *Yura* (Adnjamathanha Trainees Newsletter) for material from Vol. 1, Nos. 4, 7, 11 and Vol. 2, Nos. 3 and 8; the Australian Institute of Aboriginal Studies for *Australian Aboriginal Paintings in Western and Central Arnhem Land* by E. J. Brandl, *for Children's Stories from the Worora* by Peter Lucich, for *Pitjantjatjara Texts* by A. Glass and D. Hackett, for *Australian Aboriginal Paintings: Temporal Sequences and Elements of Style* by E. J. Brandl, and for *Songs from the Northern Territory* by A. M. Moyle.

INDIVIDUAL STORYTELLERS

Banhdharrawuy, Milingimbi, N.T.
Barrenggwa, Angurugu, N.T.
Barunga, Albert, Mowanjum, W.A.
Corporal, Jimmy, North Queensland
Coulthard, Walter, Flinders Ranges, S.A.
Daly, Lucy, Banjalung, N.S.W.
Dhawadanygulili, Milingimbi, N.T.
Djaladjari, Elcho Island, N.T.
Djan'palil, Milingimbi, N.T.
Djawa, Milingimbi, N.T.
Elkin Umbagai, Mrs, Kimberleys, W.A.
Fletcher, Gloria, Weipa, Qld.
Gawerin, Yirrkala, N.T.
Goobalathaldin, Mornington Island, N.T.
Goodoonoo, Roper River, N.T.
Goonack, Buru, Mowanjum, W.A.
Guma, Wally, Derby, W.A.
Hall, Joyce and Ernest, Weipa, Qld.
Irinjili, Mick McLean, Simpson Desert, Central Aust.
Jalna, Waddaman Tribe, N.T.
Jambijimba, Dinny Nolan, Papunya, N.T.
Kardin-Nilla, Karraru Tribe, S.A.
Kianoo Tjeemairee, Port Keats, N.T.
Laurie, Bella, Yeagirr, N.S.W.
Lunepupuy, Milingimbi, N.T.
McKenzie, Eileen, Flinders Ranges, S.A.
Mamalunhawuy, Milingimbi, N.T.
Mandarg, Maningrida Outstation, N.T.

Manuwa, Milingimbi, N.T.
Marika, Wandjuk, Yirrkala, N.T.
Mawalan, Yirrkala, N.T.
Maymuru, Narritjin, Yirrkala, N.T.
Mayngurrawuy, Milingimbi, N.T.
Miller, Allie, Melville Island, N.T.
Mirritji, Jack, Milingimbi, N.T.
Mowaljarli, David, Mowanjum, W.A.
Mungurawi, Yirrkala, N.T.
Murray, Ben, Birdsville, S.A.
Murray, Thomas, Pitjantjatjara, S.A.
Murululmi, Spider, Maningrida, N.T.
Ngulwua, Finness River, North Aust.
Numbulmoore, Charlie, Mowanjum, W.A.
Puruntatameri, Carol, Bathurst & Melville Islands, N.T.
Rankin, Henry, Point Macleay, S.A.
Reid, Bill, Bourke, N.S.W.
Rraying, Milingimbi, N.T.
Tipimwuti, Foxy, Bathurst Island, N.T.
Uluru, Paddy, Pitjantjatjara, N.T.
Utemara, Daisy, Mowanjum, W.A.
Vesper, Alexander, Gullibul Tribe, N.S.W.
Walker, Kath, Stradbroke Island, Qld.
West, Stanley, Warburton, W.A.
Williams, Eustan, Githavul Tribe, N.S.W.
Wilton, May, Flinders Ranges, S.A.
Woolgoodja, Sam, Mowanjum, W.A.
Yanyba, Milingimbi, N.T.

TRIBES AND CLANS REPRESENTED

Adnyamatana, S.A.
Arabana, S.A.
Aranda, N.T.
Archer River tribes, Qld.
Bagundji, N.S.W.
Barwon River tribes, N.S.W.
Bibbulmun, W.A.
Bunjellung, N.S.W.
Clarence River tribes, N.S.W.
Dalabon, N.T.
Darling River tribes, N.S.W.
Dhalwongu, N.T.
Dieri, N.T.
Djauan, N.T.
Djinang, N.T.
Gullibul, N.S.W.
Gumatj, N.T.
Gunwinggu, N.T.
Groote Eylandt tribes, N.T.
Hawkesbury River tribes, N.S.W.
Iwaidja, N.T.
Jaralde, S.A.

Kandyu, Qld.
Karraru, S.A.
Kaurna, S.A.
Kujani, N.T.-S.A.
Kulin, Vic.
Kurnai, Vic.
Lachlan River tribes, N.S.W.
Lake Alexandrina tribes, S.A.
Larumbanda, N.T.
Liyagalawumirri, N.T.
Manggalili, N.T.
Maraure, N.S.W.
Maung, N.T.
Miali, N.T.
Munkan, Qld.
Murinbata, N.T.
Murray River tribes, N.S.W.-
   Vic.-S.A.
Narran River tribes, N.S.W.
Ngameni, N.T.
Ngemba, N.S.W.
Pintubi-Anmatjera, N.T.

Pitjantjatjara, N.T.
Riratjingu, N.T.
Simpson Desert tribes, N.T.-S.A.
Tasmanian tribes, Tas.
Thanaquith, Qld.
Thurrawal, N.S.W.
Tiwi, N.T.
Waddaman, N.T.
Walbiri, N.T.
Wangganguru, N.T.-S.A.
Waramiri, N.T.
Wogait, N.T.
Weilwan, N.S.W.
*West Coast of Cape York tribes, Qld.
Willilambi, S.A.
Wiradjuri, N.S.W.
Wonguri–Mandjikai, N.T.
Wonkanguri, N.T.-S.A.
Worora, W.A.
Wotjobaluk, Vic.
Yangkuntjatjara, Central Aust.
Yeagirr, N.S.W.

BIBLIOGRAPHY

Aboriginal and Islander Identity, Vol. 1, No. 1, 1970 to date.

Aboriginal Arts Board: *The Aboriginal Children's History of Australia*. Rigby, 1977.

Aboriginal Arts Board: *Oenpelli Bark Painting*. Ure Smith, 1979.

Allen, Louis, A.: *Time Before Morning*. Rigby, 1976.

Ashley-Montagu, M. F.: *Coming into Being among the Australian Aborigines*. Routledge & Kegan Paul, 1974.

Baglin, D. and Robinson, R.: *The Australian Aboriginal in Colour*. A. H. & A. W. Reed, 1968.

Bates, Daisy: *Tales Told to Kabbarli: Aboriginal Legends collected by Daisy Bates*, retold by Barbara Ker Wilson. Angus & Robertson, 1972.

Berndt, R. M.: 'Badu, Island of Spirits', *Oceania*, Vol. XIX, No. 2, 1948.

Berndt, R. M.: *Djanggawul: an Aboriginal Religious Cult of North-Eastern Arnhem Land*. Routledge & Kegan Paul, London, and Cheshire, Melbourne, 1952.

Berndt, R. M.: 'External Influences on the Aboriginal', *Hemisphere*, Vol. 9, No. 3, 1965. pp 2-9.

Berndt, R. M.: *Kunapipi*. Cheshire, 1951.

Berndt, R. M.: *Love Songs of Arnhem Land*. Nelson, 1976.

Berndt, R. M.: *Three Faces of Love: Traditional Song Poetry*. Nelson, 1976.

Berndt, R. M.: 'A Wonguri-Mandjikai Song Cyle of the Moon-Bone', *Oceania*, Vol. XIX, No. 1, 1948.

Berndt, R. M.: 'The Wuradilagu Song Cycle of Northeastern Arnhem Land', in *The Anthropologist Looks at Myth* (compiled by M. Jacobs; J. Greenway ed.). University of Texas Press, Austin, for the American Folklore Society, 1966.

Berndt, R. M. and C. H.: *Arnhem Land, Its History and Its People*. Cheshire, 1954.

Berndt, R. M. and C. H.: 'The Discovery of Pottery in North-Eastern Arnhem Land', *Journal of the Royal Anthropological Institute*, Vol. LXXVII, 1947 (published 1951). pp. 135-6.

Berndt, R. M. and C. H.: *The First Australians*, rev. ed. Ure Smith, 1974.

Berndt, R. M. and C. H.: *Man, Land and Myth in North Australia: the Gunwinggu People*. Ure Smith, 1970.

Berndt, R. M. and C. H.: 'Secular Figures of Northeastern Arnhem Land', *American Anthropologist*, Vol. 51, 1949.

Berndt, R. M. and C. H.: *Sexual Behaviour in Western Arnhem Land*, Viking Fund Publications in Anthropology, No. 16. New York, 1951.

Blainey, Geoffrey: *Triumph of the Nomads: a History of Ancient Australia*. Macmillan, 1975.

Brandl, E. J.: *Australian Aboriginal Paintings in Western and Central Arnhem Land*. Australian Institute of Aboriginal Studies, 1973.

Carroll, Peter J.: 'Mimi from Western Arnhem Land' in P. J. Ucko (ed.) *Form in Indigenous Art: Schematization in the Art of Aboriginal Australia and Prehistoric Europe*, Prehistory and Material Culture Series No. 13. Australian Institute of Aboriginal Studies, 1977.

Clegg, J. K., 'A Metaphysical Approach to the Study of Aboriginal Rock Painting', *Mankind*, Vol. 8, No. 1, 1972.

Cole, Keith: *Totems and Tamarinds: Aborigines and Macassans in Eastern Arnhem Land*. Nungalinya Publications, 1973.

Crawford, I. M.: *The Art of the Wandjina*. Oxford University Press, 1968.

Dargin, Peter: *Aboriginal Fisheries of the Darling-Barwon Rivers*. Brewarrina Historical Society, 1976.

Edwards, R.: *The Kaurna People of the Adelaide Plains*. South Australian Museum, 1972.

Elkin, A. P.: *The Australian Aborigines*. Angus & Robertson, 1961.

Ellis, C. J.: *Aboriginal Music Making: a Study of Central Australian Music*. Libraries Board of South Australia, 1964.

Fison, L. and Howitt, A. W.: *Kamilaroi and Kurnai*. Robertson, 1880.

Glass, Amee and Hackett, Dorothy: *Pitjantjatjara Texts*, Australian Aboriginal Studies No. 19; Linguistic Set No. 7. Australian Institute of Aboriginal Studies, 1969.

Gray, Dennis: 'Aboriginal Mortuary Practices in Carnarvon', *Oceania*, Vol. XLVII, No. 2, 1976.

Grey, Sir George E.: *Journals of Two Expeditions of Discovery in North-West and Western Australia*, London, Boone, 1841.

Groger-Wurm, Helen M.: *Australian Aboriginal Bark Paintings and Their Mythological Interpretation*, Vol. 1, Eastern Arnhem Land. Australian Aboriginal Studies No. 30. Australian Institute of Aboriginal Studies, 1973.

Hallam, Sylvia J.: *Fire and Hearth*, Australian Aboriginal Studies No. 58. Australian Institute of Aboriginal Studies, 1975.

Harney, Bill: *Tales from the Aborigines*. Rigby, 1976.

Harvey, Alison: 'A Fishing Legend of the Jaralde Tribe of Lake Alexandrina, South Australia', *Mankind*, Vol. 3, No. 4, 1943.

Henry, C. J.: *Girroo Gurrll, the First Surveyor and Other Aboriginal Legends*. Smith & Paterson, 1967.

Hercus, Luise: 'Eaglehawk and Crow: A Madi madi Version', *Mankind*, Vol. 8, No. 2, 1971.

Hercus, Luise: 'Tales of Ngadu-dagali (Rib-Bone Billy)' by Ben Murray and Mick McLean Irinjili, translated by Luise Hercus. *Aboriginal History*, Vol. 1, No. 1, 1977.

Hiatt, L. R. (ed.): *Australian Aboriginal Mythology*, Social Anthropology Series No. 9; Australian Aboriginal Studies No. 50. Australian Institute of Aboriginal Studies, 1975.

Holmes, Sandra le Brun: *Yirawala: Artist and Man*. Jacaranda Press, 1972.

Horne, G. and Aiston, G.: *Savage Life in Central Australia*. Macmillan, 1924.

Isaacs, Jennifer: *Oenpelli Paintings on Bark*, exhibition catalogue. Aboriginal Arts Board, 1978.

Kartomi, Margaret: 'Tjitji Inma at Yalata', in *From Earlier Fleets: Hemisphere – An Anthology*, 1978.

Lamilami, Lazarus: *Lamilami Speaks: an Autobiography*. Ure Smith, 1974.

Lofgren, M. E.: *Patterns of Life: the Story of the Aboriginal People of Western Australia*, Information Series No. 6. Western Australia, n.d.

Lucich, Peter: *Children's Stories from the Worora*, Australian Aboriginal Studies No. 18. Australian Institute of Aboriginal Studies, 1969.

McConnel, Ursula: *Myths of the Munkan*. Melbourne University Press, 1957.

McCrae, Hugh (ed.): *Georgiana's Journal, Melbourne 1841-1865*. Angus & Robertson, 1934.

Macknight, C. C.: *The Voyage to Marege: Macassan Trepangers in Northern Australia*. Melbourne University Press, 1976.

Maddock, Kenneth: *The Australian Aborigines: a Portrait of their Society*. Penguin Books, 1975.

Maddock K.: 'Myths of the Acquisition of Fire in Northern and Eastern Australia' in R. M. Berndt (ed.) *Australian Aboriginal Anthropology*. University of Western Australia Press, 1970.

Massola, Aldo: *Bunjil's Cave: Myths, Legends and Superstitions of the Aborigines of South Eastern Australia*. Lansdowne Press, 1968.

Massola, Aldo: *The Aborigines of South-Eastern Australia as They Were*. Melbourne, 1971.

Mathews, R. H.: *Ethnological Notes on the Aboriginal Tribes of N.S.W. and Victoria*. Sydney, P. W. White, 1905.

Mathews, R. H.: *Folklore of the Australian Aborigines*. Hennessy, Harper Co., Sydney, 1899.

Meanjin, Aboriginal issue, 4/1977.

Meyer, H. A. E.: *Manners and Customs of the Aborigines of the Encounter Bay Tribe*. South Australia, 1846.

Mincham, Hans: *The Story of the Flinders Ranges*. Rigby, 1974.

Mirritji, Jack: *My People's Life: an Aboriginal's Own Story*. Milingimbi Literature Centre, 1976.

Mountford, C. P.: *Ayers Rock*. Angus & Robertson, 1965.

Mountford, C. P.: *Nomads of the Australian Desert*. Rigby, 1976.

Mountford, C. P.: 'Rainbow Serpent Myths of Australia' in Buchler, I. R. and Maddock, K. J. (eds.) *The Rainbow Serpent: A Chromatic Piece*. The Hague and Paris, Mouton, 1978.

Mountford, C. P.: *Records of the American-Australian Scientific Expedition to Arnhem Land*, Vol. 1, Art, Myth and Symbolism. Melbourne University Press, 1956.

Mountford, C. P.: *The Tiwi: Their Art, Myth and Ceremony*. Phoenix House, 1958.

Mountford, C. P.: *Winbaraku and the Myth of Jarapiri*. Rigby, 1968.

Moyle, A. M.: *Songs from the Northern Territory*. Australian Institute of Aboriginal Studies, 1974.

Nangan, Joe: *Joe Nangan's Dreaming: Aboriginal Stories of the*

North-West. Nelson, 1976.

Ngirramini Ngini Parlingarri: Tiwi. School of Australian Linguistics, Batchelor, Northern Territory, 1976.

Osborne, C. R.: *The Tiwi Language*, Australian Aboriginal Studies No. 55; Linguistic Series No. 21. Australian Institute of Aboriginal Studies, 1974.

Parker, K. Langloh: *Australian Legendary Tales*. Angus & Robertson, 1954; The Bodley Head, 1978.

Peck, C. W.: *Australian Legends: Tales Handed Down from the Remotest Times by the Autochthonous Inhabitants of Our Land*. Lothian, 1933.

Pike, W. T.: *Thirty Years among the Blacks of Australia*. London, 1912.

Reece, Rev. L.: 'Wailbri Beliefs', *Newsletter of the Institute of Human Ideas on Ultimate Reality and Meaning*, Vol. 1, No. 1, 1922.

Reed, A. W.: *Aboriginal Myths: Tales of the Dreamtime*. A. H. & A. W. Reed, 1978.

Reed, A. W.: *Myths and Legends of Australia*. A. H. & A. W. Reed, 1976.

Robinson, Roland: *Aboriginal Myths and Legends*. Sun Books, 1968.

Robinson, Roland: *The Feathered Serpent*. Edwards & Shaw, 1956.

Robinson, Roland: *Legend and Dreaming*. Edwards & Shaw, 1967.

Robinson, Roland: *The Man Who Sold His Dreaming*. Rigby, 1977.

Roth, W. E.: 'Superstition, Magic and Medicine', *North Queensland Ethnography Bulletin*, No. 5, Brisbane, 1903.

Roughsey, Dick: *The Giant Devil-Dingo*. Collins, 1973.

Roughsey, Dick: *Moon and Rainbow: the Autobiography of an Aboriginal*. A. H. & A. W. Reed, 1971.

Smith, W. Ramsay: *Myths and Legends of the Australian Aborigines*. Harrap, 1930.

Spencer, Sir W. Baldwin: and Gillen, F. J.: *The Native Tribes of Central Australia*. Macmillan, 1899.

Spencer, Sir W. Baldwin: *The Native Tribes of the Northern Territory of Australia*. Macmillan, 1914.

Stanner, W. E. H.: *On Aboriginal Religion*. Sydney University Press, 1964.

Stanner, W. E. H.: 'The History of Indifference Thus Begins', *Aboriginal History*, Vol. 1, No. 1, 1977.

Strehlow, T. G. H.: *Aranda Traditions*. Melbourne University Press, 1947.

Strehlow, T. G. H.: *Songs of Central Australia*. Angus & Robertson, 1971.

Tench, Watkin: *Sydney's First Four Years, being a reprint of A narrative of the expedition to Botany Bay; and A complete account of the settlement at Port Jackson*. Angus & Robertson, 1961.

Thomson, Donald F.: 'The Hero Cult, Initiation and Totemism on Cape York', *Journal of the Royal Anthropological Institute*, Vol. XLIII, 1933.

Tindale, N. B.: 'Eagle and Crow Myths of the Maraure Tribe, Lower Darling River, N.S.W.', *Records of the South Australian Museum*, Vol. 6, 1939.

Tindale, N. B.: 'Legend of Waijungari, Jaralde Tribe, Lake Alexandrina', *Records of the South Australian Museum*, Vol. 5, 1935.

Tindale, N. B.: 'Natives of Groote Island', *Records of the South Australian Museum*, Vol. 3, 1925-6.

Tindale, N. B.: 'Native Songs of the South-East of South Australia', *Transactions of the Royal Society of South Australia*, Vol. 61, 1937, and Vol. 65, 1941.

Tindale, N. B.: 'Notes on the Natives of the Southern Portion of Yorke Peninsula, South Australia' in *Transactions of the Royal Society of South Australia*, Vol. 60, 1936.

Tindale, N. B. and Mountford, C. P.: 'Tjibruki', *Records of the South Australian Museum*, Vol. 5, 1936.

Tjuma: Stories from the Western Desert, translated and edited by A. Glass and D. Newberry. Aboriginal Arts Board, 1979.

Tresize, Percy: *Rock Art of South-East Cape York*, Australian Aboriginal Studies No. 24; Prehistory and Material Culture Series No. 4. Australian Institute of Aboriginal Studies, 1971.

Turner, D. H.: *Tradition and Transformation: a Study of Groote Eylandt*. Australian Institute of Aboriginal Studies, 1974.

Von Brandenstein, C. G. and Thomas, A. P.: *Taruru: Aboriginal Song Poetry from the Pilbara*. Rigby, 1974.

Walker, Kath: *Stradbroke Dreamtime*. Angus & Robertson, 1972.

Warner, W. Lloyd: *A Black Civilization: a Social Study of an Australian Tribe*, rev. ed. Harper and Brothers, 1958.

Wells, Ann E.: *Skies of Arnhem Land*. Angus & Robertson, 1964.

Woolgoodja, Sam: *Lalai Dreamtime*. Aboriginal Arts Board, 1974.

Yura, Adnjamathanha Trainees Newsletter. Vol. 1, No. 4, 1977 to date.

ACKNOWLEDGEMENTS

Assistant Editor: Diana Conroy
Secretarial Assistants: Carmel Pepperell
Helen Magner, Mary Kirrane, Susan Bruce.

FIELD RESEARCH AND ASSISTANCE

Bathurst Island, N.T.
Raphael Apuatimi, Chairman, Ngaripuluwamigi Committee.
Robert Parker, Craft Adviser.

Ramangining, N.T.
Peter Yates, Art & Craft Adviser, Ramangining Art & Craft Centre.
Charlie Djota, Craft Assistant, Ramangining Art & Craft Centre.

Milingimbi, N.T.
David MacLeay, Headmaster, Milingimbi School.
David Morgan, Milingimbi Literature Centre.
Michael Christie, Milingimbi Literature Centre.
Ian Ferguson, Milingimbi Arts & Crafts Centre.

Maningrida, N.T.
Peter Cooke, Art & Crafts Supervisor.

Mowanjum, W.A.
David Mowaljarli, Wunan Crafts.

Yirrkala, N.T.
Stephen Fox, Yirrkala Arts & Crafts.

The editor wishes to thank the following advisers for their valuable contributions and comments:

Robert Edwards, Director, Aboriginal Arts Board. Originally suggested the project and offered valuable advice and guidance in the selection of themes and stories as well as selection of photographs.

Rev. W. Edwards, Uniting Church in Australia, Amata, South Australia. Checked the accuracy of the Pitjantjatjara stories.

Robert Layton, Anthropologist, adviser to Central Lands Council, Alice Springs. Checked the Pitjantjatjara/ Yangkuntjatjara stories.

Max Henry of the Paul Hamlyn Group gave generous encouragement at every stage with his enthusiasm for the book.

Elaine Godden and Chris McGuigan of the Aboriginal Arts Board offered practical assistance and Anthony Wallis of the Aboriginal Artists Agency assisted in Arnhem Land field work.

In compiling this Aboriginal history of Australia the previously published works of Australian researchers have been invaluable. Particular thanks are due to:

Professor R. M. Berndt, Department of Anthropology, University of Western Australia, who generously permitted extensive quotations from his translations of song-poetry. Many stories from Arnhem Land and extensive information about the visits of Macassans are based on his writings.

Dr Catherine Ellis, Department of Music, University of Adelaide, and Susan Reid of the Centre for Studies in Aboriginal Music who provided the Nyi: Nyi (Zebra Finch) story for Chapter 3.

Dr Ian Crawford, Western Australian Museum, who generously permitted extensive use of his records of Aboriginal comments on paintings in the Kimberleys.

Dr Howard Morphy, Australian National University, Canberra, who provided his translation of the Cockatoo song from north-eastern Arnhem Land and made general suggestions concerning stories from this area.

INDEX